*GENIUS FRIEND*

Fig. 1: *Gerald Basil Edwards* (1899-1976)
(photo: c.1926).

# GENIUS FRIEND

## G.B. Edwards
### and
## *The Book of Ebenezer Le Page*

## EDWARD CHANEY

**BLUE
ORMER**

Published by Blue Ormer Publishing

www.blueormer.co.uk

Printed by Short Run Press, Exeter.


ISBN 978-0-9928791-0-5

*for*
Katy,
Keith & Sira
(Eternal Returns)

'In every work of genius we recognize our own rejected thoughts; they come back to us with a certain alienated majesty.'

> Ralph Waldo Emerson, 'Self-Reliance' (1841).

'Truth is ugly. We have art lest we perish of the truth'.

> Friedrich Nietzsche in *The Will to Power, cit.* in Julian Young, *Nietzsche 's Philosophy of Art* (Cambridge, 1994), p. 134.

'What makes mankind tragic is not that they are victims of nature, it is that they are conscious of it.'

> Joseph Conrad; letter to Robert Cunninghame-Graham, January 1898, F.R. Karl and L. Davies eds., *The Collected Letters of Joseph Conrad*, II, p. 30.

'Art has two great functions. First, it provides an emotional experience. And then, if we have the courage of our own feelings, it becomes a mine of practical truth... The artist usually sets out - or used to - to point a moral and adorn a tale. The tale, however, points the other way, as a rule... Never trust the artist. Trust the tale. The proper function of a critic is to save the tale from the artist who created it.'

> D.H. Lawrence, 'The Spirit of the Place', *Studies in Classic American Literature* (London, 1923).

'Because I cannot hope to turn again
Consequently I rejoice, having to construct something
Upon which to rejoice'

> T.S. Eliot, 'Ash Wednesday' (1930)

'I have always believed that ... if you write about writers, that you are offering your subject the opportunity to write one more book, posthumously, of course, and in collaboration with you... I believe in private life for the living [but] when one is dead one should be a little bolder'

> Michael Holroyd, in an interview with Lisa Cohen, *The Paris Review*; Summer 2013.

'*Con altra voce omai, con altro vello
Ritornerò poeta, e in sul fonte
Del mio battesmo prenderò 'l cappello ...*'
(With another voice now, with another fleece
I shall return a poet, and at the font
of my baptism take the laurel crown...)

> Dante, *Paradiso*, XXV, lines 8-9.

# CONTENTS

PART TWO: THE BOOK OF G.B. EDWARDS

APPENDICES

# PREFACE

To my great shame, despite being a relatively cosmopolitan, half-Dutch Englishman who married an Australian in Paris and lived in Italy for seven years, I hadn't visited Guernsey until I was well into my forties, and then only as a result of what I describe in this book. I feel especially honoured, therefore, to have been made an honorary life member of the Guernsey Society. This is yet another benefit I have received thanks to befriending the person I believe produced Guernsey's greatest work of art: *The Book of Ebenezer Le Page*, or *Sarnia Chérie*, as his typescript was originally entitled. The extremely enthusiastic reviews this received when it was finally published in 1981 were more than endorsed by one of the few people who had known the author in his youth, yet survived long enough to celebrate the novel's success:

> It happens that judgments such as 'to read it is not like reading but living', or 'the achievement is so intense that the reader is rendered speechless,' so far from being exaggerated are actually under-statements. It would be easy to miss the significance of the book – an unlettered fisherman reminiscing about Guernsey. It turns out to be a mirror held up to an island so that you see all the relationships; more than that it stands for every island anywhere; more than that, it mirrors all mankind. The supposed provincialism becomes a universal picture, and the supposed simple gardener-fisherman becomes a narrator of genius with material so rich and extraordinary that we frequently have to put the book down exhausted, only to feel so deprived that we soon take it up again.[1]

The author of this extraordinary book, G.B. Edwards, or Gerald as I knew him, was indeed a remarkable man; an uncompromising Guernsey donkey in the most positive sense of that normally pejorative term. (I am told this is of Jersey or 'crapaud' origin, though Lampedusa also used it of his fellow-

---

[1] J.S. Collis, 'Memories of a Genius Friend', *Spectator* (31 July 1982), pp. 21-23.

Sicilians).[2]

I first met Gerald when I was a 21-year-old art student and he was a 73-year-old recluse, living as a lodger near Weymouth, a base he chose as providing at least theoretical access to and from his native island. Part II of what follows is the revised and much extended version of a talk I gave to the Guernsey Society more than twenty years ago, by then almost twenty years since Gerald's death. The first three-quarters of this Part were published in instalments in the 1993-94 issues of *The Review of the Guernsey Society* but, for various reasons, the last quarter never appeared.

It was the Society's Vice-Chairman and IT expert, Stephen Foote, who suggested I complete my memoir within a single volume and then not only scanned the first three parts into a format I could work on, but from my faded Amstrad print-out completed this task with my concluding essay. He then organised everything required (including my procrastinating self) to see this somewhat eccentric production through the press, launching his own publishing house in order to do so. In the process he accommodated my enlargement of what had been a mere introductory chapter into a more than PhD length study of Gerald's early life, which now constitutes Part I. From the start he has made innumerable contributions to the contents of both parts of the book, but particularly on the Guernsey history and genealogy front, regarding which he has become a leading authority. Our original intention was to launch this book at the 3rd Guernsey Literary Festival in May 2014, but this has been postponed to the 4th such event in mid-September 2015.

Postponement was in part prompted by - but also allowed for - further research as I became more focussed upon the German influences upon Gerald, his early publications, the reasons his

---

[2] 'É una bella terra benché popolata da somari. Gli Dei vi hanno soggiornato...' ('It's a beautiful place, even if it is inhabited by donkeys. The Gods once sojourned there...') says the self-exiled La Ciura to his fellow islander and future protégé in 'The Professor and his Siren' (see below, p. 218.); for donkeys and crapauds, see *The Book of Ebenezer Le Page*, p. 45 . All references to the novel are to the first English (Hamish Hamilton) edition of which the first American edition by Alfred A. Knopf, and the New York Review of Books (NYRB) Classics edition are facsimiles.

friends considered him a genius and then gave up on him, his Mass Observation work and theatre production in Bolton. I was finally able to use materials I had been accumulating for decades but not fully investigated – including his correspondence with Middleton Murry and J.S. Collis and unpublished autobiographical notes by Stephen Potter.

I have now not only revised my documentary memoir, but have prefaced this with a biography of even greater length. This has taken me deep into more complex territory. If less fluent than the memoir, I hope that my study of Gerald's life between the wars also makes a contribution to our understanding of that strangely intermediate period. In these 'years of *l'entre deux guerres*', those who opted for a brand of neo-Romanticism associated themselves with Middleton Murry's *Adelphi* magazine while the more neo-Classically-inclined adhered to T.S Eliot's *Criterion*.[3] A significant number lived their lives - or indeed died - in ways which were all too driven by ideologies, albeit adapted to their particular temperaments. These ideologies often dated from before the Great War and ironically, tended to be German in origin, as if due to this great interruption they had not been properly worked through. The 23-year-old Otto Weininger was a repressed bisexual, Jewish, anti-semitic-Christian convert who believed that if one could not 'be' a universal genius it would be better to die. He accordingly committed suicide in the Viennese house of his ideal genius, Beethoven, after publishing his *Geschlecht und Charakter* (or *Sex and Character*) in 1903. Gerald struggled with an equivalently emotive credo but managed to maintain a belief in himself as a Nietzschean genius through a lifetime of personal and professional failure. To the extent to which he fulfilled his destiny, he did so - after living the second half of his life as a virtual recluse - by completing a fictional autobiography and handing it over to me to publish. Despite featuring a provincial

---

[3] *Life and Letters*, which Desmond MacCarthy edited between 1928-1935 should indeed also be mentioned in the context of this period; *cf.* also A.R. Orage's *New Age* and *New English Weekly* (Murry himself first appeared in print in the former, writing on Picasso as early as 1911) and somewhat less avant-gardedly: J.C. Squire's *London Mercury*. Finally, F.R. Leavis and L.C. Knights founded *Scrutiny* in 1932.

cast of islanders who seem at first far removed from the archetypal *Übermensch,* his novel ultimately expressed a kind of nobility that Nietzsche might have recognised.[4]

In the Modernist version of the Romantic tradition, the foundational influence on the *Adelphi* brotherhood was D.H. Lawrence, whose extraordinary status it may be hard for a post-Modernist, TV and internet society to comprehend. Immediately behind Lawrence lay a largely German *Kultur,* persistently Romantic and characterised by Goethe, Bachofen, Schopenhauer, Nietzsche, Haeckel, Freud, Weininger and Otto Gross, albeit leavened by those two great British and American autodidactic individualists, William Blake and Walt Whitman. Lawrence's German wife was crucial in transmitting to the Anglosphere a half-digested but thoroughly-lived version of her *Kultur,* largely via her increasingly celebrated husband. She maintained the momentum of this influence after his death, continuing to consort, not merely with the likes of Murry and Richard Aldington, but with Gerald himself.

In the interests of remaining more or less self-contained, Part II – which preserves the form of the documentary memoir it started as - summarises the relevant facts enlarged upon in Part I in a way, I hope, that is complementary enough to justify the occasional repetition. For the critical reception of *Ebenezer Le Page* and a more detailed account of how I came to know its author one still needs to turn to the first chapter of Part II.

To the invaluable family documentation I received during the 1980s and early '90s from the late Clary Dumond, the son of Gerald's cousin, I have been able to add a good deal of new genealogical information, up to and including details of Gerald's marriage and the births of his children, mostly provided by Stephen Foote. This supplements information supplied by Susan Ilie in Guernsey, Sally Bohan in Alderney, and especially helpful, Jane Mosse, with whom I organised the 2011 exhibition on Gerald and his book at the Priaulx Library, on which occasion the Chief Librarian, Amanda Bennett, was

---

[4] This was written when I envisaged the title of this book to be: *The Nietzschean Guernseyman,* a title which for some unaccountable reason, friends and family discouraged me from using.

also extremely helpful. More recently I have received help and crucial encouragement from Gerald's great-niece, Sarah Inman and her family.

I would like to thank the late Joan and Bert Snell and their children, in particular Liz Valentine, formerly Elizabeth Snell, for help in reconstructing life in 'Snelldonia', the name Gerald gave to the house in which he lodged when I knew him, during the last five years of his life. I thank the late Adam and Dorcas Edwards, David Simon and John Enoch Edwards, and Ben and Jeane Holmes, *née* Edwards. I thank Adam and Dorcas in particular for sympathetic support and permission to publish Gerald's letters and poems. I also thank Dame Margaret Drabble and Sir Michael Holroyd both for their encouragement in the process of 're-creation' and for practical help with the research into Gerald's friendship with J.S. Collis. Particular thanks to Michael Holroyd for permission to quote from Collis's writings, both published and unpublished, as well as permission to use his kind words as a pre-publication 'puff'. I thank the late John Fowles for his encouragement and assistance in the early stages of biographical research and for the original suggestion, in his 1981 introduction to *The Book,* that I should publish Gerald's letters.

Thanks also to Richard Ingrams for the loan of Gerald's letters to Collis and other materials, and to the late Julian Potter for copying his father Stephen's typescripts and sending them to me with subsequent permission to publish. I thank David Gilmour and Gioacchino Lanza Tomasi for providing a *nihil obstat* regarding my comparisons between posthumously-published, islander novelists Gerald and Lampedusa, as well as Marina Warner for advanced proofs of her introduction to the new NYRB Classics translation of Lampedusa's *La Sirena*. I thank Josie Walter for permission to quote from her grandfather, Franz Wilfrid Walter's account of 'The Sanctuary' near Storrington and to Peter Kenyatta and Malcolm Linfield for help in researching Gerald's connection with Peter's father, Jomo Kenyatta, who also lived at Storrington. I thank Professor James Hinton for timely help with Gerald's residence in Bolton and participation in Mass Observation there and Frances Clemmitt of Bolton's Little Theatre for crucial last minute help in finding new evidence of Gerald's theatrical activities there.

I thank the Trustees of the Mass Observation Archive and the Curtis Brown Group for permission to reproduce photographs from their archive, and Bolton Council for permission to include Humphrey Spender's photograph of Davenport Street. I thank the Alexander Turnbull Library, Wellington, New Zealand for permission to quote from Middleton Murry's diary, a letter from Gerald that remained in the archive, and permission to reproduce the photograph of Murry, D.H. and Frieda Lawrence; the Guernsey Press and Visit Guernsey for photographs; Ciprian Ilie for photographs of the Edwards family properties in Guernsey; Yvonne Widger of the Dartington Hall Trust Archive for Elmhirst family photographs; the Kunsthaus Zürich and the Estate of Suzanne Perrottet, for the photograph of Rudolf von Laban and his dancers; Darryl Ogier of Island Archives in Guernsey for permission to reproduce the Occupation identity card photos of the Edwards family; The Howard Gotlieb Archival Research Center, Boston University, for the photograph of Lancelot Law Whyte; Corbis Images for the photograph of Jomo Kenyatta; The National Portrait Gallery for the photographs of Stephen Potter by Lady Ottoline Morrell, Tom Harrisson and Charles Madge; Sheffield Council for the photograph of Walt Whitman and Harry Stafford from the Edward Carpenter Collection and Trinity College, Cambridge, for Sir Richard Rees's self-portrait. Finally, on both personal and practical levels, I thank Ann Barnes, Gillian Bastow, Jaspreet Singh Boparai, Katy Budge, Jessica, Lisa and Olivia Chaney, Richard Davenport-Hines, Roy Dotrice, Michelle Drew Nielsen, Richard Fleming, Andrew Fothergill, Edwin Frank, Vittorio Gabrieli, Peter Goodall, the late Ian Harris, Al and Jo Horn, Bryan and Clare Hornsby, Sarah Inman, Keith and Sira Jacka, Peter Kenyatta, Philip Mansel, Michael Shipley, Jonathan Snell, Michael Thomson-Glover, Anneliese Walker, Irving Wardle, Anthony Willey, Bobby Williams, John Worthen and James Zabiela.

E.C., Southampton. June 2015

# PART ONE: REDISCOVERED LIFE

## 1: ENCOUNTER IN UPWEY

When, in March 1981, almost five years after the death of its author, Hamish Hamilton published the first edition of a fictional autobiography set in Guernsey, scarcely a punctuation mark in his typescript needed altering.[1] Like Giuseppe Tomasi di Lampedusa, who also wrote a retrospective novel set entirely in the island of his birth but based on a world of reading, Gerald Basil Edwards had worked hard to ensure that the completeness and quality of his *magnum opus* justified the relatively unsatisfactory nature of his life. At least as authors, both men exemplified the dictum attributed to George Eliot: 'It is never too late to be what you might have been.'[2] Both had hitherto published only relatively minor, albeit incisive works of criticism.[3] Then, towards the ends of their lives each completed a great novel based on a traditional island archetype with which - and whom - they profoundly identified. Both typescripts were rejected by their preferred publishers: in Lampedusa's case: Mondadori and Einaudi; in Edwards's: Faber, Cape, Cassell and Calder and Boyars; and then they died. After their deaths,

---

[1] See the beginning of Part II for the reviews that welcomed *The Book* and its various editions.

[2] Rebecca Mead, 'Middlemarch and Me: What George Eliot teaches us', *New Yorker*, 14 February 2011. The quotation was attributed to her in 1881, within a year of her death.

[3] See below for Gerald's often brilliant critical writing in *The Adelphi* between 1926 and 1931. Lampedusa's few published articles (including one on 'W.B. Yeats e il Risorgimento Irlandese') appeared in the same period as Gerald's, in the late 1920s, when he got away from his mother-dominated home and visited England, his uncle being Italian ambassador there; see now (coincidentally), his adoptive heir, the musicologist Gioacchino Lanza Tomasi's, *Giuseppe Tomasi di Lampedusa: A Biography through Images* (London, 2013), p. 111. This is introduced by David Gilmour, author of *The Last Leopard: Life of Giuseppe di Lampedusa* (London, 1988; 5th edition, 2007), whom I thank for checking my comparative account.

forgotten by almost all but their adoptive heirs, their novels were then published to great acclaim: Lampedusa's *Il Gattopardo* (translated as *The Leopard*) in 1958 and G.B. Edwards's *The Book of Ebenezer Le Page*, twenty-three years later.

I was an art student, spending the summer in a Dorset village, when I first met Gerald Edwards, introduced by a young pianist whose parents took in lodgers [Figs 1 and 2]. One day she told me that their new lodger had known D.H. Lawrence. This had me introducing myself more or less immediately. Whilst I was disappointed to discover that he might never have met Lawrence, I was far from disappointed by the man himself, his forthright presence, seemingly supreme self-belief and exceptionally articulate erudition. Where the claim to have

Fig 2: Pre-art school attempt at Wyndham Lewis-style self-portrait; done in great-aunt Josephine's Upwey studio (author, 1969).

known Lawrence personally is concerned, there must have been a misunderstanding, for, so far from name-dropping, Gerald rarely referred to his past at all, still less to his literary past, despite, as I only discovered years later, his once impressive list of friends and admirers.[4] He talked of Lawrence with an extraordinary authority and intimate knowledge of his work and personality but claimed only to have met Lawrence's widow, the formidable Frieda, *née* Von Richthofen. He seems to have known Frieda well, perhaps even, like his mentor John

---

[4] For the extent to which Gerald's landlady may have been informed of his range of acquaintance, however, see below, pp. 133-34.

Fig 3: John Middleton Murry, Frieda Lawrence and D.H.
Lawrence at 9 Selwood Terrace, London, after the Lawrences'
wedding on 13 July 1914.
(Alexander Turnbull Library, New Zealand).

Middleton Murry, albeit more momentarily, intimately.[5] Her
influence, based on her acquaintance with the work of Sigmund
Freud and intimacy with one of Freud's star protégés, Otto
Gross, as mediated through her celebrated second husband, can

[5] Given her character, as documented by numerous biographers, and that she
was the only woman of this era to whom I remember Gerald referring more than
once and the nature of his account of her both to me and to his landlady, Joan
Snell, it is conceivable he had the briefest of affairs with her, the next best thing
to having known Lawrence himself; *cf.* below, pp. 237-38. For her dining with
Stephen Potter in Chiswick in 1931, see below, p. 56. According to Potter, Gerald
already 'knew some German literature' in the 1920s and it is likely he spoke the
language, particularly after living in German-speaking Switzerland from 1928-
30; see below, p. 81.

hardly be over-estimated. So significant was this influence on the likes of Gerald Edwards and his circle that I have coined the term 'Friedian', complementing the more conventional 'Lawrentian', in order to cope with it.[6] The still more widely used term, Nietzschean, was common to both, indeed a cause of quarrels, both husband and wife having known at least some of the works of Nietzsche before they met.

I later discovered that Gerald met Frieda through Lawrence's ambivalent best man, Middleton Murry, the then extremely influential author and editor [Fig. 3]. He is now best known for having been married to Katherine Mansfield, with whom he co-edited Britain's pioneering Modernist magazine, *Rhythm*.[7] In

---

[6] Lawrence's self-proclaimed 'resistance' to Freud is discussed by Fiona Becket, in 'Lawrence and Psychoanalysis', *The Cambridge Companion to D.H. Lawrence* (Cambridge, 2001), ed. Anne Fernihough, pp. 217-34; but most usefully, see John Worthen, *D.H. Lawrence: The Early Years 1885-1912* (Cambridge, 1992), pp. 442-444.

[7] *Rhythm* was created by Murry and a fellow-undergraduate in 1911 when he was still at Brasenose College, Oxford, and lasted for two years, Mansfield joining Murry in June 1912 as assistant editor and becoming co-editor for the February 1913 issue. For Murry (1889-1957), see Rayner Heppenstall, *Middleton Murry: A Study in Excellent Normality* (London, 1934), F.A. Lea, *The Life of John Middleton Murry* (London, 1959), Ernest Griffin, *John Middleton Murry* (London, 1969), Sharron Greer Cassavant, *John Middleton Murry: The Critic as Moralist* (Alabama, 1982), *ODNB* and, albeit not cited in the latter, the chapter on him in John Carswell, *Lives and Letters* (London, 1978). See also his daughter, Katherine Middleton Murry's *Beloved Quixote: The Unknown Life of John Middleton Murry* (London, 1986), his son, Colin's two memoirs, and Sydney Janet Kaplan, *Circulating Genius: John Middleton Murry, Katherine Mansfield and D.H. Lawrence* (London, 2010). The latter is particularly good on Murry's abandonment of the Modernist project. For Mansfield see Claire Tomalin, *Katherine Mansfield: A Secret Life* (London, 1987), Kaplan as above and *idem*, *Katherine Mansfield and the Origins of Modernist Fiction* (Ithaca, 1991). She died in Fontainebleau on 9 January 1923 after a reconciliation with Murry who had arrived at her request the same afternoon. Gerald probably met him later the same year, introduced by J.S. Collis; see below, p. 40. Having worked in the War Office in the political intelligence department 1916-19 as a translator and then editor of the Daily Review of the Foreign Press, in 1919 Murry was appointed chief censor and awarded an OBE in 1920. In the 1930s he moved from a kind of Christian or religious socialism to Communism to such extreme pacifism he argued that Hitler should be allowed to master mainland Europe. He then migrated, via quasi-Catholicism, to Anglicanism (almost taking orders in the 1930s), advocating a preventative war against Russia, then a form of Coleridgean elitism, founding an agrarian commune at Thelnetham and concluding his life as a Conservative-voting country gentleman. He expressed his concluding

terms of Modernist art he preferred the Bergsonian painter, J.D. Fergusson, to the more radical Italian Futurists or the Anglo-American avant-gardist Wyndham Lewis.[8] As we shall see, however, he did promote Gaudier-Brzeska, whose work appeared in Lewis's *Blast* and whom he commissioned Gerald to write about many years later, after Gaudier's death in the Great War.[9]

After the war Murry edited *The Athenaeum* and after Mansfield's death in 1923 he launched the *Adelphi*, the influential and long-lived journal to which Gerald became a regular contributor from 1926 until 1932.[10] Immediately following Lawrence's funeral in France, Murry briefly resumed an affair with Frieda before she more permanently resumed hers with Angelo Ravagli, whom she eventually married.[11] At Frieda's death, Ravagli returned to

---

thoughts on religion, which by then resembled Gerald's (and Ebenezer's) in *The Conquest of Death* (London, 1951), a customised edition of his translation of Benjamin Constant's *Adolphe*.

[8] Though *cf. Rhythm's* pre-*Blast* publication of a Picasso drawing; Kaplan, *Circulating Genius*, p. 30.

[9] For Gerald's review Ede's *Savage Messiah* in the *Adelphi* in 1931, see below, p. 151.

[10] The various accounts of Lawrence's 'Last Supper' at the Café Royal in late December 1923, as well as his fictional version of an earlier event: 'Gudrun at the Pompadour' in *Women in Love* (1920), evoke the incestuous ambience into which Gerald arrived from Guernsey, via Bristol University. (Gerald Crich and Gudrun were to some extent based on Murry and Mansfield.) Murry published his book on Lawrence, *Son of Woman* in 1931, after it had appeared in instalments in the *Adelphi*, Gerald commenting on these in his correspondence with the author. If Murry indeed slept with Frieda before Lawrence's death as well as immediately after, this would help explain his self-exculpatory claim that Lawrence was impotent in his final years. He was widely criticised for this book, scornfully by Virginia Woolf in her correspondence, facetiously by Wyndham Lewis, who mocked Murry and Lawrence together in *Time and Tide* (XII, 16, 18 April 1931, pp. 470-72; *cf.* T.S. Eliot in the *Criterion*), and more forcefully by Catherine Carswell, whose *Savage Pilgrimage* Murry legally suppressed in 1932 (albeit after more than a thousand were sold), but then answered in detail in his *Reminiscences of D.H. Lawrence* of 1933. Carswell's title echoes Ede's *Savage Messiah*; her clothes-conscious account of the Café Royal party is on pp. 205-14.

[11] It was Frieda who had informed Murry of Lawrence's enfeebled powers and it is clear that she at least offered herself to Murry prior to Lawrence's death; see his later letter to her in *Frieda Lawrence: The Memoirs and Correspondence*, ed. E.W. Tedlock (London, 1961), p. 282. Although Frieda twice narrates Norman Douglas's offer, after Lawrence's death, of 'a charming boy of 14 but I prefer

his former wife, having, according to Italian law at least, never been divorced in the first place.

Many years after Gerald's death, I discovered that, largely thanks to Murry's recommendation, Jonathan Cape had commissioned him to write what should have been the first major monograph on Lawrence.[12] This would have explained Lawrence and his Messianic message to the world and thereby ensure Gerald obtained a significant starting position from which to launch himself into literary history. That he failed to accomplish this task was partly the result of the great man dying on the eve of their proposed meeting but the postponement of this meeting beyond its possibility epitomises Gerald's tendency to procrastinate. It may also be that Murry's recommendation had been less helpful in eliciting Lawrence's cooperation than Gerald would have required. Gerald's procrastination *vis à vis* the larger Lawrentian, or 'Friedian', project, however, had deeper roots, not merely in his own ambivalent psyche but in his relationship with the psycho-spiritual crisis of early 20th-century Europe.

An excerpt from a letter Lawrence sent to Gerald, dated 1 March 1929 and addressed from the Hotel Beau Rivage, Bandol, in the south of France, is included in the modern edition of Lawrence's *Letters*, though, in the immediately pre-internet age, the editors failed to identify the recipient as the prolific contributor to the *Adelphi* and subsequent author of *The Book of Ebenezer Le Page*. Lawrence begins in slightly off-putting mode:

Murry told me you were writing a book about me – which

them younger' in a somewhat superfluous attempt to damage Douglas's reputation, it suggests her own reputation; see her 1954 letters to Richard Aldington in *Frieda Lawrence and her Circle*, eds. H.T. Moore and D.B. Montague (London, 1981), pp. 105 and 109. That Aldington would have been receptive to such a negative view is clear from his jaundiced account of Douglas in *Pinorman* (1954); see Jean Moorcraft Wilson, 'Norman Douglas and Richard Aldington: A Literary Feud', *Norman Douglas: 8. Symposium: Bregenz und Thuringen, Vlbg, 10/11/10. 2104*, ed. Wilhelm Meusburger (Graz, 2015), pp. 54-59.

[12] Cape (1879-1950) started his own publishers at 11 Gower Street in 1921 and immediately recruited the brilliant reader-editor, Edward Garnett, who, having been a long-standing supporter of Lawrence (and adviser to Duckworth) may have been primarily responsible for commissioning Gerald, which would explain his particular annoyance at the latter's non-delivery; see below p. 87.

of course makes me bristle a bit – I'm sorry I haven't a copy of *The Rainbow* in the world – people always steal my books – I mean my own copies of my own work. [13]

Lawrence then becomes friendlier in tone, however, providing suggestions as to where Gerald might find a copy of the American edition of *The Rainbow* which, he says, was:

> … only one page different from the English editions – what's the odds! The omitted page is one near the end where Ursula is in a hotel in London with the young man – very harmless, I believe...[14]

---

[13] *The Letters of D.H. Lawrence*, VII, ed. Keith Sagar and James T. Boulton (Cambridge, 1993), pp. 200-01. Murry and Katherine Mansfield had stayed in the Villa Pauline, Bandol, in late 1915, where she remained when he returned to England. He returned to Bandol in 1921 when he stayed in the same Hotel Beau Rivage that the Lawrences used; see *The Letters of John Middleton Murry to Katherine Mansfield*, ed. C.A. Hankin (London, 1983), pp. 67-68 and 322.

[14] This letter, which had appeared in John Wilson's manuscripts sale catalogue in March 1981 (the month in which *Ebenezer Le Page* was published) is described as of 3 pages but since it has disappeared can be quoted at no greater length than in the Wilson catalogue (I thank Mr Wilson for trying to help me track down its purchaser, alas to no avail). The 1993 footnote in *The Letters* reads: 'Nothing is known of DHL's correspondent except that he lived in Switzerland and later reviewed Stephen Potter's *D.H. Lawrence: A First Study* (1930), in Murry's *Adelphi*… His own projected work never appeared.' Although, on the basis of our correspondence in 1995, Professor Boulton identifies Gerald more completely in a subsequent article (in which he compares Lawrence's response to him unfavourably with that to Potter), somewhat oddly, given his acknowledgement that my *Guernsey Society Review* articles had made Gerald 'come alive', he still failed to identify him as the author of *Ebenezer Le Page*; see 'Editing D.H. Lawrence's Letters: The Editor's Creative Role', *Prose Studies,* XIX, no. 2 (August 1996), pp. 211-20. *The Rainbow* had been prosecuted for obscenity when first published in 1915 and half the edition of 1250 was destroyed but it was by now back in print. Gerald was trying to obtain a rare copy of the uncensored first edition. Elsewhere Lawrence says the cuts made in the American edition made him 'sad and angry' (*Letters*, II, p. 480). In the summer of 1929, Lawrence's London exhibition of paintings was raided by the police. Interestingly Murry had himself failed to publish a letter sent in by Lawrence in the winter of 1923-4 on the subject of the 'slightly obscene desires' that women provoked in a contributor to the *Adelphi*. Lawrence compared the contributor's response to beautiful women to a coyote howling when it smells fresh meat. 'The hideousness he sees is the reflection of himself, and of the automatic meat-lust with which he approaches another individual... Even the most "beautiful" woman is still a human creature.' (exchange.nottingham.ac.uk/research/unpublished-dh-lawrence-manuscript-discovered-revealing-a-blistering-attack

A later letter from Gerald to Murry (quoted below) reveals that Lawrence had gone on to provide details of his travel plans in order to facilitate a meeting. Lawrence had written to Murry on the same day, responding similarly to a request from the latter for a first edition of *The Rainbow* on Gerald's behalf, largely because Murry was reluctant to lend his younger friend his own dedicated copy.[15]

So profoundly Nietzschean and persuasively Lawrentian was Gerald in this period – in both his conversation and writings - that the likes of Murry himself, as well as younger contemporaries such as J.S. (Jack) Collis and Stephen Potter, hailed him as 'our genius friend', as both Lawrence's John the Baptist and Evangelist; the man most likely to fill the shoes of the miner's son turned similarly-self-exiled literary Messiah [Figs 4 and 5]. This is confirmed by the tone and content of Gerald's numerous letters to Murry, which I was fortunate enough to find in an Oxford bookshop, as well as by those to Collis, which were kindly loaned to me by his biographer, Richard Ingrams.[16] Further evidence is to be found in the unpublished autobiography of Stephen Potter (of *One-Upmanship* fame), sections of which were loaned to me by Potter's son, Julian.[17]

---

-on-1920s-misogyny/)

[15] *Letters of D.H. Lawrence*, VII, p. 200. Murry had not otherwise written to Lawrence since 1926; see Harry T. Moore, *The Priest of Love: A Life of D.H. Lawrence* (London, 1974), p. 465.

[16] The Collis letters were themselves on loan to Richard Ingrams from Collis's literary executor, Michael Holroyd, for the purposes of writing his *John Stewart Collis: A Memoir* (London, 1986). Sir Michael has now deposited the letters and other literary materials in the library of Trinity College Dublin (where they are for the time being inaccessible). When in 1985 I found that James Fergusson, then managing Robin Waterfield's Oxford bookshop, had obtained the Middleton Murry archive, I persuaded him to sell me his letters from Gerald; see *Waterfield's Catalogue 50; Twentieth Century English Literature* (1985), item 1378.

[17] In April 1994 Julian Potter kindly wrote that my *Guernsey Society* article: 'brings [Gerald] to life better than anything my father wrote about him. He obviously had a mesmerizing influence on my father and Jack Collis. I think Stephen felt inhibited and patronised by what was a teacher-disciple relationship, and wanted to be free, as he wrote in the excerpt, "to choose his own authors".'(*cf.* below, p. 173).

Fig. 4: *Stephen Potter* (1900-1969), (photo: Ottoline Morrell, 1935). (National Portrait Gallery)

Fig. 5: *J.S. 'Jack' Collis (1900-1984),* (oil on canvas: John Lavery, 1940). (National Gallery Ireland).

The clearest confirmation of Gerald's status and influence on this circle is to be found in Collis's own writings after his reputation, unlike Gerald's, had been successfully revived in the early 1970s. Gerald's affinity with, and zeal for, Lawrence was such that he inspired Potter to produce a short version of the monograph he failed to deliver himself. The Irish-born but Oxford-educated Collis, on the other hand, already the author of a highly-praised book on Bernard Shaw (whom Gerald lambasted in the July 1926 *Adelphi*), based himself on those authors Lawrence had chosen as his own spiritual mentors.

Enthusing in his autobiography over the writings of Walt Whitman and Edward Carpenter, Collis reveals that even these 'were introduced to Stephen and myself by our mutual friend and mentor, G.B. Edwards, and I doubt if we would have come upon them at the right time otherwise'.[18] Collis published this in

---

[18] J.S. Collis, *Bound upon a Course* (London, 1971; reprinted in paperback 1991), p. 108. Potter continued to promote Whitman when he worked for the BBC, commissioning Stephen Spender to broadcast the first of his series, 'New Judgements,' on him in October 1941; see Julian Potter, *Stephen Potter at the BBC: 'Features in War and Peace'* (Orford, 2004), p. 122, where, Gerald-like, Potter confides in his diary that Spender 'falls short on the acceptance of the "true"

1971, a year before I met Gerald, but although the latter kept up with all the reviews and was therefore very likely to have sought out this book and been aware of this reference to him by his one-time intimate, he never mentioned it; neither he nor Collis ever seem to have attempted to renew their acquaintance.

Yet just over a decade later, and half a decade after the death of the friend he had not met for almost half a century, Collis published an extraordinarily personal (and poignant) response to the publication of the Penguin edition of *The Book of Ebenezer Le Page*. Presumably in consultation with A.N. Wilson, the then literary editor of the *Spectator*, he entitled this long review-cum-lamentation: 'Memories of a Genius Friend.'[19] By this time Gerald's novel had been widely and enthusiastically reviewed by the likes of William Golding and Guy Davenport and was being read on Radio 4 by Roy Dotrice (see Part II, Chapter 1).

Though, apart from his landlady, Joan Snell, I was the closest, effectively the only friend of this 'Genius' in the last years of his

---

Whitman.'; *cf.* Alan Jenkins, *Stephen Potter: Inventor of Gamesmanship* (London, 1980), which confirms that Potter was indeed introduced to *The Leaves of Grass* by Gerald (pp. 62 and 78); *cf.* Potter's unpublished autobiography, vol. II, on which this is based, kindly loaned to me by his son, Julian, quoted below, p. 50 (now University of Texas). Gerald linked Whitman and Shakespeare and compared both favourably (and facetiously) with Bernard Shaw in his critical essay on the latter in the *Adelphi* for July 1926; see below, p. 58. He also wrote to Murry from Erstfeld on 24 September 1929 that he had begun an essay on Whitman; below, p. 101. One of the last things Murry wrote was the essay on Whitman as poet-prophet of the free society, the first of his four *Unprofessional Essays*, published in 1955, two years before he died. In *Bound upon a Course*, Collis wrote eulogistically of Carpenter's *Art of Creation* and his *Pagan and Christian Creeds*, both 'extraordinarily illuminating, the latter especially with regard to the upshot of Frazer's *The Golden Bough*. Then again there was the man himself, a bright particular star of the English genius' (*ibid.*, pp. 108-9). The extent of Gerald's influence upon Collis is above all confirmed in the unpublished novel, presumably the *Progress of an Artist* to which Ingrams refers, pp. 57 and 118. It describes a visit by Gerald to Collis's Rotherhithe flat in the wake of his mother's death and the 'Socratic dialogues' they would have at this time, 'that is to say they were not dialogues at all, they were more like question and answer, one side taking the other giving… In thus surrendering himself to another man Mark [Collis] showed little character' (p. 141). In this dialogue, Collis remembers Gerald quoting from Carpenter's *Towards Democracy*; see below, p. 240.

[19] Collis, 'Memories of a Genius Friend', pp. 21-23; *cf.* below, pp. 48, 177, 224, 237, 341.

life, I knew next to nothing of his previous seven decades. What follows is my attempt to document these decades as thoroughly as possible, from his birth in Guernsey in 1899 until his death in Upwey in 1976.

## 2: GUERNSEY ORIGINS

The only son from the second marriage of a Guernsey quarry owner, Gerald Bazil Edwards was born in the substantial family home, Sous Les Hougues, St Sampson's, on 8 July 1899 [Fig. 6]. In his first letter to me, dated 28 November 1972, he wrote that the name 'Edwards' was fairly common in Guernsey:

> My particular branch, no doubt, stems from Wales, as do the others; but the earliest ancestor I know of on my father's side was Zackariah Edwards of Dalwood, Devon, who married a gipsy and begat a brood of stalwart sons, who migrated to every quarter of the globe. He was my great-grandfather.[20]

Gerald's paternal grandfather, whom he calls 'Tom', but who seems to have been christened George, 'married one Mary Organ of Honiton and migrated to Guernsey at the age of 19 for

Fig. 6: *Sous Les Hougues, St Sampson's, Guernsey* (photo: Ciprian Ilie).

---

[20] See below, p. 244, for full text.

the "stone rush", when the quarries of the north were opened'.

This, and a good deal else of his somewhat romanticising account, does not correspond with the Guernsey records.[21] According to the latter, Gerald's great grandfather was not called Zachariah, but rather more mundanely, John (his biblical son), born in 1801, the son of James, who was born in 1762. He and his father, however, were indeed from Dalwood (in fact part of Dorset until 1844), as were their Edwards predecessors, usually baptised John, going back at least as far the seventeenth century.[22] James's wife's parents are documented as resident in Thorncombe, across the border in Dorset, she herself having been baptised there as Arnella White on 18 April 1771.[23]

In 1826, Gerald's great grandfather, John, married an Elizabeth Gage (about whom so little is known she might indeed have been a gipsy). They had four sons, one of whom was indeed called Tom but ostensibly, at least, it seems to have been his older brother George (born c.1835) who fathered Thomas (born 1861), who in turn fathered Gerald in 1899 [Fig. 7]. Categorised as a 'Carrieur' or quarryman, George is recorded as having married Isabella Underdown of Colyton (born 1835) in the Town Church, St Peter Port, on 7 February 1858.[24] Mary Organ was George's second wife whom he married in 1897 and was from

---

[21] Gerald's father's baptism in St Sampson's Church records *his* father's name as George. This George is in turn referred to in several Guernsey records as being the son of John, for example 'Partage des rentes venantes appartenant de la succession du feu Monsieur George Edwards fils Jean,' dated 2 September 1915 (Contrats de Partage, Greffe). I thank Stephen Foote for this information.

[22] John Fowles continued to interest himself in Gerald's biography after writing the introduction to *The Book of Ebenezer Le Page* (he reprinted this in his collection: *Wormholes* in 1998). He wrote to me in August 1997 about the possibility of a 19th-century botanist, the Reverend Zachariah Edwards of Combpyne in Devon being an ancestor but he doesn't seem to have been related. Despite Gerald's claim that his early ancestors were Welsh there are Dalwood Edwardses dating back at least as far as the mid-seventeenth century.

[23] Daughter of John and Arnella, or Eleanor White, baptised 18 April 1771. (www.opcdorset.org/ThorncombeFiles/ThorncombeBaps1.htm - original in Dorchester Record Office). James and Arnella had other sons, including the eldest James, born in 1799 who married an Ann from Honiton.

[24] Isabella was the illegitimate daughter of Ann Underdown; Colyton baptisms register, 1835; I thank Stephen Foote for this reference.

Fig. 7: Gerald's father, Tom Edwards (centre); Bordeaux Quarry, c.1910.

Clanfield in Hampshire rather than Honiton. George and his three brothers all settled in Guernsey in the 1850s. His eldest brother, John, died shortly after his marriage to Emilia Priaulx, and James raised a family of nine children whilst pursuing a career at sea. George's younger brother Thomas, after whom Gerald's father was presumably named, settled in St Sampson's, marrying a girl from Bridport named Thirza England in April 1864. They had at least eleven children and still have many descendants on the island, including Jeane Holmes, *née* Edwards, who kindly helped with this genealogy.

In Guernsey, George acquired his own quarry and relatively early handed this over to his son, after which he acquired Câtel Farm and took up cattle dealing.[25] That son, Gerald's father, was

---

[25] See the 1891 census for Hougue du Pommier, Câtel, where the household consists of George, 'Cattle dealer' and his wife Isabella, both listed as of 56 years of age (interestingly, in the 1861 Census, she had been two years older than her husband, with George, son aged 21, 'Farm labourer born Vale' and William aged 14 (see below, p. 27): 'Carpenter's App[rentice] born Vale'. After Isabella's death in 1896, George remarried and moved to Alderney. His second wife, widow Mary Organ, demonstrates that Gerald's account of his family history was non-fictitional in parts. They were married in 1897 in the English Wesleyan Chapel in Alderney, and lived there for 18 years until his death in 1915. The 'Morts dans l'ile d'Auregny' for 1 May 1915 describe George Edwards as having died aged 78 from 'senile decay' as a 'Retired Farmer'. I thank Sally Bohan in Alderney for

baptised Thomas in St Sampson's in June 1861.[26]

Reverting to Gerald's account: 'at twelve [Tom] ran away from his strap-wielding father and his mother, who had a bosom of iron, to the softer usages of sailing ships.' After seeing the world he eventually returned home, having apparently 'never overcome his tendency to sea-sickness,' and according to Gerald, 'married at the age of 26'. I double-checked his writing at this point and he clearly writes '26' though it was in fact on 11 April 1882, when he was still only 20, that his father married his first wife, whom the records tell us was Louisa Alice Simon.[27]

Gerald informed me that he was the only child of his father's second marriage, 'from the first of which two half-sisters of mine survived' [Figs 8 and 11]. The records reveal that there were in fact seven other children by the first marriage, but that five of these died of various ailments before the age of three, including the first-born who in 1883 was baptised Isabella Louise, presumably after her grandmother and mother. Their mother, Tom's wife, Louisa Simon, died in 1892 at the age of 29 of 'inflammation of the throat', in the same week as her youngest child, Janet Christine, died of 'consumption of the spine.'[28]

Tom's second wife, Gerald's Calvinist mother, Harriet Mauger, hailed from a far older and larger Guernsey family, descended, he claimed, from a Norman who married a Guille, having been exiled to the island by William the Conqueror [Fig. 9].[29]

---

these references.

[26] Born Tuesday 28 May 1861; baptised Sunday 16 June 1861. Baptismal sponsors were George Edwards, Thomas Edwards and Isabella Underdown (his mother). See Fig. 7 for photograph of Gerald's father Tom, posing in what is described as the Bordeaux Quarry with his men.

[27] St Sampson's Church, Marriages register 1882, p. 93 (microfilm copy, Priaulx Library).

[28] Civil Deaths Register 1892, Greffe, folio 274, entries 39 & 40 (microfilm copy, Priaulx Library)

[29] See his letter detailing this below, p. 245. This is a Guernsey legend that William the Conqueror's uncle, Archbishop Mauger, criticised William for marrying his cousin, Matilda. William therefore banished the Archbishop to Guernsey, where he fell in love with a girl of the Guille family, and established the ubiquitous Mauger family; see Edgar MacCulloch, *Guernsey Folk Lore* (London 1903), pp. 444-45: 'All who bear the name, even in the humblest ranks

Fig. 8: *Gerald Edwards*,
aged 8, c.1907.

Fig. 9: *Harriet Edwards*
(*née Mauger*), Gerald's mother.

Fig. 10: *Hawkesbury*, Braye Road, Guernsey (photo: the author).

of society, have heard of the Archbishop, and pride themselves in their supposed descent from him.'

In January 1900, Thomas acquired a field in the Braye Road for himself and his wife and built a large house called 'Hawkesbury' upon it. The 1901 census records Tom and Harriet, having already moved out of Sous Les Hougues into the new house [Fig. 10].[30]

With them and the one-year-old Gerald was his half-sister, the 16-year-old Kathleen, Tom's eldest surviving daughter by his previous marriage to Louisa Simon.[31] According to Gerald's cousin, Clary Dumond, Gerald 'was very fond of' Kathleen or Kate, born in 1884 (the year of her one-and-a-half-year-older sister's death), and might thus have been the inspiration for Ebenezer's sister, Tabitha.[32] The latter is the most straightforwardly sympathetic depiction of a woman in a novel not otherwise overflowing with positive depictions of the female of the species.[33] In the light of recent research any such

---

[30] On 24 September 2008 we unveiled a Blue Plaque in honour of Gerald's residence on the façade of 'Hawkesbury'. Not long before this was erected the house was valued at £2,000,000, a reminder, if ever one were needed, not to identify Ebenezer too closely with Gerald, the only child of the second marriage of relatively prosperous parents.

[31] There was another daughter, Rose Evaline, by this marriage but despite being a year younger she is not listed here. After her father's second marriage she went into service and in the 1901 census is listed as a housemaid in the service of Laura Thursden, La Herronière, The Banks, St Sampson's. By 1911, she had progressed to cook for Thomas de Sausmarez at Springfield, King's Road. She left Guernsey in 1915, and a year later took a job as a 'munitionette' at Woolwich Arsenal. She was walking across one of London's bridges with a group of other workers when two girls slipped and fell. One girl broke her hip, the other her leg. Rose stayed with them until an ambulance arrived but caught a chill and died on 13 February 1917. Her sister, Kathleen, travelled to London for the funeral (Liz Walton, 'Guernsey Women and the Great War', *Channel Islands Great War Study Group*, greatwarci.net, 2011 citing 'Death of a Guernsey War Worker: The Late Miss Rose Edwards', *Guernsey Evening Press*, 24 Feb 1917). I am grateful to Susan Ilie for finding this reference. Rose's great-niece Sarah Inman, informs me that Rose was buried, with two others, in Plumstead Cemetery.

[32] This son of Gerald's cousin, Hilda Dumond, the late Clary Dumond to whom I am very grateful for information on such matters as well as family photographs and memorabilia, though here perhaps, as occasionally elsewhere, he tended to conflate Gerald's fiction with supposed facts. Since he also says 'I know very little about her [Kate] but she died', it is even possible Clary was confusing her with her younger sister, Rose. The 86-year-old Clary, who used to address me as 'Neville Falla', was fatally injured by a car on Christmas Eve 1998.

[33] As ever I thank Stephen Foote and Jane Mosse for genealogical work on this,

straightforward identification seems unlikely and indeed Kathleen was at least in part the source for one of Gerald's most negative vignettes. When she married the young jeweller's assistant, Augustus Thoumine, at the Greffe on 11 October 1904 Kathleen would have been visibly pregnant, for baby Augustus Eric was born 10 December 1904. When their daughter, also named Kathleen then left Guernsey and married an Englishman, Frederick Felgate 'Eric' Stone, in Hendon in 1927 Kathleen senior left her husband and son and went to live with them as a sort of housekeeper in London [Fig. 11].

Fig. 11: Gerald's half-sister, Kathleen Thoumine, *née* Edwards, with her daughter, Kathleen and grandson Michael (photo: Sarah Inman).

If Gerald and his half-sister Kathleen were close in his early years, Kathleen's grandchildren cannot confirm any contact between them during the period that both lived in humble

---

but special thanks to Kathleen's granddaughter, Gerald's great-niece, Sarah Inman, for further details and her generous willingness to share more personal reminiscences. The name Tabitha, that Gerald gives Ebenezer's sister, is the Aramaic version of the Greek 'Dorcas', he gave his own daughter. Tabitha/Dorcas of Joppa/Jaffa is raised from the dead by St Peter in the *Acts of the Apostles*, as depicted in the Masaccio/Masolino Carmine fresco in Florence. Augustus Thoumine's sister, who emigrated to America with her mother, was also baptised Dorcas (see next note). Ebenezer's own name is, incidentally, derived from the Hebrew: 'Eben ha-Ezer' meaning 'stone of the help'.

circumstances in London during and after the war, Kathleen dying in 1960.[34] And so far from positive memories of his half-sister, Gerald clearly based the following passage in *Ebenezer Le Page* on what he heard of his brother-in-law's fate. Having passed a flirtatious note to a well-developed girl wearing a tight blue velvet frock in his Sunday School class, the younger Ebenezer was dismayed that instead of responding positively to his declaration of love she immediately reported him to their teacher and he was accordingly punished:

> I never looked at Marie Le Noury again. She married Reg Symes, an English chap in the Artillery stationed at Castle Cornet. He was a great boy with the Indian clubs and used to give displays at military concerts; but he came out of the Army to please her and opened a little shop in the Commercial Arcade for mending clocks and watches. He worshipped the ground she walked on. When she got to middle age she left him and went to live with her married daughter in England; and he put his head in the gas oven and was found dead in the morning. I was lucky, really.[35]

That 'Reg Symes' had a watch-mender's shop, that his wife left him to live with her married daughter in England and that he died by putting his head in a gas oven, make it certain that the whole incident was based on Gerald's half-sister's decision to leave her husband and its complex consequences.

Not only did the abandoned 61-year-old Augustus Thoumine [Fig. 12] indeed commit suicide by gassing himself, his granddaughter, Sarah Inman, has informed me that her mother and grandmother had a terrible relationship, the reasons for which her mother would never discuss.[36] Kathleen junior (Kitty)

---

[34] Kathleen seems to have received Red Cross messages from her step-mother, Rosina, in 1942 reporting that she and her father, Thomas, were working in the vinery (*Channel Islands Monthy Review* [Stockport, August 1942], p. 43). One wonders whether Gerald was kept similarly informed. If Gerald did meet his half-sister again it seems most likely they would have met in Guernsey, rather than London, at their father's funeral in early 1946, when both would also have met Rosina. Her grand-daughter Sarah, however, informs me Kathleen never revisited Guernsey; see below, p. 199.

[35] *Ebenezer Le Page*, p. 12.

[36] Augustus had already been abandoned by his sister, Dorcas, who emigrated

24

had a son, Michael, by first husband Eric, but this marriage did not survive and in 1939 she remarried in Kensington, Charles Montague Cahn, by whom she had two children, Sarah (later Inman) and Catherine. Sarah eventually discovered that after Eric lost his job in the depression and her mother, Kathleen junior, was therefore obliged to go out to work, the still-married Kathleen senior had an affair with her daughter's stay-at-home husband. Kathleen junior's marriage ended partly as a result and she never forgave her mother. Her children by both marriages remember terrible rows and Kathleen senior living elsewhere in London in relative poverty.

Fig. 12: *Augustus Thoumine* (1882-1943), Occupation ID, 1941 (Island Archives).

Apart from the already somewhat creative account of his antecedents in his first letters to me, Gerald likewise never discussed his family, preferring to project or sublimate his life's sometimes sordid realities into a novel in which he could temper Verga-like 'fate-embracing' realism with satirical or occasionally quasi-Proustian romance.[37]

In terms of romance but also evidence of the care with which his novel is constructed, the note that the young Ebenezer had

---

to New York with her husband, George Godden. Their mother, also Dorcas, died in Manhattan whilst visiting them there in 1920. According to an article on p. 2 of the *Guernsey Press* of 4 October 1943, Augustus's still warm body was found by his son, Gus, at his home in 6 Commercial Arcade, St Peter Port. He was lying in bed with a gas tube in his mouth. A fellow employee said he shook hands with his workmates on Saturday (at the Jewellers and Silversmiths and Co., also in Commercial Arcade) and said he would not be at work on Monday. He had often spoken of suicide, saying 'If I could snuff my life out like turning on the electric light, I would'.

[37] Gerald writes to Murry offering to review Proust's *Sodom and Gomorrah* in April 1929; see below, p. 96. For Giovanni Verga, see, p. 213. In his perceptive *New York Times* review of *Ebenezer*, Guy Davenport wrote: 'This is a Proustian work in two senses. It conceals its major theme in a river of sharply observed, seemingly trivial events, and leaves it to us to chart the course of the river and

passed to the girl behind him - on a page torn out of his hymn-book - was inscribed simply: 'Je t'aime, Marie':

> I thought she would write back 'Je t'aime, Ebenezer', but instead I heard her saying, 'Look, Miss Collas, what one of the boys has given to me!'

At the end of the novel, the aged Ebenezer's young friend drives him to see the love of his life, Liza Quéripel, who is by now a little old lady tending her chickens. She reciprocated in the way he had hoped Marie Le Noury would some seventy years before.

> She came to me then, and caught hold of me; and I held her close and kissed her on the mouth. She was small and frail, smaller than me now; but her mouth was hungry yet, and she was soft as a young woman in my arms. 'Je t'aime, Liza,' I said. She said, 'Je t'aime, Ebenezer.'[38]

Another early episode in the novel involved the suicide of Ebenezer's uncle. In the process of writing this book it has emerged that this was based even more closely on family history. Here as elsewhere the fictional version may enhance our understanding of what really happened. The comparison also illustrates Gerald's cryptic way of dealing with what he presumably means was Ebenezer's uncle's homosexuality, with the implication - given the similarity between the two stories - that Gerald's uncle may have dreaded marriage for the same reason. On occasions like this it is as if Gerald is writing largely for himself (albeit as Ebenezer) yet here as elsewhere this strangely personal style results in a heightened sense of authenticity.

> My father thought the world of his young brother. Willie was a great sportsman and won the championship cup three years running at the Cycling Track. His photo was in Bucktrout's window down High Street, standing by his

---

realise its shape, its gesture, on a map of which Ebenezer is necessarily unaware. Like Proust, Edwards can make us feel the passage of time as a tragic force. Like Proust, he has a surprise for us that can only be convincingly revealed in the fullness of time. For this is a novel you must read every word of, or miss the deeply human meaning altogether.'

[38] *Ebenezer Le Page*, p. 391.

penny-farthing bicycle, which was nearly as high as him, with the big silver cup at his feet. He laughed at my father for bothering about what was going to happen to the Boers. 'Look after Number One, Alf,' he said, 'and let the world manage its own affairs.' He didn't manage his own affairs very well, my Uncle Willie. He was gardener for Mr Roger de Lisle from the Grange and a friend of the son and lived in the house: then if he didn't let himself be dragged into getting engaged to a girl Le Couture from St Martin's. The evening before the wedding he said he was going to shoot rabbits on Jerbourg. When long after dark he didn't come back, young de Lisle went to look for him and found him shot dead through the head. It was decided at the inquest it was an accident; but everybody knew he had done it on purpose. He was used to handling a gun from a boy, and had won prizes at Bisley. I knew why he had done it, the poor chap. He did the brave thing. After waiting a year, the Le Couture girl married old Cohu from Les Petites Caches for his second wife and he left her well off.[39]

Gerald never mentioned that on 24 May 1901, on the eve of marrying a Miss Bisson of L'Ancresse, one of his father's younger brothers, William, described in the *Press* as living with his married brother at Câtel Farm, shot himself in a nearby field.[40]

Câtel Farm [Fig. 13], near the Hougue du Pommier, had been the family home since the 1880s when Gerald's grandfather, George, had handed the arduous quarrying business over to his eldest son, Gerald's father Tom, to opt for the less strenuous trade of cattle dealing. When his wife Isabella died, George senior remarried and moved to Alderney, leaving the farm in the care of his two youngest sons: the unfortunate William; and his elder brother George [Fig. 14].

---

[39] *Ebenezer Le Page*, pp. 6-7.

[40] 'Fatality at the Castel', *Guernsey Evening Press*, Saturday 25 May 1901. I thank Jane Mosse for this reference. William is described as aged 23 in the Press but was born on 10 April 1875 so was in fact 26 at the time of his death. A still younger brother, Archie, had died in 1884. George and Rachel's son, Archie, who went to America, was presumably named after him; see below p. 31.

Fig. 13: *Castel Farm, Rue de la Charuée, Guernsey* (photo : Ciprian Ilie).

Fig. 14: *Rachel Edwards*
*(née Mauger)*
(1864-1937).

Fig. 15: *George Edwards* (1869-1949)
Occupation Identity card, 1941.
(Island Archives).

George junior was married to Rachel Mauger [Fig. 15], the elder sister of Harriet, whom Tom married after his first wife died. Thus the two Edwards brothers ended up married to two Mauger sisters who, even if not quite as formidable as La Prissy and La Hetty, clearly inspired the Martel family structure that dominates the first half of *The Book of Ebenezer Le Page*.

Fig. 16: *The Maugers of Le Petit Désert*: top row, left to right: Mary Ann,
Louisa, Daniel senior, Charlotte (who married Nicholas Le Page).
Front row: Rachel (married George Edwards), Daniel junior, Harriet
(Gerald's mother), Charlotte (*née* Trachy), c.1873.

The parents of Rachel and Harriet, Daniel and Charlotte
Mauger, had one surviving son and at least three other
daughters, one of whom, the eldest, also Charlotte, married
Nicholas Le Page, whom his great-nephew, Clary Dumond,
believed was a significant source for Ebenezer [Figs 16 & 17].[41]

---

[41] But Clary also says, in a letter to the author, that Nicholas, who died aged 65
in 1921, was 'the one who was in the Pigsty with the hat on' (*cf. Ebenezer Le Page*,

Fig 17: *Nic Le Page*, Gerald's cousin.

Fig 18: *Harry Bougourd and Mary Ann (née Mauger).*

The middle sister, though it seems the least good-looking, was Mary Ann Mauger, who married the even less handsome Henry (Harry) John Mahy Bougourd [Fig. 18].[42]

This couple had a daughter, Hilda, who became the mother of Clary Dumond [Fig. 19]. The latter claimed that his mother was the source for the Mary Ann in *Ebenezer Le Page*, 'who had set her heart on a white wedding, but La Prissy said, "Mon Dou, but

Fig. 19: *Clary Dumond* (photo: the author, c.1991).

p. 8). When he finally names Ebenezer's mother, Gerald decides to call her Charlotte. I first published this photograph of the Mauger family 20 years ago but for various reasons the identification of several of the sitters was incorrect; see *Review of the Guernsey Society*, Spring 1995, p. 21.

[42] Mary Ann died aged 52 on 14 January 1918.

Fig. 20: *Archie Edwards* (1896-1955)
with daughter Marjorie (1924-2014).

Fig. 21: *Herbert Edwards*
(1906-1945).

you wouldn't have the cheek, you!" so the bridesmaids was in white, but she wore a blue dress cut loose and with a long train…'.[43]

That the vivid family dramas which characterise *Ebenezer*'s early chapters were inspired by the ambience in which Gerald grew up is confirmed by the saga of George and Rachel's son, Gerald's eighteen-year-old cousin Archie, who in 1914 got a girl 'into trouble'[Fig. 20].[44] His father wouldn't let him marry her so she was sent to stay with his step-grandmother in Alderney where the baby was still-born. Archie was meanwhile packed off to

---

[43] *Ebenezer Le Page*, p. 34.

[44] Letter to me from Clary Dumond who, however, probably conflated fact with fiction in naming 'Isobel Mansell' as the girl impregnated by the real Archie as well as the fictional Horace ('the only girl he ever really liked'; *Ebenezer Le Page*, p. 50). Clary also says the baby was still-born: 'oh said Rachel, Prissy oh will [*sic*] every thing turned out for the best. So time came Isobel married a sergeant in the army, in Alderney.' It seems unlikely that Gerald would have used her real name in his novel. For a revealing reference by Gerald to a minor character in *Ebenezer Le Page* as Archie Mauger, see below, p. 272. It was in 1914 that Gerald's mother (perhaps knowing that her husband was already partial to their widowed housekeeper?) drew up her will; see below, p. 40.

America, just as Raymond's cousin, Horace, is packed off by *his* father, Percy Martel, in the novel. Whereas Horace came back to Guernsey, however, with all that ensued, Archie returned just once in April 1937, presumably to see his ailing mother who died the following December. [45] He returned to America after less than a month and eventually died in Saginaw, Michigan, in June 1955.

Although, according to Clary Dumond, she initially supported the idea of sending him away, Archie's emigration ultimately so upset his mother, Gerald's aunt Rachel, that having failed to 'go over to the U.S.A. and join her son', she took to drink and abandoned Câtel Farm to George and their other son Herbert, who then starved to death as a result of the German occupation [Fig. 21]. [46] A contributory factor in her decline, though common enough, may have been the death of her second son, who was indeed named Horace, 'dearly beloved child of George and Rachel Edwards who died May 29th 1909, aged 4 years, 7 months and 8 Days', according to the invitation to his funeral [Fig. 22]. [47] No doubt this inspired the fictional fate of Horace's younger brother, Cyril Martel, who died aged 5, leaving La Prissy distraught. [48]

---

[45] Passenger List, SS *Berengaria*, arrival Southampton from New York , 21 April 1937 (TNA, BT26/1134/5, Ancestry.com. UK, Incoming Passenger Lists, 1878-1960) and Passenger List, SS *Acquitania*, departure 27 May 1937, Southampton to New York (Passenger Lists leaving UK 1890-1960, findmypast.co.uk). I thank Stephen Foote for these references.

[46] Letter from Clary Dumond: 'His father [George] wouldn't even except [*sic*] the Red Cross parcels. The only one cow they had left was one night killed in a field at the back of the house only the skin was left, could have been the Germans who did the job.' He actually died on 3 August 1945, several months after the Liberation. Rachel died at Castel Farm in 1937 of 'morbus cordis' according the records; Castel Civil Deaths Register, folio 535 entry 120, Greffe.

[47] According to Clary Dumond, 'when Horace died his mother Rachel left Horace's bed as it was... Herbert was found lying on the same bed. My mother [Hilda] Mary Ann in the book was still going there up to about a month just before he died. Uncle George ... now being on his own made setain [*sic*] advances to my mother so she promptly put on her coat and left the house and never went there again.' 'Uncle George died soon after the Liberation, Archie had written, but uncle said he'd rather go broke than except his help; so ends a very sad story of George Edwards of Câtel Farm.'

[48] *Ebenezer Le Page*, p. 26

Fig. 22: Funeral card for Horace Edwards,
who died in 1909 aged 4.

As the little Horace's nine-year-old first-cousin, Gerald would probably have joined his funeral procession on 2 June (as the young Ebenezer follows his grandmother's), included among the 'Men and Women,' (women were often not expected to attend a funeral). The funeral card printed by undertakers N. Mahy in English rather than French advised them: 'To leave the House, "Câtel Farm, Guernsey," at half-past Two o'clock'. As relatively recent immigrants, the surviving funeral cards for the Edwards family tend to be in English while those for the Maugers are, with few exceptions (e.g. that for Louisa Mauger, widow of Michael Thomas Balcke) in French.

Gerald would refer to Patois as the 'the speech I was born into' (see below, p. 281), but although he may have spoken Guernsey French as a small boy, he is unlikely to have spoken enough to rival his literary hero, Joseph Conrad, in claiming to be a non-native-speaking English novelist. Ebenezer's grandmother: 'didn't speak the English, and could only read the Bible in French. My mother spoke the English a little, and the big Bible was in English.'[49] But the first school Gerald attended was the Misses Cohu's school at the Albion Terrace, Vale Road, the same that he had Raymond attend in the novel, and therefore likely to reflect his own history in this respect:

---

[49] *Ebenezer Le Page*, p. 8; *cf.* Peter Goodall, ' "The Rock whence ye are hewn": *The Book of Ebenezer Le Page* and Guernsey Literature and History', *The Modern Language Review*, 103, no. 1 (January 2008), pp. 22-34, n.23.

There was one thing [Raymond] was ashamed of his mother for, and that was the way she spoke English. He was everlastingly teasing her for saying 'tree' for 'three' and 'true' for 'through' and for not sounding her aitches and all the rest of it. I didn't like him for that. It was partly Hetty's own fault, because she had never let him speak in patois, from the days he went to the Misses Cohu's School. She wanted him to grow up to speak English like the gentry...[50]

One of the passages that Hamish Hamilton omitted from the *Book* as published, provides more on the Misses Cohu:

He [Raymond] was five and a half or nearly six, when he started going to the Misses Cohu's school. He wasn't strong enough and was excused from going before; though by law he ought to have gone when he was five. He made me laugh over the Misses Cohu. There was two Misses Cohu. Miss Annette Cohu and Miss Louise Cohu. Miss Annette was very short and very upright; and had a face like a walnut with whiskers. He said the older she got, the shorter she got and in the end, she didn't die: her head and her feet met...[51].

From this junior school, in April 1909 Gerald entered the Hautes Capelles. No doubt this was where he learned history, as Ebenezer did at the nearby Vale School:

History was dates. I have forgotten most of it now, but I know it began in 55 B.C. when Julius Caesar landed in Britain; and I remember A.D. 1066, because that was the year we conquered England.[52]

A photograph survives of Form IIIa (1911-12) in which Gerald is probably the boy almost obscured by the one in front of him, on the extreme left of the third row; his friend, Wilfrid Burgess, is more clearly visible, third from right at the front [Fig. 23].[53]

---

[50] Raymond is sent there, because his mother 'wanted him to grow up to speak English like the gentry' (see *Ebenezer Le Page* p. 25 and p. 96). Raymond was also taught the piano by Miss Annette Cohu (p. 30).

[51] *Ebenezer Le Page*, original typescript, p. 410. Sadly, page 411 of the typescript, which continued this cut section, seems to have been destroyed by the publisher.

[52] *Ebenezer Le Page*, p. 10

[53] For Wilfrid de Lisle Burgess, see below, pp. 37-38.

Fig. 23: Hautes Capelles: form IIIa, 1911-12, form master Mr. W. Buckley.

From here Gerald won a scholarship to the Boys' Intermediate School, now the Grammar School. Gerald returned to the Hautes Capelles as a pupil-teacher but transferred to the Vauvert School in St Peter Port in July 1914 after his mother decided he was becoming too fond of fellow-teacher, 'Miss Waymouth'.[54] Combining Burgess's reminiscences with the 1911 census it is very likely that this was Alice Christine Waymouth, the youngest daughter of Richard Henry

---

[54] Reminiscences of Clary Dumond, who was a five-year-old pupil at the school when Gerald taught there, in an undated letter to me from the early-1980s: 'Gerald was in love with Miss Waymouth he wanted to marry her but of course Aunt Harriet wouldn't have it Miss Waymouth was not good enough for her son Gerald. When after the war Gerald turned up with his new wife to be to [sic] us kids and Mum thought she was very nice…'. Clary had been the principal source for the illustrated article on Gerald's early life by Nick Le Messurier in the *Guernsey Evening Press*, 18 June 1981. In his Ebenezerish letters to me he laments that Gerald didn't marry the Waymouth girl and have a happier existence. In an undated letter from Harry Tomlinson to John Fowles, which the latter forwarded to me in September 1980, Tomlinson says that Gerald was admitted to the States Intermediate School from Misses Cohu's school on 26 April 1909 and then became a pupil teacher at Vauvert in July 1914, with no mention of his being a pupil-teacher at Hautes Capelles. For D.H. Lawrence's pupil-teachership, teaching to subsidise one's ongoing education, see Worthen, *Lawrence: The Early Years*, p. 114. As a shy boy, Gerald's initial experience of this was no doubt as difficult as it had been for the 17-year-old Lawrence, albeit, one would hope, not as traumatic as Ursula Brangwen's in *The Rainbow*.

Waymouth, the baker at L'Islet, who was originally from Ilsington, Devon [Fig. 24].[55] It seems likely that La Hetty's unsuccessful attempts to prevent Raymond's marriage to Christine Mahy reflect an equivalent success on the part of Gerald's mother.

Fig. 24: Miss Waymouth with her class, Haute Capelles School, c.1923.

Although during the Great War he joined the Royal Guernsey Light Infantry some time after it was formed in December 1916, Gerald seems not to have been sent to France, where the regiment suffered heavy casualties, but ended up in Portsmouth instead. [56]

Some of those he knew fared less well. The death of Ebenezer's best friend Jim Mahy may not be based on an equivalently traumatic loss in real life, but other episodes in the novel conjure up a convincing enough picture of the terrible consequences of war:

> Jim Le Poidevin was the last of the three Jims; and lived for many years after Jim Machon died. He wasn't as big as my Jim, but slim and well-built when he was a young chap; and, before he went to France, used to go to dances a lot. He was engaged to Étienne de la Mare from the Vauquiédor and, when she heard what had happened to him, she said she would marry him if he had lost both legs; but he hadn't been back a week before the engagement was broken off. It was him did it. He was blamed by many people and he let them blame him, but I think he did right. He told me that

---

[55] 1911 Census, L'Islet, St Sampson's, Guernsey (RG14, reg. district 636, schedule num. 59).

[56] In his 1975 letter via me to Calder and Boyars, he wrote that he 'was only old enough to serve more or less unadventurously in the Second Battalion'; see below, p. 282.

once, when she was all soft and loving, he said to her brutally 'How are you going to like having a stump in your bed?' and he saw the look of disgust pass across her face, before she could say 'Darling, it don't make any difference.' 'I wouldn't put any girl through that,' he said to me. I don't know what happened to her in the end...

Jim Le Poidevin could have got an artificial leg and pottered about at home. His people was growers and quite well-to-do; but he said he didn't want to be dependent on them for the rest of his life. He made up his mind he would learn a trade and decided to be a cobbler. Clarrie Bellot from by the Tin Church, who was a sapper in France all through the War and came back without a scratch, taught him for nothing: which is just the sort of thing Clarrie would do, though it might mean less business for him. I'm glad to say it didn't, because he was such a steady chap and so much liked he always got more work than he could do.[57]

Apart from the likes of Sir Ambrose Sherwill and the King and Queen, Clarrie Bellot was one of the few characters in the novel who featured as himself [Fig. 25]. Despite this, and surviving the war, either he or mutual friend Wilfrid Burgess (or a mix of two) may also have been the inspiration for Ebenezer's beloved Jim.[58]

---

[57] *Ebenezer Le Page*, p. 158.

[58] In the early 1980s, I corresponded with Burgess, who was also a model for Jim's younger brother, his near-namesake, Wilfred, inasmuch as both took a ship-load of cattle to America. When *Ebenezer* was published, the 82-year old Burgess wrote me a very interesting letter – which he kindly followed up with a long and fascinating 34-page 'Commentary' on the book. Wilfrid Burgess passed away, in 1997 aged 99 in North Carolina. Among other interesting revelations in his letter and commentary (from 'Sarnia', Jamestown, Rhode Island) is Burgess remembering a visit to 'Hawkesbury' during which Gerald recited Alfred Noyes's 'The Highwayman' and 'a walk up to the Victoria Road Wesleyan Methodist Chapel in St Peter Port one Sunday evening – ostensibly to hear some minister. My real reason for wanting to go, however, was to hear the soloist, Chrissy Mahy, from The Figtree. My mother told me of her having sung "The Long, Long Trail" at some women's affair at the St. Sampson's Wesleyan Hall opposite our home' (Burgess letter, dated 19 September 1981, p. 3). In his commentary, Burgess recalled Bellot inviting him and Gerald to the cottage he lived in with his parents on the eve of his departure for France with the Royal Engineers. 'It was a Sunday afternoon. Although there was no piano there, I recall that we sang the song "A Perfect Day". I've just remembered the name of the lane on which they lived … the Robergerie. As Ebenezer relates, Clarrie

Wilfrid's younger sister, Phyllis Burgess, seems to have been the inspiration for Jim's sister, Lydia, and complemented the account her brother kindly wrote for me with the information that 'Clarrie told me the man he taught ended up doing fancy leather work like purses and bags.'[59] She also confirmed that:

> Clarrie volunteered for the Royal Engineers... Wilfi was passed as fit for Home Duties only and spent some time under canvas on L'Ancresse Common. Gerald Edwards did the following year. Gerald and Wilf corresponded for some time after the latter went to America. Then Wilf went to an Agricultural College, Gerald went to Bristol University and both became so busy the correspondence ceased...

At some stage, presumably prior to Gerald's leaving the island, he and Clarrie were photographed together, in a pose

---

became a cobbler when he returned from the War. He still lives in a house near the East end of Braye Road, and is in his nineties. Brenda and I visited him and his wife Blanche in 1968 and 1977. We still exchange letters with the Bellots, mostly at Christmastime. I remember inquiring about Gerald in 1968, but Clarrie had also lost touch with him...'

'It is terribly sad that we could not have picked up the threads of our friendship at that time, for I feel sure that it would have meant pleasure for all of us. Who knows, he might even be still alive, for he was born after Clarrie and me.' Burgess returns to this theme subsequently, referring to *Ebenezer Le Page* as 'a condensation of so much history of a Guernsey that is no more, so authentic a picture of my homeland as I knew it ... such a re-run of my youth ... that I am deeply grateful the book was written. Many fellow-natives must feel the same for, as far as I know, no one else has filled the need.

To have known Gerald as intimately as I did was a marvellous piece of good fortune; to have lost track of him something I deeply deplore. We did make inquiries in both 1968 and 1977, and I rather imagine that I did in 1934 [when Burgess first returned for a visit from America] ... but he seemed to have dropped out of sight.

I feel strongly that had we met again he and I could have quickly taken up where we left off; and I can't help but wonder if the latter part of his life might not have been a lot happier than it was.'

[59] Although we met and discussed such matters, this and the following quotation are actually from the Penguin copy of *Ebenezer Le Page* that Phyllis Burgess annotated for the late Ian Harris, school teacher and pioneering Ebenezer expert, who with his wife, Deirdre, kindly hosted me and showed me around the island during my first visit in 1991. Shortly prior to this Deirdre had published her wonderful map of Ebenezer's Guernsey. After Ian's poignantly early death she gave me his annotated copy as a memento.

reminiscent of the one adopted by the seated Walt Whitman and his young protégé, Harry Stafford [Figs 25 and 58].

Fig. 25. *Clarrie Bellot and Gerald Edwards*
(photo: J.A. Hamson, Guernsey, c.1918).

# 3: THE MOTHER'S WILL

Gerald indeed matriculated at Bristol University in 1919.[60] It appears he never graduated but migrated instead to London where, with surprising ease (as a Guernsey-born elementary-school teacher), he befriended J.S. Collis and through him Middleton Murry and Stephen Potter. Thus he entered the literary circle associated with Murry's *Adelphi* at around the time of this influential magazine's inception. Its headquarters were established in June 1923 at 18 York Buildings, Adelphi, WC2, which eponymous address appropriately recalled the Greek 'Adelphoi' for brothers, recalling in turn the four Scottish Adam brothers who built it, but reflecting also Lawrence's aspiration to form a 'blood brotherhood' with Murry and others. Murry and the *Adelphi* were never too far from the British Museum Reading Room and J.S. Collis's 2nd floor flat at 5 Guilford Street where Gerald stayed prior to getting married from that address in September 1926.[61]

Meanwhile, back in Guernsey on 3 February 1924, Gerald's 53-year-old mother Harriet, died bequeathing to her only child all her worldly possessions, worried perhaps that his father might otherwise exclude him in his will [Fig. 26]. In characteristically melodramatic style, he (re-?)told the story to his cousin Hilda Dumond as to how he tore up his mother's will, ostensibly out of pity for his father but perhaps also by way of rebellion against maternal control beyond the grave. This was clearly the source for the episode in the novel when Raymond does the same in the

---

[60] He was recorded as being in attendance at the University in March 1920. He passed his Intermediate Exam for the degree of B.Sc. in June 1920 (*Western Daily Press*, 25 June 1920, p. 5). John Fowles told me he had found evidence of Gerald still being at Bristol University in the summer of 1923.

[61] Though by then Gerald had moved to Switzerland, in 1929 the *Adelphi* offices moved closer to the B.M. Library, 58 Bloomsbury Street. For Collis's account of this ambience, of his friendship with R.H. Tawney and with Jacob Epstein's two Indian models, of whom Tagore disapproved when he visited Guilford Street; see his *Bound upon a Course*, pp. 107-14 (in the 1920s Epstein lived at 23 Guilford Street and had five children from extramarital affairs; his first wife shot rival, Kathleen Garman, in the flat there in 1923); *cf.* Collis's description of the nearby B.M. Reading Room which he says he has known 'for a trifling fourteen years' (thus since 1923) in *An Irishman's England* (London, 1937), pp. 50-57

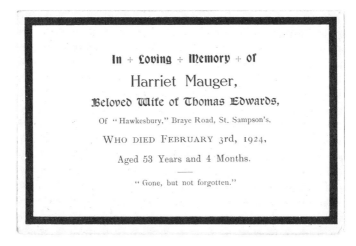

In + Loving + Memory + of

Harriet Mauger,

Beloved Wife of Thomas Edwards,

Of "Hawkesbury," Braye Road, St. Sampson's,

WHO DIED FEBRUARY 3rd, 1924,

Aged 53 Years and 4 Months.

———

" Gone, but not forgotten."

Fig. 26: Funeral card of Harriet Edwards, 1924.

presence of his father Harold:

> All Raymond's sympathies went over immediately to his
> father and, if it hadn't been for that horrible Mrs Crewe, it
> might have been all right yet between father and son. They
> went upstairs together. The doctor had been, but the
> envelope was still in her hand. Raymond looked at his
> mother lying dead. Her face when she was alive had always
> been full of soft feelings. Raymond said in death it was
> frozen stern and hard as marble. He only felt a great load
> was lifted from his shoulders. Harold said, 'Aren't you
> going to read what your mother has written to you?'
> Raymond had a fear of what it might be from the shape of
> the envelope. He read it downstairs while my Cousin Mary
> Ann, saying nothing but all ears, was moving about on
> tiptoe making tea for the two of them. It was a will. Hetty
> had managed to get a lawyer to draw it up, whether it was
> legal or not… It left everything to Raymond with only a life-
> interest for his father. Raymond gave it to his father to read;
> but, of course, Harold couldn't understand it. Raymond
> was used to such things. He explained. Harold said, 'Well,
> it is your mother's will, son.' Raymond tore it across and
> across and threw the pieces on the fire. My Cousin Mary
> Ann was the only one who ever knew; and she didn't tell a

soul until she told me years after they was all dead.[62]

Gerald's creative account may have been further enhanced by Clary but the latter's colloquial re-telling of the tale conveys a vivid sense of the transition from fact to a fiction according to which the house as well as its contents were left to Gerald:

Now it was his own fault he could not come back home to Hawkesbury. His mother knew if anything happened to her, his father could never do without a woman in the house, he would never have coped on his own. The house was in her name so she went and had a will made, leaving it all to Gerald. Mr Randell the solicitor handed him the will at Court Row St Peter Port Guernsey.[63] In 1967 he came to Guernsey to see my mother Mrs Hilda Dumond; he asked her for a Photo of his mother same as the one I have sent you [Fig. 9]. Mum had one made for him. I was there in the room when Gerald spoke at some len[g]th about what had happened when his mother died. He said he had done a very silly thing when his mother had died. He said, When I came out of 'Randells' I still had the will in my hand, and all I would think of was poor dad, poor dad he had nothing. I have it all[.] So, I looked at it, I stopped, then I tore it up to shreds and scattered it to the wind.[64] He said he was so sorry for dad, If only I had given it more thought. So I went back to England, and what did he do. dad just sold the lot for old Mrs Cook, the house keeper and married her with the

---

[62] *Ebenezer Le Page*, p. 193. Harriet Edwards's will stated that 'subject to the said life enjoyment of my said husband I give and bequeath the whole of my said Personal Property to my son Gerald Bazil Edwards.' Despite Gerald's claim to have destroyed it, his mother's will was registered at the Ecclesiastical Court on 16 February 1924 (see Wills of Personalty files at the Greffe). Whilst Gerald (and Clary) may have believed that this included her share of Hawkesbury, this would not have been the case, unless as is hinted in the account of La Hetty's will in the novel it was not an official one. Because Thomas and Harriet had jointly owned the house, under Guernsey inheritance laws, on Harriet's death, Thomas automatically became the sole owner.

[63] Harold Hickman Randell, born 1874 and a partner in the firm who are still practising at 1-6 Court Row (www.randellandloveridge.gg). My thanks to Susan Ilie for this information.

[64] Clary Dumond recalls this story, told to his mother by Gerald in his presence: 'He said to mum I am sorry I did that'.

money perchest Les Rosiers, Baubigny, St Sampson's. What a fool he'd been. Its my own fault, I threw my inheritance away. Gerald said Good Bye to us and said he'd come again to see us. He was staying at a Mrs Mead at Les Galliennes, Torteval. After a few years we wonderd what had become of him. Time went … by then my mother died in 1977 aged 85 years…

Fig. 27: *Tom Edwards* (1861-1946), Occupation Identity card, 1941 (Island Archives).

Fig. 28: *Rosina Edwards* (Mrs Cooke) (1870-150), Occupation Identity card, 1941 (Island Archives).

In July 1927, Gerald's father indeed married the housekeeper, a Mrs Rosina (Rose) Cooke, just as Raymond's father, Harold, marries the scheming Mrs Crewe after the death of *his* wife [Figs 27 and 28].[65] Clary Dumond recalls that his mother, Hilda:

> was working in the washhouse when Uncle Tom and Mrs Cook was rolling around on the lawn like two young kids. Mum said she was disgusted considering their age. A few days after Mrs Cook approached my mother and extended her hand before her, and said 'Look what I've got.' She had on her finger a new engagement ring. It was soon after that my mother left there. Hawkesbury was sold, and they

[65] Rosina Annie Cooke, *née* Purssey, was born in Dover in 1870 (Civil Births Register, England & Wales), and married Colour Sergeant Charles Thomas Oxford Cooke there on 11 April 1888 (Diocese of Canterbury Marriages). He spent 20 years as an Army Pay Master with the Royal Guernsey Militia, and died in 1910 (Civil Deaths Register, Greffe). Clary Dumond confirmed that she was very much as Gerald describes Mrs Crewe, even telling similar anecdotes.

perchest [*sic*] a cottage Les Rosiers at Baubigny, St Sampson's [Fig. 29].[66]

Fig. 29: Les Rosiers, St Sampson's (photo: Ciprian Ilie).

It was indeed in November 1927 that Tom Edwards bought Les Rosiers, Les Effards, and in April 1929 he sold Hawkesbury. Had he kept the latter it would indeed eventually have come to Gerald; instead Gerald was not merely disinherited but effectively exiled, given Guernsey inheritance laws and his purported concern that this housekeeper-turned-step-mother might do away with him if he came to stay.[67] When Tom died in January 1946, Rosina inherited and buried him with her previous husband rather than with his previous wife, Gerald's mother; she did not, however, then have herself buried on top of the both of them as is in the novel [Fig. 30].[68] She then quickly

---

[66] Letter to me dated 12 March 1986; part based on one sent to Hamish Hamilton in 1981. Clary quotes La Prissy on the subject of Mrs Crewe in *Ebenezer Le Page*: 'She owned a house in the Rohais and another at the Vrangue; and had a niece she was paying for at the Ladies' College, who she was going to leave all her money to', and then writes in his letter to me: 'Well Mrs Rose Cook who married Uncle Tom, Gerald's father told us the same story word for word'.

[67] See below p. 50.

[68] According to Clary even this detail was as in the novel but Stephen Foote has found that Rosina was not buried in the same grave (I thank Nigel Le Sauvage

sold Les Rosiers and moved back to the house she had shared with her first husband, Charles Cooke. When she died in 1950 she bequeathed her possessions (as distinct from property) to her English sister and nieces.[69]

Gerald seems to have been fully aware of what had happened, *i.e.* the discrepancy between his (and Raymond's) dramatic gesture, and reality, for in transmuting his fate to Raymond, he has Ebenezer explain the law to his widow, Christine Mahy, who returns to Guernsey to claim the house for their son Abel.[70] At first Ebenezer thinks that by 'property', Christine (whose

Fig. 30: Foulon Cemetery plot CC38, where Rosina buried Gerald's father on top of her first husband.
(photo: Stephen Foote).

enquiry may reflect Gerald's wife, Kathleen's real-life disappointment) is referring merely to Raymond's few clothes and books, and is indignant that she could think he might have kept them:

> 'Now listen to me, Christine,' I said. 'Raymond when he went away from here left behind a few rags of clothes I wore, or Tabitha used for mending, during the Occupation. His suitcase I suppose Liza Quéripel kept; but there can't have been much in it, perhaps the relics of a few things I got

---

and the staff of the Foulon Cemetery for finding plot CC38 and confirming this); *cf.* below, p. 199.

[69] Will proved in Ecclesiastical Court, Guernsey, 29 July 1950. Meanwhile, the property in Coronation Road that Rosina had shared with her first husband went to his nieces (Date [Real Estate Transactions], ref 187/423, Greffe, 16 March 1951).

[70] As well as reminding us of parallels with Gerald's wife, Kathleen, and her sons by two different men in the lead up to the anecdote, we are reminded of the irony that Raymond ended up living, albeit chastely, with Liza Quéripel, the love of Ebenezer's life.

for him. His books and everything else he had he left at Rosamunda.' She was only half listening. 'Oh, of course,' she said, 'he lived with Liza Quéripel at the end I had forgotten. Gwen did mention it in a letter. Well, well, I didn't think he had it in him.' 'He didn't live with Liza Quéripel in the way you mean,' I said. 'I couldn't care less, if he did,' she said. 'It is not his suitcase I am thinking about. It's the house.' 'What house, for goodness sake?' I said. 'His father owned a house, didn't he?' she said. 'I know he sold one: but he bought another. It's Abel's now.' 'It is not Abel's,' I said. I tried to make her see how Wallabaloo would have been Abel's, if Harold had not sold it; but the house he bought when he married again he was in his legal rights to leave to Mrs Crewe when he died: and she left it to her niece when she died. 'I think you might at least have gone to law about it,' she said, 'seeing you were so fond of Raymond.' I let her think what she liked. It was hopeless.[71]

The concluding reflection of responsibility for having failed to claim Raymond's house back upon Gerald's *alter ego*, Ebenezer, is of fascinating psychological interest, whether conscious or not.[72]

The autobiographical nature of Gerald's depiction of Raymond is confirmed by Gerald's use of real names in the incidents of his life, from his own birth to the birth of his son, Abel, in both cases delivered by a nurse who actually existed. Raymond fetches Nurse Wright when Christine was about to deliver: 'It was Nurse Wright who had brought Raymond himself into the world, and she had a soft spot for him. She let him stay with Christine until nearly the time, and everything had gone wonderfully well.'[73] Clary Dumond informed me that the real Nurse Wright delivered him in 1912, by which time 'she was very old', but presumably no older than she is supposed to be when she delivers Abel, having delivered his fictional father before him.[74]

---

[71] *Ebenezer Le Page*, pp. 326-27.

[72] *Cf.* his letter to me, p. 245.

[73] *Ebenezer Le Page*, p. 213; *cf.* p. 159.

[74] The real 'Nurse Wright' is probably Ellen/Helen Wright from Lancashire, who

Though such speculation runs the risk of pushing identification too far, it is nevertheless worth considering the extent to which the paragraph in the novel that follows, might also be based in autobiographical rumination. Christine is first accompanied by Gideon, her son by Raymond's cousin and best friend, Horace, the fictional equivalent of the son that Gerald's wife, Kathleen, had with *his* best friend. If what follows doesn't necessarily reflect Gerald's attitude to Kathleen's relationship with their legitimate, also biblically-named son, Adam, it at least suggests he had him in mind, knowing, perhaps from his daughter - with whom he was at least periodically in touch when writing *Ebenezer Le Page* - that Adam became a successful engineer. 'How is Abel?', asks Ebenezer:

> 'Abel bores me!' said Gideon. 'The question was addressed to me,' said Christine. There wasn't much love lost between those two. I reckon they was too much alike. She went on and on about Abel; and though every word was a word of praise, by the time she had done I was sick of the sound of him. There never was anybody so perfect. He was good, he was patient, he was kind; and from a small boy had but one idea in his mind: which was to take care of his mother. He had been the head boy of the school, he had passed all his examinations first class, he had done three years as an officer in the Army in Germany for his National Service; and now he was doing very important work for the Government. 'He is an electrician, isn't he?' I said. 'An electronic engineer,' she said, as if he was the Prime Minister of England. 'Well, what do he do?' I said. 'Ah, that is a secret,' she said, 'even I, his mother, am not allowed to know.' 'Why, is he ashamed of it, then?' I said. 'He lives for his work,' she said. I had been thinking she had lost her holy voice, but it came back when she was speaking of Abel.[75]

---

appears in the 1901 and 1911 census in Guernsey as a district nurse, though in 1911 she was still a mere 44. Given her presence on the island in 1901 it is possible that Gerald features her because she had delivered him also. She also delivers Horace's son, Gideon; see below, p. 160.

[75] *Ebenezer Le Page*, p. 327. Adam's maternal grandfather, Robert Frank Smith, was listed as an engineer on Gerald and Kathleen's marriage certificate, though was a master iron-monger on her 1904 birth certificate; see below, p. 59.

Poignantly, when soon after, Ebenezer meets Abel, he considers him a potential heir until he discovers that Abel's research involves atomic weapons:

> If he had stuck a knife into me, he couldn't have hurt me more… I had been having a wonderful dream all to myself. I would leave him what I got and make up to him in a small way for what he had lost through his father; and then he would always have a home in Guernsey where he belonged… I can understand fighting, man against man … but to make things to go and kill millions of people you don't know, don't see even, because somebody sitting in a big office say you got to, no: I couldn't leave him what I got to do that! I couldn't.[76]

# 4: LITERARY LONDON

Given such grubby and/or gothic goings-on in Guernsey and Gerald's escapist tendencies, life in literary London must, for the time being at least, have seemed considerably more appealing. Collis summarised his friend's flourishing, still-bachelor status in this period in the 1982 review-article he wrote for the *Spectator*:

> These were his happiest days, I think. He was being admired, and feared by lots of people, including Middleton Murry to whom I had introduced him. Stephen Potter, Edwards and myself thought Murry a fascinating personality, very learned and gifted, and a great force. We knew his faults, but we did not know that he had been cast in the role of villain and charlatan by various luminaries who would have regarded the three of us very much *de haut en bas*.[77]

These were the years of Edwards's Great Expectations… He

---

[76] *Ebenezer Le Page*, p. 331.

[77] For Collis's view of Murry's faults, which included Lawrentian humourlessness and the repressing of Collis's instinct to visit Murry's ailing wife, Violet, upstairs in the Coastguard Cottages in Abbotsbury when he was staying there, see *Bound upon a Course*, pp. 118-20.

always had several works in hand. 'A book of essays,' I quote from his correspondence with me, 'a book of poems, a book of stories. In each case to be published separately before together. I have sent Murry a copy of Margaret and received a letter from him offering to help me by giving me £10 at once if I'd write some articles for *The Adelphi*.[78] It was a most friendly letter. I accepted, of course, and last week got the cheque.' And in another context, 'Millstones is finished, at least the dialogue. I am now occupied re-writing it and putting in stage directions. It is a very masculine production. It doesn't touch the teaching of females by females. Also I think you had better warn any of your women students who are weak minded (probably 7/8 of them) that if they come they come at their own risk.[79] Please try to collect some men'.[80]

---

[78] It might be relevant that Collis was engaged to Margaret Lindsay, the sister of Kenneth Lindsay at around this time; see below, p. 133.

[79] For Nietzsche on the weak-mindedness of women in Gerald's edition of *Beyond Good and Evil*, see below pp. 71-73, and for the Schopenhauer-Nietzsche-Weininger consensus on the subject, Chandak Sengoopta, *Otto Weininger: Sex, Science, and Self in Imperial Vienna* (Chicago, 2000), pp. 29-31. Since it is not in the article as published, Richard Ingrams is perhaps quoting from a pre-cut version of Collis's 'Memories of a Genius Friend' when he writes that 'Collis wrote in an epitaph [for Gerald] which could just as well have been his own: "He suffered throughout his life from three terrible things: poverty, publishers and women".' (Ingrams, *Collis*, p. 58).

[80] This is Collis's exact transcription of a letter of which, courtesy of Richard Ingrams and Michael Holroyd, I now have a copy, dated 18 March 1925, from Ide Hill, Sevenoaks in Kent. It begins 'Jack / In great haste. I'm not coming up Friday. Nor am I speaking to the TSA at a future date. / I've completely lost my temper again – with Catchpool! I've written to Potter asking him to come down. Do tell him it's tolerable, will you?' The letter ends: 'Till the 26th, GB.' Egerton St John (Jack) Catchpool (1890-1971) was a Quaker of great influence in the history of philanthropy; *cf. ODNB* and M. Freeman, 'Fellowship, service and the "spirit of adventure": the Religious Society of Friends and the outdoors movement in Britain c.1900-1950.' *Quaker Studies,* XIV, pp. 72-92. Catchpool no doubt knew Gerald through being first a resident (after returning from Russia) and then, between 1921-29, subwarden of Toynbee Hall. He represented the Workers' Travel Association at Toynbee Hall in 1921 and at the inaugural conference of the Youth Hostel Association whose founding secretary he became in 1930. Catchpool and his brother, Corder, who also lived at Toynbee Hall in this period, were both advocates of nature conservation and the 'Quaker tramps' which, along with Octavia Hill's saving of Ide Hill for the National Trust may

So his spirits were high, though little came of these projects. His mother had just died, and he hoped for help from his father and ultimately the family inheritance in Guernsey. But he did not go and see his father and soften him up, he allowed the housekeeper to marry him and inherit the property. He feared that she would poison him if he went to stay with his father. So his finances were low…[81]

Although Ebenezer may be Gerald's ostensible *alter ego* therefore, Raymond is at least a complementary one and one who more clearly epitomises the fate his spirit might have suffered had he remained on Guernsey. We continue to see the extent to which he suffered (and to some extent embraced) a similar fate despite his escape from the island.

Meanwhile, it is clear from Stephen Potter's unpublished memoirs, that it was Collis who introduced Gerald to Potter as well as to Murry. The impact of Gerald's arrival in the Collis, Potter and Murry milieu, to the extent of influencing both their literary and life styles is most vividly (and amusingly) conveyed in the unpublished sections of Potter's autobiography.[82] He and Collis were discussing their own relationship and the proofs of Collis's book on Bernard Shaw, published by Cape in 1925:

> Jack looked at me. 'Simple … yes, the situation did have a simplicity about it?'
>
> 'What?'
>
> 'There was something basically opposed between us'
>
> This was not Jack's usual way of talking. 'Who has been here to lunch?,' I said suspiciously. Jack was repeating my words as if he, not I, was the only one to understand them.
>
> 'You aren't in love again, are you?'
>
> 'No, my dear Stephen. I'm not "in love". No – as a matter

---

lie behind Gerald's choice of Ide Hill as his home in this last year of his bachelorhood. Collis himself moved to a cottage in Sevenoaks in 1932.

[81] Collis, 'Memories of a Genius Friend', p. 22; *cf.* above, p. 42.

[82] Copy of typescript kindly made for me with subsequent permission to publish by the late Julian Potter. This seems to have been written in the 1950s, continuing the memoir of his first nineteen years which was published in 1959 as *Steps to Immaturity*.

of fact it was some-one who might have interested you. A man called Gerald Edwards. I'll tell you about him'…

They then resume their discussion about Bernard Shaw, Potter articulating in his charmingly self-effacing style admiration mixed with mild envy of Collis's personal correspondence with Shaw: 'It was all too glorious. There were Shaw's notes in the wide open clarity of Shaw's hand…'. But he concludes this passage with a hint that Collis's admiration for Shaw was being qualified by conversation with his new friend.[83]

I left soon after. What was Jack driving at? Had he gone off Shaw, suddenly? He was on such a wave of Shaw, and writing so well about him, that I had concealed my own doubt, instilled by Tom and D. and had wanted to get back to good draughts of Jack enthusiasm once more. And who on earth was Gerald Edwards?[84]

The next few paragraphs of Potter's autobiography describe his first meeting with Gerald, set up by Collis:

'I prefer not to be called Gerald'.

Jack had fixed this meeting and then gone off and left us together. Edwards had a wide smile, and a good strong mobile face, a pleasant plebeian nose, dark hair thinning back off a good forehead, and eyes the frankness and candour of which made me feel fidgety. 'I'm usually called 'G.B.' – I'm G.B. Edwards'.[85]

---

[83] This may already be reflected in Collis's book as published. Shaw's notes on his first draft were to be included in the publication but Gerald's sceptical (pre-publication) views post-date these and seem to be reflected in Collis's final version.

[84] 'Tom and D.' were a young couple, 'flat-in-Chalk-Farm-top-floor-of-Mecklenburg-Square people', Slade School of Art students, like his wife-to-be Mary; see Jenkins, *Potter*, p. 77. Potter was in Platonic love with the beautiful 'D', referring to 'the corduroy Slade student' on and off for the rest of his life.

[85] The fashion for substituting first names with less personal (and gender neutral) initials was widespread in this period, being adopted by both Lawrences, Eliot, Auden, Wells, Cummings, Tolkien, Lewis (C.S.) and a host of others including the mere H.D. (for Hilda Doolittle); interestingly, the inventor of One-Upmanship took the advice of his mentor, Henry Arthur Jones on the matter: 'I notice you sign yourself S.M. Potter. Don't do that. *Stephen Potter* – much better' (Jenkins, *Potter*, p. 70). Not that the fashion shows any sign of

All I knew about this man was that he had started Jack rocketing off on a new line which I didn't know anything about. There was no doubt Jack's talk had somehow changed direction in the last few weeks. Jack was reading D.H. Lawrence, and wouldn't talk about him. Where was Jack's splendid ordinariness, his common sense? I knew Lawrence myself – enough to talk about him. 'His descriptive writing is the best ... he has this thing about sex', I said.

G.B. stared at me encouragingly.

'He's obsessed by it', I tried.

'Possesses it. A difference between possession and obsession.'[86]

'I must say I got stuck in Kangaroo.' I kept on.

'I don't think you would get *stuck*, if it was really you reading it' –

G.B. had a wonderfully warm quality in his voice.

I had really got stuck in this my first Lawrence novel. 'Chapter One of course was marvellous,' I said, not wishing to overdo my negative. 'Describing the back-endedness of Sydney.'

But I really had had the feeling I would never get the real essence – there was a wall, here, which I felt I would never be able to climb.

G.B. wanted me to read 'Sons and Lovers'. 'But look, Stephen, you wouldn't expect even the greatest anatomist the world has ever seen to understand the human body from one slice. A cross section is an abstraction, an anatomical fantasy.'

Or he would say, his eyes searching me for a spark of understanding: 'Each of the Lawrence books is a *process*... I

---

fizzling out given the range of contemporary authors from A.A. Gill to J.M. Coetzee, not to speak of that most under-rated of modern painters, R.B. Kitaj.

[86] This seems to echo a passage of reported speech in Jessie Chambers, *D.H. Lawrence: A Personal Record* (London, 1935), p. 76: 'I'm not *possessed* with an idea, I'm *obsessed* with it.'

think Lawrence might have a lot for you.'

This was rather encouraging – perhaps he might. But must I now then re-orientate once more?

Butler had got me under way… Wells and progress and left-wing had given me a rudder: Bernard Shaw was my turbo-jet engine: Bloomsbury levelled the boat: Slade and Fitzroy has given it a new coat of paint. Was I to be submerged in a new wave from another direction altogether?

*'There cometh one'* … Every new god needs his John the Baptist, and there are times when the St. John is more forceful than the Messiah himself. G.B., with his wide brow, piercing eye, his fine head and his ability to wear an ordinary shirt as if it were rough aboriginal wear or even a goatskin, made a good St. John. He was uncomplicated by misplaced education, though his reading was wide. He knew some German literature. He was completely unbranded with the ex-undergraduate mark. He was a mystery. I never knew his parents – never knew where he was born. Guernsey, was it? He was uninterested in Butler.[87] Shaw was 'sometimes truly bad'. Shaw was 'untrue to his own demon.' Who were the people to read and know? His men were not my men. He liked to speak of the great by their Christian names sometimes.

'How Vincent did hate his own character.' This was about the Van Gogh letters.[88] Half the time I didn't understand what G.B. was talking about. Occasionally I did understand and it made the whole bunch of Huxleys and Wells to say nothing of the philosophers as different as

---

[87] Gerald's lack of interest in the closet bisexual Samuel Butler (1835-1902), distinguished him from Butler's Bloomsbury admirers. He would no doubt have regarded his critique of their Victorian predecessors, in the posthumously-published *Way of All Flesh* (1903), as inadequately Nietzschean.

[88] Gerald's identification with this aspect of Van Gogh, suggested here and decades later in his correspondence with me, is telling. Both men were intensely gregarious, yet incapable of sustained relationships, in part due to their uncompromising existential dogmatism and tendency to manic depression. Both qualities are reflected in their remarkable letters, Van Gogh's being published in a variety of editions and translations in this period.

Bertrand Russell and F.H. Bradley, seem as thin as cards. But G.B.'s Messiah, though it was more than one man, was chiefly one man – Lawrence.[89]

If only I could find here the first sentence or words which let me in, so to speak – which gave me the clue.

That would be absurd (I can still hear G.B.'s voice), because it is not one thing, but a process – changing me, or ting[e]ing me: taking hold of a cautious bit of immaturity and giving me some kind of bearings relative to life. There is no 'moment' of this kind of truth.

Where were the words, in G.B. or Lawrence? G.B. was never eloquent in words, only in presentation. 'Don't start with Kangaroo, whatever you do. You don't begin the day at four o'clock in the afternoon'. Quite so. Quite so. You don't introduce yourself to Shakespeare by reading Coriolanus. It must have been *Women in Love* which put me in the stream. *In the stream.* G.B. could give special force to the most simple images. Keeping out of the backwaters and the weeds on the bank – join yourself to the stream, to the tide.

How could I go 'with' such a book? Every single character was unattractive. None had a trace of charm. Hermione Roddice had an air of being a symbol, and I thought I disliked symbolic figures.[90] But everything is a

---

[89] Gerald clearly encouraged this feeling in Murry, despite the latter having known Lawrence long before and in person. Towards the end of his life in the mid-1950s, Murry was still writing 'In my bones I am sure I am right: he [Lawrence] is the Jesus of our times…'; Lea, *Murry*, p. 348.

[90] 'Hermione Roddice' was Lawrence's quasi-caricature of his former hostess, Lady Ottoline Morrell, in *Women in Love* (1920). After Frieda left Garsington in a rage, Ottoline and her husband Philip Morrell tried to persuade Lawrence to leave her. After yet another row, about Nietzsche, she wrote to her lover, Bertrand Russell: 'If only we could put her in a sack and drown her.' Like Katherine Mansfield, who wrote to her on this, they thought Lawrence had ruined his life by marrying her, a view implicitly shared by Gerald in his first letter to me; see below, p. 246 and Brenda Maddox, *D.H. Lawrence: The Story of a Marriage* (New York, 1994), p. 208. After Lawrence's death Ottoline Morrell wrote a very appreciative letter to Murry, concluding that although he was 'disastrously unhappy … L. was really most pure'; see *Waterfield's Catalogue no. 50,* item 1343.

symbol. It's a question of degree, G.B. would say. Birkin, the protagonist, the Lawrence figure was the least attractive of all. How he would have disapproved of me, my fairness, and my lack of deep sexual experience. O my God was I too 'dying the white death' like Gerald Crick[*sic*]? But *Women in Love* was my Lawrence Primer.[91]

Potter remembers that his Slade friends, Tom and D. 'couldn't bear Lawrence and seemed to think that reading him was something like believing in phrenology, or worse'. But, he continues:

> 'Yes' instead of 'No'. It was a big chance, though the best in Shaw leads you to it. G.B. could always supply new draughts of Yes when I wanted them. He was even Yes about my No friends. 'There [*sic*] sensitiveness is beautiful. There [*sic*!] intelligence would be beautiful if it were not ingrowing, pot bound.'

Soon other writers were to be revealed to us by our St. John. I found myself presented with some of the least expected authors. 'But he really has the heart of the matter – he is wonderful – such marvellous strength.' This was Nietzsche, and of Nietzsche's books, especially Zarathustra. I couldn't believe it. Superman. German militarism. I would be ashamed even now to record the extent of my misapprehension of Nietzsche even if it were not that Bertrand Russell's summing of him in his *Western Philosophy* is still more comically inadequate.[92] This modern danger of 5% knowledge which must always be worse than

---

[91] Potter, unpublished autobiography, vol. II , pp. 173-74. It is interesting that Gerald thought so highly of *Women in Love* given Murry's notoriously negative review of it in the *Athenaeum* of 13 August 1921. In the novel Gerald Crich, who freezes to death in the Alps after almost throttling Gudrun (inspired by Katherine Mansfield) was part-based on Murry.

[92] Gerald had already referenced Russell's crude caricature of Nietzsche in his 1926 article on 'Shaw', p. 20. Behind this lay the proto-Nazi interpretation of Nietzsche's writings promoted by his anti-semitic younger sister and editor, Elisabeth Förster-Nietzsche (1846-1935). For Russell's tendency to journalistic simplification, see Ray Monk, *Bertrand Russell: The Spirit of Solitude 1872-1921* (London, 1996) and *Bertrand Russell 1921-70: The Ghost of Madness* (London, 2000).

complete ignorance.

I had to bring my utmost powers of concentration to crack this great nut: but the kernel was always worth having, and gradually, as the reading acquired a context, the labour became easier.[93]

This section of Potter's autobiography continues with a reminiscence which further underlines the extraordinary influence that Gerald wielded over him, even as he gently avenges himself on his occasionally provincial mentor with a bit of incipient one-up-manship:

G.B. would come to No. 36 and show me his copy of *Beyond Good and Evil*.[94] I never saw the room where G.B. lived: but whenever he came to us he started proceedings by having a bath. Surrounded by the corpses of Father's dressing gowns, he would test the virtuosity of Ewart's Lightning Geyser to the limit, and lavish himself in steam and great gas bonfires of hot water...[95]

For all the lightly facetious tone that became his trademark, Potter's account of Gerald's Lawrentian Nietzscheanism provides us with a vivid reminder of this most intense form of early 20th-century Neo-Romanticism, one which he distinguishes from the gentler *fin-de-siècle* versions that both Modernists and Neo-Classicists sought to sweep away:

There were certain less positive voices, tinged with sentiment or a love of nature which was half back to earth romanticism. Margin voices. Carpenter. Jeffreys.[96] On the

---

[93] *Ibid.*, p. 176

[94] This was presumably Helen Zimmern's translation of Nietzsche's 1886 publication; see below, p. 66.

[95] No. 36 Old Park Avenue, SW12, was Potter's parents' home, where he was born and continued to base himself until his marriage in 1927 when he and Mary moved to Two Riverside, Chiswick Mall (where in 1931 they entertained Frieda Lawrence). Conflating two anecdotes in Potter's memoirs, Jenkins has Gerald bathing at Potter's parents' house in the same period as he lived 'on the edge of a wood near Eltham ... with a wife and five children who wore no shoes'; *cf.* below, p. 163.

[96] By 'Jeffreys' Richard Jefferies is clearly intended; the nature writer and novelist, whose autobiographical *Story of my Heart*, first published in 1883, anticipates with its advocacy of 'now' and authenticity of expression, some of

other side were voices which were so near the very centre of knowledge that their meaning could only be felt dimly: Dosteievsky, Christ.

Scored through immediately after the reference to Christ is the following, still legible passage which serves as a reminder as to how influential Gerald's Guernsey-bred articulation of the King James Bible and the story of Jesus had proved:

> Half the most famous sayings of Christ had seemed to me like sermon platitudes. Now I realised that I had spent half my life without ears to hear them – that I had only taken them at face value.[97]

The answer to the question Potter then poses himself, at least where the British intelligentsia is concerned, partly suggests itself in Gerald's unconventional cultural background:

> What is this extra zest to knowledge and understanding which yet sometimes never touches the best brains in the world? This understanding which in my own case even if it were only partial made my previous mental exercise seem by comparison something more arid than, and almost as trivial as, filling up a crossword puzzle?

> Hitherto I had always been disappointed with philosophy - with the great official philosophical writing, except as a beautifully exact mental game…

> 'They don't really *do* anything, ' I said to G.B. 'Thank goodness I didn't do Greats at Oxford.'…

> 'No. Yet they have the feeling that they are adding a brick to the pyramid of objective truth: but there is no such

---

what would be advocated by Lawrence and others. An interesting account of Jefferies' influence on an author who later took over the editorship of the *Adelphi* can be found in Anne Williamson's fine biography of her father-in-law, *Henry Williamson: Tarka and the Last Romantic* (Stroud, 1995), *passim*. John Fowles was a great admirer of both TB sufferers, Jefferies and Lawrence, writing introductions to both *After London* and *The Man who Died*. For Edward Carpenter, see *ODNB* and below, p. 240.

[97] Potter, unpublished autobiography, vol. II, p. 178. Murry published his *Life of Jesus* soon after meeting Gerald in 1926, initially in instalments in the *Adelphi* (it was published in America in the same year as *Jesus – Man of Genius*). For Gerald on *Jesus*, see below, p. 109. Lawrence published *David: a Play* in 1926.

brick and no such pyramid.'

'No philosophy is true unless it is the expression of a personal experience.' What 'ism' is this called in the text books?

But it was no ism to G.B. Words like 'experience' were as lively as a cat in his mouth. I soon learnt well enough that Lawrence's 'dark Gods' and 'centres of unconscious' writing, which in terms of official philosophy was a sort of fifth rehash of Freud and a thousandth retake of the noble savage, was essential Lawrence, if you were to take him seriously at all. That books like *Fantasia of the Unconscious* were boiled down essence of Lawrence, not 'a pity' – not something to be skipped.

We were all very happy on this wave, of which it must be noted that the young men in the grip of such a change feel that this has never happened to anybody before, and that the writer, the man who opens up this world for them, whoever it happens to be, is the one and only.

We discussed the weakness of Shaw: and as for the common-sense, scientific, straight-line-progress attitude from which we ourselves had so recently evolved, all that seemed like old tin.

G.B. himself was in print only occasionally: but when he was, as in his essay on Shaw in the *Adelphi*, it seemed to Jack [Collis] and me that the writing had real originality and power.[98] G.B. cut this article out and sent it to me as a present. 'I am absolutely certain', I said to Jack, holding the whispy little pack of pages up in front of his eyes 'that some day this will be worth quite a lot of money'. I was an authority on this kind of thing...

'Now my dear Stephen, you're overdoing it', said Jack who was already beginning to drift away from G.B. a little.

'I am absolutely certain.'[99]

---

[98] For Gerald's essay on Shaw, published in the July 1926 of *Adelphi*, see below, p. 62 and Fig. 32. That Collis admired Gerald's indictment is significant given that he had published his enthusiastic account of Shaw just a year before.

[99] Potter, unpublished autobiography, vol. II, pp. 179-80.

# 5: NIETZSCHEAN MATRIMONY

In his *Spectator* review-article, Collis writes of Gerald still being single during this preliminary period of his 'Great Expectations':

> – no need to halve himself by marriage. He once said to me that when a man marries he becomes alone for the rest of his life – which Ebenezer also says.[100] But in 1928 he appeared on my doorstep in Guilford Street with a wife who looked like Alice in *Alice in Wonderland* [Fig. 31].[101]
>
> They had a son whom they called Adam, and a daughter whom they called Eve [*sic* for Dorcas]. Then two more children.[102] They lived in frightful squalor. 'It is an achievement to keep alive,' he would say to me over and over again. An achievement for the children too, I thought. 'Aren't we responsible for children we bring into the world?' I asked. He did not hedge. 'Yes we are. But we must not spare ourselves the harder truth – that every living creature who ever was, is, or shall be on earth, always was, is, and shall be there on its *own* responsibility.' (*cf.* p. 89)

Gerald may already have visited Guernsey with his fashionably-dressed fiancée, but putting all the evidence together it seems more likely that he came in 1924 for his mother's funeral and only subsequently with his fiancée, or indeed bride. For Collis misremembered (or misreported) the couple's arrival on his doorstop as the 27-year-old Gerald not only married Kathleen Maude Smith, the 22-year-old daughter of engineer, Robert Frank Smith and Hannah Roberts, in the St Pancras Registry Office on 14 September 1926, rather than 1928, but he gave as his

---

[100] In fact it is Jim who says this after marrying Phoebe, as reported by Ebenezer (p. 104). Ebenezer himself had already concluded chapter 5 of his *Book*: 'Marriage is a terrible thing, when you come to think of it. Perhaps it's as well I've never married. Mind you, I've had it a few times under the hedge.' (p. 32). Elsewhere Raymond asks: 'Is marriage only war at close quarters?' (p. 236).

[101] Alice, was the name Collis gave a character inspired by Kathleen in an unfinished story he wrote some decades later, entitled *The Realist* (see below). In this Collis describes 'Jack' (*i.e.* Gerald) bringing 'Alice' to see him one day, both 'in a spectacular state of love'.

[102] See below, p. 159.

Fig. 31: Gerald with Kathleen Smith
at around the time of their marriage in September 1926.

place of residence on the marriage certificate Collis's flat at 5 Guilford Street.[103] One of the two witnesses at the wedding,

---

[103] Marriage certificate, General Register Office, England and Wales marriages 1837-2008, St Pancras, Vol. 1b, p. 183. A more celebrated Bloomsberry, the previously predominantly homosexual Maynard Keynes, had married the ballerina Lydia Lopokova, in the same registry office a year earlier; see Richard Davenport-Hines, *Universal Man: The Seven Lives of John Maynard Keynes* (London, 2015), p. 240. Keynes had been Murry and Katherine Mansfield's Gower Street landlord a few years earlier.

moreover, was Collis's twin brother, Robert, the other being an Elizabeth Briggs.[104]  On the certificate Gerald and Kathleen were both described as elementary-school teachers, as Lawrence had been twenty years earlier in Croydon. Kathleen's address is given as 47 Doughty Street, just around the corner from Collis's flat. The house next door to this was that in which Charles Dickens had lived between 1837-39 and had been turned into a museum the previous year.[105]

The couple seem to have remained in London through the rest of 1926 and the following year, Gerald building up his reputation as a literary star, greatly assisted by Middleton Murry's belief in him. At the beginning of the year, Lawrence had written to Murry suggesting he shut down the *Adelphi*, which, given the extent to which it had been founded with Lawrence in mind, would have been a serious blow to his disciples:

> Let the *Adelphi* die, and say to it: Peace be to your ashes! I don't want any man for an adelphos [*i.e.* brother], and adelphi are sure to drown one another, strangling round each other's necks. Let loose! let loose![106]

---

[104] Perhaps the 'Elizabeth' criticised by Gerald in his letter to Collis from Ascona dated 11 March 1929. Collis's twin brother, W.R.J. Collis, or Robert, known as Bob, was a paediatrician and author who later witnessed and wrote of the horrors of Belsen and lived and worked in Nigeria. He married his first wife in 1927 and published a very successful autobiography: *The Silver Fleece*, in 1936. The twins' elder brother was the even more popular (and prolific) author Maurice Collis. Curiously, none of these fraternal-authors have been accorded even a group entry in the *ODNB*, while the entry on Christy Brown, whom Robert assisted in the writing of *My Left Foot*, manages to misdescribe J.S.'s first wife, Eirene, who also helped Christy, as Robert's sister rather than sister-in-law; *cf.* for other errors and omissions (including G.B. Edwards) my review in the *British Art Journal* (Winter 2004), pp. 88-92.  See now, for useful entries on all three Collis brothers by Frances Clarke, the *Dictionary of Irish Biography* (2009).

[105] Dickens published his first novels, *Pickwick Papers, Oliver Twist*, and *Nicholas Nickleby* whilst  resident here. Vera Brittain and Winifred Holtby shared a flat in No. 52 Doughty Street, a few doors further south,  in the early 1920s.

[106] 9 January 1926; Lawrence, *Letters*, V (1989), p. 380. Murry had already declined Lawrence's suggestion that the *Adelphi* should 'attack everything ... and explode in one blaze of denunciation.' In connection with this, and Lawrence's invitation to New Mexico, Murry confirms that 'the main purpose of the *Adelphi* had been to make a place for Lawrence'; *Reminiscences*, pp. 110-11.

Ten days later he wrote again, now hinting at the feelings of betrayal that lay behind this suggestion:

> I would rather you didn't publish my things in the *Adelphi*. As man to man, if ever we were man to man, you and I, I would give them to you willingly. But as writer to writer, I feel it is a sort of self-betrayal. Surely you realise the complete incompatibility of my say with your say. Say your say, Caro! – and let *me* say mine. But for heaven's sake, don't let us pretend to mix them.         Yrs DHL.[107]

It was to some extent symbolic, therefore, that Murry published an important article by his brilliant new protégé, G.B. Edwards, in the July 1926 issue of the *Adelphi* [Fig. 32].[108] Entitled simply 'Shaw', though it didn't prevent the great man receiving the Nobel Prize that year, this profoundly critical account created something of a stir, accusing Shaw as it did of 'sterility' and of betraying Courage and Love.[109] In support of this, whilst succinctly surveying Shaw's oeuvre to date, Gerald argued the superiority of Nietzsche (and indeed Whitman) in what they offered a post-Darwinian world. 'Nietzsche is a prophet: Shaw is not':

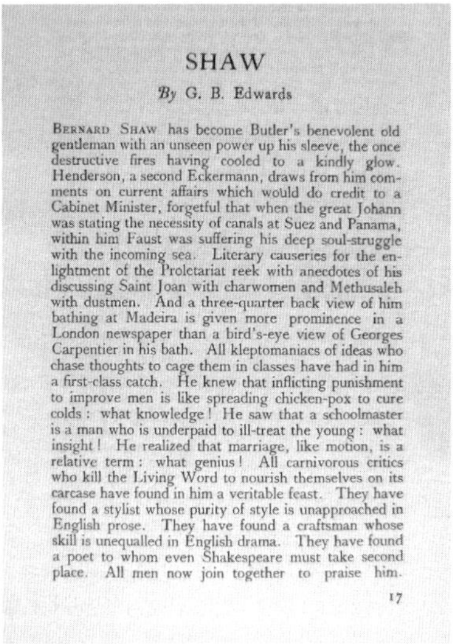

### SHAW

#### *By* G. B. Edwards

BERNARD SHAW has become Butler's benevolent old gentleman with an unseen power up his sleeve, the once destructive fires having cooled to a kindly glow. Henderson, a second Eckermann, draws from him comments on current affairs which would do credit to a Cabinet Minister, forgetful that when the great Johann was stating the necessity of canals at Suez and Panama, within him Faust was suffering his deep soul-struggle with the incoming sea. Literary causeries for the enlightment of the Proletariat reek with anecdotes of his discussing Saint Joan with charwomen and Methusaleh with dustmen. And a three-quarter back view of him bathing at Madeira is given more prominence in a London newspaper than a bird's-eye view of Georges Carpentier in his bath. All kleptomaniacs of ideas who chase thoughts to cage them in classes have had in him a first-class catch. He knew that inflicting punishment to improve men is like spreading chicken-pox to cure colds : what knowledge ! He saw that a schoolmaster is a man who is underpaid to ill-treat the young : what insight ! He realized that marriage, like motion, is a relative term : what genius ! All carnivorous critics who kill the Living Word to nourish themselves on its carcase have found in him a veritable feast. They have found a stylist whose purity of style is unapproached in English prose. They have found a craftsman whose skill is unequalled in English drama. They have found a poet to whom even Shakespeare must take second place. All men now join together to praise him.

17

Fig. 32: Gerald's article on Bernard Shaw, *The Adelphi*, July 1926.

> Both have that great longing which is a great contempt and

---

[107] Lawrence, *Letters*, V (1989), p. 380.

[108] *Adelphi*, IV, no. 1 (July 1926), pp. 17-32.

[109] See below, p. 95. Shaw is still the only author to have received both a Nobel Prize (1925-26 for Literature), and an Academy Award (1938 for his adaptation of *Pygmalion*).

both use prevalent biological ideas to express it: to Shaw Evolution is the path to Godhead, and to Nietzsche Man is a bridge to the Superman. But here similarity ceases. To Shaw Godhead is omniscience and omnipotence: to Nietzsche it is innocence. To Shaw the Superman is an Ancient who aspires to become Force without Form: to Nietzsche the Superman is a Child. Shaw's Ancient seeks a heaven where contemplation shall be his only joy: Nietzsche's Child seeks nothing but to stand as man upon the natural earth and be a man with men. But there is a still deeper significance. Shaw sees a moment only as a point on an infinite straight line, and imagines the only Life Eternal to be Everlasting Life; but Nietzsche, knowing otherwise, cancelled the Dogma of the Superman by the equal and opposite Dogma of the Eternal Return so that every moment's living should be Eternal Life...

Shaw, Gerald concludes, 'has betrayed Courage':

he has denied creation for contemplation: he has denied living for thought. But it is creation, not contemplation, which is an unending discovery and an unceasing conquest: it is living, not thought, which is the only absolute action and the one indestructible deed.[110]

More superficially, Gerald critiqued Shaw's somewhat hubristic celebrity status - a phenomenon that remained personally problematic for the assertive yet almost obsessively private Gerald - though this was more gently mocked by others, including William Rothenstein, who said he admired Shaw for not waiting 'until he was famous to behave like a great man.'[111]

Interestingly, in view of Gerald's negative view of Wyndham Lewis, the latter's mockery of Shaw resembled his own. Gerald compares Octavius's romantic rhetoric in Shaw's *Man and Superman* with Ferdinand's equivalent declaration of love in *The Tempest* and concludes that in contrast to the former, who 'is untrue, unpoetic, and ridiculous', Ferdinand 'is true, poetic, and

---

[110] 'Shaw,' p. 32.

[111] Michael Holroyd, *Bernard Shaw: 2. The Pursuit of Power* (London, 1989), p. 183.

sublime. Shakespeare is a poet: Shaw is not.'[112] A decade later, Lewis writes of 'that noisiest of old cocks':

> I am rather what Mr. Shaw would have been like if he had been an artist – I use 'artist' in the widest possible sense - if he had not been an Irishman, if he been a young man when the Great War occurred, if he had studied painting and philosophy instead of economics and Ibsen, and if he had been more richly endowed with imagination, emotion, intellect and a few other things. (He said he was a finer fellow than Shakespeare. I merely prefer myself to Mr. Shaw.)[113]

Gerald's reservations about Shaw's seriousness as a thinker (articulated more than a decade before Lewis's) were surely vindicated by the former Fabian's future endorsement of both Communism (including its Stalinist manifestations) and Fascism:

Fig. 33: *Bernard Shaw* 'taking his sun bath cure at Madeira' (1925).

> Bernard Shaw has become Butler's benevolent old gentleman with an unseen power up his sleeve, the once destructive fires having cooled to a kindly glow... Literary causeries for the enlightenment of the Proletariat reek with anecdotes of his discussing Saint Joan with charwomen and Methuselah with dustmen. And a three-quarter back view of him bathing in Madeira is given more prominence in a London newspaper than a bird's-eye view of

---

[112] 'Shaw', p. 19.

[113] *Blasting and Bombardiering* (London, 1937), p. 3. As late as 6 August 1954, in a review of a new book on Mathew Arnold in the *TLS*, Lewis wrote that 'Shaw was always a philistine.'

Georges Carpentier in his bath [Fig. 33].[114] All kleptomaniacs of ideas who chase thoughts to cage them in classes
have had in him a first-class catch… He realized that
marriage, like motion, is a relative term: what genius![115]

Written in the year of Gerald's own marriage, this sardonic
reference to Shaw's sceptical view of marriage and advocacy of
liberalising divorce as truistic was perhaps ominous. As distinct
from Shaw's celibate wife, Charlotte, Kathleen Edwards had
conceived their first child and gave birth to Adam at 60 South
Hill Park, Hampstead, on 17 December 1927.[116]

The following spring the young family joined a commune in
West Sussex. A newspaper feature dating from August 1928,
features a photograph of a complacently smiling Kathleen,
sporting a fashionably feminist hair-cut and carrying a naked
Adam in a sling. It is entitled: 'THE SIMPLE LIFE' [Fig. 34] and
captioned:

Mrs. G. Edwards with her baby, Adam, whom she carries
in a sling, native fashion, at The Sanctuary, the Sussex
colony founded by Mrs. Dennis Earle, daughter of the late
Sir George Pragnell. Adam never wears clothes.[117]

---

[114] Gerald's comparison is amusing given Shaw's proclivity for posing in the
nude or in sporting Jaeger stockinette; see several relevant photographs in
Michael Holroyd's four-volume biography, but behind it may also lie familiarity
with Shaw's interest in boxing. Three years after this article was published we
find Shaw writing in detail to Norman Clark, a fellow boxing enthusiast, about
Georges Carpentier (1894-1975), the French boxer turned Hollywood actor-cum-
popular author; see *Bernard Shaw: The Collected Letters 1926-1950*, ed. Dan H.
Laurence, vol. 4 (London, 1988), pp 130-31.

[115] *Adelphi*, IV, no. 1 (July 1926), pp. 17-32. Shaw married in 1898 but he
disapproved of the institution and his own was probably never consummated;
see Holroyd *passim* and Shaw's *Getting Married* of 1908.

[116] Birth certificate, General Register Office, England and Wales births 1837-2006,
Hampstead, vol. 1a, p. 753. Uncannily, in attempting to research the connection
between Gerald and Jomo Kenyatta (*cf.* notes 247 and 353), I was helped by the
latter's son, Peter, who was born in Storrington (see below) but now lives next
door to this Hampstead house in which Gerald's son was born.

[117] 'The Simple Life', *Daily Express*, 10 August 1928. I am grateful to Julia
Westgate of the Storrington & District Museum for this scan from their
newspaper cuttings file. In his 1986 letter to me, Clary Dumond writes that 'He
came back to Guernsey to Hawkesbury to see his mother and father bringing
with him his intended wife 1923 [*sic*; in the version he sent Hamish Hamilton he

Given the cult of D.H. Lawrence that prevailed in the circle in which Gerald had situated himself - and increasingly dominated as most empathetic apostle to this literary Messiah - it is likely that Kathleen aspired to play an equivalent role to Lawrence's older, cosmo-politan and sexually-liberated wife, Frieda. According to Collis, aspects of this role came naturally to her, at least in the thinly disguised version of her he created for a short story that featured them both:

Fig. 34: 'The Simple Life'
Kathleen with Adam, as published in the
*Daily Express*, 10 August 1928.

Alice [*i.e.* Kathleen] possessed an unusual power of self-idealisation. She saw herself as a Wonderful Person… She always knew how to look after herself. She was the least monogamous woman I have ever known. She could have done with ten men. And whatever she did was done in the same idealistic, pure, natural way. If she stripped naked and played on a couch with a man, she would say – 'Clothes are so stupid. I simply

wasn't sure of the date and it may well have been later, in which case perhaps after his mother's death. If she came over in 1923 she would have been nineteen]. I was only a boy then, I was there at Hawkesbury the evening of the day they came… The Lord knows what his mother thought of it at the time. They went back to England where they were married… Gerald came to Guernsey when his mother died in 1924. He was alone.' Clary implies that Gerald came back alone after his marriage but as we have seen he did not marry for another two years and may not yet have met Kathleen. The use of the word 'simple' in connection with Kathleen, reminds one of Christine Mahy's description of herself as 'a simple soul', and Ebenezer's facetious echo of this: 'She was a simple soul. She might have been the Virgin Mary in person', in *Ebenezer Le Page*, p. 176. When Frieda first met Lawrence in her husband's house she said 'he seemed so obviously simple.' (Worthen, *Lawrence*, p. 380).

go dead dressed up and without the sun. I don't feel I'm myself.'[118]

Since Clary Dumond could not have known this account, his recollection of the couple's mid-1920s visit to Guernsey tends to confirm that Collis's fictionalised account reflected reality:

> The young lady appeared very nice, to me rather high class. It was said later she was a dedicated nudist. She it was said in our newspaper believed in what she called 'the simple life'.[119]

If Kathleen naturally rivalled Frieda in sexual promiscuity, her emulation of Frieda's literary pretentions proved less convincing. Frieda justified her libertarian life-style by generalised reference to that creative brand of German philosophy and Viennese psychoanalysis which, however incompletely digested, via its influence on Lawrence, became a major influence on his 'New Romantic' contemporaries and successors.[120] Inasmuch as either woman might justify their bohemian behaviour in terms of the new thinking, however, Gerald may already have been harbouring Nietzschean reservations regarding the female character, even as enhanced by Otto Weininger.[121] In his more 'religious' (post-William Jamesian) approach to such matters he may indeed have influenced Murry and in turn Sir Richard Rees with whom he travelled abroad in 1930.[122] In his *Theory of my Time*, Rees quotes

---

[118] *The Realist* (unpublished short story); whereabouts of original unknown but relevant excerpts kindly sent me by Richard Ingrams. Not found among the Collis papers donated by Michael Holroyd to Trinity College Library, Dublin.

[119] Dumond seems to be referring to the *Daily Express* photograph above.

[120] Given subsequent praise, in her correspondence with Richard Aldington, of his debunking of Norman Douglas and T.E. Lawrence, it is interesting to read the latter's observation, published in the 1938 edition of his *Letters* by David Garnett, that the equivalently celebrated D.H. Lawrence 'was too much on the make.' (T.E. Lawrence, *Letters*, p. 755).

[121] See below, p. 71. The casual reference to Weininger (linked with Oscar Wilde) by Murry in his 1916 novel *Still Life,* suggests a familiarity with his work among this circle; see Kaplan, *Circulating Genius*, p. 30.

[122] See below, p. 100. Sir Richard Rees (1900-70) was an Eton- and Cambridge-educated baronet who painted, wrote, taught at the WEA in London and in 1930 succeeded his friend Murry as co-editor of the *Adelphi* (which he also funded).

the 'Christian heretic' Murry's *Reminiscences of D.H. Lawrence* with approval:

> Psycho-analysis, without knowing what it is doing, has assumed the responsibilities of a religion without having religious duties to impose or religious satisfactions to offer.[123]

Rees [Fig. 35] offers up as an alternative the saintly Simone Weil, whose 'brave' life and work he promoted and compared

Fig. 35: *Sir Richard Rees: Self-Portrait* (oil on canvas, c.1960)
(Trinity College, Cambridge)

with that of the more Nietzschean D.H. Lawrence, for though apparently very different: 'each of them possessed, or was possessed by, a religious genius. They were two of the greatest spirits of this age.'[124]

---

[123] Murry, *Reminiscences*, pp. 241-42 as quoted by Rees, *Theory of my Time: An Essay in Didactic Reminiscence* (London, 1963), p. 43. This attitude contrasts with Auden's elegy 'In Memory of Sigmund Freud', in which he praised the latter for enabling us to 'approach the Future as a friend.'

[124] Rees, *Theory of my Time*, p. 194; *cf. Brave Men: A study of D H Lawrence and*

# 6: FRIEDIAN PHILOSOPHY

In August 1899, the twenty-year-old Frieda Von Richthofen married the Nottingham University philologist, Ernest Weekley, in Freiburg and went on to have three children by him. During visits home to Germany, however, she had several affairs, much the most significant of which was in 1907-08 with the brilliant young psychoanalyst (or psycho-anarchist), Otto Gross, whose enthusiasm for sexual libertarianism (and mutual psychoanalysis) influenced Jung and Ernest Jones, and worried Freud, who was initially also an admirer.[125] Jones acknowledged Gross as his first instructor in psychoanalysis and thought him: 'the nearest approach to the romantic idea of a genius I have ever known... Such penetrative power of divining the inner thoughts of others I was never to see again.'[126] Beyond Freud and

---

*Simone Weil* (London 1958), Simone Weil, *Seventy Letters: translated and arranged by Richard Rees* (Oxford, 1965) and Rees, *Simone Weil: A Sketch for a Portrait* (Oxford, 1966).

[125] Martin Burgess Green, *Otto Gross: Freudian Psychoanalyst 1877-1920: Literature and Ideas* (New York, 1999); *cf.* Ken Robinson, 'A Portrait of the Psychoanalyst as a Bohemian: Ernest Jones and the "Lady from Styria"', *Psychoanalysis and History*, XV (July 2013), pp. 165-189; Jones had studied with Gross so was well-qualified to reprimand Frieda when she complained that Lawrence was trying to murder her: 'From the way you treat him I wonder he has not done so long ago', Maddox, *Lawrence*, p. 216; *cf. idem, Freud's Wizard: The Enigma of Ernest Jones* (London, 2006), p. 122. Jones's first letter to Freud, dated 13 May 1908, concerned Otto Gross, both Frieda's and their multiple sexual relationships: *The Compete Correspondence of Sigmund Freud and Ernest Jones 1908-1939*, ed. R. Andrew Paskauskas (Cambridge, Mass. and London, 1993), pp. 1-2. It includes Jones's observation that 'Gross gets great delight in getting other men to love her [his wife]', a phenomenon/philosophy relevant to both Lawrence and Gerald's experience (and one that Jones seems to have taken advantage of in this instance). In 1907 Gross had stayed in Heidelberg with the Webers and had a child with both his Frieda, with whom he had agreed a free-love pact, and by Else Jaffé. Both couples named both sons Peter; see Martin Green, *Mountain of Truth. The Counterculture Begins. Ascona, 1900-1920* (Hanover and London, 1986). Thoughts on these aspects of Gross (from a largely Jungian perspective) are to be found in Gottfried Heuer ed., *Sexual Revolutions: Psychoanalysis, History and the Father* (Hove, 2011). A major documentary source is now Esther Bertschinger-Joos, *Frieda Gross und ihre Briefe an Else Jaffé: Ein bewegtes Leben im Umfeld von Anarchismus, Psychoanalyse und Bohème* (Marburg, 2014); *cf. Otto Gross: Selected Works 1901-1920*, ed. Lois L. Madison (New York, 2012).

[126] Martin Green, *Mountain of Truth*, p. 178; *cf.* Maddox, *Freud's Wizard*, p. 55.

Nietzsche and the latter's leitmotif: 'repress nothing', Gross was inspired by the matriarchal anthropology of the Swiss scholar, Johann Jakob Bachofen (1815–1887).

Though 'Gross was not homosexual … he saw bisexuality as a given and held that no man could know why he was loveable for a woman if he did not know about his own homosexual component', a credo, albeit in more conflicted form, that proved relevant to Gerald.[127] It was in Munich's bohemian suburb, Schwabing, where Frieda went to stay with Otto and Frieda Gross, that in the early years of the 20th-century, interest in Bachofen's *Mutterrecht* revived, the anti-patriarchal Gross being a particular admirer.[128] Combined with the anti-repressive aspects of feminism, Bachofen's account of primeval matriarchy encouraged a form of *fin-de-siècle* awe of women which was not, for the time being, fearful.[129] Building on Bachofen, however, Nietzsche promoted preemptive tyranny over the female tyrant:

The happiness of man is: I will. The happiness of woman is:

---

[127] Gottfried Heuer citing Gross's 1913 article in *Die Aktion*, in 'Otto Gross, 1877-1920: Biographical Survey', 1: www.ottogross.org/english/documents/BiographicalSurvey.html. For further discussion *vis à vis* Gerald, see p. 185.

[128] Green, *Mountain of Truth*, pp. 161-62 and www.ottogross.org/english/documents/BiographicalSurvey.html); *cf. Myth, religion, and mother right: selected writings of J. J. Bachofen*, translated from the German (*Mutterrecht und Urreligion*, ed. Rudolf Marx) by Ralph Manheim, with a preface by George Boas and an introduction by Joseph Campbell (London, 1967). Green also discusses Bachofen's contribution to the idea of *Sonnenkinder*, or *The Children of the Sun*, the title of his 1977 'Narrative of 'Decadence in England after 1918'. The most recent study of Bachofen is *An English Translation of Bachofen's Mutterrecht (Mother Right) (1861): A Study of the Religious and Juridicial Aspects of Gynecocracy in the Ancient World*, ed. David Partenheimer, 2 vols (Lampeter, 2003 and 2007). I am very grateful to Dr Partenheimer for sending me the complete text of his translation. Reference to Bachofen's *Mutterrecht*, albeit via Jane Harrison, as the 'fantasy … that there was once a peaceable matriarchy overthrown by war-mongering men,' is made in Camille Paglia, *Sexual Personae: Art and Decadence from Nefertiti to Emily Dickinson* (New Haven, 1990), p. 42.

[129] See for example, Bram Dijkstra's *Idols of Perversity: Fantasies of Feminine Evil in Fin-de-Siècle Culture* (Oxford, 1986), though he nowhere mentions Bachofen. In his subsequent, *Evil Sisters: The Threat of Female Sexuality and the Cult of Manhood* (1996) Dijkstra speculates on the supposed link between turn of the century gynecide and later genocides, citing Otto Weininger whose pejorative narrative connecting the female with Judaism appealed to Hitler, despite his being a Jewish homosexual (pp. 401-03).

he wills. 'Behold, just now the world became perfect!' — thus thinks every woman when she obeys out of entire love. And women must obey and find a depth for her surface. Surface is the disposition of woman: a mobile, stormy film over shallow water. Man's disposition, however, is deep … woman feels his strength but does not comprehend it.[130]

*Thus spake Zarasthustra* was succeeded by *Beyond Good and Evil*. The copy that Gerald brought with him to Stephen Potter's parents' house (where he would have a hot bath), was no doubt Helen Zimmern's 1906 translation, which played a major role in encouraging English interest in Nietzsche and led to her being commissioned to translate *Human, All Too Human*, which appeared in 1909 and was likewise included in Oscar Levy's multi-volume edition.[131] This very talented German-Jewess seems to have no qualms about publishing her friend, Nietzsche's views on women, though her own career (and that of her collaborator-sister, Alice) could be said to have called these into question:

To be mistaken in the fundamental problem of 'man and woman,' to deny here the profoundest antagonism and the necessity for an eternally hostile tension, to dream here perhaps of equal rights, equal training, equal claims and obligations: that is a *typical* sign of shallow-mindedness; and a thinker who has proved himself shallow at this dangerous spot — shallow in instinct! — may generally be regarded as suspicious, nay more, as betrayed, as discovered; he will probably prove too 'short' for all fundamental questions of life, future as well as present, and

---

[130] *Thus spake Zarathustra*, as quoted by Ofelia Schutte, *Beyond Nihilism: Nietzsche Without Masks* (Chicago, 1986), p. 178.

[131] Nietzsche considered Zimmern 'extremely clever' and as the woman 'who introduced Schopenhauer to the English'; Walter A. Kaufmann, *Nietzsche: Philosopher, Psychologist, Antichrist* (Princeton, 4th ed. 1975), p. xiii. Helen Zimmern wrote children's books, studies of Lessing as well as of Schopenhauer (1876). She collaborated on literary projects with her more feminist sister, Alice, critiqued German anti-semitism and eventually established herself as a cultural historian in Florence where she died in 1934; see *ODNB*. Her *Italian Leaders of Today* (London, 1915), pp. 294-95, draws attention to the *volte face* of the Nietzschean Mussolini in advocating war in favour of France, after advocating neutrality in his socialist magazine *Avanti*.

will be unable to descend to *any* of the depths. On the other hand, a man who has depth of spirit as well as of desires and has also the depth of benevolence which is capable of severity and harshness, and easily confounded with them, can only think of women as *Orientals* do: he must conceive of her as a possession, as confinable property, as a being predestined for service and accomplishing her mission therein – he must take his stand in this matter upon the immense rationality of Asia, upon the superiority of the instinct of Asia, as the Greeks did formerly; those best heirs and scholars of Asia – who as is well known, with their *increasing* culture and amplitude of power, from Homer to the time of Pericles, became gradually *stricter* towards women, in short, more Oriental. *How* necessary, *how* logical, even *how* humanely desirable this was, let us consider for ourselves!

The weaker sex has in no previous age been treated with so much respect by men as at present.[132]

Although, like most of his acquaintance in this period, Gerald may have tended to the political left, his particular enthusiasm for Nietzsche prevented progress towards egalitarian gender politics, as did his understanding of the fate of D.H. Lawrence as one who overcame domination by the mother only to succumb to domination by the *Mutter*-figure who played the crucial role in liberating him.[133] In *Sons and Lovers*, if not in life, Lawrence hastens the ailing mother's death with morphine, thereby challenging Freud's Oedipal norm in the manner articulated by the then almost as influential - albeit Freud-, Bachofen- and Nietzsche-influenced- Jane Harrison (1850-1928).

---

[132] *Beyond Good and Evil,* §238-39. If Nietzsche were alive today he would no doubt confirm this as being at the root of the Muslim fundamentalists' fight against further progress towards Westernization. It is with the opposite notion of women's 'weakness' that Dr Johnson justifies the maintenance of their inferior legal status: 'Nature has given women so much power that the Law has very wisely given them little'; letter to the Rev. Dr Taylor 18 August 1763, *Letters of Samuel Johnson*, ed. Bruce Redford, 5 vols (Oxford, 1992), I, p. 228.

[133] See below, his reviews of Potter's book on Lawrence, p. 118, and of Velona Pilcher's war play, *The Searcher,* as discussed below, p. 137, as well as his letter to me, p. 246.

She wrote that:

> Man cannot escape being born of woman, but can, and if he is wise, will, as soon as he comes to manhood, perform ceremonies of riddance and purgation.[134]

Gerald defied his real mother more firmly in fact than in fiction. He left Guernsey long before her death and immediately after it tore up her will, having over-hastily interpreted it as out-manoeuvring assistance in a struggle with the father. Yet his early advocacy of love, or at least faith in life, as a quasi-religious necessity only seems to have faltered with the failure of his Friedian, albeit even more polyamorous marriage. Until the early 1930s, his letters and surviving articles maintained a tone of supreme confidence bordering on conceit, no doubt concealing insecurities too deep to be acknowledged. The extent to which he disappeared after the break-up of his family and abandonment of his children may be explained both by embarrassment at his failure to prevail with his once so-confidently articulated philosophy and his profound disillusionment with women.[135]

Had the followers of early-20th-century anarcho-libertarianism been as conscious of the fate of Otto Gross and some of his associates as they were of Otto Weininger's, they might have proceeded more cautiously. In Ascona, where Otto and Frieda Gross moved in 1910 (to be visited there by Frieda Weekley the

---

[134] Harrison's *Themis* of 1912 (2nd edn, 1927) was influenced by Freud's *Totem and Taboo* (1913; but first published in the previous year in *Imago*), itself heavily influenced by James Frazer's *Golden Bough*, 3rd edition, 12 vols (1911-15) and beyond that by Nietzsche, who coined the concept of the 'id' and whom Freud said had 'a more penetrating understanding of himself than any man who ever lived or was likely to live'; Walter Kaufmann, *Freud, Adler, and Jung: Discovering the Mind*, III (New Brunswick, 1992), p. 266. Harrison praises Nietzsche's 'instinct of genius', in discerning the Dionysian ingredient in *The Birth of Tragedy*; *Themis*, 2nd ed., p. 436. Nietzschean Bronislaw Malinowski (see below, p. 181) became a critic of Frazer, as well as of Freud, problematizing both patricidal theorizing and the universality of the Oedipus complex. For his casual racism and a defence of the Freudian notion of 'eternal desire to be and be rid of the Father', see Armstrong, *Compulsion for Antiquity*, p. 251, and my review, *cit.* below, footnote 124, p. 306.

[135] In his *Son of Woman*, Murry suggests that Birkin in *Women in Love* is trying 'to escape from the misery of his own failure with a woman'; *cf.* Kaplan, *Circulating Genius*, p. 182.

GENIUS FRIEND – PART ONE

following year), he supplied poison to a suicidal young woman called Lotte Hattemar and there were rumours that Ernest Jones might have murdered his young wife.[136] Freud himself contributed to the death of his friend and patient Ernst Fleischl in 1891 due to his faith in the therapeutic value of cocaine; he meanwhile maintained an intimate relationship with his wife's sister.[137] Gross fathered a child with Frieda Weekley's more intellectual sister, Else Jaffé, who was in turn the lover of both Alfred Weber (1868-1958) and his more famous brother Max (1864-1920), whose student she had meanwhile married.[138] Frieda briefly contemplated leaving Weekley for Gross, who encouraged her to believe in herself as 'the Woman of the Future', and that 'if only sex were "free" the world would straightaway turn into a paradise.'[139] She then had an affair with Gross's disciple, the anarchist painter Ernst Frick, who was also

---

[136] For Ernest Jones's possible contribution to the death by chloroform of his wife, the singer Morfydd Owen, see Maddox, *Freud's Wizard*, pp. 142-43.

[137] Rumours, including those spread by the no longer admiring Jung, of Freud's sexual relationship with Minna Bernays, tend to be confirmed by the recent discovery that they shared a double bed in the Schweizerhaus, an inn in Maloja, in the Swiss Alps, north east of Ascona. Jung meanwhile almost certainly had an affair with a protégé-cum-patient of both his and Freud's, Sabina Spielrein; see John Launer, *Sex versus Survival: The Life and Idea of Sabina Spielrein* (London, 2014).

[138] Worthen, *Lawrence*, pp. 378-89, Martin Green, *The Von Richthofen Sisters: The Triumphant and The Tragic Modes of Love* (London, 1974) and Sam Whimster and Gottfried Heuer, 'Otto Gross and Else Jaffé and Max Weber', *Theory, Culture & Society*, XV (August 1998), pp. 129-160. Gross's correspondence with Frieda was conducted via Edgar Jaffé, her sister's husband (1866-1921). According to Lawrence, 'Jaffe was a Jew and Professor - rich – and went and became Finanzminister to the Bavarian Bolshevik Republic or whatever it was, in 1920 - and died of funk, poor thing.' (*Letters of D.H. Lawrence*, VI, pp. 281-82). For Jung's correspondence with Freud on the subject of the 'extraordinarily decent' Otto Gross, who was ultimately diagnosed as schizophrenic, see *The Freud/Jung Letters*, ed. William McGuire (London, 1979), pp. 112-16. Lawrence and Frieda's first flat together (in Icking) was loaned to them by Alfred Weber. It was here that Frieda instructed her husband in the libertarian ways of Ascona for which Alfred was also an enthusiast. This seems to have encouraged him, literally, to imitate Otto Gross, when walking alone in Italian Switzerland and perhaps even to visit Ascona; see the discussion in Maddox, *Lawrence*, pp. 137 and 177.

[139] Worthen, *Lawrence*, p. 381. The chapter in Frieda's unfinished memoir, *Octavio*, is based on her affair with Otto Gross and Lawrence's unfinished *Mr Noon* is based on her reminiscences of the same; see below, p. 81.

the lover of Gross's wife, the other Frieda. The latter stayed in Ascona when Otto moved to Berlin in 1913, and indeed after his drug-and-depression-related death in 1920. The Lawrences remained friends with Frieda Gross, having Secker send a copy of *Women in Love* to her in 1921 after the trade edition was finally published.[140] Frick remained in Ascona and died there in 1956.[141]

It is very likely, therefore, that it was due to their knowledge of this circle – not least through Murry's intimacy with the Lawrences - that Gerald and Kathleen chose to stay at the lakeside paradise of Ascona, the base camp at the foot of the Alps of the sexually-liberated community at Monte Verità.[142]

# 7: ADELPHIAN SANCTUARY

It is all the more likely that Gerald and Kathleen, with their baby, Adam, were drawn - albeit indirectly - to Ascona due to the reputation of Monte Verità, because prior to leaving England they lived in a similarly libertarian commune in Sussex. As it happens, this was not far from the more bourgeois community visited by Murry and the Lawrences during the Great War. In 1912 the Meynell family had acquired the 80-acre estate of Greatham, near Storrington, West Sussex. Lawrence was

---

[140] *Letters of D.H. Lawrence*, IV, p. 39. Meanwhile, Secker's wife, Rina, had (at least) a romantic association with Lawrence, and the voracious Ernest Jones had an affair with Frieda Gross; see Richard Owen, *Lady Chatterley's Villa. D.H. Lawrence on the Italian Riviera* (London, 2014) and Robinson, 'A Portrait of the Psychoanalyst as a Bohemian', *cit.*, pp. 165-189; *cf.* Maddox, *Freud's Wizard*, *passim*.

[141] There was recently a conference-cum-book launch there in his honour; see Esther Bertschinger-Joos and Richard Butz, *Ernst Frick 1881-1956: Anarchist in Zürich, Künstler und Forscher in Ascona, Monte Verità* (Zurich, 2014); *cf.* E. Bertschinger-Joos, *Frieda Gross*. See below, p. 114, for Olga Fröbe-Kapteyn's establishment of a conference room at the suggestion of Jung near her home in Ascona in 1928, subsequently used for the Eranos summer school.

[142] See below, p. 88. For the best account of the significance of Ascona by an author who had already written the biography of Frieda Lawrence and her sister, see Green, *Mountain of Truth*. For the role of Ida Hofman and Henri Oedenkoven in the establishment of the Monte Verità community, see now Robert Landmann, *Ascona – Monte Verità. Auf der Suche nach dem Paradies* (Munich, 2009).

meanwhile dreaming of his ideal community, which he called Ranamin ('my Island idea'), even designing badges for members, featuring a Phoenix on a black background. The Meynells had a similar ideal, to the extent of calling their estate 'the Colony'. One of their first guests was fellow-Catholic, smock-wearing and extreme sexual-libertarian, Eric Gill, who having moved out of Ditchling village, founded his own family-based community on the edge of the Common.[143] The newly married Lawrences, plus servant Hilda, moved into Viola Meynell's smartly-converted cow shed in the spring of 1915 and were soon joined by visitors to the neighbouring cottages on the estate, including Lady Cynthia Asquith, Bertrand Russell, his mistress Ottoline Morrell and E.M. Forster.[144] Perhaps most significantly, in terms of Gerald's community-minded inspiration just over a decade later, Middleton Murry also came, suffering from flu and heartache, Katherine Mansfield having fled to Paris with her temporary lover, Francis Carco, to whom she had been introduced by Murry himself.[145] When she unexpectedly returned to London, Murry immediately abandoned Lawrence to go to her.[146] After one of her frequent quarrels with Lawrence, Frieda also left for London but they soon reunited, only to separate again, this time after quarrelling

---

[143] He was to publish a relevant article about it entitled 'The Scythe' in the *Adelphi*; Fiona MacCarthy, *Eric Gill* (London, 1989), pp. 112-18. MacCarthy's courageously objective reporting of Gill's acts of paedophilic incest at Ditchling and elsewhere caused an uproar whilst ever more crudely-defined accounts of child abuse continue to flourish. The last thing Lawrence wrote, days before his death, was an essentially enthusiastic review of Gill's *Art Nonsense*, while Murry wrote an obituary of Gill in *Blackfriars* in February 1941.

[144] Maddox, *Lawrence*, pp. 195-200; the last two pages summarise Lawrence's aggressive behaviour to still virgin homosexual Forster who left first thing next morning and wrote back: 'I do not like the deaf impercipient fanatic who has nosed over his own little sexual round until he believes that there is no other path for others to take'. Viola Meynell had been the lover of Martin Secker before they separated and he met Rina en route to Capri; see Owen, *Lady Chatterley's Villa*, p. 69. Lawrence completed *The Rainbow* at Greatham.

[145] Francis Carco, a French poet and contributor to Murry's first magazine, *Rhythm*; see *The Letters of John Middleton Murry to Katherine Mansfield*, ed. C.A. Hankin (London, 1983), pp. 42-43. Photographs of him go some way to explaining Murry's confidence that Mansfield would come back to him.

[146] Maddox, *Lawrence*, p. 200.

about Nietzsche over dinner at Garsington.[147]

Garsington was a rather more up-market community than either Ditchling or Greatham. Gilbert Cannan's briefly celebrated Buckinghamshire windmill, around which the Murrys and Lawrences had clustered before the war has been described as 'a poor man's Garsington'; it was indeed Cannan who introduced Lawrence to Ottoline Morrell.[148] But in 1922, to the other side of Storrington, the anti-capitalist daughter of a textile magnate, Vera Pragnell, acquired 50 acres of land in order to establish a more authentically humble Utopia, closer in character to Gill's Ditchling [Fig. 36].

Vera had worked for a while with volunteers in the slums of East London. Like both

Fig. 36: *Vera Pragnell*, *Daily Chronicle*, 24 Jan 1925. (Storrington Museum)

---

[147] Interestingly, in view of other somewhat snobbish accounts of Frieda, despite her quasi-aristocratic status about which Lawrence tended to boast, Murry managed to be simultaneously condescending about her intelligence, whilst sneering at the owner of the cottage in which they were staying, Monica Saleeby, daughter of the long-suffering Wilfrid and Alice Meynell, and sister of Viola: 'She's fat, quite amiable & kindly, and perfectly stupid, *so stupid* that Frieda L. seems a paragon of wit and ingenuity beside her.' (*Letters, ed. cit.*, p. 41). Gerald would at least have known of the Meynells from Stephen Potter, who was a friend of Viola's brother, Francis, later Sir Francis, co-founder of the Nonesuch Press.

[148] Kaplan, *Circulating Genius*, p. 65 and below, p. 162. J.M. Barrie's secretary, Cannan had an affair with his actress wife, Mary, who divorced Barrie and married him. He eventually went mad and spent the rest of his life in Holloway Sanatorium; see Diana Farr, *Gilbert Cannan: A Georgian Prodigy* (London, 1978);

Lawrence and Gerald, she was an admirer of Edward Carpenter and his community at Millthorpe in Derbyshire, and like Murry strove to combine Christianity and Communism. At its peak in the mid- to late 1920s, there were more than a dozen families, along with assorted characters such as the pagan, 'Dion' Byngham,[149] encamped in improvised accommodation clustered around Vera's cottage on Heath Common, between Washington and Storrington. Their once controversial presence is recalled today merely by the names 'Vera's Walk', 'Bohemia Row' and Sanctuary Lane [Fig. 37].[150]

Fig. 37: *Sanctuary Cottage, Storrington* (photo: the author).

Given their growing interest in the theatre, Gerald and Kathleen's residence at 'The Sanctuary' may have been linked with that of the slightly older family of artist-actor, Wilfrid Walter. A relevant excerpt from his unpublished memoirs has

---

*cf.* Lisa Chaney, *Hide and Seek with Angels: A Life of J.M. Barrie* (London, 2005).

[149] *Vere* Harry Byngham who chose the name Dion as short for Dionysus, was, like his friend Victor Neuburg, a follower of Alistair Crowley, and, Ascona-style, enjoyed posing nude with or without his girlfriend; see Ronald Hutton, *The Triumph of the Moon: A History of Modern Pagan Witchcraft* (Oxford, 1999), pp. 166-68. Byngham was Ernest Westlake's successor as British chief of the Order of Woodcraft Chivalry which was founded in 1916, to save society from the cul-de-sac of intellectualised religion.' Neuberg ran the Vine Press at nearby Steyning, publishers of Vera Pragnell's *Story of the Sanctuary*; see below, p. 81.

[150] Chris Hare, *The Washington Story: The Forgotten Story of a Downland Village* (West Chiltington, 2000), pp. 62-77.

been transcribed, courtesy of his granddaughter Josie:

My days of modest security at the Old Vic were over. After five weeks I was out of work, pending a decision on the conditions of my contract, which entitled Drury Lane to keep me out of work for 12 weeks in the year. Mai Mai [Walter's first wife] and I plus our two boys Will and Richard went to live in a caravan at the Sanctuary near Storrington. Here was springy heather surrounded by silver birch and pine, with a grand vista of the South Downs. It was a remarkable encampment.

Vera Pragnell was a young woman of means with an overpowering desire to share her wealth with others but wise enough not to give it away wholesale. She had therefore bought some acres of wild hillside and invited its free occupation by those in need of it. As may be imagined she was soon surrounded by a motley crew, including ourselves in our caravan. Vera was of magnificent stature. Her great encompassing eyes gleamed gaily through a lock of chestnut hair that escaped most wilfully from a long 'kerchief, reminiscent somehow of a veil and the release of those unruly locks. Her first act of bounty had been to take a cottage by a high road and allow any tramp to rest and sleep there... It was a bold act for a very beautiful young girl...

When she moved to the Sanctuary she kept a tramp room always open, attached to a little chapel. Numerous plots were taken up, cultivated, and bungalows built, and there was a floating population of tent and caravan dwellers. An old London omnibus without wheels was used too. All the misfits came there to be mothered and tendered [sic] in illness, and to be understood in their particular difficulties by this golden-haired, rather divine but very human girl...

There was Betty, a bona-fide lady of the fair grounds, living in a caravan whose polished brass shone amid the heathers. Ours was a huge road-menders' caravan with four beds, which Mai Mai amazingly converted... There was an Indian married to a white wife, a builder with a horde of children and a drunken mother; there were folk with impossible theories of natural ways of living. There were inept craftsmen, convalescents, and a nudist couple. It was a trifle disconcerting to have a tent flap opened suddenly by a young woman in the nude, with whom one attempted to make trivial conversation by inquiring whether she found the return to London life rather trying after this state of nature…

Then there was the continuous procession of those who came to woo. Vera's soul was very much the concern of all; but especially of young men of the Church; and there were poets and artists, and highly civilised and altogether too intellectual young men…

Then one day two painter pals of mine drifted in and lived in the red London bus without wheels. After an arduous and bitter contest, Vera laid aside the veil – in favour of Dennis Earle.[151]

In 1928 there had already been a somewhat valedictory tone to Vera Pragnell's privately published account of this social experiment.[152] The following year she indeed married Dennis Earle and, partly as a result of scandals stirred up in press, some of 'the settlers' began to disperse. In 1932 Pragnell and Earle, together with another couple, migrated to a chateau near Montpellier but returned to the Sanctuary after a year and then, having generously granted ownership to the remaining residents, settled down to a more bourgeois existence until her death in 1968. By this time a democratised (and consumer-capitalised) version of the ethos she had so nobly promoted was well underway.[153]

---

[151] 'The Sanctuary through the Eyes of Franz Wilfrid Walter', *Times Past*, No. 41, Spring 2012, www.storringtonmuseum.org

[152] Under the name Vera G. Pragnell, in a limited edition of 600 copies, she published *The Story of the Sanctuary* (Vine Press, Steyning, 1928); *cf.* review in the *Aberdeen Press and Journal* for 9 August 1928.

[153] Hare, *Washington Story*, pp. 71-2.

# 8: ASCONAN THEOSOPHY

By the time Victor Neuberg was printing Vera Pragnell's *Story of the Sanctuary*, Gerald and Kathleen had left it and indeed England. In early June 1928, in the same month as the Lawrences left their villa outside Florence for Switzerland, the Edwardses also headed there, settling in Erstfeld, a route-town Lawrence had visited on his walk into Northern Italy fifteen years earlier [Fig. 38].[154] Drawn perhaps by its reputation as a superior version of the Sanctuary, Gerald and Kathleen may already have been planning to head further south to Ascona where they indeed stayed for several months the following year; but above all Gerald was hoping to meet Lawrence. Most likely equipped with Cape's compact, 1926 Travellers' Library edition of *Twilight in Italy*, it seems he was preparing for such a meeting by treading in Lawrence's footsteps. Lawrence had in turn trod in Frieda's and indeed her lover's footsteps when he first travelled this route in September 1913, even to the extent of impersonating 'a doctor from Graz', *i.e.* the same Otto Gross, who was travelling between Munich and Ascona, throughout this period.[155]

---

[154] After Christmas together in Tuscany, Aldous and Maria Huxley had encouraged Lawrence to come to Switzerland for the sake of his health at the beginning of 1928; see *Letters of D.H. Lawrence*, VI, p. 246. His delay in leaving was in large part due to the completion and publication (by Orioli) of *Lady Chatterley's Lover* in Florence. In July the Lawrences settled in Kesselmatte, 4,000 feet up, near Gsteig bei Gstaad, on the German-speaking side of the Pillon pass leading to French-speaking Diablerets.

[155] 'The Return Journey', *Twilight in Italy and other essays*, ed. Paul Eggert (Cambridge, 1994 and 2002), pp. 209 and 296. Eggert's deduction that Lawrence was thinking of Otto Gross is supported by Lawrence's pretence that 'my father was a doctor from Graz', Otto's authoritarian father being the celebrated criminologist, Hans Gross, who was born and died in Graz. Lawrence never met either but was clearly impressed by Frieda's account of Otto, as evidenced in his unfinished novel *Mr Noon*, in which Gross features as Eberhard, 'the wonderful lover'; 'he was so beautiful, like a white Dionysus'; 'He was almost the first psychoanalyst, you know--he was … far, far more brilliant than Freud' (though he may have been encouraged by Freud in his dependence on cocaine). Gross and Franz Kafka met in 1917 and compared notes regarding their authoritarian fathers. He also seems to have influenced Anton Kuh regarding the tendency of both Judaism and German *Kultur* to favour patriarchal monotheism which had supposedly driven out ancient matriarchal religion, a theme related to Kuh's coining of 'Jewish self-hatred' as articulated in *Juden und Deutsche* (Berlin, 1921),

Fig. 38: *Erstfeld, Switzerland* (postcard: c.1930).

On 17 June 1928 Gerald wrote to Murry from Erstfeld, excusing himself for not having completed promised articles - partly because he and Kathleen had contracted scabies - and asking him if he would meanwhile consider publishing some of Kathleen's stories.[156] Given his later tendency to chauvinism, it is worth noting his more positive, almost uxorious tone that still prevailed at this stage in their marriage:

> Kathleen wants me to send you three short stories she has written, and though I hate doing so before I can send something of my own, I can't keep them back any longer. You'll get them soon after you get this. In a way I'm the last person to judge them, though actually I'm always violently

---

which in turn influenced Theodor Lessing's *Der Jüdische Selbsthaß* (Berlin, 1930).

[156] Gerald's letter to Murry dating from more than a year later on 15 July 1929 reveals that an essay of his, presumably his review of West's *Annie Besant*, has been accepted, 'And Kathleen wants to thank you for taking her "Quaker Meeting". In his long, 17 April 1929 letter to Murry from Ascona, Gerald writes that he loves George Fox 'for sitting on a haystack, the crowd clamouring round him, waiting for him to speak, and him silent, waiting for the Lord. That's the only way.' Had he followed this method instead of defying the Lord, he says, 'Cape would probably have had his book by now and published it, and I might easily be on my way with another.' Interestingly, he quotes the Quaker founder Fox on Christ by way of conclusion to his review of West's *Annie Besant*: 'He teacheth every man that cometh into the world' (*New Adelphi*, September-November 1929, p. 48). For Gerald meeting Annie Besant, see p. 134.

critical of whatever she writes. But I do think them good, and one of them very good. She has in mind many others of the same kind, and is, in fact, writing another at the moment, but she says she very much wants some honest outside word about them – she distrusts my partiality; and also, though she hardly dares believe it possible, I know she hopes one may find its way into the Adelphi. And I hope so too. Anyhow, I will ask you to read them, though I know how occupied you must be with other things: and I'd be glad of a line or two about them, and for any hint as to how to dispose of them.

Only now, after promoting his wife's writings, does Gerald say something about his own work:

The fact that I didn't manage to get anything to you for this quarter's Adelphi is something I don't like to think about. I am inexcusably to blame – and yet not to blame at all – as one usually is... The Essay on Sex grew longer and longer even after I'd cut out the 'attack', until it was obvious that it was going to be much too long for the Adelphi... And the days passed. Then I turned frantically to the Life of Annie Besant...[Fig. 39]

The latter refers to the newly-published biography of Annie Besant by Geoffrey West which Murry seems to have sent him for review, probably thinking it appropriate, given Besant's quasi-intimate relationship with Shaw before she embraced Theosophy:

I read it. It isn't a good book, but the people interested me very much, and it raised issues which seems to me important. I began to review it – in 2,000 words, I hoped. No good. I tried and tried, but I just couldn't get

Fig. 39: *Annie Besant* (1847-1933), (photo: c.1897).

it in. I fretted, and more days passed. At last I had to give
up hope of getting anything off to you in time.

He concludes that he most sincerely hopes to have something
substantial for Murry for this quarter and thanks him for his
delicacy in not hurrying him on, '- and for more than that'.

This letter is merely addressed as from 'Erstfeld, Kanton Uri,
Switzerland' but the next specifies that they were resident 'c/o
Gerhard Spinner', a liberal Lutheran pastor who may have been
an acquaintance of Collis's given that Gerald refers to him
(critically) in a later letter as if Collis knew him.[157] The young
family seems to have stayed with Spinner for more than six
months for on 23 February 1929, Gerald writes to Murry from
the same address asking 'if you would lend me, or put me in the
way of borrowing, Lawrence's 'Rainbow' as it was originally
published.'[158] He also asks if Murry knows anyone in Heidelberg
where 'we are thinking of moving shortly unless some better
possibility presents itself' and if so whether he will give him an
introduction.

Until the early successes of the Nazi party there, Heidelberg had
a scholarly, left-liberal (and libertarian) reputation, not least
associated with psychiatrist-cum-existentialist, Karl Jaspers
(who had a Jewish wife), and with Max Weber and his brother
Alfred, both of whom had affairs with Frieda Lawrence's
married sister, Else Jaffé.[159] The city had a romantic reputation

---

[157] He is perhaps the young theologian and author of *Die Engel und Wir*, praised
by Karl Barth on the subject of Aquinas in his *Church Dogmatics, III, part 3, The
Doctrine of Creation* (London, 2010), p. 400. In 1929 Spinner is recorded as a young
(born 1901) Swiss pastor (and graduate of Zurich and the University of
Heidelberg) who speaks English as well as German living in Erstfeld. In the
Swiss National Library is a document recording his resignation as Pastor
(Pfarrer) Gerhard Spinner dated 18 November 1942: www.helveticarchives.ch/
detail.aspx?ID=204587. By 1953 he was living at Alte Landstraße 24 in Horgen,
near Zurich. If Gerald heard of his resignation he may have had him in mind
when describing Raymond's.

[158] See above, p. 12.

[159] Max was also godfather to Else's son by Otto Gross. For Jaspers' dismissal
from his post in 1937 but survival in Heidelberg through the war whilst
promoting Weber, see Green, *Von Richthofen Sisters*, pp. 290-92; Green argues for
a parallel between Jaspers' attitude to Weber and Murry's to Lawrence,
concluding, however, that Leavis's adulation of Lawrence was even closer. In

associated with the hugely popular 1901 play *Old Heidelberg*, which was turned into a film from 1915 on, and the 1926 song and film: 'Ich hab mein Herz in Heidelberg verloren/I Lost My Heart in Heidelberg.'[160] In 1921 Goebbels had taken his doctorate in Romantic literature there, following this by publishing his autobiographical (and Christian socialist) novel *Michael,* eventually published in 1929. By 1926 he had been appointed Nazi Gauleiter in Berlin.[161]

Apart from being Spinner's *alma mater*, however, the most relevant connection with Heidelberg was Lawrence's. Thanks to his sister-in-law's long-term intimacy with Alfred Weber, Lawrence often stayed there, writing in June 1914:

> … I am now with Prof Weber in Heidelberg hearing the latest in German philosophy and political economy. I am like a little half fledged bird opening my beak *very* wide to gulp down the fat phrases. But it is all very interesting.[162]

On the basis of this and subsequent visits, in 1928 Lawrence wrote his now well-known, race-based 'Letter from Germany', with its 'prophetic' account of Heidelberg, though this remained unpublished until 13 October 1934 when it was appeared in the *New Statesman*:[163]

> Heidelberg full, full, full of people. Students the same, youths with rucksacks the same, boys and maidens in gangs

---

March 1928 Alfred visited the Lawrences at the Villa Mirenda, near Florence, with Else: 'they've been as good as married, and as bad, for many years'; *Letters of D.H. Lawrence*, VI, p. 317. Alfred had written to Lawrence from Ascona 'quite enchanted with the paradisal days there' in November 1927; *ibid.*, p. 214.

[160] By the actor-director Arthur Bergen, who died in Auschwitz in 1943.

[161] Peter Longerich, *Goebbels: a Biography* (London, 2015).

[162] See Carl Crockel, D.H. *Lawrence and Germany: The Politics of Influence* (London, 2007), p. 137, quoting *Letters of D.H. Lawrence*, II, pp. 63, 186. Else Jaffé eventually translated several stories, such as *The Woman Who Rode Away*, into German.

[163] See Michael Burleigh, *Sacred Causes: Religion and Politics from the European Dictators to Al Qaeda* (London, 2006), p. 28. In January 1933 Hitler was elected Chancellor and on 1 May Heidegger was elected Rector of the University of Freiburg. Ten days later he joined the Nazi party and a few weeks later gave his notorious Speech to the Student Association of the University of Heidelberg. In 1929, meanwhile, Eric Voegelin 'had the good fortune' to be taught by Alfred Weber in Heidelberg; Voegelin, *Autobiographical Reflections*, p. 15.

come down from the hills. The same, and not the same. These queer gangs of Young Socialists, youths and girls, with their non-materialistic professions, their half mystic assertions, they strike one as strange. Something primitive, like loose, roving gangs of broken, scattered tribes, so they affect one. And the swarms of people somehow produce an impression of silence, of secrecy, of stealth. It is as if everything and everybody recoiled away from the old unison, as barbarians lurking in a wood recoil out of sight. The old habits remain. But the bulk of the people have no money. And the whole stream of feeling is reversed.

So you stand in the woods about the town and see the Neckar flowing green and swift and slippery out of the gulf of Germany, to the Rhine. And the sun sets slow and scarlet into the haze of the Rhine valley. And the old, pinkish stone of the ruined castle across looks sultry, the marshalry is in shadow below, the peaked roofs of old, tight Heidelberg compressed in its river gateway glimmer and glimmer out...

Something about the Germanic races is unalterable. White-skinned, elemental, and dangerous. Our civilisation has come from the fusion of the dark-eyed with the blue. The meeting and mixing and mingling of the two races has been the joy of our ages. And the Celt has been there, alien, but necessary as some chemical reagent to the fusion. So the civilisation of Europe rose up. So these cathedrals and these thoughts.

But now the Celt is the disintegrating agent. And the Latin and southern races are falling out of association with the northern races, the northern Germanic impulse is recoiling towards Tartary, the destructive vortex of Tartary.

It is a fate; nobody now can alter it. It is a fate. The very blood changes. Within the last three years, the very constituency of the blood has changed, in European veins. But particularly in Germanic veins.

At the same time, we have brought it about ourselves — by a Ruhr occupation, by an English nullity, and by a German false will. We have done it ourselves. But apparently it was not to be helped.

*Quos vult perdere Deus, dementat prius.*[164]

In the letter Gerald writes to Murry from Erstfeld soon after Lawrence had written his from Heidelberg, he is more focussed upon his writing. He asks for comments on a manuscript he is sending, which he says has been turned down by Cape, Heinemann, and Chatto and Windus:

Chatto and Windus were very nice about it, praised it, wanted to see anything else I did, but still would not take it. Heinemann was non-committal. Cape was violent: at least, Edward Garnett was – I don't know if Cape himself saw it [Fig. 40]. But Garnett was abusive. I think I can see some literary reasons for this, but I think it was also due to some extent to the unconscionable time my partly prepaid Lawrence book has been in arriving. And on this score I have felt, and still feel, very guilty. Though I think there were some less reputable and personal reasons for this abuse.[165]

Fig. 40: *Edward Garnett*
(1868-1937)
(photo: Lucia Moholy, 1937)
(National Portrait Gallery)

---

[164] 'Whom God wishes to destroy, he first makes mad' (after Samuel Johnson).

[165] Edward Garnett (1868-1937) was the author and publisher's editor who effectively discovered Joseph Conrad and was instrumental in getting Lawrence's *Sons and Lovers* published in 1913, having already become his friend and confidant. He was the son of Richard Garnett, keeper at the British Museum Reading Room, husband of the translator, Constance, and father of fellow-author and bisexual, David (Bunny) Garnett, who in turn fathered four daughters with Angelica, the daughter of Vanessa Bell and his former lover, Duncan Grant. David Garnett published the edition of T.E. Lawrence's *Letters* with Cape in 1938. For D.H. Lawrence telling David Garnett 'because I love your father … you must leave these "friends", these beetles … come away, and grow whole, and love a woman, and marry her…'; see *Letters*, II, pp. 320-21. See now, Sarah Knights, *Bloomsbury's Outsider: a Life of David Garnett* (London, 2015). Stephen Potter was commissioned to write his book on Lawrence well before the latter's death in March 1930 so it is likely that Cape had already given up on

GENIUS FRIEND – PART ONE

In an unappealingly indignant letter presumably written soon
after, having left Spinner's address, Gerald asks Collis to:

> ... please tell me how we are to get to Heidelberg or
> anywhere else to teach or to do anything else when we have
> 12 francs in hand of which we owe 25, when we have to
> leave these rooms the day after tomorrow, and when,
> should we accept another week's shelter elsewhere we shall
> be 30 francs more in debt the day we move in?
>
> And if you ask me why we did not stay on indefinitely
> at Gerhard's I will tell you that with him – as with you
> apparently – a straight relationship was impossible while
> with respect to him we had the status of beggars.[166]

In the end, Gerald and Kathleen, with baby Adam, did not move
to Heidelberg. Presumably, introductions from Murry were not
forthcoming and anticipated offers of teaching English there
also failed to materialise; perhaps they were already hearing
reports of the city's move to the Right. In any case they moved
in the opposite direction, remaining in Switzerland and heading
due south to the more permanently liberal (and beautiful)
Ascona on Lake Maggiore.

Tending to confirm common interests with those of the Monte
Verità community is the fact that Gerald was finally completing
his review of West's *Life of Annie Besant*. Though recent claims
that Besant actually stayed in Ascona lack documentation,[167]
there had been strong theosophical connections from the start.
There were indeed ongoing links with the likes of Jung and
Hermann Hesse, who by this time had moved nearer Italy, albeit
still in the Ticino, to Montagnola, where he was correcting the
proofs of the English translation of *Steppenwolf* which was first

---

Gerald.

[166] Letter headed merely 'Thursday', kindly loaned by Richard Ingrams. It seems
that the family had fallen out with the progressive pastor Gerhard Spinner, for
whom see above, p. 84.

[167] Robert Temple, 'Eranos: Past and Present', in John van Praag and Riccardo
Bernardini eds, *Eranos Reborn: The Modernities of East and West ; Perspectives on
Violence* (Einsiedeln, 2010), p. 82: 'Krishnamurti lived at Monte Verità; so did
Annie Besant...'

published by Martin Secker in 1929.[168] Like many such contemporaries, Gerald was interested in both Krishnamurti and Tagore (both of whom he very likely met), as well as the still-more celebrated Mahatma Gandhi, who was encouraged by the Theosophy he encountered in England to study Hinduism and the Bhagavad Gita, consolidating his Eastern image generally as a result of his encounters with Western orientalism.[169] According to Martin Green, 'Tagore's poems had been recited and danced to in Ascona'.[170] Such dances were choreographed by the theosophical Nietzschean, Rudolf von Laban (1879-1958), who as Isadora Duncan's successor in Ascona, in collaboration with the eurythmical Suzanne Perrottet and Mary Wigman (Marie Wiegmann) developed his Expressionist (and quasi-racist) ideas in Ascona between 1912-14 [Fig. 41].

In the midst of this period, Duncan's two children drowned in the Seine after a car accident. Laban abandoned his own children (as Gerald would do), including his son by Suzanne, André Perrottet, who subsequently committed suicide.[171] In 1937, after failing to please Goebbels with his insufficiently coordinated choreography for the Nazi Olympics, Laban joined his former student, Lisa Ullman, at the Jooss-Leeder School of Dance at

---

[168] For the various connections, including Hesse's stay at Monte Verità in April 1907 (he revisited Ascona at least once in 1927); see the texts for the 2006 exhibition at the Hermann Hesse house, 'Seekers of Truth. Hermann Hesse and Monte Verità' www.seriehesse.usi.ch/allaricercadellaverita/en/pdf/monte_verita_EN.pdf (accessed 30 September 2014). The revival of Hesse's reputation in the 1960s (and the adoption of the name 'Steppenwolf' by an archetypal rock band) tends to confirm that the more or less elitist, or upper-bourgeois, phenomena under discussion culminated in the (some might say disastrously) democratised version of the same.

[169] Gandhi praised Theosophy as rising above the divisions between Hinduism and Islam, though he was more impressed by Madame Blavatsky than by 'credulous' Annie Besant, and eventually thought Leadbetter a fraud; see Martin Burgess Green, *Gandhi: Voice of a New Age Revolution* (London, 1993), p. 259.

[170] Green, *Mountain of Truth*, p. 112.

[171] Evelyn Dörr, *Rudolf Laban: the Dancer of the Crystal* (Lanham, Maryland, 2007), p. 206. The 10th article of Ida Hoffmann's family statute for the community at Monte Verità proclaims that: 'Since the day of his birth, the child belongs to himself.' www.seriehesse.usi.ch, as above; *cf.* Gerald's similar credo, p. 59.

Fig. 41: *Neopagan Ascona*: (right to left) Rudolf von Laban, Betty Baaron
Samoa, Suzanne Perrottet (Laban's mistress and mother of one of his
children), Katja Wulff, Maja Lederer (Laban's wife and mother of five of his
children) and Totimo, 1914.
(Kunsthaus Zürich, Estate of Suzanne Perrottet)

Dartington.[172]

But for all their interest in mind-body oneness, Gerald and
Kathleen were primarily moving south in order to meet D.H.
Lawrence. On 7 March 1929 Gerald writes to Murry from c/o
Alfredo Weilenmann, Carpanteria, Ascona, reporting that he
has received the letter from Lawrence already quoted:

> I was going to write again as I said I would, then came a
> letter from Lawrence, and now yours with the cheque. You
> really are very good to me. And Lawrence's letter was most

---

[172] Having given Laban an eleven months contract, on 21 June 1936 Goebbels
recorded, somewhat incoherently, in his diary: 'Dance festival rehearsal; taken
from Nietzsche, a bad contrived thing. I object to much of it. It is all so
intellectual'; Dörr, *Laban*, p. 169. Laban remained at Dartington until 1940 when
he was moved on as an enemy alien considered too close to the naval base at
Dartmouth, after which he migrated to Manchester with Ullman and set up a
new dance school there. A former artist, Laban evolved a new method of dance
notation known as Labanotation or Kinetography Laban.

friendly and helpful. He put me on the track of a Rainbow, and invited me to write to him if I want to ask him anything. Unfortunately he has gone to Spain this week, and Spain is out of financial reach. But I have written to him, and if not just yet I hope we'll meet before long.[173]

The move here was made as being on the way to him. Our stay at Erstfeld – except at the end - was a cold and barren trial – everything and everybody frozen hard in and out. This place is unbelievable after it, and I am almost afraid to think how well we are here -- we've fallen into excellent cheap rooms, and found an interpretess who has shown us the back way into cheap Italian shops. At the moment we feel like staying on here indefinitely until Lawrence comes nearer, or it becomes possible for us to go and see him.

In a subsequent letter to Murry from 'Alte Liebe', Ascona, dated merely 'Thursday 11th', but presumably April 1929, Gerald thanks Murry for another cheque and continues in his peculiarly procrastinating way:

These last weeks I have been working on an essay which at the outset I hoped would be of some use to you. It's on Lawrence – not extracts from my book, but something quite new… I think it would be a good thing if you were to curb my free hand a bit by suggesting some definite things you want, or by sending me some books to review.

'I haven't heard from Lawrence again', he continues:

but when I wrote to him I said I'd send him this essay about himself when it was done… He gave me an address of a hotel in France from which letters could be forwarded but that was some time ago, and if you have some more

---

[173] Lawrence did not in fact leave for Spain until the following April, after spending almost a month in Paris, returning to Italy - 'Italy rather bores me after Spain' (though the latter 'was too hot') - in late June; *Letters of D.H. Lawrence*, VII, p. 344. Whilst Gerald was hesitating, the slightly younger, gay Welsh novelist, Rhys Davies, invited himself to visit the Lawrences in Bandol, first in late November 1928 and again in early March 1929 - just when Lawrence was writing to Gerald - whence they travelled up to Paris together; see Davies, *Print of a Hare's Foot* (London, 1969) and Meic Stephens, *Rhys Davies: A Writer's Life* (Swansea, 2010).

permanent address of his it would be useful…

In a 13-page letter dated Wednesday 17 April [1929], Gerald responds loftily to Murry's criticisms of *Margaret*, the unpublished play he had sent him. Most interestingly, he defends this in terms that are close to those he used in defending the typescript of *Ebenezer Le Page* against my more gently posited comments almost half a century later:

> Your criticism of my play delighted me. Of course you are substantially right – though I think you're too good to me on the way it's done: but then I can see its patches, and I know my own tricks and wickedness. But you're quite right about its being sentimental: it is, and Barrie-ish, may be…

Given the similarity between Gerald's defence of his play here and, decades later, of his novel, it is significant that he cites the author who insisted beyond most on fiction as intuitive fantasy, despite or because of life's disappointments. Significantly, if Murry was snooty about J.M. Barrie, Lawrence was not, having recommended *Sentimental Tommy* and its sequel, *Tommy and Grizel*, to Jessie Chambers a week after breaking up with her. He quotes the fantasist (and sexually inadequate?) Tommy: 'I want to love you, you are the only woman I ever wanted to love. But apparently can't.' In 1916 Lawrence recommended Barrie to the Dutch author, Augusta de Wit.[174] Barrie may have been in both Murry's and Gerald's minds partly because it was in this month, April 1929, that he gave the *Peter Pan* copyrights to Great Ormond Street Hospital, where Collis's twin brother, Robert, who had been a witness at Gerald's wedding, worked as a paediatrician.[175]

Continuing with his lofty defence of *Margaret*, Gerald echoes back to Murry phrases the latter had used which he was to re-

[174] See Philip Callow, *Son and Lover. The Young D.H. Lawrence* (London, 1998), p. 150; see Lawrence, *Letters*, VIII, p. 19, where he also praises Thomas Hardy and is correspondingly dismissive of Arnold Bennett. For Barrie's subsequent promotion of Lawrence, see L. Chaney, *Hide and Seek with Angels*, pp. 133, 362.

[175] *Ibid.*, p. 59. Most of the rest of Barrie's estate went to his friend and former secretary, also Lawrence's close friend, Lady Cynthia Asquith. He did, however, leave a substantial legacy to his ex-wife Mary, another friend of Lawrence's despite her having abandoned him for Cannan; for whom see below, p. 162.

echo in his 1974 letter to me defending the roles of Neville Falla and Adèle in *Ebenezer Le Page*. He follows this with a facetious expression of pity for Murry's failure to keep his reason from checking his healthier, more holistic initial response, in a way that reminds one of Iain McGilchrist's recent work on left brain domination and its cultural consequences:[176]

> … you say: 'The troubles of those two are only beginning.' Too true. And you add: 'Your "live-happy-ever-after" ending simply won't wash for me." I'm sorry about that happy-ever-after-ending. And whatever you do I can't bear to think of you turning against yourself because it moved you, and proved on examination not to be worth doing so. After all, it's more to your credit than to Barrie's if you're moved by him; and it's better to weep over him, than to laugh over, say, Anatole France.[177] There's something about that ending which <u>is</u> wrong due to the something wrong all along. But the ever-afterwards part of it is not the point. (And, by the way, I think I do acknowledge that I know they won't live happily ever afterwards. Isn't there a line to the effect 'nor be ashamed to tell whatever joys or <u>pains </u>may come'? They'll 'live happily ever afterwards' in Eternity, as Blake would say, and no where else.

Given Gerald's reference to Blake's 'Eternity,' it is worth quoting as underpinning both Lawrence's and his own life-philosophy:

> He who binds to himself a joy
> Does the winged life destroy;
> But he who kisses the joy as it flies
> Lives in eternity's sun rise.

This and other references call into question whether it was really Murry's assistant and editorial successor, Max Plowman [Fig. 42], who had published his *Introduction to the Study of Blake* in 1927 but who only met Murry two years later, rather than

---

[176] *The Master and his Emissary: The Divided Brain and the Making of the Western World,* 2nd ed. (New Haven and London, 2012). This also reminds one of the fact that the left-brain-dominated Gerald Crich in *Women in Love* was partly inspired by Murry; see above, p. 55.

[177] The Nobel Prize-winning Anatole France was a more fashionable novelist whose reputation had, however, declined since his death in 1924.

Gerald himself, who primarily inspired Murry's subsequent enthusiasm for Blake. Murry's devoted daughter, Katherine, writes that:

> Max Plowman ... failed to influence my father in the matter of his marriage to Betty, but he did succeed in firing him with an enthusiasm for William Blake. That autumn [of 1931] he spent many hours alone in his study, with the photographs of his two dead wives beside his desk, mourning them as he prepared his book on Blake which was to be published in 1933.[178]

Fig. 42: *Max Plowman*
(1883-1941)
(photo: E.C. Large, 1936).

Gerald had already enthused about Blake in his essay on

---

[178] *Beloved Quixote*, p. 67. Murry's *William Blake* argues that he was both a profound Christian and 'a great Communist'; see Gerald Bentley's introduction to *William Blake: The Critical Heritage* (London, 1975), p. 23. Mark (Max) Plowman was a pacifist on the quasi-Blakean principle that 'killing men is always killing God'. He became a friend and colleague of Murry's in 1929 and of Murry's second wife, Violet (see below, pp. 147-49). He has been described as 'one of the great men of the first half of the twentieth century' (Davies, *The Adelphi Players*). He certainly seems to have been a good one and had a deeper insight into human nature than his younger mentor, Murry, with whom he became only temporarily disillusioned during Violet's final illness and Murry's hasty marriage to his housekeeper; *cf.* John Carswell, *Lives and Letters* (London, 1978), pp. 238-39. By this time Plowman was co-editing the *Adelphi* with Richard Rees, who considered him 'one of the gentlest and noblest characters I ever knew' (*A Theory of my Time*, p. 27). Plowman encouraged D.H. Lawrence's former fiancée Jessie Chambers (Miriam in *Sons and Lovers*) to publish her *Personal Record* of the author in 1935 and published Dylan Thomas in the *Adelphi*. From 1937-38 he was Secretary of the Peace Pledge Union. In 1939 he took over the Adelphi Centre commune Murry had founded at The Oaks, Langham, Colchester, and invited the likes of George Orwell, Herbert Read and Vera Brittain to stay and lecture. He died there on 3 June 1941, 'a sick man worn out by the complications and responsibilities of running' it (*ODNB*). Murry and Plowman's widow, Dorothy, brought out a collection of his essays the following year (*The Right to Live*). The

Bernard Shaw in the July 1926 *Adelphi*, his excuse being Shaw's supposedly analogous strength but, he writes:

> Blake conceived a man to be a focus of infinite energy, a vortex of pure force, whose body is that form of himself of which he is aware by means of his five senses, whose past is that form of himself of which he is aware by means of his memory, whose future is that form of himself of which he is aware by means of his imagination...[179]

It was partly due to mutual enthusiasm for Blake, that the 26-year-old Gerald articulated as positively existentialist a philosophy as Lawrence's, though the more recent encourager of both was Nietzsche, whose credo Gerald summarises as: 'every moment's living should be Eternal Life.'[180]

In his April 1929 letter to Murry, Gerald continues to justify his now lost (but perhaps yet to be discovered) play, mentioning one of his characters in the discussion of his own post-Christian version of Blake's 'Eternity', highlighting:

> Karl's line near the end, a line about 'intercourse', which I wrote quite thoughtlessly, and which I still believe expresses something of that which is the ultimate solution of Sex...

There are more hints in the first half of this long letter that Murry had been disappointed with *Margaret*. Gerald writes: 'you say that I am younger than you thought I was,' and responds facetiously, but ultimately downheartedly. Then, having dealt with the first of Murry's two letters he returns to the subject of

---

major source on Plowman is his widow's edition of his letters, published under the title *Bridge into the Future*, ed. D.L.P[lowman]. (London, 1944), which has a reference to Murry being 'seduced into reading Blake' and coming into his 'orbit' on 5 March 1931; *cf.* letter to Murry himself dated 27 February, celebrating the fact that he was 'getting his teeth in Blake' (pp. 368-71). Potter recalls Gerald wondering whether Collis's 'understanding of Blake isn't really in the head' c.1926; see below, p. 171.

[179] 'Shaw', p. 21. It was clearly from Blake's use of the this term that Wyndham Lewis and Ezra Pound derived the term Vorticism, though Blake himself derived it from Plotinus.

[180] 'Shaw', p. 32. In his 1931 review of Ede's *Savage Messiah*, Gerald writes that Gaudier-Brzeska 'was as surely a genius as D.H. Lawrence was, or William Blake'; see below, p. 151.

'that Lawrence essay'[181]:

> It isn't good enough either and must be scrapped.
> Unfortunately some of it is excellent, but it is eked out to an
> interminable length by critical analytic cackle which I can
> spin out by the page quite speciously when I am only
> present 'in absentia'. And that's no use. Lawrence is still
> alive, for one thing, and I believe he is a man in whom we
> may still put great hope. For my book to be worth while, or
> anything I write about him, it must contain somehow my
> love for him, and yet my impact against him. I may say that
> your review of his Poems entirely satisfied this condition…

> But now I have a copy of the last 'Adelphi' and have read
> it through. Your two articles interested me very much, and
> have given rise to many thoughts in me on Marriage and
> Homosexuality, so I have been led to think of an essay on
> the two together … my adventure on the Lawrence essay
> has taught me what I have known all along – that I can only
> write freely in a context of people and a situation, either real
> or imaginary. So the essay I propose to write will be in some
> measure an attack on you, and I think I will quote extracts
> from your articles, if I may. Though, believe me, I have
> some scruples about doing this. I wouldn't mind at all
> attacking you in private, but it's a different matter writing
> a controversial essay in your own paper…

> About reviews, I really don't know. I haven't a copy of
> 'Lady Chatterley's Lover', but I have read it, and have some
> extracts. I may be able to write a review of it.[182] But has
> Proust's 'Sodom and Gomorrah' been reviewed in 'The
> Adelphi' yet? If not I would like to read it… I've read
> several reviews … which, if the book is what I imagine it to

---

[181] 'Not extracts from my book, but something quite new', *i.e.* not the book for
which he had been paid an advance.

[182] Lawrence's last novel was a scarce item. It had been printed privately by
Norman Douglas's friend, Pino Orioli, in Florence, the previous year, the type
set by Italians who were supposed not to recognise the offensive English words
that delayed an unexpurgated reprint until Penguin republished it in 1960
(anticipating Philip Larkin's *Annus Mirabilis* by three years).

be, all seemed to me entirely irrelevant.[183]

Gerald concludes his epic epistle on another uxorious note: 'Kathleen wants me to say that she is so glad to be remembered by you, and she wants to enquire after your wife.' The slightly arch, or self-conscious style he adopted when enquiring as to one's well-being, is still recognisable in his correspondence with me almost half a century later. Here, having asked after Murry's own recent operation, he then, somewhat awkwardly, enquires after the precarious health of Murry's second wife, Violet Le Maistre, who was already suffering from the tuberculosis that killed his first wife and would kill Violet two years later.

On 11 March, meanwhile, Gerald wrote to Collis from Ascona, reporting on his correspondence with both Murry and Lawrence, confirming that he had indeed asked the former for his dedicated copy of *The Rainbow* before trying the latter. He continued with a summary of what seems to have been substantial work in progress:

> I suppose it's bathos to add that I'm well into three of the books, and that especially the Poems are doing well. (At the moment, I can't send you a specimen, as I can't yet decide whether to uproot them out of their context. They are to be all related, almost a 'narrative'…)
>
> As for Ascona, well, I won't say anything about it, for if the Lord were to know how pathetically I love it, he might send me away to teach me sense. If you don't know Geography, I'll tell you that it's in Italian Switzerland, on Lake Maggiore, not far from Locarno.
>
> We've rooms here, by the way, as we might have in Hampstead. Two rooms and use of kitchen – charge, inclusive of everything, with attendance – 5 francs a day.

---

[183] The reference to this title as such, volume 4 of *À la recherche du temps perdu* and the last that Proust saw personally through the press before his death in 1922, is noteworthy as Scott Moncrieff's translation appeared in 1929 under the innocuous title of *Cities of the Plain*. Because of its detailed account of 'inverts' this first English edition appeared only under the New York imprint of Knopf; see Jean Findlay, *Chasing Lost Time: The Life of C.K. Scott Moncrieff – Soldier, Spy and Translator* (London, 2014). The reviews were similarly reticent about the sodomitical themes.

That means we live cheaper than we ever did in England – except when we had rent-free at The Sanctuary.[184] Kathleen collected a pound or two, I earnt a few pounds teaching English in Erstfeld, and then came Murry's ten. That's how we've got here, and are secure here for a month yet.

Gerald then resumes his lofty tone with belated views on a poem Collis had sent him but thanks him for sending a copy of the *Observer*. As if the tone of this letter weren't imperious enough – and having said on the 11th that he was secure for a month - on the 28 March Gerald sent a telegram from Ascona to Collis at 5 Guilford Street consisting of just three words: 'WIRE TWENTY FRANCS'.[185]

# 9: LAWRENTIAN FLÜELEN

Whether or not Gerald received the twenty francs from Collis, by July 1929 he, Kathleen and little Adam were back in Erstfeld, albeit no longer, it seems, chez Pastor Spinner's. In a letter to Murry simply headed 'Erstfeld, Kanton Uri, Switzerland', he writes:

> I'm so glad my essay'll do – oh, it's such a relief. And Kathleen wants to thank you for taking her 'Quaker Meeting'.

Though I cannot find that Murry published Kathleen's short story, the 'essay' to which Gerald refers must be his critical review of West's *Annie Besant*, which he had told Murry he was struggling with as long ago as June 1928 and which would finally appear in the September-November 1929 issue of *The New Adelphi* under the title 'Humanism versus Theosophy.'[186]

---

[184] *I.e.*, at Storrington, just as the Lawrences had stayed rent-free at 'The Colony' not far away at Greatham.

[185] Photocopy of the original, courtesy of Richard Ingrams and Michael Holroyd.

[186] Pp. 36-47. Given West's likely feelings about this relatively recently published review it may have been Gerald, rather than Murry himself, to whom Plowman refers in a reply to Murry dated 26 March 1930: 'Of course we shall be delighted to see Geoffrey West & can keep him talking about a mutual acquaintance if you should be late...' (*Bridge into the Future*, p. 344). It is clear from numerous references in this edition of Plowman's letters that he and West also became

This begins:

> There are two people in this book – Annie Besant and Geoffrey West. And there is quite as much of Geoffrey West as of Annie Besant. That is all right. But then Geoffrey West is an exasperating man…

It is yet another mark of Murry's belief in Gerald at his time that he published such a review given that West seems to have been a friend, though judging by West's *bien pensant* review of three new books on Soviet Russia published in the July 1933 edition of the *Adelphi*, Gerald may have been justified in finding him exasperating.[187]

 Gerald continues his letter to Murry in grateful, personable mode, at least in the short term:

> And thank you for telling me of your troubles. I myself find it the hardest thing in the world to 'fess up to my own woes. Yours though leave me stunned. What can I <u>say</u>? My bull-in-china-shop tactics wilt before them. It's what made even the Review I sent you the hell of a job to write. And it's what makes me hang fire even now in the midst of my attack on your Sex articles. I always feel there is a better way. In this mood I turn to my stories and plays – I feel nearer it there.
>
> You don't want another essay till November. You shouldn't have told me that – it seems such a long way off. But you must send me the Keyserlings as soon as you can. I'll read them, anyhow.

'The Keyserlings' presumably refers to the two new books published by the prolific, philosophical traveller, Count Hermann Keyserling: *Creative Understanding* and *America Set Free*, but it seems Gerald wrote on neither in the end, the latter being reviewed by Richard Rees in a subsequent edition of the

---

friends, united not least in their admiration of Murry, who according to a letter from Plowman to West in February 1938 was: 'the most valuable man alive … the poet of all our lives since 1920. His drunken excess shows us our course … never fail to regard him as the *most significant* man alive' *(ibid.,* p. 618).

[187] *Loc. cit.,* pp. 303-05.

*Adelphi.*[188]

Instead he tackled a subject more closely continuous with his study of the Theosophical Annie Besant, concluding his July letter to Murry with the note:

> You say: 'I send a little book of Krishnamurti's addresses.' I am wondering whether you put it in with Kathleen's MSS. The envelope got torn in the post and a little book could easily have dropped out. If you still have it I'd like you to send it with the others.

That's all, I think.

Yours very sincerely

G.B. Edwards

Gerald's surviving correspondence with Murry during the late

---

[188] Sir Richard Rees (see also above, p. 67-68.) took over the editorship of (and financed) the *Adelphi* (assisted by his friend Max Plowman) from October 1930-September 1938 (though in *A Theory of my Time*, p. 62, he says 'I severed my connection with *The Adelphi* in 1936 and saw little of Murry after that until the late 1940s' (after Plowman's death). For the first part of this period he rented a cottage in Yateley near Murry's Hampshire bungalow (he may have been there when Gerald visited). Plowman and his wife had meanwhile stayed in a converted-pub-guest-house in nearby Eversley 'to be near the Murrys' (see *Bridge into the Future*, p. 361). Latterly the *Adelphi* 'was edited from Rees's flat, over a newsagent's shop in Cheyne Walk, overlooking Albert Bridge' (Rayner Heppenstall, *Four Absentees* [London, 1960], p. 36). Rees and Plowman befriended and published George Orwell, whose literary executor Rees eventually became (inheriting his library), and translated editions of the writings of Simone Weil (he was also R.H. Tawney's literary executor). In 1958 he published *Brave Men: A study of D H Lawrence and Simone Weil* with Victor Gollancz, and three years later *George Orwell: Fugitive from the Camp of Victory* with Secker and Warburg, who had published *Animal Farm* after Faber and Gollancz had both rejected it; see Bernard Crick, *George Orwell: A Life* (London, 1980), *passim*. Rees's *A Theory of my Own Time* concludes with high praise of Weil and Murry jointly. The loyalty Murry inspired in men of Rees and Plowman's quality prompted one to pause before condemning him for his all to obvious failings (*cf.* above p. 99). Looking back, Rees wrote that Murry was 'probably the ablest man I have ever personally known and certainly the most disinterested.' (*Ibid.*, p. 79). Aside from Gerald and Plowman, Rees's principal rival for having 'understood [Murry] perhaps better than anyone' (C.M. Murry, *Shadows*, p. 184), was his secretary and biographer, Frank Lea, whose loyalty is confirmed if not comprehended by Jeffrey Meyers in his introduction to the 2002 edition of his *Katherine Mansfield: A Darker View*, p. xix.

summer and autumn of 1929 is sparse but he must have received and reviewed Jiddu Krishnamurti's *Life in Freedom* with relative efficiency for his fine essay on the subject appeared in the December issue of the *New Adelphi*.[189] If his review of *The Life of Annie Besant* might be regarded as continuous with his critique of the reputation of Bernard Shaw, so his essay on Krishnamurti could be construed as continuous with that on Besant who in

Fig. 43: *Jiddu Krishnamurti* (1895-1986), (photo: c.1920).

1909 'discovered' the 14-year-old South-Indian boy in Adyar and thenceforth promoted him as the wished-for 'World Teacher' [Fig. 43].

In late September, Gerald was still in Erstfeld but expecting to move on soon. On the 24th he wrote to Murry thanking him for 'that letter' and a note: 'I'm glad my debt has been diminished by so much.' Reverting to his somewhat imperious tone, he writes:

> I've been expecting those Keyserlings to come along, and you can still send them if you like. But I doubt now whether I'll need them. I have in mind – and have, in fact, actually begun – an essay on Whitman, the excuse for it being a new cheap edition of 'Leaves of Grass' recently issued by Macmillan. Unfortunately, I haven't the edition in question (a mere detail, though); but still, if they have sent you a copy, perhaps it would be as well for me to have seen it.[190]

---

[189] 'Krishnamurti', *The New Adelphi magazine*, III, 2 (December 1929), pp. 146-70.

[190] Unfortunately this letter, from the collection I acquired at Robin Waterfield's bookshop, lacks any subsequent pages. Collis refers to Keyserling as a 'modern philosopher' in the unpublished novel that prominently featured Gerald (p. 141)

By early November the young family had migrated north to the head of Lake Lucerne, in the centre of that part of Switzerland particularly associated with the history of freedom. The address on the first of the next batch of Gerald's letters to Murry I have, dated 9 November 1929, is: 'bei Frau Rämi, 'Konsum', Flüelen, Kanton Uri, Switzerland' and his next seven letters are all from the same ancient town, most specifying the same address.

Since the early thirteenth century, when the St Gothard Pass became one of the most popular routes in and out of Northern Italy, Flüelen had been an important lakeside port.[191] Since the eighteenth century it had prospered as a result of the development of Alpine tourism, not least the 'discovery' of Mount Rigi which looms above Lake Lucerne; it was praised by Goethe and painted by Cozens and Turner [Fig. 44].[192]

Fig. 44: J.M.W. Turner, *Flüelen from Lake Lucerne* (oil on canvas: 1845).
(Tate Britain)

To get to Flüelen, at the far end of the lake, the Edwards family would have sailed out of Lucerne past Tribschen, where

---

and provides a detailed (and admiring) account of meeting him in *Bound upon a Course*, pp. 139-47.

[191] Lawrence 'took an express steamer 22 miles to Flüelen' and stayed in an inn there, before walking, via Erstfeld, towards Italy; see Mark Kinkead-Weekes, *D.H. Lawrence: Triumph into Exile 1912-1922* (Cambridge, 1996), p. 95

[192] Turner painted The Rigi more than 30 times between 1802-45.

Nietzsche had visited Wagner at his lake-side villa in 1869 before revisiting this father-figure and fellow Schopenhauerian some twenty-five times more over the next three years.[193] In 1882, revisiting the centre of Lucerne, at Paul Bonnet's studio, Nietzsche posed for what became a famous photograph, featuring himself and Paul Rée being whipped by their beloved Lou Salomé as they pull her in a cart [Fig. 45].[194]

Fig. 45: *Lou Andreas-Salomé, Paul Rée and Friederich Nietzsche* (photo: Paul Bonnet, 1882).

Gerald might have known Flüelen as somewhere similarly visited by Nietzsche during his trips from Basel to Tribschen. But as the friend and protégé of Murry who corresponded with Lawrence throughout his early travels and as a major authority on the complete range of his writings, Gerald was most likely to have known Flüelen as the setting for one of Lawrence's most memorable encounters, *Ebenezer*-like in that the sheer intensity of expression triumphs over the ostensibly mundane narrative content. Lawrence's principal protagonist was a 'perishingly victorious' Streatham clerk whom he describes in terms of

[193] Carl Pletsch, *Young Nietzsche: Becoming a Genius* (New York, 1991), p. 116. Only after Wagner's return, in more ways than one, to Imperial Germany did the relationship deteriorate, not least due to Nietzsche's disapproval of the latter's anti-semitic nationalism.

[194] It has been convincingly suggested (following a hint by Cornelius Verhoen) that Nietzsche posed this photograph in emulation of a relief on a Roman altar depicting Kleobis and Biton pulling Hera to her temple, see Babette Babich, 'Reading Lou von Salomé's Triangles,' *New Nietzsche Studies*, VIII, Nos. 3 and 4 (Winter 2011/Spring 2012), pp. 95–132. In *Thus spake Zarasthustra* (XVIII), it is into the mouth of an old woman that Nietzsche puts the words: 'You are going to a woman? Forget not thy whip.' Salomé was subsequently the friend of Freud and the lover of Rilke (1875-1926), who was fifteen years her junior.

Nietzsche's 'small man.'

On 22 September 1913 Lawrence reported to a friend that, having left Frieda with her sister at Wolfratshausen, in Bavaria, he was:

> going across Switzerland on foot. Came over the Rigi today to Lucerne, and now am going down the lake to Flüelen. When I get an address in Italy, I will send it you.[195]

Planning to meet up with Frieda again in Milan, Lawrence indeed 'climbed over the back of the detestable Rigi, with its vile hotel, to come to Lucerne.'[196]

Having met a lost young Frenchman who could speak no German, they 'sat on a stone and became close friends', Lawrence promising to meet him again in Algiers though knowing, even as he agreed to do so that this was unlikely. But, he writes:

> … my friend is my friend for ever, though I have lost his card and forgotten his name. He was a Government clerk from Lyons, making this his first foreign tour before he began his military service. He showed me his 'circular excursion ticket'. Then at last we parted, for he must get to the top of the Rigi, and I must get to the bottom.[197]

Gerald would relate to people he chanced upon in just this way. So too does Ebenezer, who is likewise never not an intrinsic part in what he is describing. The following more or less self-contained set-piece from *Twilight in Italy* has the added interest that it may have inspired Gerald's residence in Flüelen, *en route* as he thought he was, to meeting Lawrence himself. Having descended the mountain to Lucerne, Lawrence writes:

> Lucerne and its lake were as irritating as ever — like the

---

[195] Letter to May Holbrook, the sister of Jessie Chambers; *Letters of D.H. Lawrence*, II, p. 77.

[196] Lawrence's negative remarks on Rigi, known by this time as 'Queen of the Mountains' reflects its status as a damaged tourist site. Queen Victoria was carried up it in 1868, two mountain railways were constructed in the 1870s and Mark Twain wrote about his 1879 visit soon after King Ludwig II of Bavaria had visited the indeed rather 'vile' hotel that was built upon its peak.

[197] *Twilight in Italy*, see Eggert ed., p. 209.

wrapper round milk chocolate. I could not sleep even one night there: I took the steamer down the lake, to the very last station [Flüelen]. There I found a good German inn, and was happy.

There was a tall thin young man, whose face was red and inflamed from the sun. I thought he was a German tourist. He had just come in; and he was eating bread and milk. He and I were alone in the eating-room. He was looking at an illustrated paper.

'Does the steamer stop here all night?' I asked him in German, hearing the boat bustling and blowing her steam on the water outside…

… I started almost out of my skin at the unexpected London accent. It was as if one suddenly found oneself in the Tube.

'So am I,' I said. 'Where have you come from?'

Then he began, like a general explaining his plans, to tell me. He had walked round over the Furka Pass, had been on foot four or five days. He had walked tremendously. Knowing no German, and nothing of the mountains, he had set off alone on this tour: he had a fortnight's holiday. So he had come over the Rhône Glacier across the Furka and down from Andermatt to the Lake. On this last day he had walked about thirty mountain miles.

'But weren't you tired?' I said, aghast…

I was sorry for him in my soul, he was so cruelly tired, so perishingly victorious…

'What time will you be going on?' I asked.

'When is the first steamer?' he said, and he turned out a guide-book with a time-table. He would leave at about seven.

'But why so early?' I said to him.

He must be in Lucerne at a certain hour, and at Interlaken in the evening.

'I suppose you will rest when you get to London?' I said.

He looked at me quickly, reservedly.

I was drinking beer: I asked him wouldn't he have something. He thought a moment, then said he would have another glass of hot milk. The landlord came —'And bread?' he asked.

The Englishman refused. He could not eat, really. Also he was poor; he had to husband his money. The landlord brought the milk and asked me, when would the gentleman want to go away. So I made arrangements between the landlord and the stranger. But the Englishman was slightly uncomfortable at my intervention. He did not like me to know what he would have for breakfast.

I could feel so well the machine that had him in its grip.[198] He slaved for a year, mechanically, in London, riding in the Tube, working in the office. Then for a fortnight he was let free. So he rushed to Switzerland, with a tour planned out, and with just enough money to see him through, and to buy presents at Interlaken: bits of the edelweiss pottery: I could see him going home with them.

So he arrived, and with amazing, pathetic courage set forth on foot in a strange land, to face strange landlords, with no language but English at his command, and his purse definitely limited. Yet he wanted to go among the mountains, to cross a glacier. So he had walked on and on, like one possessed, ever forward.[199] His name might have been Excelsior, indeed.[200]

But then, when he reached his Furka, only to walk along the ridge and to descend on the same side! My God, it was killing to the soul. And here he was, down again from the mountains, beginning his journey home again: steamer and

---

[198] Albeit relatively commonplace, *cf.* Gerald's use of the metaphor of the machine, in particular for the dehumanizing city, but in mitigation of his tendency to misogyny characterised as a specifically male phenomenon (see below, p. 299, in relation to 'the New Jerusalem').

[199] Perhaps an inspiration for the fate Lawrence had in store for the similarly driven (and machine-like), Gerald Crich, in *Women in Love*; see above, p. 55.

[200] 'Excelsior' is the name of Longfellow's 1841 poem in which a young man with a banner emblazoned with this 'strange device' marches 'mid snow and ice' to his death.

train and steamer and train and Tube, till he was back in the machine...

I could not bear to understand my countryman, a man who worked for his living, as I had worked, as nearly all my countrymen work. He would not give in. On his holiday he would walk, to fulfil his purpose, walk on; no matter how cruel the effort were, he would not rest, he would not relinquish his purpose nor abate his will, not by one jot or tittle. His body must pay whatever his will demanded, though it were torture.

It all seemed to me so foolish. I was almost in tears. He went to bed. I walked by the dark lake, and talked to the girl in the inn. She was a pleasant girl: it was a pleasant inn, a homely place. One could be happy there.

In the morning it was sunny, the lake was blue. By night I should be nearly at the crest of my journey. I was glad.

The Englishman had gone. I looked for his name in the book. It was written in a fair, clerkly hand. He lived at Streatham. Suddenly I hated him.[201] The dogged fool, to keep his nose on the grindstone like that. What was all his courage but the very tip-top of cowardice? What a vile nature — almost Sadish, proud, like the infamous Red Indians, of being able to stand torture.

The landlord came to talk to me. He was fat and comfortable and too respectful. But I had to tell him all the Englishman had done, in the way of a holiday, just to shame his own fat, ponderous, inn-keeper's luxuriousness that was too gross. Then all I got out of his enormous comfortableness was:

'Yes, that's a *very* long step to take.'

So I set off myself, up the valley between the close, snow-topped mountains, whose white gleamed above me as I crawled, small as an insect, along the dark, cold valley

---

[201] Given that Gerald would live a mile west of Streatham for perhaps as long as fifteen years after the war whilst working as a minor civil servant one hopes that these are non-sequiturs.

below.[202]

Gerald's letter of 9 November 1929 from Flüelen acknowledges the rejection of an article and the receipt of Murry's latest book:

> I haven't read much of it yet, but enough to know that it is beyond any bombastic criticism of mine. And yet in the end I think I will differ from you as much as before. But I don't think I'll want to review it for the Adelphi… I only wish we could have some long talks together.

Three days later Gerald writes to confirm that he will not be reviewing the book, perhaps partly in response for Murry's rejection of his piece. The latter was probably the essay Gerald said he was writing on his beloved Whitman the previous September but the book Murry wanted Gerald to review must have been: *God, being an Introduction to the Science of Metabiology*, which Cape had just published.[203] This was a quintessentially Murryan production, which sought to define religion in quasi-Jungian, harmonious universalism, according to which 'the very essential element in the whole of Catholic Christianity has its equivalent somewhere in the system outlined here', a system which was one where 'conscious Science and conscious Religion become absolutely identical.' Given his adoption of Shaw's neologism 'metabiology' Murry thought to send the great man a copy. Shaw scribbled at the bottom of Murry's letter, which he then returned:

> The subject is hackneyed: but if the book is readable I'll read it. But I warn you that if you show the faintest symptom of sentimentality, the book will knock the bottom out of the waste paper basket.[204]

Gerald wrote that he would be sending the book back in a day or two, adding, somewhat facetiously: 'I don't want you to be

---

[202] *Twilight in Italy*, Eggert ed., pp. 209-12.

[203] One of Murry's most chaotically autobiographical books, the manuscript was acquired in 1989 for £1,250 by Edinburgh University Library. Though sometimes thought to be a neologism coined by Joseph Salk, the discoverer of the Polio vaccine, the term meta-biology had been used in 1921 by Shaw as the subtitle of his *Back to Methuselah: a meta-biological Pentateuch*.

[204] Lea, *Murry*, p. 158. It seems that Shaw's subsequent deposition had the effect of ending their friendship.

out of pocket.' Murry seems to have responded immediately still seeking to persuade Gerald to review his book for on 14 November Gerald wrote to him again:

> There is one region of yourself from which you are always so good to me that you put me to shame. But, though I've been tempted, I still hold by my decision to do nothing more about your book...

In a P.S. Gerald adds, quasi-apologetically:

> I must say, though, that I don't like again deranging your plans for the Adelphi. But from any practical point of view perhaps a later review by somebody else will be just as useful... For the February number I think I will be able to let you have something on Jesus. It'll be quite impersonal.

On 2 December, still from Flüelen, he responds at length to an 'abrupt postcard' from a presumably disappointed Murry which had apparently queried Gerald's account of him as 'only a theologian' in both a recent article and (still) in *God*. Gerald is at pains to point out that he hadn't written (or at least meant) this because he believed a theologian to be only 'a part-man ... and by the nature of things it can't be anybody's business to be that ... you're quite right ... when you say that I think theology neither necessary nor good. Yet you must add something else.'

A month later, on 1 January 1930, Gerald reports that he had 'written to Lady Lutyens and asked her to acknowledge the "New Adelphi".' This was presumably the December 1929 issue featuring his latest publication, the review of Krishnamurti's essays, which he must have asked Murry to send to that enthusiastic promoter of both Besant and Krishnamurti, Emily Lutyens, the theosophical wife of the long-suffering Sir Edwin and mother of the 22-year-old Mary, whose autobiographical *To be Young*, describes the relevant context so poignantly.[205] Gerald's article was taken seriously enough to be republished by the Theosophical Society in Australia in their *International Star Bulletin* a few months later, after Krishnamurti had caused

---

[205] As a young girl, Mary Lutyens fell in love with Krishnamurti's brother, Nitja, about whom she wrote - long after he died - in *To be Young* in 1959. She eventually edited Krishnamurti's writings in 3 volumes (1975-88). Her sister, Barbara, married Idina Sackville's first husband Euan Wallace; *cf.* below, p. 141.

Fig. 46: *Flüelen with Bristenstock* (postcard, c. 1930).

consternation by leaving the Society, to be followed by Lady Lutyens and her daughters.[206]

He meanwhile announces he has returned to writing his no doubt 'all too human' interpretation of *Jesus*, the first chapter of which he would send Murry, assuring him it was 'quite self-contained'. On 7 January, he changes his mind about refusing a £10 cheque until Murry 'has something in hand', asking instead for it to be sent 'to me as soon as you like':

> We're in a situation which I'm afraid occurs to us only too often for our sins (next week sans food, this week sans rent), and this time your cheque is the only way out I can see… And I don't really feel so very bad about it. My chapter is not actually finished, but is half done and still going quite well – and is only a few pages off its end. Besides, I think it'll have to go into two parts for the *Adelphi*; and that means that one part (about the length of my thing on Annie Besant) is already done… Though these last days I've been thinking that if you like it at all I could let you have for a subsequent

---

[206] The issue of 15 May 1930, pp. 25-29. Given that Gerald had sent her the relevant issue of the *New Adelphi*, as a regular contributor to the *International Star Bulletin*, Lady Lutyens may have entrepreneured this reprint.

number the next chapter on the temptation – his [Jesus's] first dose of 'de-toxification', so to speak.[207]

Gerald wrote to Murry from Flüelen again on 13 January thanking him for the cheque but having still not finished the first chapter/article on Jesus: 'another paragraph or two – that's all. But it *is* long.' That he finally submitted the chapter and received a positive response is clear from his letter of 27 January. But, as he had anticipated, Murry thought it too long to publish and it was in any case, too late for the February issue. Gerald then informs Murry he is going to send him a play he had written before *Margaret*, asking him to read it through for potential recommendation. He also asks for the return of the manuscript of *Margaret* for revision.

## 10: THE MAN WHO DIED

Having discharged himself from a sanatorium, D.H. Lawrence died of the effects of tuberculosis at the Villa Robermond in Vence on 2 March 1930, a year and a day after writing to Gerald. He had survived so many health crises since his near-fatal bout of pneumonia whilst teaching in Croydon in 1911 that only those immediately surrounding him knew how imminent his death was.[208] It seems that a by now heavily pregnant Kathleen had returned to Britain with Adam shortly before the beginning of March when Gerald received this terrible news. Seven weeks of 'enforced separation on top of everything else' in the lake-side town in which Lawrence encountered his poor, isolated Englishman had already:

> made this time for all its compensations the most terrible I've known. Then when the news of Lawrence came I

---

[207] This is an interesting reference given Gerald's later enthusiasm for Kazantzakis's *Last Temptation of Christ* (1953), in which the ultimate temptation was to avoid the crucifixion. See also the poem 'The Temptation' in Appendix 3. One of Gerald's few unpublished poems not included here, is entitled 'The Genealogy of Jesus' and concludes by emphasizing that he was the son of 'MAN'.

[208] Though see below, p. 121, for Arnold Bennett warning Stephen Potter of the imminence of Lawrence's death.

walked about wildly for two days. It was among mountains and all that sounds very romantic. But I assure you it wasn't – it was only my prosiest way of trying to keep sane. Yet he was nothing to me and his going left the place desolate. But to you he was the best of all friends. You will understand that I couldn't write to you.[209]

Knowing he would now never meet his hero and, it seems, having already abandoned his book on him, Gerald returned to London the following week and on 16 April 1930 his second child, Dorcas, was born at 59 Victoria Road, Stroud Green, Finsbury Park.[210] There are three letters to Murry from this address in April and early May, all dealing principally with works in progress and showing an increasing interest in promoting both these and previous typescripts. In that dated 17 April, the day after his daughter's birth, Gerald writes first about his now almost complete book on Jesus:

I've heard from Cape and there's nothing doing...[211] He

---

[209] Gerald writes that he had received an anonymous cutting, which he assumes is from *The Times*: 'a short article on Lawrence by "A Correspondent", and I think you did it.' This presumably refers to Murry's piece on Lawrence which appeared in the *Times Literary Supplement* of 13 March 1930 (reprinted in *Reminiscences*, pp. 277-81). The letter is from Flüelen but merely dated 'Thursday' (presumably in early April). He says he hoped Murry wrote this appreciation 'for it made me weep for him, and for you.' Murry had written that 'Lawrence was the most remarkable and most lovable man I have ever known'. Gerald concludes by saying he has 'been thinking a lot about your book on "God" and about the passing of The Adelphi' as if it were to be terminated as a result of Lawrence's death. His intended address in London was given as c/o Nathan Paskin, 237, Green Lanes, Clissold Park, N.' to the east of Finsbury Park, near Manor House, but in the end he seems not to have moved there.

[210] Birth certificate, General Register Office, England and Wales births 1837-2006, Edmonton, Middlesex, vol. 3a, p. 873.

[211] Presumably Jonathan Cape was now dealing with Gerald personally, Garnett having given up on him (indeed, as above, p. 87, fallen out with him) due to his failure to deliver the part-pre-paid book on Lawrence. Gerald's no doubt Nietzschean *Jesus* would probably have referenced Lawrence, who referenced himself as Jesus in one of his last publications, *The Escaped Cock,* completed near Gstaad in 1928 and published the following year in Paris by Harry Crosby (who committed suicide soon after). It was subsequently (1931) and since published as *The Man Who Died*. In his *Son of Woman* (1931), pp. 371-82, Murry wrote enthusiastically of this 'masterpiece of a great and dying genius' and of Lawrence's identification with the risen Christ who enjoys being truly human at last.

suggested that Faber and Faber might be willing to do something about it. I thought it over and wrote back to him suggesting that I kept the Jesus by me for the time being and (if he should want it) set to work at once on a book on Lawrence – a new and shorter one... I went on Monday. He was quite friendly but not very keen on another Lawrence book, expecting crops of them just now ... he is willing to let the old advance stand by for the time being and recognises that it's necessary for me to try elsewhere. I'm extremely glad that the whole thing has come out in the open, for it has long been a secret jar in my machinery...

After more stream-of-consciousness on the subject of what to do about getting things into print, he concludes:

The new infant has arrived, by the way. It came yesterday morning – a girl. Kathleen is very well indeed and (as such things go) didn't have a bad time – 2½ hours only. The infant itself is nondescript, and to my mind not up to the first one; but they say it's all right.

That's all. I think.

Yours very sincerely,

G.B. Edwards

 As a postscript to this somewhat posturing piece of tough-mindedness, he reverts briefly to his career, not least in order to be able to support said infant:

Oh, one thing more. Can you send me back 'Waysmeet'. Whyte said something about some theatre people who might be interested in it, and I'll ask him to put me on to them.

The 'Whyte' to whom Gerald refers here and who indeed tried to help must be Lancelot Law Whyte (1896-1972), the now unjustly forgotten, Scots-born, Cambridge-educated polymath [Fig. 47].[212]

---

[212] Like the three Collis brothers, Sir Richard Rees and Gerald himself, at least as extraordinary is the fact that Whyte has no *ODNB* entry. At the time of writing, James Pepper Rare Books of Santa Barbara, California, has a copy of Murry's *Son of Woman* signed (a few days after his marriage): 'For Lotte & Lance Whyte, Affectionately, John Middleton Murry. May 26, 1931.' For biographical

The son of a Presbyterian minister, Whyte was educated at Bedales and after combat in the Great War went to Trinity College, Cambridge, where he studied physics under Ernest Rutherford. In 1929 he won a Rockefeller scholarship to work in Berlin where he met Einstein and published two articles in the *Zeitschrift für Physik*. From 1937 to 1943, having been an early admirer of Frank Whittle's jet engine, he became chairman and

Fig. 47: *Lancelot Law Whyte* (1896-1972). (photo: Boston University)

managing director of Power Jets Ltd and played a key role in persuading the government to back it. His second wife was the cultured German, Lotte Heller, whom he married on Christmas Day 1926, and who died in 1941. In his autobiographical *Focus and Diversions*, he talks of meeting both her and Murry in 1925 and of his enthusiasm for the *Adelphi*, to which he occasionally contributed (e.g. on psychology in March 1928 and on Einstein in February 1931).[213] In the early 1950s, Whyte was invited to speak and stay at Olga Fröbe-Kapteyn's *Eranos* summer school at Ascona where he met Jung.[214] His later publications included

---

information not available elsewhere, as well as interesting excerpts from Whyte's diaries, now in the archives at Boston University, see: www.inquisition21.com/index.php?module=pagemaster&PAGE_user_op=view_page&PAGE_id=92. It may have been Lotte who provided Gerald with some of his German connections. His third wife, Eva, wrote the useful 'Biographical Note on L. L. Whyte', in *Contemporary Psychoanalysis* (1974), X, pp. 386-388. Testimony of his ongoing devotion to Goethe survives in the form of a Christmas card featuring the reproduction of his portrait, quotation and Whyte's commentary signed by him and Eva in December 1948; currently for sale from Dr Richard White; www.richardfordmanuscripts.co.uk/catalogue/2578.

[213] Whyte, *Focus and Diversions* (London, 1963), pp. 63-67.

[214] Whyte, *Focus and Diversions*, pp. 184-86. Olga first visited Monte Verità above Ascona in 1920 with her Dutch father who, a few years later, bought the Casa Gabriella, where she spent the rest of her life, dying in her house in 1962. She was connected with the School of Wisdom run by Count Hermann Keyserling,

*The Unconscious before Freud* (London, 1960), and the following year, a pioneering volume on the similarly under-rated 18th-century Jesuit polymath who was an important early influence on Nietzsche, Roger Joseph Boscovich FRS.[215]

Gerald's next, long letter to Murry is dated 23 April 1930 and begins by discussing the pros and cons of completing his book on Jesus, as distinct from his 'several other things nearing completion':

> I have a curious confidence (new with me) that I'd be able to discharge for certain what I undertook…
>
> Applying this to my 'Jesus' I can only say that I'll go on with it for as long as I possibly can, but that when there's more of it I may (if I still feel easy about it) have a shot at getting some money on it. One thing I still feel strongly with you is that there should be in any case more than one chapter – especially since to my mind Jesus after the temptation is very different from Jesus after his conversion. I was even uneasy about sending you this one half-view only – except that I thought (as I suggested at the time) that if it went in the Adelphi it might be followed by the antithetical chapter.[216]
>
> Apart from this I have a thing about school life (the one thing Edward Garnett liked me for) which I'll send to Faber and Faber off my own bat – there's always a chance it may

---

whom Gerald references in his correspondence and his review of Potter's *Lawrence* (see p. 118). In 1928, at the suggestion of Jung, she built a conference room near her home (construction must have been in progress when Gerald was in Ascona). This led to an annual meeting under the name of *Eranos*, first suggested by the religious historian Rudolf Otto; see Hans Thomas Hakl, translated by Christopher McIntosh, *Eranos: An Alternative Intellectual History of the Twentieth Century* (London, 2014). Her more international legacy is the Archive for Research in Archetypal Symbolism, or ARAS, part of which was deposited at the Warburg Institute in 1946, and was a major source for Erich Neumann's *The Great Mother: An Analysis of the Archetype* (London, 1955).

[215] Lancelot Law Whyte ed., *Roger Joseph Boscovich: Studies of his Life and Work on the 250th Anniversary of his Birth* (London, 1961), p. 118 and Greg Whitlock,'Roger Boscovich, Benedict de Spinoza and Friedrich Nietzsche: The Untold Story', *Nietzsche Studien* 25, 1 (1996), pp. 200–220.

[216] One would hardly guess from this that Murry had himself published *The Life of Jesus* in 1926.

hit a sympathetic reader.[217] And then Whyte has put me into touch with some people who just may be interested in Waysmeet. And Margaret I'm sending to Geoffrey Whitworth who read Waysmeet just before I went to Switzerland and was very keen about it. I lost my chance then because my play (and my person too, I believe) annoyed his wife. But this time I'll send my MSS. to his business address.

Fig. 48: *Geoffrey Whitworth* (1883-1951)
(oil on canvas: Roger Fry, 1934)
(Victoria & Albert Museum).

Geoffrey Whitworth (1883-1951) [Fig. 48] was the first director of the British Drama League, which was launched at the Theatre Royal Haymarket in June 1919 and, via the creation of amateur 'Little Theatres', culminated in the foundation of the National Theatre in 1963.[218] He had previously published an illustrated book on *Nijinsky* (1913) and lectured for the WEA to the Vickers munitions workers in Crayford, Kent, where there is now a theatre named in his honour. By 1923 there were 360 affiliated drama societies. By 1927 the League's monthly journal, *Drama*, was distributing 3,000 copies and the one-act play, a medium in which Gerald was manifestly interested, flourished as never before.[219]

---

[217] One assumes it failed to do so. Gerald used a similar phraseology when we were negotiating with publishers almost half a century later; see below, pp. 271 and 283.

[218] Similarly successful at the more local level was the establishment of the All-England Theatre Festival.

[219] William Kozlenko ed., *The One-Act Play Today: A Discussion of the Technique, Scope and History of the Contemporary Short Drama* (London, 1939). In 1934, Bernard Shaw described Whitworth as 'one of the most important people in the

Whitworth's wife, Phyllis Bell, with whom Gerald had evidently not hit it off, also directed and managed plays (including D.H. Lawrence's biblical failure, *David*), and between 1924 and 1931, ran the 'Three Hundred Club' for staging plays with a limited public.[220]

Returning to the contents of Murry's letter, Gerald now responds to his reassurances regarding his successor as editor of the *Adelphi*:

> I'm glad you think Max Plowman will take my stuff. I have liked him the twice I've met him and will be only too pleased to do the best I can for him – and even try to keep strictly within bounds of time and space. And I'm extremely glad that you're giving me one of those lectures. That's really an opportunity I'm grateful for. Thanks very much.[221]

He then segues into his more familiar style:

> And now about your little lecture at the end. Well, I can't say much – except that you're free and welcome to lecture me as much as you like. After all, I am ten years your junior and have no scruple about lecturing you when I feel like it… Certainly I want you to know that there is very much indeed about my 'way of life' for which I myself haven't the least admiration. But I wonder if it's the same as that which makes you uneasy… And if you knew all the facts I think you'd be forced to admit that in an ultimate analysis my

---

theatre today' (*ODNB*); *cf.* G. Whitworth, *The Theatre of my Heart*, rev. edn (London, 1938).

[220] Maddox, *Lawrence*, pp. 415-16. Given Gerald's combination of interests and connections, not least with co-founder Max Plowman, he is likely to have been involved in the formation of the Adelphi Players, associated with Murry's 'Community,' The Oaks, Langham, near Colchester; for which see Cecil Davies (ed. Peter Billingham), *The Adelphi Players: The Theatre of Persons* (London, 2002). See below, pp. 183-97, for Gerald producing plays in 1938-39 at the Bolton Little Theatre, where he also acted in one by Sydney Box, *alias* Cedric Mount, who in the same year contributed an article to Kozlenko's collection, *cit.* above.

[221] Murry lectured widely, including at the Mary Ward Centre in Bloomsbury. Given that Christine may have fallen in love with Raymond when he preached at the Birdo Mission (*Ebenezer Le Page*, p. 235), perhaps Kathleen fell for Gerald when she saw him lecturing here or elsewhere in London.

way (the one I'm on *most* of my time) isn't very much different from the one you're on most of yours. I know yours looks steadier – but that's only incidental, surely, and isn't it a little deceptive?... But there is (in the midst of my apparent muddle) a 'way' which I feel is essentially *my* way (and which I firmly believe is yours also). And I believe that if and when I can get down to that and keep there my surface complications (yes, £.s.d. included) will gradually disappear...

On the 12 May 1930, writing his last extant letter from 59 Victoria Road, Gerald tells Murry:

I got your card this morning. Thanks very much. I now want to cancel a note I sent you a few days ago asking you to pay me for my article. I took the proofs of it to the office today and was paid for it.

I've heard from Faber and Faber. But nothing definite though it leaves an opening. But I had already dropped the pamphlet to return to my plays.[222] And there I am now, and I verily believe that there I will stay.

My address from the end of this week onwards will be:

Moor House,
Westerham,
Kent

<u>G.B.E.</u>

Gerald's notification of this change of address signalled a move that lasted for at least the rest of the summer and from which he continued to send in articles and reviews for the *Adelphi*. Perhaps his most significant, as well as over-the-top contribution was entitled: 'Lawrence and the Young Man'.[223] *The Young Man* had been the title of Stephen Potter's well-received autobiographical novel, published by Cape the previous year and featuring friends including Gerald himself as the 'genius'

---

[222] This pamphlet may have been 'the thing about education' he was thinking of sending to Fabers above, perhaps relating to 'The Education of John Jones' he would lecture on at Dartington in February 1931.

[223] G.B. Edwards, 'Lawrence and the Young Man', *The Adelphi*, new series, III, 4 (June-August 1930), pp. 310-16.

Gessler.[224] This, however, was a review of Potter's *D.H. Lawrence: A First Study* [Fig. 49], so that Gerald's reference to the earlier title was no doubt intended facetiously, as well perhaps as echoing (semi-consciously avenging?) Murry's recent remark that Gerald was younger than he had thought.[225]

D·H·LAWRENCE
A First Study
by
STEPHEN POTTER

London · JONATHAN CAPE · Toronto
JONATHAN CAPE & HARRISON SMITH
New York

D. H. LAWRENCE
1929

Fig. 49: Stephen Potter, *D.H. Lawrence: A First Study* (1930).

The facetious tone, however, failed to disguise the frustration Gerald felt at not having delivered his own book on Lawrence, particularly as Potter's project was so indebted to his influence. According to Potter's unpublished memoir, it is clear that Gerald even critiqued the manuscript before publication.[226] On the other hand, although he was clearly upset by the review, it says a lot for Potter's good nature that Gerald's patronising

---

[224] Stephen Potter, *The Young Man* (London, 1929), p. 88. Gessler (Gerald) is admired by the Potter character, David Voce, quasi-erotically in the opinion of 'J', the Collis character.

[225] Gerald was a mere six months older than Potter. Gerald's 6-page review featured far more prominently than the 2-page one in the same issue by the slightly younger E.A. Blair (soon to be known as George Orwell) of Sherard Vines, *Alexander Pope by Edith Sitwell and The Course of English Classicism,* one of his earliest publications.

[226] See below, p. 176.

scorn seems to have been forgiven.[227] To give both men their credit, Potter may have recognised a degree of truth in the account of his character; certainly his later career suggests acknowledgement that he was not cut out for confronting Nietzschean profundities or even the life of a lecturer.[228]

Probably at Edward Garnett's suggestion, Jonathan Cape must have commissioned Potter to write the book as soon as he concluded that Gerald was not going to deliver. Potter followed in Gerald's footsteps to the extent of writing to Lawrence, albeit without leaving England, with a greater variety of questions and more confident request that they might meet.[229] Lawrence replied politely from the Villa Beau Soleil in Bandol on 9 January 1930, just as he had responded to Gerald in March of the previous year:

Dear Mr Potter

I believe my books are published pretty well in the order in which they were written… Only *Women in Love* was finished by end of 1916 and didn't get published till some years later – was it 1922? – I haven't got any important unprinted works: and I don't think any exist.[230]

---

[227] Though when, at his request, I sent Julian Potter a copy of the review he recalled that his father 'was deeply upset by it' (letter dated 20 February 1994). Evidence for this is to be found in another autobiographical passage in an unpublished typescript Julian kindly copied for me in which his father writes of the review: 'It was by G.B. It was coldly and regretfully crushing.' Potter then recalls his friends' response to Gerald's review: 'So that's how I shall go down to posterity… I felt mortally stung; or rather stunned… I did not know how to think, where to move. My work and enthusiasm all done for nothing. Quite irrationally and with no special plan, I wanted to see Murry himself…' which he did.

[228] J. Potter, *Stephen Potter at the BBC*, passim.

[229] One cannot help suspecting that for all Gerald's grand style, his relatively provincial and non-Oxbridge background left him with less confidence than Collis and Potter could count upon when approaching literary celebrities such as Shaw or Lawrence, or when Arnold Bennett telephoned. Bennett praised Potter's biography as 'an excellent book' in the *Evening Standard*. Gerald's failure to meet Lawrence and deliver the book on him, proved fatal where his career and much else in his almost tragically unfulfilled life was concerned.

[230] An interesting remark in view of the posthumous publication of *Mr Noon* (initially in 1934). Potter published this first part of Lawrence's letter on the final

We are here till the end of March, and I shall be pleased to see you if you really want to come down – though I hate reading about myself and my 'works.' The Hotel Beau Rivage here is quite pleasant, costs about 45-50 francs a day – and is ten minutes distant from here.

About a photograph – perhaps my sister would lend you one that was taken for my 21st birthday, clean shaven, bright young prig in a high collar like a curate – guaranteed to counteract all the dark and sinister effect of all the newspaper photographs.[231]

I don't know the name of your novel, or I would order it. Please tell me.

All good wishes

D.H. Lawrence

Lawrence's promise that he and Frieda would be pleased to see Potter in Bandol any time until the end of March proved poignantly optimistic for he died on the 2nd of that month in Vence. Contextualising the contents of Lawrence's letter, a copy of which his son, Julian, kindly sent me, Potter had written, in the early 1950s: 'Thirty one years ago I put this letter in an old tin box: and then, last month, dug it out again.' He then recalls his thoughts about whether or not to visit, persuading himself that he should, but concludes somewhat disingenuously, in view of the date he would have received the letter (as distinct from a fellow-author's phone call):

I would certainly go out next week, straight away. I felt apprehensive and excited. Then came a ring from Arnold Bennett. 'I have to say, I'm afraid, d-d-<u>don't</u> go out to s-s-<u>see</u> Lawrence. (The stammer was bad.) 'He will be dead by the time you get there.'

Lawrence died ten days later.

---

page (159) of his book. For the rest, see *Letters of D.H. Lawrence*, VII, p. 620.

[231] This part of Lawrence's letter to Potter was also published in *D.H. Lawrence: A First Study*, on page 7, with the acknowledgement: 'For permission to reproduce this portrait of her brother I am greatly indebted to the kindness of Mrs. King', *i.e.* Lawrence's sister Emily. The whole phrase is repeated as a caption beneath the photograph facing p. 38.

Gerald's review of Potter's book begins promisingly enough with a melodramatically revealing meditation on the theme of Potter's youthful novel:

> Lawrence loved young men: loved them erotically, loved them sentimentally, loved them religiously. As Whitman did. Of course he'd have shrieked a denial…[232]

That this book had been published so soon after Lawrence's death was 'extraordinarily opportune', writes Gerald promisingly:

> The fact that it was written (except for a few paragraphs) before Lawrence died makes little difference. Any word of him is welcome. Here we are, still loitering, talking about him, thinking about him: in our half-feeling way afraid to weep for him; in our half-believing way half-hoping for the resurrection of his spirit among us.[233] And now comes this book by one who says he owes to Lawrence his greatest debt – another John. We hardly dare to read it. Will it be by some young man writing cheap anecdotes, information, journalism only; or some stupid attack or superficial appreciation: or something done out of indiscriminate fervour, sentimentality? Or will he be John indeed and have seen the godhead in the man he loved, as a woman sees it, and yet be fixed in that vision, as no true woman is, so that his whole life after will be broken and unfree? That is possible – and all too likely. Or will he see what John would not see? Will he see how his leader failed him, and be free and brave enough himself to lead where his leader would

---

[232] *Cf.* Lawrence's plea to the young David Garnett to 'Go away … and try and love a woman'; *Letters*, II, p. 321 and above, p. 87. Gerald seems in this respect more libertarian; *cf.* pp. 184-5. Harold Bloom calls Lawrence, after Eliot, Wallace Stevens and Hart Crane, 'the fourth true Whitmanian poet in the language.' For Lawrence on Whitman, see Bloom's *Western Canon*, pp. 288-89. On the survival of both the reputations of Gerald's heroes, Bloom writes: 'Like Shelley and Hardy before him, Lawrence will go on burying his own undertakers, even as Whitman buried several generations of dismissive morticians.' *Cf.* the discussion in Jeffrey Meyers, *D.H. Lawrence: a Biography* (London, 1990), passim.

[233] That this intentionally references Christ's Resurrection is confirmed by the following sentence; *cf.* note 211 above, for Lawrence identifying himself with the Resurrected Christ in *The Escaped Cock* (*The Man Who Died*).

not, and so be the more faithful in his love? But all such thoughts are needless, irrelevant – no, almost ridiculous and comic in connection with this book. This book is, I know for a fact, written by a young man (a man under thirty, I mean). But it is not young.

> It is incredible. If one didn't know so many other young men these days who might have written it (though I doubt whether any one of them could have done it as well) it would be impossible to believe that it came from anybody under forty. Its intellectual maturity is (to me, at least) staggering.

But the next facetious twist makes it clear that this is a piece of epideictic rhetoric reminiscent of Mark Antony's praise of Brutus at Caesar's funeral:

> And I am not meaning that intellectual maturity is necessarily bad; nor, for the moment do I want to judge the book. I only want to describe it – as an object say … it is excellently set out, excellently planned. It is well written too. Even when it is almost academic it is not formal – he can speak naturally, yet without looseness… It's in good taste (almost offensively so to me, I fear) and it is clear – interesting to read, without being superficial. Its terms of thought derive from Plato, Spengler, Keyserling, Whitehead, most of them modern, you see: all of them reputable… And the main thesis of the book has all these qualities … and proceeds from thought to thought with as slick precision as the Theorem of Pythagoras.

> … He divides the book into four parts. Part One: *Neri and Bianci* (that is, blacks and whites) – Lawrence philosophy.[234]

From Potter's misspelling of 'Bianchi' here, repeated throughout Part One in the book's running-title, and Gerald's uncritical repetition of what would be a very different-sounding (and non-existent) word in Italian, it is clear that neither author knew this language. Its survival through Cape's editorial procedures also reminds one of the rush there must have been to bring this book out after Lawrence's death. To his

---

[234] 'Lawrence and the Young Man', p. 312.

more cosmopolitan credit, had he lived long enough, Lawrence would have noticed the error immediately; he had checked with Pound's American friend, Grace Crawford, how to pronounce the hard 'ch' in the more useful word: 'Chianti' when he was the same age as Gerald and Potter.[235] But having missed this opportunity to score a pedantic point, Gerald nevertheless proceeds in full school-masterly mode:

> He doesn't explain the philosophy. Good. He shows how it came – briefly. He concludes that the philosophy is not the clue to Lawrence, but merely part of his self-description. Excellent (as far as it goes)…

Here, however, matters become more overtly ominous:

> It's true that at other times I want to say: 'But I don't see it quite that way.' When he deals with the failure of love, for instance, he seems to me to speak from a strangely arid imagination; and when he deals with the failure of friendship he seems to me to speak not his own thoughts at all, but somebody else's he has imagined and no more.

That Gerald has himself in mind at this point he confirms in his next two sentences:

> But I may be wrong. And in any case such criticism carried further can only lead to the presumption that I want him to be me – which is absurd. We each have to write within our own human limits and whatever freedom we may achieve is still within them. So I won't try to speak as a god-like critic of a critic, but as another human being. And as one (perhaps it is only fair to add) in years only imperceptibly older.

Knowing Gerald as he did, by this point in reading the review, Potter must have felt a sense of dark foreboding, a feeling fully justified by what follows:

> But, as such, I would say that in spite of all its good *qualities*, this book seems to me as bad a *book* as a book on Lawrence

---

[235] *Letters*, I, 175. According to a review of Alan Jenkins's biography of Potter (*Times Literary Supplement*, 17 October 1980, p. 1185), it suffered from another regrettable misprint, rendering *Sea and Sardinia* as 'Sex and Sardinia' but this seems to be untrue, unless some copies of the first edition were corrected.

could be. And why bad? Because it is utterly heartless.

'Heartless and intellectual' was the accusation that fifty years later, Gerald would level at my gift to him of Wyndham Lewis's *The Lion and the Fox* [Fig. 50].[236] Unfortunately one can't help thinking here of Lewis's satirical (similarly patronising but intentionally more amusing) account in *Paleface* of Lawrence, 'good little Freudian that he has always been'.[237] Discuss-

Fig. 50: *Wyndham Lewis* (1882-1957), self-portrait (1932).

ing *Mornings in Mexico* (chapters of which had first appeared in the *Adelphi)*, Lewis blames Spengler and Bergson as well as Freud for the fact that 'Everything Flows!' in contemporary culture, which was reverting to a sentimental, neo-Romantic primitivism:

> In art the Mexican Indian approximates closely to the ideal of the contemporary Bolshevik theatre… It is evidently just like life. It is a form of naturalism, the mystical form. And above all there is no bunk about mind. Mind is kept in its place, in the indian idea of drama!

I now see more clearly why when, albeit already somewhat provocatively, I commended Lewis to Gerald in the mid-1970s it didn't go down well. The irony is that Lewis's classical, or at least anti-Romantic aesthetic, belied (or was the result of) a nature that was at least as instinctual and more sexually driven

---

[236] See below, p. 250. Lewis's *The Lion and the Fox* had been critically reviewed by 'the Journeyman' in the February 1927 issue of the *Adelphi* (pp. 510-14), the same issue that published 'The Mozo' chapter of Lawrence's *Mornings in Mexico*.

[237] *The Enemy vol. 2* (September 1927), p. 53.

than that of Lawrence, Collis, Potter or even Gerald. Settling for uxoriousness relatively late in life - having meanwhile acquired a debilitating venereal disease and fathered several illegitimate children he abandoned even more promptly than Gerald - Lewis's almost paranoid discretion about his private life reminds one of his friend T.S. Eliot's put-down of those who seek to 'express themselves' or their *Zeitgeist*:

> Poetry is not a turning loose of emotion, but an escape from emotion; it is not the expression of personality, but an escape from personality. But, of course, only those who have personality and emotions know what it means to want to escape from these things.[238]

Even in his somewhat slapdash linking of Lawrence's Mexico with what he presumably means is Diaghilev's Ballets Russes, Lewis's particular brand of stream of consciousness - to which he was ostensibly so opposed - prompts associated ideas. Having failed to stay sane in a marriage contracted partly in order to escape Diaghilev's domination, in March 1919 Nijinsky was admitted to Ludwig Binswanger's private sanatorium in Kreuzlingen on Lake Constance. The following month he temporarily convinced Binswanger he was cured by performing a dance in the sanatorium's central hall.

Despite being unusually up-to-date with German *Kultur* and sharing an enthusiasm for Nietzsche in particular, Lawrence may not have known of Aby Warburg, who succeeded in persuading Binswanger to pronounce him cured and free to leave the same sanatorium four years later.[239] On the basis of a visit he had made to Oraibi, Arizona, in 1896, Warburg gave a lecture to doctors and fellow-inmates on the symbolic function

---

[238] 'Tradition and the Individual Talent' (1917), p. 21. Eliot was less entertainingly critical of Lawrence than Lewis in *After Strange Gods: A Primer of Modern Heresy* (London, 1934), though was likewise capable of recognizing his essential qualities. For Lewis, whose chauvinistically-treated women remained devoted to him, see Paul O'Keeffe, *Some Sort of Genius* (London, 2000) and Paul Edwards, *Wyndham Lewis, Painter and Writer* (New Haven and London, 2000).

[239] Ludwig Binswanger and Warburg, *La guarigione infinita. Storia clinica di Aby Warburg* (2005); cf. E. Chaney, "R.B. Kitaj (1932-2007): Warburgian Artist', *emaj issue 7.1* (November 2013): emajartjournal.com/2013/11/30/edward-chaney-r-b-kitaj-1932-2007-warburgian-artist/, pp. 8-9.

of the Hopi snake ritual. The year after Warburg's 1923 lecture, Lawrence was taken by Mabel Dodge Luhan to nearby Hotevilla, where the surviving traditionalist Hopi had migrated, to see what had by now become something of a 'circus performance'. Three thousand spectators, 'even negroes' were in attendance and Lawrence dwelt on their 'greedy … curiosity' as well as the gulf that had opened between contemporary white culture and what remained of the blood consciousness of 'the darker races'.[240] He nevertheless wrote an account of the event which he told his agent not to let Murry cut and said was his favourite chapter in what was eventually published as *Mornings in Mexico*.

Meanwhile Gerald continued to preach a literary version of what Warburg had promoted as *pathosformel* or artistic empathy, based on bodily and emotional rather than intellectual responses.[241] Albeit more concerned with the creation of new art than in interpreting past masters, the critical theme that underpinned his review of Potter's *Lawrence* was the one that characterised both his 1926 essay on Shaw and his responses to Lawrence Hyde's *Prospects of Humanism* five years later: that such authors lacked the courage to create or promote an art that was at one with authentic life, going the way Lawrence 'would have had us go – only further'; thus about as far from Eliot's classically impersonal aesthetic as it would be possible to go, even whilst sharing something with that advocated by George Santayana:[242]

---

[240] *Letters of D.H. Lawrence*, V (31 August 1924), p. 110.

[241] In this sense, therefore, more along the lines of the Darwinian tradition exemplified by Vernon Lee's writings in this field; see Carolyn Burdett, '"The Subjective inside us can turn into Objective outside": Vernon Lee's Psychological Aesthetics', *19: Interdisciplinary Studies in the Long Nineteenth Century*, no. 12 (2011), DOI: dx.doi.org/10.16995/ntn.610.

[242] For Gerald's review of Hyde, see below, p. 207. Like Lewis, albeit less entertainingly, Hyde drew attention to the dangers of 'mindlessness' in 'New Romantic' thought. The Spanish-born, Harvard-educated philosopher George Santayana (1863-1952) was recognised by Hyde as an influence on Murry's group of authors. Murry had indeed published him in the *Athenaeum* of 1919 (David Goldie, *A Critical Difference: T.S. Eliot and John Middleton Murry in English Literary Criticism, 1919-1928* [London, 1998], p. 34) and the *Adelphi* published his *The Genteel Tradition at Bay* as a separate pamphlet in 1931, the year of Gerald's

And that is not a criticism: it is a judgement. And in my judgement this book is bad because the young man behind it, while knowing a great deal about Lawrence, and having a keen perception of many of his qualities, and a certain sort of sympathy with him and certain admiration, has yet never let himself for one moment … be touched by him. Everything he says is right: and he says practically every right thing that can be said. But he himself is not in action: his book is a 'study' not a deed. It follows that he does not even see Lawrence. It is only a soul in action that can glimpse the reality of another soul, but he is keeping himself as static (and as safe) as any human soul can be and continue to live. And blind to the reality of the man he cannot judge him; and without judgement he cannot forgive him. He feels he has been let down by him – and he had been. But in his book he forgives him nothing: there is no generosity in it, not even generous anger. There is no reverence for the sufferings of the man, no sorrow for his failure… It is barren, sterile, dead. He as good as says that the significance of Lawrence is not in his work considered as Art, Philosophy, or even Religion, but in the very nature of his soul and what he was impelled to try to do on earth. And that is an invulnerable conclusion. But he means it so little that he can yet write a theorem on him, and dissect him like a dead insect.

---

critical review of Hyde's book. (Hyde had meanwhile also contributed to the magazine, in one case somewhat critically of D.H. Lawrence; see 'Glands and Chakras', *Adelphi*, December 1930, pp. 252-4). Santayana's now largely forgotten *Bildungsroman*, *The Last Puritan*, was published in 1936 when it became a best-seller. The sad trajectory of Santayana's protagonist, Oliver Alden, may have encouraged Gerald to continue resisting his similarly puritanical background, particularly pronounced in the northern parishes of his native Guernsey. Santayana's more overtly autobiographical *Persons and Places*, with its post-Nietzschean credo that 'integrity or self-definition is and remains first and fundamental in morals…' (p. 170) can only have encouraged Gerald's characterization of the more robust Ebenezer, whose love of Jim Mahy reminds one of Oliver's love of Jim Darnley in *The Last Puritan*. For Santayana's criticism of Nietzsche, see *The German Mind: A Philosophical Diagnosis* (Iowa, 1968), chapters 12 and 13.

And what was Lawrence then?

And with this introductory cue Gerald now delivers a cluster of paragraphs of powerful prose, which since they provide the best indication of what he would have said had he completed the book Cape and Garnett commissioned him to write, we quote from here. Taking up the theme of Lawrence as a Messiah-like phenomenon, he emphasises his Christ-like humanity, but a humanity furiously frustrated by the handicaps of his nature and nurture. Lawrence merely wanted to be a man among men (and women) on earth. Most of us are beneath this, 'submerged souls', merely *thinking* about being men:

> And his heart's desire was to remain on earth, to have a woman with him there, and to call men to him (each with his woman too) that they might live together. It was perfectly simple and what everybody wants. And this he knew too, but he would not believe it – he would have had to admit how much he liked everybody then. And he was reluctant, unwilling, ashamed (and also too hurt) to do that. So his work is not simple – it is the work of an obstinate man. It is complex, indirect, esoteric, its surfaces warped and distorted and shattered by the very strength of the unfree passion in him.

With a combination of the confidence gained from his relatively recent marriage and fatherhood, and no doubt less positive insights derived from even more recent experience of the same, supplemented by his correspondence and conversations with Murry and above all his empathetic reading of almost everything Lawrence had written, Gerald wrote what amounts to a prophetic critique of Modernism in a plea that we should judge Lawrence as a passionate paleo-conservative.

Sometimes, Gerald writes, Lawrence would let his judgements harden into unforgiveness, 'and stem the free flow of his love, and his thoughts became a heretic to the religion of his heart.' Then he would speak:

> new strange words (as though there could be a new language, a new truth, a new life) instead of the old elemental words of the earth whose meaning none knew so well as he – man, woman, husband, wife, father, brother,

love, hate, anger, joy, religion, God.

The Religion in his heart was the religion of all the religions…

What follows is even more Lawrentian in style and content, a manner encouraged by Murry who seems in turn to have been influenced by his young protégé but whose strangely naive brand of self-exculpatory confessionalism was largely his own. The wilfully subjective nature of the writing leads one to suspect that the statement: 'His death was his final failure – a premature, unnecessary end', expresses an at least half-conscious lament for his own failure to effect a meeting prior to that end, a failure not articulated as frankly as Potter had done but no doubt felt even more disturbingly.

The rest of this more or less self-contained paragraph consists of an impassioned account of the vital, ongoing importance of Lawrence, 'a person (a presence that can never leave us) whose very existence on earth was a call and a challenge to our souls'. Then Gerald returns to his personal brand of back-handed complimentary scorn, as strongly worded as it is, perhaps, because only he knew the extent to which Potter had been inspired by his own advocacy of Lawrence as the modern Messiah. Not conventionally vulgar enough to point this out, he instead suggests his own superior courage in living rather than merely 'knowing' the gospel according to St Lawrence:

> And the young man who wrote this book as good as says all this – and what he doesn't say he knows. The Young Man of these days is not stupid – only cowardly. And this one, more than most, knows, knows, *knows*. Every one of his hundred true intellectual perceptions comes from such knowledge. But knowledge is not enough … he will not face him as a person – he will only see his qualities and try to believe that thereby he knows the man. Yet when a man loves a woman does he love the *qualities* of his beloved? No. He loves *her*. And to know a man is precisely the same. But to know a man this way, as to love any living soul, is to open to oneself a world which it is dangerous to enter, though it is the only world we can live in and be at peace. And this Stephen Potter knows too; but in fear he denies what he cannot help but desire…

And so he continues, ever-crescendoing towards a climax of undoubtedly sincere but sublimely patronising prose about his half-year-younger friend being an:

> old Young Man who is anything over forty in his head … but a baby boy in his heart. And he is afraid and ashamed of it. But he must not be. And he need not be…

It says a lot about Murry's regard for Gerald and his own strange brand of 'New Romanticism' that in this, the last issue of the *Adelphi* he was to edit for a decade, albeit already with help from Rees and Plowman, he passed such an extraordinary outburst for publication (even though bound to prompt Potter's protest). It is likewise a reminder of the extraordinary status (at least for some) that Lawrence had achieved by the time of his death at the age of forty-four. Gerald concludes:

> Yes, he (and all of us) must go the way that Lawrence would have had us go – only further. Wherever we are, we must go on towards where he should have led us, till we emerge and see and know each other (with that other knowledge which men who have dared to be shameless have called love) and live there together – young men on earth.[243]

# 11: DARTINGTON DRAMA

Gerald's relations with Murry, Collis and Potter (and perhaps even with Plowman and Rees) were no doubt sorely tested by the lofty, preaching tone which prevailed in such reviews. This was especially evident in his review of Potter's Lawrence, but was also expressed in letters laying down literary laws or soliciting rarely-repaid loans, following failure to please or to provide promised typescripts to publishers. But it seems to have been only after it became clearer that he would not, at least any time soon, fulfil their great expectations of him by producing a work of genius, that their patience finally evaporated. Gerald's procrastination was all too closely connected to his uncompromising perfectionism, as he destroyed work which failed to meet his own particularly high standards, whether an

---

[243] 'Lawrence and the Young Man', p. 316.

article, play, novel or 20,000 word 'Essay on Sex'.[244] Gerald also wrote powerful poems which were never published and in this period, I suspect, were not even submitted for publication, though we shall see that he attempted to have at least one of them printed after the war, sent a few to me and retained a handful of other works in progress until his death (See Appendices 1, 2 & 3).

In late August 1930 Gerald wrote to Murry from Pillar Box Cottage, Moor House, Westerham, Kent; Moor House being the less specific address he had anticipated the previous May:

> I've got to ask you to do something for me again. It's this. There's an American woman, one Mrs. Elmhirst (formerly Mrs Strait) of Totnes, Devonshire, who has an interest in the sort of thing I'm trying to do and who might be helpful, and a friend of mine, Kenneth Lindsay, who has some influence with her, hopes to interest her on my behalf. But he thinks it would make things very much more likely if he could send her a statement from you about my work. I gather she has been done in a good deal by friends recommending friends rather vaguely, and now she is on her guard, so he wants to be able to send her something definite on what you've published or read of mine – with a sort of 'this-pupil-shows-promise' footnote, he said. Will you do this for me [*sic*; perhaps significantly lacking a question-mark]. You can send it to him or to me. I'll give you his address. Kenneth Lindsay, 32, Clareville Street, S.W.7.[245]

---

[244] It is hoped, even if typescripts were usually returned, that one or more of Gerald's works might eventually turn up in a publisher's office. In February 1929 he reports to Murry that his play, *Margaret*, had been 'turned down by Cape, Heinemann, and Chatto and Windus.' *Waysmeet* also seems to have been a completed play which he no longer possessed at his death but which may yet survive in a private or publisher's archive. For other lost titles, see bibliography.

[245] If Collis hadn't introduced them, Lindsay may well have known Gerald from (or indeed introduced him to) Toynbee Hall, where he taught between 1923-26 before becoming an MP in 1935 and Parliamentary Secretary to the Board of Education. Collis was engaged to Lindsay's sister, Margaret, and another sister, Christine, had dated Potter (Jenkins, *Potter*, p. 81). Collis praises the Dartington project in terms of reviving English manor houses as 'the mental and spiritual and moral nurseries of the future – if England is to have a future. They should supply the need which is no longer supplied by the Church of England'; *An*

No doubt recommended by Murry, therefore, as well as by the future National Labour MP, Kenneth Lindsay, Gerald and Kathleen now became acquainted with Leonard and Dorothy (*née* Whitney) Elmhirst, the wealthy Anglo-American couple who in 1925 acquired Dartington Hall in Devon, and founded there the liberal school and experimental estate [Fig. 51]. As well as hosting a well-funded community, the Elmhirsts shared the younger couple's theatrical interests. Kenneth Lindsay was a particular favourite of Dorothy's; she thought him 'a bit of a genius', and had written to husband-to-be, Leonard (to whom Lindsay may have introduced her): 'I love him dearly'.[246]

Fig. 51: *Dorothy and Leonard Elmhirst* (photo: c.1928) (Dartington Hall Trust).

The introduction to Dartington effected short-term benefits - with a broadening of scope for Gerald and Kathleen - as well as longer-term ones for their children, given the otherwise restricted range of alternatives. Despite his reluctance to discuss the past, I recall Gerald mentioning having met the Nobel Laureate Rabindranath Tagore [Fig. 52]. Mrs Snell

---

*Irishman's England* (London, 1937), p. 84. His *segue* to the unhappiness and indeed suicides that result from 'the mastery of the Machine', and concomitant loneliness, could have been written by Gerald.

[246] Michael Young, *The Elmhirsts of Dartington: the Creation of a Utopian Community* (London 1982), p. 74.

Fig. 52: *Rabindranath Tagore* (1861-1941), bronze by Jacob Epstein (1926).    Fig. 53: Jomo Kenyatta (1889-1978) meets Sylvia Pankhurst at the LSE's Abyssinia and Justice conference (1937). (Hulton-Deutsch Collection/Corbis)

independently remembered that Gerald had told her 'he had also known Tagore and Annie Besant quite well.'[247]

---

[247] Fowles, 'Introduction', *Ebenezer Le Page*, p. xiii. According to Joan Snell, he also knew Jomo Kenyatta [Fig. 53], with whom 'he ate tripe – and hated the stuff'; see Wilson, 'The Quiet Man of Upwey'. Kenyatta arrived in London in 1929 and, apart from a spell in Moscow, spent much of the next decade in Britain, first at Woodbrooke Quaker College in Birmingham, and then at University College London and the London School of Economics, where he studied social anthropology under Bronisław Malinowski. The latter, who was a supporter of the Mass Observation project that Gerald joined in 1938 (as Malinowski left for America), helped Kenyatta write *Facing Mount Kenya*, his critique of the colonial system which made him something of a celebrity - though one wonders what Sylvia Pankhurst (1882-1960), as the feminist daughter of a suffragette, whom he met the previous year, would have thought of his defence of female circumcision; see below, p. 181. His post-1939 friendship with his Storrington landlord, Roy Armstrong, the Southampton University and WEA lecturer who founded the Weald and Downland Open Air Museum, provides another possible point of contact with fellow-WEA lecturer Gerald; see Malcolm Linfield, 'Jomo Kenyatta,' www.lindfield.org/longshot/volume_5/jomo_kenyatta.html. I thank Mr Linfield for sending me a revised version of this interesting article; *cf.* Hare, *The Washington Story*, pp. 75-76.

If they had not already met through Collis, who describes Tagore's 'majestically poetic personality' after his visit to Guilford Street, it is likely that it was through the Elmhirsts that he would have done so, Gerald's interest in the Bengali poet and polymath having perhaps been stimulated by his reading of West's *Life of Annie Besant*, who had founded a college in India over which Tagore subsequently presided.[248]

Having employed Leonard Elmhirst soon after the Great War, in the summer of 1930, whilst on his European Grand Tour, Tagore visited his friend at Dartington - which was to a large extent modelled on their jointly-run Institute of Rural Reconstruction at Santiniketan.[249]   Tagore's July visit was recorded in the Dartington *News of the Day* magazine. On 18 November of the same year, the same news sheet announces:

> Drama - postponement of the play which Mr G B
>     Edwards is producing.
>     Cast:
>     A Fisherman - Gerald Edwards
>     His Wife - Kathleen Edwards
>     Their son - Solomon Ben Simon.[250]

Then in the *News of the Day* for Tuesday 25 November is the announcement of 'a play called "Sonny" by G.B. Edwards on Saturday' (presumably the 29th).[251] I also recall Gerald talking once of a close friendship with (the son of?) a Rabbi in this period and participating in Jewish ceremonies as a result. It

---

[248] Tagore expressed his 'heartfelt sympathy and gratitude to Mrs Besant when she was interned' for campaigning for India Home Rule in 1917; *Selected Letters of Rabindranath Tagore*, ed. K. Dutta and A. Robinson (Cambridge, 1997), p. 183. For Tagore 'turning up' in Guilford Street, see above, p. 40.

[249]   Dartington  Hall  Trust  Online  Archive  (www.dartington.org/ archive/display/LKE/TAG). In 2012 the art school at Dartington was merged with Falmouth School of Art and subsequently closed. The School's collection of paintings by Tagore was meanwhile sold.

[250] *News of the Day*, vol 4, no. 192: Dartington Hall Trust Online Archive (www.dartington.org/archive/display/T/PP/EST/1/006). For the possible influence of Giovanni Verga's *La Malavoglia*, which is about Sicilian fishermen - though it is of course possible it was already about a Guernsey one - see below, p. 213.

[251] *Ibid*.

seems that, according to the best libertarian (Friedian?) principles of the day, his friend Solomon Simon soon became intimate also with Kathleen.[252]

By late 1930 therefore Gerald and presumably his enhanced *ménage* had entered the Dartington circle and were renting accommodation near the estate. Dartington's historian, Michael Young, writes that although the Elmhirsts themselves 'were never seen naked in public ... they were to be a magnet for the devotees of naked bodies and cabbage juices', including those whom George Orwell caricatured as the 'high-minded women and sandal-wearers and bearded fruit-juice drinkers who come flocking towards to the smell of "progress",' whom he thought gave socialism a bad name.[253] Orwell's focus on feminism in a complementary critique is cited by the post-feminist author of *Heterophobia*, Daphne Patai in *The Orwell Mystique: A Study in Male Ideology*:

> One sometimes gets the impression that the mere words 'Socialism' and 'Communism' draw towards them with magnetic force every fruit-juice drinker, nudist, sandal-wearer, sex-maniac, Quaker, 'Nature Cure' quack, pacifist, and feminist in England.[254]

Albeit bearded, the too dapper to be sandal-wearing Gerald may not have needed Orwell to elaborate on the downsides of socialism or, by this time indeed, feminism. The Germanic mix of *Mutterrecht*, Nietzsche, Weininger and 'Friedian' sexual libertarianism was proving a deeper and more deadly diet than middle-class suffragettism among the English elite in general and Gerald's personal life in particular.[255] Though he had relatively recently promoted his wife's writing, a decline in marital relations, perhaps reinforcing nostalgia for Nietzsche, may be reflected in his views on the role of women, including literary women in relation to motherhood. If somewhat

---

[252] See below for the birth a year later of David Simon Edwards, p. 159.

[253] Young, *Elmhirsts*, pp. 132-34 (quoting Orwell's *Road to Wigan Pier*).

[254] *The Road to Wigan Pier* as cited by Patai, *The Orwell Mystique* (Cambridge, Mass., 1984), p. 85.

[255] Ann Taylor Allen, *Feminism and Motherhood in Western Europe, 1890-1970: The Maternal Dilemma* (New York and London, 2005).

obliquely articulated, these views are expressed in Gerald's article on Velona Pilcher's *The Searcher: A War Play*.[256] He writes that war will be prevented:

> Not by propaganda. Not by votes or laws or leagues. Nor by all wives saying to all husbands: 'You shan't go!' Nor by all mothers calling to their sons: 'Come home!'... None of these. Not by violence. But by being – women. And what does that mean? If women were women would men make wars? If men knew the peace that is beyond war and peace would they fight to order for what they do not know? Then what does being a woman mean? Does it mean writing drama, for example? *Can* she write drama? Dare one ask? She can speak, sing, dance, pray. She can shape and decorate. She can know and understand. She can pity, she can love, she can bless. But can she do all these round the germ of man's unformulable faith? Can she? Can man bear a child?[257]

Unless exclusively specifying drama, this seems to overlook the fact that women write at least as well as men, but is an effective indictment of egalitarian feminism in the Nietzschean if not even more pessimistic Schopenhauerian tradition. It was, however, clearly not effective enough to prevent the kind of

---

[256] G.B. Edwards, 'The Drama, the War, and Woman', *Adelphi*, vol. I, no. 2 (November 1930), pp. 161-64. Typically, Gerald doesn't mention *The Searcher's* very fine wood engravings and dust-jacket by Blair Hughes-Stanton (despite the latter being Lawrentian in more ways than one). For Pilcher, see Charlotte Purkis, 'Velona Pilcher and Dame Ellen Terry 1926', *Ellen Terry: Spheres of Influence*, ed. K. Cockin (London, 2011), pp. 119-132. For help with Velona Pilcher I thank Dr Purkis who writes to me that: 'what [Gerald] has to say about her play is the most perceptive and intelligent review I have read. After all the odd bits of journalese his voice really speaks to me about the conundrum of the play and the conversations audience members may have had - so a very thought-provoking find.'

[257] *Ibid.*, p. 164. Although Ebenezer's voice is characterised by tragi-comic irony this is not self-evidently (or at least exclusively) the legacy of the Great War, the argument advocated by Paul Fussell's *The Great War and Modern Memory* (Oxford, 1975). As this review suggests, his mind was already focussed on (even) larger human issues. In this respect, Gerald was evidently less impressed with Sean O'Casey's *The Plough and the Stars*, which he saw when it opened in 1926: 'wars are less the cause of tragedy than vice versa. And he is Irish before he is human.' (Collis, 'Memories of a Genius Friend', p. 22).

progress ironised by Orwell, which has culminated with women serving on the front line and freezing their eggs to prioritise their careers; its most recent manifestation (as we go to press) being the sacking of a Nobel laureate for having joked to a meeting of scientific journalists about falling in love with women who weep in laboratories.[258]   While unprecedented attention is paid to child sexual abuse (pornography meanwhile flourishing as never before), state-subsidised abandonment of children facilitates capitalist manipulation of feminism, resulting in children being deprived of affection at home, or abused in institutions, whilst women themselves are deprived of motherhood whether or not they wish to be.

But the deeper emotional context from which Gerald's gender politics emerged is retrospectively revealed in the letter with which he formally introduced himself soon after we met in 1972:

> My boyhood, adolescence and young manhood was an increasingly intense fight to the death against my mother; and indeed all my relationships with women have been a fight to the death. I survive, but in grief; for I have sympathy with what I fight against, and sorrow at the necessity. That should make clear to you my disorientation from Lawrence, with whom in other ways I have much in common.[259]

Though Lawrence's denunciations of women fascinated Frieda from the moment they met, Lawrence was far from the sole source of this common cause in Gerald's circle and was in any case, as this letter suggests, more sanguine about *Mutterrecht*.[260] In his autobiography, Collis wrote of his hypochondriacal mother: 'From the hour of my birth she hated me.'[261] Despite this most extreme conclusion, Collis seems to have settled for a compromise attitude towards 'the female will', somewhere between Lawrence's and Gerald's, though he survived in only slightly better shape and in many ways more regretfully than

---

[258] *I.e.*, Sir Tim Hunt FRS, dismissed from posts at UCL and the European Research Council's Science Committee (10 June 2015).

[259] See below, p. 246, for full text.

[260] Worthen, *Lawrence*, p. 389.

[261] *Bound upon a Course*, p. 21.

the Gerald I remember.[262]

In his novel, Gerald casts Raymond rather than Ebenezer as the principal victim of Womankind: 'I made a great mistake when I was a young chap. I used to think girls were human beings like us; but they are not…'.[263] Where feminism *per se* is concerned, it is interesting that the awful Mrs Crewe cites gender politics when rebuffing Ebenezer, who had been delegated to try and prevent her burying her late husband with his predecessor instead of with his first wife, Ebenezer's aunt:

> I was only a man: how could I be head of a family? Was I so ignorant! Hadn't I heard of Women's Rights?[264]

Because of the left-of-centredness that was then as much an assumption in this milieu as now, and perhaps because of its relative infancy, feminism, as the ultimate manifestation of egalitarianism, was not yet coherently critiqued, even if the combined advocacy of sexual and political liberation on the part of women made for a threatening mix where large numbers of males were concerned. It was surely no mere coincidence that between 1870 and the 1920s the birth rate in England fell from five children per woman to two.[265] In the midst of this period the 23-year-old homosexual Jew, Otto Weininger published his gender-polarizing and anti-semitic *Geschlecht und Charakter (Sex and Character)* before arranging to commit suicide in 1903 in the

---

[262] Ingrams, *Collis*, passim, though see in particular Potter's poignant report back to him from New York of the beautiful 'Marion' (*vere* Elizabeth), the now married woman he had waited too late to propose to but who still cherished his memory. Collis quoted Othello on having thrown a pearl away (pp. 119-22). Ingrams hints at Gerald having had a role in this as it happened when Collis 'was setting out, under the influence of G.B. Edwards, to follow his destiny'. Collis remained more fascinated by celebrity than Gerald, which may have encouraged his failure to keep in touch with his far less productive friend. For Collis's later views on 'the Battle of the Sexes' (and unromantic women), see his *Marriage and Genius: Strindberg and Tolstoy: Studies in Tragi-Comedy* (London, 1963), pp. 3-6.

[263] *Ebenezer Le Page*, p. 121.

[264] *Ibid.*, p. 298.

[265] See David Spiegelhalter, *Sex by Numbers: What Statistics Can Tell Us About Sexual Behaviour* (London, 2015).

Viennese house in which Beethoven had died.[266]

A particularly vivid account of a victim turned determined enemy of womankind was published by someone who managed friendships with both Lawrence and Wyndham Lewis, the musician and musicologist, Cecil Gray (1895-1951). He warms to this Weiningerian theme via an account of his maternal uncle, Robert Ernest Miller, who like his father (Gray's grandfather) was warned not to marry his future bride by his prospective brother-in-law.[267] In an account not notable for its political correctitude, both grandfather and beloved uncle die wretchedly as a result of ignoring these warnings, thereby arming Gray Junior with a pre-emptively defensive philosophy resembling Gerald's:

> One begins to understand how and why there are so many homosexuals about when one contemplates this little family history, which is assuredly not unique. It is Mr. Somerset Maugham's story, *Of Human Bondage*, extended over generation after generation…
>
> The sad truth of the matter is, I am afraid, only too plain and evident. In marriage there can be no equality; one or the other must dominate, and Nature has decreed that it should be the male. Modern civilization has decreed

---

[266] Combining misogyny with anti-semitic Christianity and the cult of genius, Weininger's book achieved notoriety partly due to his dramatic suicide. Wittgenstein's brother, Rudolf, committed suicide 'in an equally theatrical manner', six months after Weininger, a fact that heightened the philosopher's fascination with the man and his book: Ray Monk, *Ludwig Wittgenstein: The Duty of Genius* (London, 1990), p. 20; *cf.* Weininger's influence on Strindberg, below, p. 141.

[267] See *Musical Chairs or between two stools: Being the Life and Memoirs of Cecil Gray* (London, 1948). Gray was a close friend and collaborator of that even more libertarian member of the Lawrence circle, Peter Warlock, *vere* Philip Heseltine (1894-1930), recently identified by Brian Sewell as his father, who committed suicide on 17 December 1930, seven months after Sewell's birth after his Catholic mother refused to have a termination. Gray and Heseltine co-authored a book on the aristocratic composer Carlo Gesualdo, who murdered his wife and her lover in Naples in October 1590. Gray also wrote a play about Giles de Rais. He was the father of the beautiful bisexual, Hilda Doolittle's only daughter, Perdita. Jeffrey Meyers argues that Gray had an affair with Frieda during Lawrence's lifetime though offers as little evidence as I do for Gerald's possible liaison; *Lawrence*, pp. 206-07.

otherwise, and the male has accepted the situation.[268] He fondly believed that woman only wanted equality, and she may have believed herself that she did; but in practice it has not so worked out. Man, civilised man to-day, genuinely desires equality – he has no wish to dominate, and he has abdicated. Woman, instead of accepting the dominion status offered freely, has established a tyranny, an ascendancy over the male – and nowhere is it more evident than in Anglo-Saxon countries…

The first premonitory symptoms of the female ascendancy which has since spread like a blight over the entire world, is to be found in Scandinavian literature, and drama particularly, especially in Ibsen and Strindberg… It is no mere coincidence that my unfortunate uncle's wife was a Scandinavian – an unholy combination of the worst elements in the heroines of both these dramatists – … in the end she drove the poor man mad, literally, certifiably mad, after which he shortly died, mercifully.[269]

The institutionalised forms of feminism and indeed of homosexuality that prevail now that formerly discrete life-style ideologies have been democratised would no doubt have horrified those who wreaked such havoc in Nigel Nicolson's *Portrait of a Marriage*.[270] Enjoying her affair with Virginia Woolf

---

[268] *Cf.* Collis's summary of Gerald's concerns: 'In what way did we see him as a genius?… It was what he said – his angle of approach… He derived support from D.H. Lawrence in his feeling that modern civilization was uncivilising masses of people.' ('Memories of a Genius Friend', p. 21).

[269] *Musical Chairs*, pp. 61-62. Strindberg, whose *Easter* Gerald produced for the Bolton Little Theatre in 1939, veered from an occasionally feminist position in his youth to an often vehemently misogynistic one by middle age; see Sue Prideaux, *Strindberg: A Life* (London and New Haven, 2012). Whilst largely the result of the experience of his marriages, intellectually this transition complements his enthusiasm for Nietzsche and Weininger's *Sex and Character*, which he believed solved the 'woman problem'. Strindberg contemplated his own suicide in relation to Weininger, who is not referenced by Prideaux but see Strindberg's letters to Arthur Gerber:   www.huzheng.org/geniusreligion/ aphlett.pdf. and above, p. 139. Gerald would no doubt have known Nietzsche's correspondence with an admiring Strindberg, published in various venues from 1913.

[270] *Portrait of a Marriage* (London, 1973; illustrated ed. 1990).  Among the most extreme manifestations of the consequences of the amoral pursuit of pleasure

in the aftermath of her more destructive one with Violet Trefusis, the bi- but predominantly homo-sexual Vita Sackville-West wrote to her bi- but predominantly homo-sexual husband, Harold Nicolson:

> If you were in love with another woman, or I with another man, we should both or either of us be finding a natural sexual fulfilment which would inevitably rob our own relationship of something. As it is, the liaisons which you and I contract are something perfectly apart from the more natural and normal attitude we have towards each other, and therefore don't interfere. But it would be dangerous for ordinary people.[271]

If Gerald's wife had found sexual fulfilment with a woman rather than, more 'naturally', with one of his best friends, perhaps his marriage, like the Nicolsons, might have survived - along with some sort of relationship with his children - into the more repressively respectable post-War period. For after the war, albeit *en route* to the later twentieth-century liberation of 'ordinary people', the freedoms formerly enjoyed even by upper class feminists and homosexuals were for a while more restricted. The laws against homosexuality in particular, including Henry VIII's 1533 Buggery Act, were more fiercely enforced than they had been in the first part of the century, when

---

were those associated with Vita's cousin, Lady Idina Sackville, who abandoned husbands and children for colonial Kenya with Josslyn Hay, Lord Erroll, her character inspiring Michael Arlen, Evelyn Waugh, Nancy Mitford and the book and film *White Mischief*; see *ODNB* and her great-grand-daughter Frances Osborne's *The Bolter* (London, 2008). Their affairs culminated in Erroll's murder and the accused's suicide with collateral damage along the way. Albeit less dramatic, painful consequences may also be found (albeit between the lines) in fellow libertarian Angela Culme-Seymour's extraordinary autobiography, *Bolter's Grand-daughter* (Oxford, 2001). Her third husband, the bisexual Patrick Balfour, Lord Kinross, entitled the novel inspired by her: *The Ruthless Innocent (1949)*. She subsequently ran off with her half-sister, Janetta's husband, the scientist, Derek Jackson. Her 'bolter' grandmother was Trix Ruthven, Idina Sackville's rival as Nancy Mitford's inspiration in the *Pursuit of Love*. Interestingly both Harold Nicolson and Lord Erroll became members of Mosley's Fascist 'New Party' in the early 1930s.

[271] Hermione Lee, *Virginia Woolf* (London, 1996), p. 488. See now also Matthew Dennison, *Behind the Mask: The Life of Vita Sackville-West* (London, 2014) which documents the destructive chaos which culminates in a fine garden.

well-known figures such as Edward Carpenter, Lytton and James Strachey, Maynard Keynes, William Plomer,[272] Brian Howard, Harold and William Acton and Norman Douglas survived fairly flamboyantly without being blackmailed or imprisoned.[273]   The social revolution of the 1960s, often associated with Penguin's popular republication of *Lady Chatterley's Lover*, was characterised by the democratisation of self-consciously libertarian behaviour, hitherto associated with a privileged elite. It has culminated in a 'Conservative' government in the UK and a 'plebiscite' in Ireland licensing gay marriage for the first time since the reigns of Nero and/or Elagabalus. Meanwhile and not unrelatedly there lurks a worrying undercurrent of aimless indignation or puritanical groupthink. It is now surely misleading to suggest, as it may already have been in 1985 when Alan Bennett wrote of 'The Wrong Blond', that we are more liberal than we were in the 1930s, or indeed 1911 when Norman Douglas 'picked up' 12-year-old Eric *en route* for Old Calabria:

> Back in 1939, Auden is typically bold, not to say boastful about his affair. Even nowadays … a middle-aged man would think twice about meeting the family of the 17-year-old son he's knocking off. Auden had no such scruples…[274]

---

[272] The 25-year-old Plomer published an article on the Anglophile Japanese novelist, Natsume Soseki, immediately after Gerald's 'Humanism versus Theosophy' in the September-November 1929 issue of *The New Adelphi*, p. 53.

[273] Acton and Douglas lived abroad; the former born there and the latter only after an incident in the Natural History Museum that would have led to a European arrest warrant today. Both were able to behave indiscreetly even after World War II in Italy but  the likes of Lord Montagu of Beaulieu and his cousin Michael Pitt-Rivers (who later married George Orwell's widow), were all imprisoned in the 1950s and Alan Turing chose oestrogen injections as an alternative; *cf.* the victims of the so-called Lavender Scare in America. For Strachey, see Michael Holroyd's pioneering biography which, not coincidentally, appeared in 1967 as liberating legislation was being passed; *cf.* now, Richard Davenport-Hines, *Universal Man: The Seven Lives of John Maynard Keynes* (London, 2015), which documents only occasional scares despite Keynes's actively eclectic pre-marital sex life. For Acton and Douglas, see my *ODNB* entry and Mark Holloway, *Norman Douglas: A Biography* (London, 1976).

[274] Alan Bennett, 'The Wrong Blond', *London Review of Books*, VII, no. 9 (23 May 1985), pp. 3-5; review of Dorothy Farnan, *Auden in Love* (London, 1984). Richard Davenport-Hines compares Auden's disillusion with Republican Spain with

# 12: DEVONSHIRE ADELPHOS

On 9 January 1931, from what may already have been a caravan site, 'Ayreville, Totnes Road, Paignton, Devon',[275] Gerald wrote a mellower, if still oddly melodramatic letter to Murry, suggesting he come and see him at Yateley, at the large Hampshire bungalow in which he lived and wrote during most of the week:[276]

> And what will happen if I do come? I don't know. Perhaps I will meet your children and look at your garden and come away again. I am a very weak human being. But perhaps I will speak to you – about your reminiscences of Lawrence, if you like.[277] I don't know. But I have sat next to you at table and known you as a real man. And I have read Lawrence till I know his suffering spirit almost as I know my own soul. And I have seen your failure and the agony of it. There are many who are despising you, blaming you: they do not understand. But I have nearly nearly failed your way. I do not despise or blame you: and I believe I understand.
>
> Sincerely,
>
> Gerald Edwards [278]

---

Simone Weil's, which culminated in her conversion and his less dramatic equivalent; *Auden* (London, 1995), pp. 168-69; while the Germany that had helped sexually liberate Auden elected Hitler when confronted by a choice of two extremes. Meanwhile, thanks to Douglas's educative role, the 12-year-old Cockney, Eric Wolton, became Chief Superintendent of the Tanganyikan Police; see Chaney, *The Evolution of the Grand Tour*, 2nd ed. (London, 2000), p. 141.

[275] There is still a holiday home site called 'Ayreville' on the Totnes Road.

[276] From October 1928, Murry, initially with his second wife and the two children, lived in a large (now demolished) bungalow called 'South Acre'; see Michael Holroyd, 'John Middleton Murry in Yateley', in *The Yateley Society Newsletter*, no. 27 (July 1986), pp. 2-3. He left it later in 1931, moving from Yateley to Norfolk with his third wife in July. Murry meanwhile joined the Independent Labour Party this year, together with Richard Rees, who played Engels to his Marx, not least in the sense that once it became a monthly, in 1930 'I took complete financial responsibility.' (*Theory of my Time*, p. 57).

[277] Murry's *Son of Woman* appeared this year but his *Reminiscences of D.H. Lawrence* not until 1933, though these were already appearing in instalments in the *Adelphi*.

[278] This letter (in my collection) is dated 'Friday, January 9th 1930' but 1931 was

144

On 6 February 1931, Dartington's *News of the Day* had announced that at the:

> Backbenchers' Club - Mr G B Edwards late of Toynbee Hall will discuss 'The Education of John Jones'.

The only candidate for John Jones I can think of here is the seemingly far-fetched one of Lawrence's Croydon landlord, the school attendance officer who became irritated by the friendship that developed between Lawrence and his wife Marie; a situation not dissimilar to that which was to prevail between Gerald and his landlady, Joan Snell, decades later. According to Lawrence's biographer, John Worthen, Jones supplied Lawrence with a pair of condoms but Gerald would no doubt have argued that it was the young Lawrence who in essence educated the older man[279]. It is just possible that Gerald knew of Lawrence's still unpublished short story which was inspired by his relationship with the Jones family. In this Freudian tale, with its echo of Frazer's *Golden Bough* – and the patricidal theory implicit in its title, 'Old Adam' - the Lawrentian figure fights victoriously with his landlord, in effect for the wife, who is, however, ultimately marginalised when the younger man pities his (and her) victim.[280]

On 25 February, Gerald writes again from 'Ayreville' still in sympathetic mode though having apparently received a letter from Murry which did not include an invitation to visit. Instead

---

clearly meant, not least because Gerald refers to Lawrence in the past tense. 9 January 1931 was indeed a Friday.

[279] See Worthen, *Lawrence*, p. 308.

[280] See Brenda Maddox's fascinating (though Frazer-less) comparison, including that between Lawrence's quasi-sexualised observations of Jones's young daughters and the three-year-old Mary in this dramatic short story (*Lawrence*, pp. 44-45). If one bears in mind the extent and intimacy of Gerald's knowledge of Lawrence in this period, as well as his predilection for pointed or punning titles (such as 'Lawrence and the Young Man' and 'The Lost Boy') it is possible, if he knew the origin of this story, though not published till 1934, that he used the educationalist Jones as a way of discussing the superiority of Lawrence's educational ideal over the orthodoxy of the day. Lawrence's sympathy for the father-figure, a sympathy shared by Gerald, distinguishes them both from the orthodoxly Oedipal Freudian, who insists on the son's urge to commit parricide and ultimately supersede God; Amstrong's *Compulsion for Antiquity* (p. 251) on 'the eternal desire to be and be rid of the Father.'

Murry has asked him to read (review?) his book, presumably
*Son of Woman,* which was about to appear as a single volume,
but had appeared in instalments in the *Adelphi,* thus earning the
vilification to which Gerald had referred in his previous letter.
Gerald doesn't seem to know that these essays were appearing
in book form. He turns instead to Murry's latest self-vindicating
series of articles destined to appear in book form:

> When I read your next instalment on Lawrence in the
> Adelphi (the February one I mean), I felt it so strongly that
> I nearly wrote to you again. I'm sorry I didn't now.
>
> About that book of yours you want me to read – is it
> written yet, is it published? Of course I will read it if you
> want me to. But I haven't seen anything about it
> anywhere… What a funny man you are to say I've got to
> read your latest book before we can meet. Goodness, I've
> read volumes of yours already. And you don't change – not
> at bottom. Nor do I. We're alike in that. Only we mustn't
> get hard and cold…
>
> But I can buy a copy if I want to, and I expect I would if
> I saw one, and I do when I buy a copy of the Adelphi
> whenever I see one. Though you can give me one if you like.
> But I don't wish to ask for anything this time. And as to
> whether we're to meet or not – that I must leave to the Lord.
> I am content. Yet as I look back I see how I have failed you
> all along the line. And I still pray for a chance to pay my
> debts.
>
> Sincerely,
>
> G.B. Edwards [281]

The February 'instalment' to which Gerald refers was Part VI of
the 'Reminiscences of D.H. Lawrence', an often queasily
personal memoir of Murry's relationship with Lawrence, which
both prompted and, in book form, responded to Catherine
Carswell's *Savage Pilgrimage* of 1932 (see above p. 11). The

---

[281] A copy of this letter was kindly supplied by the Alexander Turnbull Library,
Wellington, though it is clearly one that went astray and should have been
among the otherwise complete collection of Gerald's letters to Murry I
purchased at Robin Waterfield, Oxford, in 1985.

previous instalment, published in the January edition, was almost as much about Katherine Mansfield as about Murry or Lawrence, dealing with the notion that Gudrun, in *Women in Love*, was indeed based on Mansfield and explaining how if true, 'it confirms me in my belief that Lawrence had curiously little understanding of her'.[282] It also deals with Murry's relative enthusiasm for 'what I regard as the two finest of his later books – *Fantasia of the Unconscious* and *Aaron's Rod*.'[283]

Reading through the Murry-Gerald correspondence (having to infer most of Murry's side), one is reminded both of Katherine Mansfield's 1913 quip about her husband, that 'Jack can't fry a sausage without thinking of God' and indeed of the reviewer of Lea's fine, albeit official, biography of Murry who pointed out that he 'set up to lecture us about life and knows nothing directly of it.'[284] Gerald now decided to break their relational deadlock with a more proactive charm offensive for on 3 March 1931 (a year and a day after Lawrence's death) he turned up at Murry's bungalow. Murry's dying second wife, Violet, was meanwhile being cared for by Max Plowman and his wife in their house in Golders Green and when he drove up to London Murry took Gerald with him.[285] His diary entry for the Friday, 6 March 1931 documents Gerald's success in at least temporarily restoring their close friendship:

> On Wednesday I went to London, taking with me in the car one gramophone and a bowl of crocuses for V[iolet]. Also G.B. Edwards, who suddenly descended on me in the evening of Tuesday. I liked him very much this time, more genuinely than ever before: he talked of Lawrence and me with much understanding, though naturally with incomplete knowledge. Finally he said he wanted to do

---

[282] *Adelphi New Series*, vol. I, no. 4 (January 1931), p. 322. Murry reviewed *Women in Love* somewhat negatively in *The Athenaeum*. Lawrence was irritated by what he considered was Murry's over-promotion of Mansfield.

[283] *Ibid.*, p. 329 and pp. 199-224 of Murry's *Son of Woman*.

[284] Hilary Corke, review in *Encounter* (January 1960), pp. 75-77. Mansfield's sausage-frying quip opens Basil Payne's review of Lea in *Studies: An Irish Quarterly Review*, XLIX, 195 (January 1960), pp. 338-40.

[285] In his letters Plowman described their address: 12 Woodside, Erskine Hill, NW11, as Hampstead Garden Suburb; see *Bridge into the Future*, p. 380.

something with me. I didn't shrink back, but said (what I felt) that I thought it very probable that we could do something together: only he must not be impatient.[286] Just now I was in the condition of moulting, and until the situation outside and inside me had resolved itself there was nothing to do but wait. We parted in the morning with real love of some sort between us, and I promised to write to him soon, which I will. One remarkable thing he said: that I could always have trusted Lawrence's love for me.[287]

The concluding sentence here probably speaks more of Gerald's charm and Murry's peculiarly self-regarding tendency towards wishful thinking than of Lawrence's likely feelings on the matter. But that Murry, who unlike Gerald had known Lawrence personally over many years, should find what Gerald said to him 'remarkable' is itself remarkable testimony to the esteem and affection in which he held the younger man at this time.

That he indeed wrote to Gerald at least once before Gerald wrote to him is suggested by the latter's next extant letter, dated 18 April. This tends to confirm the success of Gerald's visit, which seems to have included a night in London together, possibly at

---

[286] Murry's belief in himself as 'in every fibre of my being heterosexual' (and his flight from Lawrence's blood-brotherhood), makes this likely to have been a proposal to work together rather than anything else; see Kaplan, *Circulating Genius*, p. 29.

[287] Middleton Murry's unpublished diary in the Alexander Turnbull Library, Wellington, New Zealand, MS-Group-0411, p. 145. According to Lea, Murry drove up most Wednesdays. For the argument that Lawrence was indeed in love with Murry; see his daughter, Katherine Middleton Murry's *Beloved Quixote*, pp. 21-24. Despite her best (defensive) intentions, by quoting Murry's journal she exposes her father's apparently high-minded yet profoundly self-centred failure to understand himself and/or his effect on others, not least in his behaviour towards her mother. She recalls her father visiting Violet (at the Plowmans') 'as often as he could. There she died without my father being there.' Two days after receiving Plowman's phone call reporting her death (and driving up to London, which, interestingly, his daughter doesn't mention), Murry records in his journal: 'I told the children [it is not clear how long since they last saw their mother]. Weg thought a little while, and said: 'It's a good thing you didn't die, Dadda. Then we should only have had Maud [a nurse] and Miss Cockbayne.' (*Beloved Quixote*, p. 66). He married the latter on 23 May having already begun their affair despite warnings from friends and even her relations (*cf.* the parallel with Cecil Gray's uncle, above, p. 140).

the Plowmans' house but more likely at Murry's flat, where he stayed most Wednesdays in order to work at the *Adelphi* office in 58 Bloomsbury Street. Writing from: 'Vue Charmante', Liverton, Newton Abbot, Devon,' Gerald hopes that Richard Rees (who also lived in Yateley) has forwarded his message, which must have been one of condolence on Violet's death, Murry having apparently written to inform him of the news. The visit that Murry made to his wife when he accompanied Gerald to London must have been one of the last times, if not the last, that he saw her for she died in his absence (and that of her children) at the Plowmans' Golders Green house in the early morning of 30 March 1931. Gerald apologises for not having responded in writing: 'It wasn't because I wasn't moved by your letter. But what could I say?' He then writes cryptically:

> It touched pretty deeply my own situation, and I didn't know where to begin telling about that. Nor could I send you sympathy and that sort of thing: I felt rather that you could now go on stronger than before. I really only wanted to thank you for having let me know so soon.

Whatever Gerald meant depends to a large extent on what he was responding to in Murry's letter, but to judge from the latter's confessional style Murry would already have indicated the fading of his love for Violet before her death, exacerbated by the (understandable) transfer of her affections to Plowman, who was taking far better care of her. Murry is also likely to have at least hinted at his burgeoning relationship with the housekeeper, Betty Cockbayne, whom indeed he married, to most people's astonishment, less than two months later.[288]

Gerald continues this short letter by saying that he is sending Murry his review of 'Hyde's book'.[289] 'There's no need to send it on to Rees as I'm sending him a copy too. There are two paragraphs more or less about you.' He then asks Murry to 'Remember me (as that funny man with a black beard) to Weg and Col', *i.e.* Katherine and 'Collin', or John Middleton Murry Jr

---

[288] Lea, *Murry*, p. 184.

[289] For Gerald's review of Lawrence Hyde's *Prospects of Humanism*, which appeared in the June issue of *Adelphi*, and his important follow-up article on religion which appeared in October, see below, p. 207.

whom he had met at Yateley before accompanying Murry to London and who were now motherless. His concluding sentence asks Murry to 'come down as soon as you can.'

In a natural (rural) transition via, it seems, occasional lecturing at Toynbee Hall, from at least as early as 31 May 1931, the black-bearded Gerald had probably already found a position with the Workers' Educational Association (East Devon Extension Scheme) as well as accommodation at 'The Brackens', Raymond's Hill, near Axminster.[290] He now writes to Murry thanking him for his card and expressing his disappointment that he had not visited:

> I do want you to come. I'm going with Rees to Holland from July 3rd to the 8th, and may leave here a few days before that, so try and come some time in June, the sooner the better.

Meanwhile, he asks for reviewing work, not merely for the *Adelphi*, explaining (by now, one might have thought, somewhat superfluously):

> It's absolutely necessary I should get hold of some more money somehow.
>
> My [WEA] job here is more formal than real until September. There's no lectures to give and precious little organizing is possible. I'm writing again: a sort of hybrid play-novel – free drama if you like. But it's nothing startlingly new – in form anyhow. It's going quite well, I think, and I'm full of it.'[291]

Apart from the fact that a second wife had died and that he had just married a third, who was already proving positively dangerous, having by now read Gerald's review of Hyde's *Prospects of Humanism*, with its back-handed defence of Murry, including the view that 'he has misled many (and sometimes lost himself) in a maze of self-hypnotic intellectualism,' it is not entirely surprising that Murry did not hasten westwards to visit.

---

[290] This position may have been obtained through Rees who had worked for the WEA since 1922 and eventually became its treasurer.

[291] The AGM of the South West District of the WEA (Plymouth) confirmed the appointment of G.B. Edwards as tutor-organiser on 18 July 1931.

Gerald seems meanwhile to have offended Collis. On 31 August he writes to him on smart WEA notepaper, headed: 'The Workers' Educational Association, South Western District, East Devon Extension Scheme. Tutor-Organizer: G.B. Edwards. The Brackens, Raymond's Hill, Axminster':

Dear Jack,

This formidable paper is not to impress you but to tell you in brief where I am and what I am up to. If you can forgive me enough to write and curse me, will you do so – and intersperse with the curses news of how you are and what you are doing. I would like to know.

Ever,

G.B

By the time the June issue of the *Adelphi* appeared featuring Gerald's review of Hyde's book, he was writing another, this time on H.S. Ede's *Savage Messiah* [Fig. 54].

Fig. 54: H.S. Ede's *Savage Messiah* (1931).

This appeared the following September as: 'A Lost Boy', which title would have reminded the *Adelphi* readership of Lawrence's *The Lost Girl*, the novel about the daughter of Midlands draper who runs away with a Neapolitan performer.[292] Ede's pioneering (though post-Poundian) book about the brilliant sculptor Henri Gaudier-Brzeska (1891-1915), was probably recommended to Gerald by Murry who, having befriended Gaudier largely thanks to Katherine Mansfield, then lost his friendship and that of his mistress, Sophie Brzeska, even faster and more completely than they lost the Lawrences'.[293]

Gerald hints at such inside information whilst praising the artist in superlative terms:

> Henri Gaudier, the sculptor, was a singular being. He was a genius, a genius in his own right: his birthright. There's no doubt about that. He was as surely a genius as D.H. Lawrence was, or William Blake.

Or, Gerald, might almost have said, the author of this review, for his segue on the difficulty of dealing with the 'demon' of his genius smacks of identification; Gerald may well have seen himself as the third of Murry's 'discoveries', after Gaudier and Lawrence:

> All who met him must have felt it; and he must have felt strangely alone among them, and different from them all. He was soon at odds with most of them. Not that he couldn't love people: he did love – passionately and tenderly. But he could not, would not be contained...[294]

Gerald then diplomatically summarises the story of Gaudier's bust of Murry, which would have resembled the celebrated head of Ezra Pound that was illustrated in Wyndham Lewis's *Blast* in 1915:

> The violence of his revulsions is terrible, his rage terrifying. He makes friends with Middleton Murry, sculpts his head, then, when Murry angers him, destroys the head with stones.[295]

---

[292] *Adelphi*, new series, III (September 1931), pp. 541-44. For *The Lost Girl* , see the edition by John Worthen (Cambridge, 1981).

[293] Lea, *Murry*, pp. 34-35; *cf.* the fuller account of this 1912 incident in John Carswell, *Lives and Letters*, passim.

[294] 'The Lost Boy,' p. 543.

[295] Gaudier and Sophie had planned to stay with Murry and Mansfield, who

This reference to an instance of iconoclasm is one of just two to specific works of art in Gerald's account; he says nothing else of Gaudier's superb sculpture or drawings though these are illustrated throughout the book. What he does provide, however, is an account of the Gaudier-Brzeska partnership, which even if, and partly because, it might be inspired by the state of his own relationship, is yet described with such clarity that he manages to universalise Lawrence's psycho-philosophy in a way that the less patient Messiah himself often failed to do:

> He demands of her that she be friend, mother, sister, mistress to him, and each at the moment of his choice: she in turn wants indulgence for her every intellectual preconception and pity for her every resuscitated pain. But they're both human, so the battle rages: and after every reconciliation it begins again… Her worst weapon against him is her intellectual detachment (a pose of which he is absolutely incapable without killing himself): his best weapon against her is relentless truth – though sometimes it well-nigh kills. Sometimes he writes to her like a father, or at least a big and wise brother cheering her on: at other times there is a tone of pleading, an ache of loneliness, a homesickness for something, as to a mother from a boy. In his strength there is his just portion of weakness, and human need…

On the subject of Gaudier's death at 23 in the Great War, Gerald comments, significantly in view of the long life left him:

> He was not broken, he was only killed. His demon power ensured that he would not break; in the trenches he could still carve a maternity group on the butt-end of a rifle. It is

---

were co-editing *Rhythm* at this time; but after a series of slights, mainly negative responses to Sophie by Mansfield, they instead organised a gathering at which they ritually destroyed the bust. Though there were other incidences, including one in which Gaudier traumatised Murry by slapping his face (Kaplan, *Circulating Genius*, p. 31), the final quarrel was caused by Gaudier overhearing Murry and Katherine discussing their reservations about the prospect of Sophie joining them at their house in Runcton, near Chichester. Fellow-admirer and publisher of work by Gaudier, Wyndham Lewis must have been amused by this talk of demons, which in *Paleface* (1928/9) he mocks as the Lawrentianly 'dark demon', to be distinguished from the good (white) 'daimon' of Socrates.

true that his strength was not strong enough (whose is?); that perhaps it was too much of animal power, too little redeemed by human spirit… But far better for him to be as he was than to be broken into a million dissociated bits and spend the rest of his life in conceited contemplation of his own complexity. He remained simple; his feeling direct, his thoughts relevant and utterly sane…

Gerald's expressive alliteration here conjures up the impression that he too would opt for death over 'conceited contemplation of his own complexity.' Though he would persevere in his quest for the authentic life and eventually outlast Santayana's 'Last Puritan', he meanwhile suffered something of the fate he admires Gaudier for avoiding.

Gerald had presumably been paid for his review of *The Savage Messiah* but on 7 September, he writes to Murry again:

Can you spare me £5 for the time being? I am in a fix this month. The rent is paid and other bills: but my account is overdrawn and I haven't cash for food. Nor have I time to write an article just now as I am absolutely swamped with W.E.A. work.

I'm sorry to have to ask you.

Ever,

G.B.E.[296]

There is bathos in what Murry wrote in his diary on receiving this request on 8 September. Ominously he records:

Letter from Edwards this morning [asking for a cheque] which I sent: but I shan't do it again. I don't think his is a fair way of living.[297]

One assumes that Gerald had by now written his 3-page response to Lawrence Hyde's response to his review on the subject of 'Religion' for this appeared in the October issue of the

---

[296] Letter in my possession.

[297] Alexander Turnbull Library, Wellington, New Zealand, MS-Group-0411, p. 221.

*Adelphi.*[298] It seems that Murry paid up, but unbeknownst to Gerald this was probably the last time he did so. Like both Lawrence and Wyndham Lewis, Gerald was prone to bite the hands that fed him and on 22 November he was writing again, back in bibliodorous-cum-blood-brotherhood mode, with a quotation from Whitman's *Leaves of Grass* thrown in as if to justify the intensity of his polemic. Though somewhat opaque without the other half of the correspondence (Gerald seems to have destroyed all his letters, except the one from Lawrence), the onslaught seems to be directed against Murry's latest conversion from his own version of Christian, or at least religious, socialism to a personal brand of pre-Soviet Communism.

To his credit Murry had already written off Leninism (albeit with somewhat optimistic time-scale) as: 'so humanly disastrous that I take it upon myself to prophesy that Russian Communism will not survive for very long in its present form.'[299] In the wake of his second wife's death and the battering he was beginning to receive from his third he had, however, plunged into Marx's *Kapital.* Recalling the effect this had on him a few years after the event he wrote:

> I do not suppose that many men to-day, and certainly not many Christians, know the experience of being consumed even to tears by the reading of Das Kapital.[300]

With dry humour, at this point, Murry's biographer and former secretary, Frank Lea, comments: 'It does seem unlikely'. Murry wrote *The Necessity of Communism* in two weeks and on 9 November, the day he completed it, he wrote ecstatically to the ever-faithful Plowman:

> Ah, you don't know – yes, *you* do – how profoundly happy I am. The old impersonal act of faith in founding The Adelphi is justified. – all the bitter, bitter struggle justified. All the pangs – the awful rendings from Katherine, from Lawrence, from Violet, even from you – justified. The dead

---

[298] See below, p. 207.

[299] Lea, *Murry*, p. 190, citing *Adelphi*, September 1929?

[300] Lea, *Murry*, p. 190.

live. Blessed be the unutterable name of the Lord.[301]

He presumably wrote to Gerald in similar spirits, including at least an excerpt from the book. After what Gerald, along with most other admirers of Lawrence, already regarded as his 'destructive hagiography',[302] *Son of Woman* [Fig. 55], this latest phase in Murry's development (if not too positive a word), prompted another negative response:

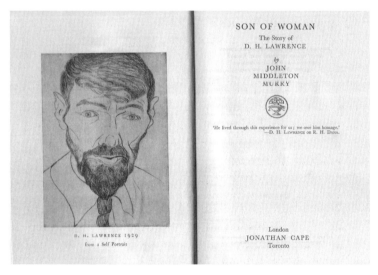

Fig. 55: Middleton Murry's *Son of Woman* (1931), with Lawrence's 1929 self-portrait.

My dear Murry,

Thanks for the book. And for your letter (many many

---

[301] *Ibid.*, pp. 193-94.

[302] This was Aldous Huxley's description, for which see Keith Sagar, *The Art of D.H. Lawrence* (Cambridge, 1966), p. 2. Huxley had briefly worked for Murry as assistant editor on the *Athenaeum*; he depicts him unflatteringly as Dennis Burlap in *Point Counter Point* (London, 1928) and calls him a 'slug' in his *Letters*, ed. Grover Smith (1969), p. 355, which is, however, not based on the original document; see *Waterfield's Catalogue 50* (1985), item 1106. When *Son of Woman* was published Murry received a post-card from America from a complete stranger with the message: 'Son of Woman, indeed! You son of a bitch!'; see the account by Richard Rees, *A Theory of my Time*, p. 59. Rees had in fact heavily edited the original manuscript which is now in the Alexander Turnbull Library in New Zealand.

thanks) and for the extract which I'm returning.

I have written to Max [Plowman] about you as follows: 'I can't tell you much except that your visit to him must have had an extraordinarily strong effect for he is now rushing helter-skelter into the arms of the Devil. That is not altogether bad (nor by any means unflattering to you) for he must have a pretty big god after him to flee netherwards as fast as that. So don't despair of him. Rather hope more than you have done for a very long time; hope and pray and hope again, for the Lord has put his mark on John and all the pig-washing in the world (even with nice clear communistic water) won't wash it out.'

And I believe that. Another false simplification you think. All right, doesn't matter. Call it crude nonsense and go your full circle — but you'll come back. Mind you, I don't want you to go. Never have – if for no other reason but that I'm lonely and because with me there's plenty room. But if you must go, go. Only don't imagine I will follow. I have never hoped you would lead <u>me</u> — would to God you could! 'If you tire, give me both burdens, and rest the chuff of your hand upon my hip, And in due time you shall repay the same service to me, For after we start we never lie by again —'[303] that is the only 'leadership' that can ever be between us. And 'if I won't come your way, you've no use for me at all' — is that it now? Don't be too sure. I may come your way; but it will be only to drag you back. I am as weak and as cowardly as you (or nearly) but I know where I belong – and where you belong: and it is the same place. 'It is not the voice of conscience,' you say: 'not the voice of God: simply the urge of life towards new forms.' But that's

---

[303] Whitman, 'Song of Myself', Part 46. That Wyndham Lewis is conscious of the importance of Whitman to the Lawrentians is confirmed by his inclusion in *Paleface* of a section entitled: 'Was Whitman the Father of the American Baby?', an amusing metaphor given that Whitman may never have had sex (*Enemy 3*, pp. 25-26). For Whitman's status as the 'Center of the American Canon', see Harold Bloom, *The Western Canon* (London, 1994), chapter 11; *cf.* since, his introduction to the Penguin edition of the 1855 *Leaves of Grass* (2005), in which he describes Whitman as 'the greatest artist his nation has brought forth … [whose] peers are Milton, Bach, Michelangelo, baroque masters of sublimity.'

a lie. The urge of life is <u>not</u> towards new forms – it only passes them by as it goes.[304] You 'pledge the whole of your life upon your <u>word</u>', you say. Fool! You can't. God won't let you. It is His Word only you can pledge your life upon – and His Word have never been spoken. – 'You are <u>gone</u>', you say: 'you <u>are</u> not'. Liar again. You are <u>trying</u> to go; you are giving yourself to a Church (and shouting about it): but you won't lose yourself - you have yourself left on your hands; the Church won't be big enough to take you — again only God can do that. G.B.E.[305]

## 13: LITTLE STRANGERS

On 25 November 1931, Gerald wrote to Jack Collis from 'The Brackens', Raymond's Hill,  fulsomely apologising for not having replied to his last, which may have been requesting repayment of a loan, had clearly been of a serious nature and included the announcement of the birth of his daughter: 'I'd like to come and make her acquaintance. I don't know when I'll be in London, but perhaps around Christmas'.[306] Gerald explains that his meagre salary doesn't cover his normal expenses and that he is having to ask Plowman for some help so he can't loan (or repay?) the £20 requested. Meanwhile, he has to give 'a lecture practically every night (and each one to be separately

---

[304] Gerald sounds commendably like Eric Voegelin here when he attacks twentieth-century Gnosticism and *The Political Religions*, the latter not published until 1938. Voegelin might not have approved of the religious terminology though he felt free to talk of the urge for 'religious renewal' of this period as 'satanic'; see *The Collected Works of Eric Voegelin*, vol. 5 (Columbia and London, 2000), p. 6. For his definitions of Gnosticism, beginning with dissatisfaction with one's situation and ending with 'readiness to come forward as a prophet who will proclaim his knowledge about the salvation of mankind' (fitting Lawrence better than Gerald), see *ibid.*, pp. 297-98. For a more complete account of Gnosticism as profoundly negative, see Keith Jacka, *To be a Briton* (forthcoming).

[305] Letter dated 'Nov. 22nd' in my possession.

[306] Collis had two daughters, Elizabeth and Gabrielle, by his wife Eirene, but was at a low ebb and increasingly living apart from his family; see Ingrams, *Collis*, pp. 64-68. In 1932 he went to live in a cottage near Sevenoaks which his father bought for him. During the war the family went to America while he remained behind working on the farms about which he was to at last write with success.

prepared), I have other classes to organise and oversee and official letters to write (try to imagine me at it!).'

There is then a long Lawrentian response to Collis's presumably conditional proposal of renewed friendship:

> it is so desirable - and so difficult... I suppose I believe in friendship more than ever I did – perhaps, even, I am more capable of it. But between you and me (if it is ever to be) it means much pain and much patience...

Prior to concluding 'always, and as always, G.B', Gerald informs Collis that he has:

> several friends to see from time to time as well as a full and complicated household (Kathleen and Solomon and Adam and Dorcas - plus a little Stranger due at any time).[307]

The latter was a reference to the child that Kathleen was expecting by his friend Solomon Simon, who had performed in the postponed play with them at Dartington a year earlier and had presumably been living in a *ménage à trois* since at least that time. David Simon Edwards was born on 11 December.[308] It was clearly this situation that inspired the ultimately traumatic consequences in *The Book of Ebenezer Le Page* of Raymond's wife, Christine Mahy, conceiving a son with *his* best friend (and first cousin) Horace. Gerald and Kathleen named their own son Adam; the legitimate son that Raymond conceived with Christine is named 'Abel' in the novel, whereas (apparently maintaining the autobiographical undercurrent) *their* 'little stranger' was named Gideon.[309] Since it forms such a central part

---

[307] Photocopy of letter kindly loaned to me by Richard Ingrams.

[308] Birth certificate, dated 23 January 1932, General Register Office, England and Wales births, Axminster, vol. 5b, p. 9. It is worth remarking that Gerald did not attest to being the father of David (the section allocated to the father's name being left blank) but allowed his name to be used three years later when Kathleen gave birth to John; see below, p. 163.

[309] According to a telephone conversation I had with him on 8 March 2010, kindly prompted by his younger half-brother, John, to both of whom I am very grateful, his father was a Russian Jewish philosopher. David himself was living in Ross-on-Wye (where John was mayor), having returned from America. According to Wilfrid Burgess, who was one of her admirers, there was a real Christine Mahy, who lived at *The Figtree* and sang solo at the Wesleyan Methodist Chapel in St Peter Port. In his September 1981 letter to me Burgess wrote that she married

of the novel and I have discovered such poignant (and, I believe, mutually illuminating) parallels between the novel and Gerald's life, I quote here Ebenezer's account of the birth of Horace's son by Christine. To the extent that Gerald was Raymond it surely places him in the most positive light we encounter, one indeed which tempts me to re-write this book in just the way I believe Gerald re-wrote his on more than one occasion:

> She had a bad time having Gideon, and was in bed yet when I went. Raymond told me he and Horace sat together by the fire downstairs the whole day, listening to her screams upstairs in the bedroom. He said he felt very close to Horace that day. They both suffered with her; but there was nothing they could do. Gwen fetched the doctor. She wanted to get them a meal, but they couldn't eat. It wasn't until nine o'clock at night it was over. When Nurse Wright came down with the doctor and said Raymond could go and see his wife and child, Raymond pushed Horace in front of him to go first up the stairs. Christine was sitting up in bed giving Gideon his first feed. Raymond said she was very pale, but had never looked more beautiful. 'Like a spirit,' he said. She didn't look at Horace, but held out the baby for Raymond to see. 'Another for your tribe,' she said. Raymond didn't know what she meant.
>
> I don't know neither. I have often wondered if, perhaps in her heart of hearts, Christine did love Raymond; or, at least, Raymond as he was the night he preached at Birdo Mission. It may be she was jealous of Horace, and wanted to get rid of him by hook or by crook. If so, I am all wrong; and Christine is greatly to be pitied. I can only say again I don't know; for women as they are to themselves are a mystery to me. I do know she couldn't bear to have Horace in the house once Gideon was born. The doctor said it might affect her mind, if she wasn't given way to; and Raymond had to ask Horace not to show himself. Raymond then devoted himself to looking after Christine and the baby. It was him gave Gideon his bath every day. He said he liked doing it. Gideon was Horace's flesh and blood. I said, 'Why

---

Louis Ogier, 'who was a friend of my brother. Both of them are long deceased'.

on earth didn't you and Christine join up again then, and bring him up as your own?' He just shook his head. 'Why not? Why not?' I said. I couldn't understand it. Liza had been with other men and had children by other men; but it hadn't made any difference to my feeling for Liza. He said:

'Humpty Dumpty sat on a wall,
 Humpty Dumpty had a great fall.
 All the King's horses and all the King's men
 Couldn't put Humpty Dumpty together again.'[310]

Even in this aspect of his personal life and morality Gerald may have taken inspiration from Lawrence who tolerated (if not, like her former lover, Otto Gross, actively encouraged) his wife's infidelities. Though this manifested itself even before his marriage, Lawrence would fly into a fury when Frieda expressed the wish to see her children, his antagonism due in part perhaps to his wanting children of his own.[311]

Those who have lived out such libertarian ideals since the Romantic period include the Hamiltons' *ménage à trois* with Lord Nelson, William Morris's with his wife Jane and Rossetti,[312] Nietzsche's (if only) with Paul Rée and Lou Salomé [Fig. 45] and Laban's with Maja Lederer and Suzanne Perrottet.[313]

---

[310] *Cf.* Olivia Chaney, 'The King's Horses', *The Longest River* (Nonesuch Records, 2015). 'All the King's horses,/ And all the King's men,/ Could not put my heart / Back together again'.

[311] Maddox, *Lawrence*, pp. 136-37. For his revealing letter to Frieda's sister, Else, who thought Frieda should indeed return to her children, see Worthen, *Lawrence*, p. 444. Lawrence's argument that the children would not benefit from her sacrifice, on the basis that 'the worst of sacrifice is that we have to pay back' is also relevant to Gerald's attitude to his children; *cf.* Strindberg's jealous attitude to his own child by another Frida, as told by Collis in *Marriage and Genius*, p. 106.

[312] Fiona MacCarthy, *William Morris: A Life for Our Time* (London, 1994), pp. 180-81.

[313] For more libertarian threesome continuities among the upper classes, see Richard Davenport-Hines, *Ettie: The Intimate Life And Dauntless Spirit Of Lady Desborough* (London, 2008). Bernard Shaw fell in love with William Morris's daughter, May, and when she married Henry Halliday Sparling, he attempted to maintain his 'mystical betrothal' to her. For the *ménage à* (at least) *trois* between Laban, Lederman and Perrottet, see *ODNB* and Dörr, *Laban*. Better-known British *ménages* include those associated with Augustus John, Henry Lamb,

When Gilbert Cannan's relationship with Mary Barrie was revealed to her celebrated husband by a spiteful gardener, Cannan proposed that the two men should share her, but partly because of predictable scandal and because he was already developing his admittedly a-sexual relationship with Sylvia Llewelyn-Davies, mother of the 'Lost Boys', Barrie opted for divorce.[314] Cannan and Mary then married and went on to host bohemian parties attended by the Lawrences and Murrys at his windmill in Cholesbury. Lawrence criticised Murry's complaisance for allowing his wife Katherine Mansfield to kiss Mark Gertler at a particularly drunken Christmas party there in 1914.[315] Cannan's marriage broke up in 1918 due to his affair with the younger and even more beautiful Gwen Wilson but the latter then married the millionaire Henry Mond, whilst he was away in America. Taking pity on him, however, the Monds had Cannan moved into the happy couple's house in Smith Square and flaunted their *ménage* with a specially commissioned relief sculpture of a naked couple by Charles Sergeant Jagger entitled *Scandal*. The arrangement did not last however and Cannan had a nervous breakdown from which he never recovered, dying thirty years later in Holloway Sanatorium.[316]

If Gerald's *ménage* was not *à quatre* towards the end of their marriage it may at least have been *à trois* for Kathleen Edwards

---

Ottoline Morrell, Vanessa Bell, Duncan Grant and several other Bloomsberries. The life (and death) of Lawrence's polyamorous publisher, Harry Crosby, perhaps best epitomises the American 'Lost Generation'. Relevant to the theme of *Mutterrecht* and his *White Goddess*, Robert Graves's marriage to Nancy Nicholson did not long survive his love for (and their cohabitation with) Laura Riding, whose attempted suicide ended what had become a *ménage à quatre* which included the Irish poet Geoffrey Phibbs; see volume 2 of Richard Perceval Graves's biography of *Robert Graves: The Years with Laura Riding: 1926-1940* (London, 1990), which the aged Riding reviewed very negatively.

[314] Farr, *Gilbert Cannan*, p. 161.

[315] Lea, *Murry*, p. 42 and Sydney Kaplan, *Circulating Genius*, p. 22. Gertler contributed articles to the *Adelphi*; e.g. on Michelangelo in July 1923. He and the Cannans were also guests at the famous Café Royal banquet (*cf.* p. 11).

[316] According to a letter from Frieda Lawrence from Cornwall dating from February 1917: 'Gilbert Cannan has had a breakdown'; then: 'He is in a Hampstead nursing home – I respect him for it – he is so poor too.' Lawrence, *Letters*, VIII, p. 20; *cf.* Eric Turner, 'Scandal', *Apollo* (October 2009), pp. 50-56.

went on to conceive a child with a third man, Gordon Cruickshank, the Communist co-editor of *Seven* who went on to work for the BBC.[317] Sometime during this period the growing family may have relocated nearer London. Paraphrasing Potter, his biographer writes that he 'took G.B. home to no. 36 for a bath because there was no bath in the bungalow on the edge of a wood near Eltham where G.B. lives with a wife and five [*sic*] children who wore no shoes.' Although this clearly conflates two different periods in Gerald's life it carries the memory of him still living with Kathleen with, presumably, at least the four of her known children.[318]

If Potter preferred the effect of five to four children here, Collis may have misremembered the date at which the family broke up for it was on 27 June 1935 at the Holborn Register Office that John Enoch Edwards was recorded as having been born to Kathleen Maude Edwards, *née* Smith, address and, it seems incorrectly, Gerald Basil Edwards - 'Lecturer in English Literature' - the previous 4 May.[319] As the 'informant' registering the baby, Kathleen gives both her current residence and the place of birth as 8 Little Bath Street (Clerkenwell). Not least due to the strain of such multiple relationships and their consequences, Gerald and Kathleen parted (if they had not already done so) and the children were more or less handed over to the Elmhirsts at Dartington. Collis's later recollection of his

---

[317] Something of an expert on Poland and 'an elusive figure in the historiographies of British communism and literary culture', according to Christopher Hilliard, *'To Exercise our Talents', The Democratization of Writing in Britain* (Boston, 2006), pp. 169. During the war he was appointed by Humphrey Swingler to edit the populist *Seven* magazine (apparently using Mass Observation methods) and co-authored at least one article with Philip O'Connor, 'Readers, you are our Writers', *Seven 2* (March 1941), p. 25.

[318] Jenkins, *Potter*, p. 62; *cf.* Potter, unpublished autobiography, vol. II, p. 177. No. 36 Old Park Avenue, Balham, was Potter's parental home, where he was born and continued to be based until his marriage in 1927. By the time Gerald and Kathleen had four (rather than five) children, Potter was married to Mary, the painter, and was living in Chiswick with two children of their own.

[319] Civil Births Register, Holborn 1935, General Register Office, 5640612-1. John was educated at Wennington School in Yorkshire and became a *Financial Times* journalist. He died in 2014, see www.ft.com/cms/s/0/519b42d6-1b03-11e4-b649-00144feabdc0.html#axzz3ZLHiAmwq.

'genius friend' was that:

> By 1933 the marriage had come to an end. And Alice [*i.e.* Kathleen] had such a way with her that I think she always managed to get rich people to take over the children.[320]

Without mentioning Gerald by name, in his book on *The Elmhirsts of Dartington*, Michael Young specifies that it was he who abandoned the marriage:

> Dorothy [Elmhirst] was … liable to be more solicitous about other people's children than her own… Dorcas's mother had been abandoned by her husband and Dorcas was befriended by Dorothy.[321]

In the context of their lives to date, the Elmhirsts' 1,200 acre Devonshire estate was merely the latest Utopian community that Gerald and Kathleen had connected with. In terms of having their children educated there they were ahead of some of the most distinguished, for Dartington's artistic and experimental reputation soon attracted parents such as Bertrand and Dora Russell (after their separation),

Fig. 56: The Elmhirsts' children with Dorcas Edwards (second from left), Adirondacks, New York, 1939 (Dartington Hall Trust).

Aldous Huxley and Ernst Freud (Sigmund's son, who sent his three sons, Lucian, Clement and Stephan there).[322] Ben Nicholson and Barbara Hepworth later sent their triplets there.

---

[320] Collis, 'Memories of a Genius Friend', p. 22. This echoes what he had already written in his unpublished short story, *The Realist*, which was about Gerald and Kathleen. He tells how 'Alice' had two children by 'Jack' (Gerald), Adam and Eve. 'She got rich women to adopt them eventually.'

[321] Young, *Elmhirsts*, p. 120. Potter also suggests that it was Gerald who left. In his unpublished fictionalised account of their marriage, *The Realist*, however, Collis writes that 'He disappeared from London when she left him'.

[322] Ernst enrolled his sons in Dartington even before migrating from Berlin.

Though sponsored by the Elmhirsts, Adam was nevertheless separated from his younger sister and fostered by a family in Totnes until the age of seven. When the family was obliged to move away he was all but legally adopted (Kathleen continued to oppose full adoption) by John and Peggy Wales, who were on the staff at Dartington School.[323] The three-year-old Dorcas had meanwhile been placed in the Elmhirst nursery and subsequently travelled with the family to America where she remained throughout the war [Fig. 56]. Both children remained connected to the Dartington Estate for the rest of their lives, giving me a warm welcome at Adam's cottage when I tracked them down and photographed them there in early 1995 [Fig. 57].

Fig. 57: *Dorcas and Adam Edwards*, outside Adam's cottage on the Dartington Estate, 26 February 1995 (photo: the author).

The only indication I have found of a feeling of fatherly guilt on Gerald's part is in one of the last of his surviving letters to Murry, dated simply 'Nov. 23rd' but presumably post-1931. As well as its references to his rejection of his children, the retrospective way this critiques Murry's *Son of Woman: The Story of D.H. Lawrence*, which was published in 1931, suggests such a

---

[323] John and Peggy Wales, were respectively the history teacher and matron at Dartington, and had three daughters of their own, with whom Adam was brought up.

dating. Gerald also criticises Murry's *Necessity of Communism*, which was published the following year, though it had appeared in instalments in *The Adelphi*. 'Yes, yes: you're quite right – and quite wrong,' he begins, without any other form of address, apparently responding to criticisms prompted by Gerald's harsher ones. In the process it hints at another love interest:

> The Lord *is* a name for my Self, but not for myself – and my Self is not separate from yours. And, of course, I have to repent (and am repenting) and one of the deeds I most repent is that of ever having stood against my children or closed my heart to them: if I did that in the name of the Lord then I did indeed take the name of the Lord in vain. But whether or not I may have done it in His name, in my heart I knew I did not do it with His blessing; rather did I do it from fear of losing a human love because I would not trust in a divine.[324] As for Lawrence, I do see him as a sign – as a warning and a promise in the heavens: himself a denier and a heretic, the Lord in him, stronger than his blasphemies, blazed the trail of the Morning Star.

> But you will only recognise a Lord who uses you totally; a Lord who is completely you. And yet you see as comic my accusing you of a terrible and tragic conceit. But are you not postponing a recognition of the Lord until either He is very small or you are very big? And if that isn't correct, what is? 'Haughty towards God, humble towards man' When the Lord does completely use you, then you will be a divine man on earth, and I, for one, will not say you cannot lead me. In the meantime you (like me) must recognise the Lord in the midst of the circumambient chaos of our natures, serve Him to the utmost till by our striving we earn our Divine stature. We are priests (you and I): not Lords of Men...

Given how nearly Murry literally became a priest in the later 1930s, Gerald's role in (at least) Murry's mental life should perhaps be better acknowledged. If he had not been so

---

[324] Lawrence cited similar justifications for encouraging Frieda to abandon her children.

dismissive of his past and (presumably) destroyed Murry's letters, we might have had a better sense of their friendship, which by this time resembled Murry's with Lawrence himself. Thus Gerald continues in that strange, 'bibliodrous' tone, which though not unique to him in this circle he nevertheless indulged in more thoroughgoingly than most. He concludes with a new style of criticism, apparently of Murry's combined project of creating the communal Adelphi Centre (on his return from America in March 1935) and embarking on a new relationship with Nehale.[325] If it was the latter, which indeed infuriated Murry's already dangerously explosive third wife, to whom Gerald was referring, then he was not far wrong. Failing to persuade his wife, Betty, to say prayers she abused him as a fool for not having let her go when she had been pregnant:

> I had all I wanted – your baby. I should have been happy. Why did you come after me?... You're a fool – a fool. Don't you know that women are all bitches – all of them?[326]

Murry concludes this reported speech in his journal with the ominous sentence: 'A doom closed down on my heart'. The episode led to Murry's abandonment of his plans for the priesthood and, eventually, in 1939 a nervous breakdown during which he lost the last traces of love (and lust) he had felt for Betty. He eventually found the love of his life in the more stable Mary Gamble and settled down to domestic bliss, marrying her four weeks after the death of Betty in February 1954.[327] He died as happily in fact as Ebenezer does in fiction, attended by doting fourth wife and daughters.[328] His late

---

[325] Even Lea is somewhat cryptic about her; see his *Murry*, pp. 234-36; *cf.* Katherine Murry, *Beloved Quixote,* pp. 139-47.

[326] Lea, *Murry*, p. 259.

[327] This was even shorter post-mortal pause than he had allowed after his previous wife's death in the spring of 1930.

[328] *Ibid.*, 352-3; *cf.* his son, John Middleton Murry junior's two memoirs, which despite experiencing more difficulties with his father than had his sister, Katherine, likewise ends on an utterly devoted note; see *One Hand Clapping: a Memoir of Childhood* and *Shadows on the Grass* (London, 1975 and 1977 respectively). Murry junior achieved a happy marriage and a successful career as an author under several names other than his own, *i.e.*: John Le Maistre (a book review in a 1945 *Adelphi*), Colin Murry, Colin Middleton Murry and Richard Cowper. Under the latter name he published several 'highly intelligent

correspondence with Frieda confirmed this as that she too had found a 'fulfilment' (with Ravagli) that Lawrence himself never experienced.[329] Murry's biographer remembers that 'his gratification was boundless' when soon after their last meeting in November 1956, he heard that the 68-year-old T.S. Eliot, after similarly fraught relations with the opposite sex, had found equivalent happiness with the 31-year-old Valerie, whom he married in January 1957.[330]

In the long term Murry had proved wiser than Eliot had anticipated when in 1924 he had responded to this 'apostle of suburban free thought' (as he called Murry elsewhere) for sounding far too secularly optimistic:

> But do you really consider it a good sign that the 'time of stony places is over'? If so, you are luckier than the Saviour, who found things pretty stony to the last – and would, I believe, have continued to find them so, had he not been removed at an age less ripe than yours or mine. I do not suppose that I share any other characteristic of the Founder of Christianity, but at least I have nothing but stony places to look forward to. This isolates me, of course, from those who can pass in and out of stony places with practised ease.

> Yours ever, Tom.[331]

Returning to Gerald's early-1930s letter, written in a more imperious tone than Eliot's, yet addressed to the man who was

---

science fiction novels', sharing with his father, who had been inspired in this by both Gerald and Plowman, an enthusiasm for William Blake whom he quotes in his *Recollections of a Ghost* (London, 1960), p. 25; see John Clute, 'Richard Cowper', *Science Fiction Writers*, ed. R. Bleiler, 2nd ed (New York, 1999), pp. 221–8, and same author's *ODNB* entry.

[329] Rees, *A Theory of my Time*, pp. 47-48.

[330] Though by mid-career they had become intellectual rivals, they remained on friendly terms to the end. In 1959 Eliot wrote a foreword to Constable's edition of Murry's *Katherine Mansfield and other Literary Studies*.

[331] *Letters of T.S. Eliot*, II, p. 554; 15 December 1924, referencing the agony of stony places that features in his 1922 *Wasteland*. Elsewhere, however, Eliot praises Murry's originality; Griffin, *Murry*, p.21. When Murry died Eliot wrote to Mary that a 'very warm affection existed between us'; *Letters of T.S. Eliot*, III, p. 901. Murry had offered Eliot the assistant editorship soon after becoming editor of the *Athenaeum* in 1919 though the latter was unable to accept at the time.

still his mentor and one whom most in his position would have assiduously cultivated, he elaborates prophetically on one of Lawrence's more extreme proposals:

> ... this last 'move' of yours is not due to metaphysical conviction but to physical obsession.[332] I know a very great deal about physical obsessions - and their metaphysical concomitants. And it is in a concession you are making to your sexuality (a spiritual concession, not necessarily a moral one) that is born your conviction of the Necessity of Communism. There have been times (many times) when I have made just such concessions, and my resulting metaphysical convictions (though only temporary - and false) were perilously near yours. It strikes me as significant that it is the last paragraph of my letter you did not answer... I said that you (like me) must be a priest in marriage – or out of it. Do you know what that means? It does not necessarily mean the end of generation - though it may be for this man or that. It is what Lawrence was always feeling towards (though Frieda stopped him at it) and what you were never very clear about in your Son of Woman, and what (I now suspect) you are only too ready to forget altogether. So, for a while, ponder that.

> I'd like to write a lot more to you, but I have a lecture to prepare for this evening and a visitor this afternoon. So, good-bye for the present.

Yours always,

G.B.E.

At this stage Murry did not wish to be diverted from the path down which he was being led and no doubt whilst recovering from his breakdown he didn't relish being told he had been taking the wrong one all along. In any case, apart from a single letter sent by Gerald in 1947 and kept but perhaps not responded to by Murry, what Gerald articulated in this epic epistle seems to have brought their correspondence and

---

[332] This is presumably a reference to Murry's decision to marry Betty Cockbayne, in May 1931, an event which must have reminded Gerald of his father's decision to marry his, also third, wife four years earlier.

friendship to an end.[333]

Stephen Potter, meanwhile, concluded his retrospective account of his friendship with, and admiration for, Gerald with the words:

> And now – where is he, this most wonderful man? Whenever I hear that opening line of 'What's become of Waring?' and read that wonderful poem, I think of G.B.[334] If genius is in the eye of the beholder, anyhow, we could not have been wrong about our G.B., with his splendid candor and warmth.[335]

After a positive account of Murry as one who wrote wonderfully on Keats,[336] edited what he thought the better of those rival journals *The Adelphi* and *The Criterion* and 'knew and admired G.B. and liked Jack [Collis]', Potter returns to the subject of Gerald, beginning with what sounds like class distinction but may in fact have more to do with Gerald's provincial, *i.e.*, island, background:

> G.B. Fading ... fading.
>
> All was not always well between G.B., Jack and me. Jack and I were out of such a different hat, educationally. Games-school-Oxford friends with comfortable houses –

---

[333] Though similarly incontinent in style and regarded as authentic by those who knew him well, by comparison with Gerald's more or less consistent philosophy of life, Murry's could hardly have been less stable or self-knowing. Gerald seems to have been one of the few who knew him very well but was willing to break with him, though even he attempted a reconciliation after the war.

[334] As this was written after 1939 it is likely that Potter's citation of 'What's become of Waring' may have been prompted by Anthony Powell's novel, published in that year though its title is borrowed from Robert Browning's poem: 'Waring'. Both poem and novel might have inspired thoughts of Gerald, but the former was indeed especially appropriate with its lines: 'He was prouder than the devil: / How he must have cursed our revel! / Ay and many other meetings, / Indoor visits, outdoor greetings, / As up and down he paced this London, / With no work done, but great works undone.'

[335] Potter, unpublished autobiography, vol. II, p. 190. Even if neither made great efforts to seek him out it is a sign of the extent to which Gerald wilfully disappeared that Potter and Collis so completely lost touch with him.

[336] Murry's *Keats and Shakespeare*, was first published by Oxford University Press in 1925 and remained in print until the late 1960s.

G.B. had nothing of these.[337] Sometimes we tended to be a little clannishly relieved when G.B. had gone. G.B. was lonely – he didn't have bushels of acquaintances, as we did: in fact very few. I used to imagine that he played off Jack against me and vice versa.

'I sometime wonder whether Jack's understanding of Blake isn't really in the head… There is something in Jack which holds back.' We used to begin to make up G.B. isms. He will talk to Jack, of 'Stephen's little boy immaturity, really wanting me to tidy things up for him mentally, like a nice safe family aunt.' Jack and I might parody G.B. to each other, to prove our independence of him.

About this time G.B. began pushing us in a new direction. [338] Once again – as so often – it was towards an author for whom I had long decided to have a natural distaste: Walt Whitman. Woolly … universal love … tiresome 'freedom' of literary form [Fig. 58].

Fig. 58: *Walt Whitman and Harry Stafford* (photo: Augustus Morand, 1878) (Edward Carpenter Collection, Sheffield Library)

Then I was half-annoyed to find that G.B. was right. Once again I found the preconception had almost nothing to do with the reality. Knowing the great men, knowing Keats and Blake, and Lawrence too, made

---

[337] A poignant remark in view of the fact that as the only son of a quarry owner, Gerald should have inherited the now multi-million pound house he was brought up in.

[338] Potter is presumably referring back to the late 1920s here, before he left for Switzerland.

this new voice easily recognisable and comprehensible.

In fact I began to read Whitman with delighted enjoyment and growing affection for this extraordinary old eccentric and his huge draughts of sanity. This time, I wanted to discover him for myself. Who *was* G.B. anyway? I had the feeling that G.B. would start being proprietary about Whitman, and interpret him for me.

Sure enough, he did, in a way. 'This should mean something very revealing to you... This is you, but not as you are at this moment ... don't get drawn into 'Drum-Taps:' there are only two poems which are really Whitman. He could be a bit bad – bad boy you know!'

'O.K. – OK. Thank you, G.B.'

Was it that I felt that G.B. was echoing the style of Lawrence – Lawrence being a critic? 'A bit bad' was very like D.H.L.

Whitman was so good at explaining himself. There was no obscurity, once you got the hang. I didn't want any more explaining.

Was it that my John the Baptist had performed his function – had shown me my Great Man and I didn't want him anymore? After all, we couldn't be perfectly easy with him. He wasn't ordinary enough.

Potter confesses that his chronology is confused at this point for his typescript autobiography suggests that the long West Country walk he now undertook was 'a turning point in the right direction' but he seems to be both escaping from the beauteous Slade student 'D' and therefore still not married (he married Mary in July 1927) as well as escaping from Gerald. The latter nonetheless contrives to meet him in a hotel in Chagford and then goes back to 'his friends in Dartington', which is likely to have been later than 1930. It also seems that Potter hadn't written his book on Lawrence yet, nor even, it seems, his 1929 novel *The Young Man*, which featured Gerald as a genius figure.[339] In any case, inasmuch as this account is at one with his

---

[339] 'So far I had done nothing. A few odd jobs. "<u>On paper</u> I have done nothing",

172

more or less valedictory thoughts on Gerald, it would seem most appropriate to continue quoting them here:

In fact I was concerned that I had recently been in love, and was wiping away a tear or two because it was all over. Like Jack at this moment, we were in particularly good heart, we said to ourselves, because we were falling out of love. Nothing derogatory in this to the charming and glorious and gracious lady who had taken pity on, or become irritated by, my virginity, and then after a few months gently dismissed me.

It was the freedom from G.B., not from this lady, which gave the extra zest to my walking. Henceforward I was going to choose my own reading. Among other things, I thought it would be a good idea to go back to my old friends, the early nineteenth-century poets. After all I was a literary lecturer by profession, and I would soon, if I wanted to get on, have to write a book of literary research. It was a long time since I had thought about commentaries. In my knapsack, besides a small Leaves of Grass, I carried Raleigh on Wordsworth and Garrod's little Coleridge selection…

This epic walk from Warwick, via Stratford, to St. Ives, took Potter via Chagford and a hotel in Haytor, Devon:

This I had fixed for my two comfortable extravagant nights at half time. Letters from home would be there, a new lot of maps, and my second pair of shoes. The stars were out now. Tomorrow would be peaceful and quiet round Hay Tor, where, 5 years before, I had such good walks with my sister Muriel. There would be a splendid bath before bed. It was irritating not to find the hotel at once. I was edgily tired.

They must have remembered me, in the Hotel Office. 'Mr. Potter?' somebody said. 'There's a friend of yours here. He's been waiting since six.'

A Devonshire friend? I hadn't got any.

O my God – I knew at once, before seeing him … there he was dressed in extraordinary breeches like a gamekeeper

---

I said to myself…' (p. 185).

in Jorrocks. I never did approve of his country clothes. It was G.B. He leapt up, ashine with welcome. He just stood and looked at me.

'I hoped you would come,' he said.

There follows an amusing account of their conversation, Potter being polite through gritted teeth:

'Well, this is marvellous,' I said, but do what I could, I felt as if starch was stiffening my features. 'Are you around here? 'No, I came to see you…. I rang your father… Have I done wrong?'

'Don't be so bloody silly.' I nearly said: but the awful old wave of conviction silenced me – the certain knowledge that G.B. was so much more direct and simple than myself, a better man.

'Completely not,' I said. 'Are you staying?'

'There is a room here – not such a grand one as yours I think.'

Continuing to suppress his irritation at having to engage in serious conversation instead of flopping in a bath and reading expected mail from home, Potter said 'something aimless about Whitman.'

But G.B. was quick as a woman to spot a mood – too quick, that is to say.

'I'm glad you still like him,' G.B. said. He looked rather sad. G.B. was much more generous than I was. He had come down to stop a drift apart, I suppose.

'It's those openings of Whitman poems which are so marvellous,' I said – a little late. I wanted to get back onto our old enthusiastic line'.

'Which one, for instance?'

'Give me the splendid silent sun with all his beams full-dazzling'.

I remembered reading the line of the Quantocks, when the four o'clock sun was getting fat and solid as it sank over Exmoor.

'Yes,' said G.B. 'It's a queer poem. I'm surprised you like

it. Near the end of the first part –what is it? Whitman says suddenly:

'O I see what I sought to escape, confronting, reverting my cries.'

'I see my own soul trampling down what I ask'd for.'[340]

And here, with this hilariously apposite quotation (a credit to both Gerald and Potter in this instance), I can't help anticipating Part II and my own much later experience of how brilliant Gerald still was at summoning from a vast range of sources the most appropriate lines of literature with which to illuminate the subject under discussion. Potter recalls Gerald asking:

'Don't you think that's extraordinary?'

'Yes,' I said – but I didn't, I hadn't read it, or hadn't noticed it. Was G.B. quoting it against me, in some way?

'I shouldn't have thought you were quite right for that poem, at this moment, Stephen. Or perhaps you are'.

'What the hell do you mean?'

Was I shouting? I was certainly angry...

We talked about general things, which always made G.B. get pretty rigid. I was angry with G.B. for being there – and dissatisfied with myself. Was I in some way too thin in personality for such a man - too fond of side-tracking into something to laugh at or be 'interested' in – concentration too wavering? I read the sun poem that night, and G.B. was partly right – Whitman was saying something important and I hadn't fully realised it.

Next morning G.B. went on to see his friends at Dartington. I saw him off at the station. He was a good man – a good man. I knew I wasn't quite up to him – and I guessed, rightly, that I wouldn't see him quite so much. On the platform, he looked small and rather stiff, as if he were disappearing into the distance. After my long walk was over, I wouldn't have minded seeing him again.[341]

---

[340] *Leaves of Grass*, 130 ('Give me the splendid, silent sun'); actually: 'I see my own soul trampling down what *it* ask'd for'.

[341] Potter, unpublished autobiography, vol. II, p. 192.

# 14: BOLTON OBSERVED

It is clear from a subsequent section of Potter's unpublished memoir that he did in fact see Gerald again before their pre-war parting of ways and from Collis's writings after the death of both men that they met again after the war. In fact Potter must have seen him relatively soon after the meeting at Haytor for Potter recalls Gerald commenting on the draft of his book on D.H. Lawrence which he began writing, as Gerald had done but never finished, when Lawrence was still alive, and published within months of his death in early 1930. Recalling his anxiety about publishing such a book when 'there were a hundred vocal and literate people who knew Lawrence, some very closely', Potter waxed indignant that they hadn't written the book themselves:

> *No-one – no-one* had stood up for him enough to do a book on him. Jack [Collis] seemed quite to like what he had read of my chapters, but what about, say, G.B. as a representative of the great mass of converts?[342] My friendship with G.B. was at the slow fade; I showed him the manuscript, but was cool.
>
> 'It's well written, of course'.
>
> That sounded bad.
>
> 'But your word – 'the God quality'. You know, Stephen, there's no God *quality*.'
>
> He was looking hard at me, or rather straight through my neck, it seemed to me. As if he were trying, through my jugulars, to read the laundry mark at the back of my collar.
>
> 'And there's nothing of Lawrence's love for things', He dwelt on the word 'love'. 'It made me feel miserable.'
>
> It made me feel miserable too. I wanted to answer, but couldn't get the words right. Was G.B. out-psychologising me? Or just speaking the plain truth? Or still feeling anti-because I had been anti him? It was not in me to have a

---

[342] This question, albeit rhetorical, raises the possibility that Gerald had not made it as clear to Potter as he might have done that Cape had commissioned such a book from him.

chapter heading 'Love'. When you're writing about sharpness you don't describe the edge of a razor. When you're writing about light you don't describe the centre of the sun's disk; because there's nothing to describe. I always won arguments when they were between me and myself.[343]

According to Collis, despite Gerald's excoriating review of his Lawrence book in the *Adelphi*, Potter saw him again in the 1950s. 'The war came and scattered us', Collis wrote in his somewhat self-exculpatory *Spectator* review-cum-memoir:

> In the late Fifties he got in touch with Stephen Potter. Stephen returned from the meeting with a glowing account of how GB was just as marvellous as ever, 'a supreme mind'. But he had been given no MS. Edwards had not yet found his frame...[344]

Gerald's failure to produce the great manuscripts his friends had anticipated seems to have been the primary factor in neither Potter nor Collis following up this meeting by renewing their acquaintance. They could tolerate the patronising style of an unrecognised genius en route to becoming a celebrated one but without the latter combination this style, complete with the constant appeals for charity, must have grated. Murry, Plowman and Rees likewise lost touch, the scattering of this not quite uniformly neo-Romantic group indeed preceding the war. Potter moved most obviously in a different, more worldly and media-friendly direction. He published three books in three years (two on Coleridge) between 1933-5 and then in 1937, with Cape's, *The Muse in Chains: A Study in Education*, which in terms of its critical theme, as distinct from its charmingly facetious style, could still have been influenced by Gerald. In the same year, however, he became a member of the Savile Club and secured a job at the BBC, a move out of both academe and more serious artistic endeavour that his son, Julian, considered 'in one way a defeat.' By the late 1950s, when Gerald and he met again, Potter had become a celebrity, had divorced and remarried and his beautiful 'Red House' in Aldeburgh (now a museum) had

---

[343] Potter, unpublished autobiography, vol. II, p. 192.

[344] Collis, 'Memories of a Genius Friend', p. 21.

been acquired by Benjamin Britten and Peter Pears.[345]

While Potter's fortunes peaked perhaps too early (and his One-up- and Games-manship perhaps too easily extended), Gerald's literary career declined as prematurely as his marriage. Whether through his Toynbee Hall, Dartington, WEA or theatrical connections, perhaps even via his enthusiasm for Whitman whose legacy was cherished in this Lancastrian town, in 1938 he moved to Bolton and found a job with the Corporation creating a drama school and producing plays, and subsidised accommodation with Tom Harrisson's Mass Observation project, based at 85 Davenport Street [Fig. 59].[346]

Fig. 59: *Planning Observations at 85 Davenport Street, Bolton* (Left to Right: Walter Hood, Tom Harrisson, John Sommerfield, unidentified man) (photo: Humphrey Spender, April 1938) (Bolton City Council).

---

[345] See Julian Potter's introduction to *Stephen Potter at the BBC,* Jason Shaw's entry in the *Encyclopedia of British Humorists: Geoffrey Chaucer to John Cleese,* ed. Steven H. Gale, II (1996) and the *ODNB.* Julian Potter was fully aware of Gerald's powerful influence on his father, commenting on it in his correspondence with me, for which I am very grateful.

[346] Though Whitman never travelled to Britain, two Bolton admirers, local doctor John Johnston and draughtsman J.W. Wallace, visited him in America and corresponded with him for the rest of his life, launching a Fellowship which included Edward Carpenter, who had known Whitman more intimately; see

Tom Harrisson (1911-76) was a widely-travelled anthropologist who, having studied the cannibals of Melanesia now wished to compare them with the natives of Bolton, or 'Worktown' as he called it.[347] After studying the locals for a few months, Harrisson met fellow Cambridge graduate and temporarily Communist poet, Charles Madge (1912-96), who had obtained a job on the *Daily Mirror* partly thanks to T.S. Eliot. In 1937 Eliot had Faber publish Madge's first book of poems, *The Disappearing Castle*.[348] When his 1938 marriage to fellow poet, Kathleen Raine, began to fail and he transferred his affections to Inez Spender, Madge swapped with Harrisson and moved from his Blackheath

---

www.boltonmuseums.org.uk/archives/walt-whitman-collection (accessed November 2014) and Michael Robertson, *Worshipping Walt: The Whitman Disciples* (Princeton, 2009). Given Potter's association with Harrisson, dating from at least as early as 1939, it is possible that Gerald's part-time employment by Harrisson and Madge was the result of his friendship with Potter though one might perhaps have expected the latter to mention this in his unpublished memoir had this been the case; see *Potter at the BBC*, *passim*. Davenport Street was a Victorian terrace in the centre of the town. The street still exists but the terrace was demolished and redeveloped in the 1980s. Stephen Spender's fellow bisexual brother, Humphrey photographed the house, its inhabitants and surroundings in this period. In the same year, 1939, Stephen Spender's promiscuous wife, Inez Pearn, finally ran off with Madge (see Thomas's diary for 4 July, recording their being 'up for the weekend'), having been painted the previous year by William Coldstream, whose ex-wife later married the Spenders' other brother, Michael. The latter was killed in an air crash shortly before the end of the war; Stephen Spender, *Journals 1939-1983*, ed. John Goldsmith (London, 1985), p. 57.

[347] *ODNB* and Peter Swain, introduction, *Adam Matthew Digital Mass Observation Online project*, whom I thank for access. In Bolton 'he made an asset of his chief handicap as an anthropologist: his lack of foreign languages. (Malay, his best foreign language, he never spoke beyond the bazaar level)' (*ODNB*)

[348] *ODNB*. Together with Humphrey Jennings, Harrisson and Madge solicited more than a thousand volunteers to keep diaries and describe their personal histories, publishing a summary as *Britain by Mass Observation* in 1939. Falling out with Harrisson in 1940, Madge went to work for Maynard Keynes and became a friend and collaborator of Michael Young, historian of Dartington (see above, p. 136). After the war Harrisson left Britain to take up a post as the Curator of the Sarawak museum and the organisation became Mass Observation Ltd, a Market Research company. Meanwhile, in 1939 Jennings made the film *Spare Time*, surely in part inspired by the Mass Observation project (pace the *ODNB*; *cf.* p.181 below). Both Harrisson and Jennings died accidental deaths; the former in a road-accident in Thailand and Jennings falling off a cliff on Poros in Greece; *ODNB* and Kevin Jackson, *Humphrey Jennings* (London, 2004), pp. 3-6.

Fig. 60: *Charles Madge* (1912-1996) and *Tom Harrisson* (1911-1976).
(photo: Howard Coster, 1938) (National Portrait Gallery).

headquarters to Bolton where he took on a 'very broad brief studying economic life ... which was conceived as trailing people round Woolworths and seeing how they behaved.'[349]

Back in London meanwhile Harrisson worked with Potter on a couple of BBC programmes, on at least one occasion, in 1939, using Mass Observation material in a programme on Southampton in 1941, and, subsequently, as radio critic for the *Observer*, praising Potter's feature on Compton Mackenzie and his sister Fay, recommending his *Muse in Chains* in the same review for features it owed to Gerald's influence.[350]

In the wake of Harrisson and Madge, members of Mass

---

[349] James Hinton, *The Mass Observers: A History, 1937-1949* (London, 2013), p. 115.

[350] J. Potter, *Stephen Potter at the BBC*, p. 121. D.H. Lawrence, who had met Mackenzie in 1914 and then again on Capri in 1919, infuriated him with his fictionalised account of *The Man who loved Islands*, the islands being Herm and Jethou, both of which Mackenzie acquired in 1920 but gave up on three years later, eventually moving to Barra in the Outer Hebrides. Mackenzie managed to have publication suppressed, at least in Britain, until after Lawrence's death; see David Shayer, 'Compton Mackenzie, D.H. Lawrence and Herm', *Transactions of La Société Guernesiaise*, XXII, ii (1987), pp. 327-332.

Observation, most of whom came to Bolton, included the painters Julian Trevelyan, Walter Hood, Michael Wickham, Graham Bell and William Coldstream - photographed in situ by Humphrey Spender - as well as the writers, John Sommerfield and Bill Naughton, and film-maker Humphrey Jennings.[351] Jennings and Madge maintained the artistic element in the enterprise as a whole, Kathleen Raine describing Mass Observation as 'less sociology than a kind of poetry, akin to Surrealism'.[352] There was support from the Communist Party and the likes of Marxist scientist, J.D. Bernal (father of Martin), J.B.S. Haldane, Julian Huxley, H.G. Wells and Nietzschean anthropologist Bronislaw Malinowski, who as his 'friend and teacher' wrote the introduction to Kenyatta's *Facing Mount Kenya* in 1938.[353] The latter was published by Secker and Warburg but the publisher who primarily supported Mass Observation was Victor Gollancz, though despite planning to publish a series for them on politics, religion and leisure, ended

---

[351] There is an interesting typescript account by William Coldstream in the M.O. archive, describing his activities in Bolton, including his painting from the roof of the Art Gallery (which Humphrey Spender photographed). He, Bell, Victor Pasmore and Claude Rogers had formed the Euston Road School in 1937. Bell and Coldstream painted in Bolton in April 1938 and no doubt influenced by the Mass Observation ethic sent invitations to their subsequent London exhibition to everyone [?] beginning with 'B' in the London phonebook (*ODNB*).

[352] See www.thephotographersgalleryblog.org.uk/2013/09/06/from-mass-obs-ervation-to-big-observation-anthropologies-of-ourselves-jonathan-p-watts/.
For the extent to which Jennings can be considered a co-founder see Nick Hubble's review of James Hinton's *The Mass Observers: A History, 1937-1949* (London, 2013), in the IHR's *Reviews in History*: www.history.ac.uk/reviews/review/1603; *cf.* however, Thomas's diary description as late as 19 March 1939: 'a bloke named Humphrey Jennings has turned up for out help in making shots of Bolton for a film he is doing for the New York fair. He explained that usually he makes films for the P.O....'. He had already had his affair with Peggy Guggenheim, who said he looked like Donald Duck.

[353] *Cf.* above, pp. 65 and 134; Bruce Berman, 'Ethnography as Politics, Politics as Ethnography: Kenyatta, Malinowski, and the Making of *Facing Mount Kenya*', *Canadian Journal of African Studies / Revue Canadienne des Études Africaines*, XXX, 3 (1996), pp. 313-344. Malinowski does not comment on Kenyatta's defence of female genital mutilation which constitutes chapter 6 of *Facing Mount Kenya*. According to the recordings at the M.O. archives, Tom Harrisson 'would openly describe Malinowski as a crook. I think Malinowski also described Tom Harrisson as a crook. There was a lot of sparring went on;' *cf.* Hinton, *Mass Observers*, pp. 85-6.

up producing only *The Pub and the People* in 1943.[354]

The nature of the reports, though reflecting the socio-anthropological (and occasionally artistic) proclivities of their predominantly middle-class compilers, may at least have suited the democratizing tendency of Gerald's temperament. Though prone to patronising and indeed losing his temper *à la* D.H. Lawrence, he responded to all classes of people with equivalent concern, making him an ideal (both empathetic and critical) Observer, however much he might have resented the menial (and much of the time, meaningless) nature of the work after what must increasingly have seemed like the glory days of writing for the *Adelphi*. Gerald's involvement in soliciting and assembling sociological information may even have contributed to his success in articulating the variety of voices that emerged in his great novel. More obviously relevant, however, was that he was meanwhile producing plays and performing them in Bolton's Little Theatre.

A comprehensive history of Mass Observation has recently been published in which Gerald, though not identified as the author of *The Book of Ebenezer Le Page*, makes a fleeting appearance as: 'a gay man of morose disposition from Guernsey employed by the local authority as drama organiser, who worked part-time for MO and lived rent-free in the Davenport Street attic, bringing in a flow of people involved in amateur theatre.'[355] The author of this history, Professor James Hinton, kindly forwarded copies of the sources in the Mass Observation Archive on which he based this summary. Largely thanks to his guidance, many more have now been discovered in the East Sussex County Records at Sussex University, The Keep, along with Gerald's reports on such matters as the Christmas shopping habits of the citizens of Bolton [Fig. 61].[356]

---

[354] Though in 1961 he also published Harrisson's retrospective *Britain Revisited*.

[355] Hinton, *The Mass Observers*, p. 122. Although Gerald is not indexed in this as one of the Mass Observers it is clear from what follows that he worked for the project, albeit in a part-time capacity.

[356] Gerald is also credited as one of the compilers of the 'Worktown Winter Sales' report of February 1940, now available through the *Adam Matthew Digital Mass Observation Online* project; www.massobservation.amdigital.co.uk. His most active participation seems to have been in November 1938 for which month a

In his immaculate, instantly recognizable italic hand on fine foolscap paper, these are much the best presented of the reports now to survive in the Mass Observation archives.

The most detailed information regarding Gerald, both as Mass Observer and theatre director, is to be found in two interviews conduct-ed by Nick Stanley for his PhD dissertation in the late 1970s.[357] In order to assist Madge after his removal to Bolton,

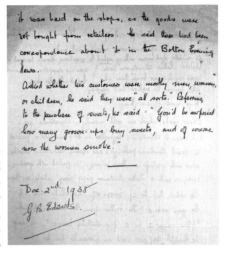

Fig. 61: An excerpt from one of Gerald's Mass Observation reports on Christmas shopping in Bolton, December 1938. (Mass Observation Archive)

Harrisson sent the aspiring young novelist Geoffrey Thomas, who had been working for Mass Observation in Fulham following a long illness, to conduct 'objective fieldwork and detailed outdoor studies of behaviour'. Like the rest of the observers, Thomas spent his time following people around shops, interviewing them on their shopping habits and studying their sexual proclivities.[358] Though Gerald was employed by Bolton Corporation to teach drama, acted in at least one play - Cedric Mount's *Dirge Without Dole* - and directed Strindberg's *Easter* at the Bolton Little Theatre, in March 1939, from late November 1938 he too worked as a Mass Observer.[359] Though he

dozen or so reports survive in the archive.

[357] Nick Stanley, *The Extra Dimension: A Study and Assessment of the Methods employed by Mass-Observation in its first Period 1937-40* (Birmingham Polytechnic [now City University], 1981).

[358] Hinton, *Mass Observers*, pp. 115-16 and pp. 118-19; *cf.* (forthcoming) David Hall, *Worktown* (London, 2015).

[359] Despite his alienation of Geoffrey Whitworth's wife, his long-standing acquaintance with Whitworth himself and his Drama organization, as well as theatrical experience with the WEA and at Dartington, may have helped him

seems to have performed the latter role assiduously, even allowing for his ambivalence about worldly achievement and the success of his theatrical productions, he must by now have felt a sense of personal and professional failure.

On the personal level there may still have been some contact with his wife and children; he at least seems to have talked of them, as also about more recent romantic interests. Interviewed about Gerald by Nick Stanley, Thomas ponders, as Potter had done: 'Yes, I wonder what happened to him? I'd love to know.' He then lists the other members of the group that lived at 85 Davenport Street, beginning with Dennis Chapman, whom Dr Stanley had already interviewed:

> Dennis turned up and I think that was in the January of '38... What did he say? And then after that Gerald turned up from nowhere. I think he [presumably Chapman] turned up a month or two after me, after St Andrews...[360] And then finally Charles [Madge] came to live in that house... That would be in late 1938 ... Christmas 1938.[361]

After he had drifted onto other matters, Stanley steered Thomas back to the subject of Gerald:

> Well I liked Gerald very much. Gerald was tall, elegant, well broad shouldered man. Slim and otherwise handsome from Guernsey or Jersey, Guernsey I think, he was a Guernseyman who could speak the patois and... but he was cross, he sometimes, he was extremely, er *very* intelligent bloke, *very* temperamental. He was gay. At the time I knew

---

obtain this post. Gerald would presumably have used the 1929 translation of *Easter* by E. Classen; the most authentic modern translation is by Gregory Motton (Oberon Classics, 2005).

[360] Chapman had worked for two years at the University of St Andrews on a project directed by Oscar Oeser, pioneer of empirical social psychology; see James Hinton, 'Mass Observation', *ODNB*. Whilst teaching at Dartington, on 19 January 1932 Oeser had married Ingeborg Emmie Dicke in Totnes, so may have known Gerald from that time and may even have provided an initial point of contact with the M.O. project (adb.anu.edu.au/biography/oeser-oscar-adolph-15396).

[361] Audiotape recording of interview between Nick Stanley and Geoffrey Thomas, 26 November 1979 (Mass Observation Archive, SxMOA 32/102/7); transcribed by Edward Chaney and Stephen Foote, 2 October 2014.

him he was having an affair with a young actor in Bolton, part-time actor, so he had all sorts of traumas and sometimes we'd sit around at midnight and talk in the awful kitchen in Davenport Street where he poured out his soul to me about this chap who I thought was a twit but nevertheless. And he had a wife Katie Edwards (you may need to censor this later on but) he had a wife Katie Edwards who was afterwards a field supervisor with the Social Survey when I was a Research Officer and Katie had, used to run a company, an amateur dramatic company of which it was said she always chose her leading man the night before. Anyway, she had, they had two children or was it three? Katie had four. The first two children were Gerald's, Adam and the girl. The other two were reported to be [a?] Rabbi's, all sorts of odd things. Katie was great fun, but you see there was a very curious mixture the two of them and…[362] He had a great contempt for Mass Observation – most of his time he spent running the productions. He did a very good production of Easter once for the Bolton Little Theatre. I remember it because I was involved in painting flats and things like that. But Gerald's interest was artistic more than anything else. I never quite knew what he did when he was in Bolton but he had nowhere and needed somewhere to be.

One perhaps needs to be reminded that the reference to Gerald being 'gay' dates from the late-1970s when this interview was conducted.[363] However destigmatising the adoption of such terminology was intended to be it has done little to depolarise

---

[362] This strangely garbled account seems to be based on a first-hand acquaintance with the family but might even be conflating Kathleen Edwards with Kathleen Box, who after a brief flirtation fell out with Tom Harrisson and then indeed worked (and co-authored a 1944 article) with Geoffrey Thomas at the Government Social Survey, Thomas eventually becoming its director in 1970 (www.socresonline.org.uk/19/3/22.html). Katie Box eventually committed suicide; Hinton, *Mass Observers*, p. 159.

[363] This was the source for James Hinton's assertion in *Mass Observers*, p. 212. It has been claimed that used with the meaning of homosexual, the word 'gay' dates back to Gertrude Stein but it only came into common use, as a preferable (politically correct?) alternative to 'queer' (which has now been returned to at least academic respectability) in the 1970s.

the twentieth-century tendency to categorise individuals according to their sexuality rather than the sexual acts they perform. Even now, with the increasingly standardised use of the term 'LGBT', the 'B' for bisexuality seems the least emphasised of the four categories, yet it could be argued that it should be the predominant one. It is certainly a more useful term to describe many of the greatest individuals of the pre-categorising cultures of the past than the exclusive 'gay', 'homosexual' or indeed 'heterosexual'. In the wake of Darwin's thoughts on primitive bisexuality, those early twentieth-century sexologists, Otto Weininger and Otto Gross, seem to have thought as much.[364] Less would-be scientifically, in *Anarchism is not Enough*, Robert Graves's muse, Laura Riding, put the case more succinctly:

> The classical type of homosexuality was far less exclusive and severe than the modern type: it was sophistication rather than specialization.[365]

Meanwhile, Gerald's wife, Kathleen, may well have been 'great fun' in the eyes of others but the strain of having their third and fourth children by two other men (the first of whom was probably one of Gerald's closest friends), seems to have eroded Gerald's faith in womankind to the extent that he looked to his fellow man for consolation. Whether such consolation included a sexual relationship is difficult to determine but Gerald's accounts of the relationship between Ebenezer and Jim Mahy on the one hand, and between Raymond and Horace (and even the more Lawrentian Harry Whitehouse) on the other, suggest everything short of this.[366] On the other, after his marriage breaks

---

[364] Dijkstra, *Evil Sisters*, p. 133. Not as historical as its title suggests, but dealing with the subject of 'bisexual erasure' on the part of both hetero- and homosexuals, is the Foucauldian Steven Angelides, *A History of Bisexuality* (Chicago, 2001).

[365] A curious book, part of which takes the form of a dialogue with 'pamphleteer of anarchism' Wyndham Lewis, published by Jonathan Cape in 1928, p. 192.

[366] Viz the episodes describing the stranding on Lihou of Ebenezer and Jim, which reminds one of Whitman's 'We Two Boys Together Clinging', and the liaison between Raymond and Harry; see *Ebenezer Le Page*, pp. 46 and 118; and pp. 144-45. A comment regarding measures that Chapman allegedly took to avoid the possibility of Gerald molesting him, added in pencil at the foot of the

up and his beloved Horace leaves for America, his second *alter ego*, Raymond, clearly consorts primarily with homosexuals. He explains to Ebenezer at one point why his close friendship with a German student broke up: 'I couldn't do it to him... I liked him too much', which more than suggests that he'd 'done' it with others.[367] In yet more confessional mode, after moving in with Ebenezer following his near suicide, he says, apparently in response to a question about what he got up to all those years: 'I had to try everything ... but there is no way out that way. It only makes chaps despise each other and behave worse than women. I was mad to hope. Man is doomed to Woman.'[368]

Despite his much-vaunted brand of existentialism, like Nietzsche himself, Gerald does not seem to have led an especially adventurous, or indeed decisive life, which may help explain his failure to establish a relationship that endured any longer than his relatively short marriage. From this portrayal of Raymond, however, it seems likely that Gerald too 'tried everything', and eventually reverted to a more conventional, if no longer very intense, heterosexuality.[369]

A complementary account of Gerald's life in Davenport Street emerges from Dr Stanley's interview with Dennis Chapman, whom Thomas recalls as having arrived in Bolton shortly before him. Chapman recalls that:

> The team in Bolton consisted of Gertrude Wagner,[370] Geoffrey Thomas, occasionally Charles Madge, myself and a mysterious character called Gerald Edwards who was

---

entry in Thomas's diary for 27 January 1939, seems to have been made in jest.

[367] *Ebenezer Le Page*, pp. 239-40.

[368] *Ebenezer Le Page*, p. 240.

[369] See below, p. 203, for what may have been his last attempt at this, when he settled in a cottage in East Coker with a certain 'Olive', perhaps a former fellow-lodger in London.

[370] Gertrude Wagner was a 33-year-old Austrian graduate of Vienna university and a refugee who was completing an MA on 'The Psychological Aspect of Saving and Spending'. She soon embarked on an affair with Bill Naughton, 'who drove a coal lorry for the Co-op and was a frequent visitor to Davenport Street after work.' Chapman himself was, meanwhile, 'carrying on with Joyce Mangnell, a constant source of contacts for MO since Harrisson first got to know her when working in a mill in 1936'; Hinton, *Mass Observers*, p. 121.

employed as drama organiser by the Bolton Corporation. So he had an income. Whether he had to pay rent or was allowed to live rent free in the attic (he had the top floor – we all had rooms of our own)... [He] gave us information and also brought other people in who were associated with drama. So there was a flow of people who came into the building for rehearsals who were also able to be picked upon.[371]

At another point in the interview, Chapman says that Harrisson:

got a commission to make a survey about public opinion about air-raid precautions for the News Chronicle which is probably somewhere in the archive. Gerald Edwards was having his hair cut that morning so he interviewed the barber. He went on the tram so he interviewed the tram conductor. I forgot how he got the other three interviews, but it made five anyhow. These appeared as percentages in the News Chronicle article. We got paid for that, quite a good fee. We got a splendid telegram the next day saying how deeply moved he [Harrisson] was by this new spirit of co-operation. We'd sent five interview answers the previous day by telegram and had duly appeared as an impressive contribution to human knowledge.[372]

Despite making money from some of their activities, money was always tight and life at Davenport Street was very frugal:

Now all through this process M-O was penniless, as you can see from the telegrams I've quoted. So that any way of getting money and of course Tom spent a great deal, so any way of getting money was important. How the rent was paid at Davenport Street was a mystery... There was a desperate central heating system which was run by coke. The ashes were never taken out of the cellar. Soon the space for coke began to diminish, and the quantities of ash ... and it became a duty to go down and do the thing. The only way in which you could do it was to go down naked and then

[371] Transcript of interview between Nick Stanley and Dennis Chapman, 23 February 1979 (Mass Observation Archive, SxMOA32/17/1), spool 1, p .7.

[372] Ibid., spool 1, p. 9.

have a bath because you were so filthy.[373]

Dennis Chapman, Geoffrey Thomas and Gerald would often sit up talking until early morning. Thomas recalls one of these discussions in his more precise diaries, also now preserved with the Mass Observation archives:

> A peculiar day. We, Dennis and I and Gerald, ended it sitting in front of the fire, with candles on, listening to the Radio and discussing life. Dennis was most revealing in view of his imminent departure. He has had a wire from his wife saying she is ill, and asking him to return at once, and it moved him to complain generally about her lack of confidence in him. She never believes that he is going to succeed at anything he does she never tries to help him to succeed… 'Why is marriage so bloody?' asks poor old Dennis. Gerald pointed out that what he wanted was a mother, wife and whore rolled into one. But Dennis wouldn't see it. He said he hated mothers.[374]

Having not kept up his diary for the next fortnight, on 12 February Thomas then records that:

> Dennis departed on the Monday 30th. Jan. to his sick wife, departing in a taxi in a night train after having had Joyce [Mangnall] in his room with him all the evening… On the Wednesday after that Gerald departed to a room in Chorley Old Road, and thereafter the house seemed empty…

Despite moving out of the centre of Bolton, Gerald seems to have remained in touch with his fellow Mass Observers, though there is evidence that his moods had caused problems with at least visitors to Davenport Street. Thomas recorded in this same summary of the past fortnight that he met one Harold Mayor for the first time since he had come to the house, 'and become involved in one of Gerald's tempers over Greta Garbo, Gerald's great favourite.'[375]

---

[373] *Ibid.*, spool 1, p. 8.

[374] Geoffrey Thomas diary, Saturday 28 Jan 1939 (Mass Observation Archive, SxMOA32/102/2)

[375] Not least due to his enthusiasm for Tolstoy, Gerald would surely have seen the Swedish-born actress in both film versions of *Anna Karenina*, of 1927 and

Whether or not he continued to work for Mass Observation, Gerald certainly produced plays for the local authority, and created the Bolton Drama School, at least two of whose highly-praised productions were staged at the Little Theatre [Fig. 62].

Fig. 62: *Bolton Little Theatre.*

Geoffrey Thomas's personal diaries include a well-informed account of Gerald's production of Strindberg's *Easter*, as he had helped out with painting flats and scenery and therefore observed Gerald's organisational, acting and directing skills at first hand.[376] On Monday 22 January 1939 he recorded that:

---

1935, the first entitled *Love*. Gerald would even more likely have read F.R. Leavis's comparison between Anna's tragedy and the 'amoral German aristocrat' Frieda Lawrence 'getting over' losing her children, as published in Eliot's *Criterion* in 1927; see the discussion in Christopher Ricks, *Keats and Embarrassment* (Oxford, 1976), p. 96. For Frieda sending Weekley, the husband she was abandoning, a copy of *Anna Karenina*, see Worthen, *Lawrence*, p. 390.

[376] This production, and perhaps others by Gerald, conceivably of plays he had written himself (see Marr, below, p. 199) is not recorded in the list of productions catalogued in Michael Shipley, Andrew Close et al. ed., *Bolton Little Theatre: 75 years of Drama* (Bolton, 2006) because it was not performed by the Little Theatre company; I thank Michael Shipley for pointing this out. He kindly informs me that in the 1930s there were two groups, Bolton Dramatic Society and Bolton Little Theatre. The latter formed the Bolton Little Theatre and eventually found a building to convert, which they moved into in 1934 and began running plays, usually six a season, until 1941. The BDS struggled along after the war, before finally closing in the 1960s. Michael Shipley's father acted as BDS secretary in the 1940s, and he and indeed Sir Ian McKellen both acted at the theatre; see

Tonight Gerald Edwards came home in a conscious fury [*sic*]. Once he said he was so furious that it was almost funny. He had gone to his class (The Bolton Drama School he established at the end of November, and which he incited to take on Easter as a play to do in March) completely fed up with the roles he and the class were playing in relation to the play. He thought that all the drive was coming from him which was wrong. To-night, it seems, he tried to get them to drop it, became furious, raved at them, read the Psalms he was using for voice practice like a bull, and could <u>not</u> persuade them to drop Easter. Those who had been most against it in the beginning were now most for it. He mentioned that he had been roused to fury early because he had arranged his seats in a big circle, so that none could sit in the back row, as they loved to do. But three women came in later, and took three chairs from the pile by the wall, to place them outside the circle. It seems that he started by raving at <u>them</u>. For the rest of the evening he paced up and down in the circle like a caged lion. Later (when Dennis had returned from an adventure with Joyce) and he had picked up his cap, scarf and blue coat, preparatory to going to the attic, he said that he was a standing joke, a complete bore, and really expressed that peculiar swing between complete arrogance and a complete self-contempt which is his. Maybe he has, as he expressed it once, a feeling that there is something in him which is capable of doing things, and the comparison between that and what he actually does arouses him to the bitterest damnation of himself. Tea and cigarettes apart, this is a sufficient stimulant for him. At 39 he is still in some ways unset. His interest in Drama is a purely personal one. He remarked that this was one of the troubles with his school. He had no real interest in teaching Drama, or producing, no real creative interest in showing other people what to do.[377]

Two days later, presumably after a day's Mass Observing, Thomas and Dennis Chapman got home to find Gerald,

---

below, p. 197, for his comments on the reviews of 'Easter'.

[377] Mass Observation Archive, SxMOA32/102/2.

presumably back from rehearsals:

> sitting in the kitchen with a single candle, the lights having
> gone out. There we sat also, and drank tea, and were
> philosophical, to the extent of Dennis lighting candles in a
> row along the mantelpiece.[378]

It seems that rows between Gerald and members of the cast continued until the eve of the performances which took place on the 10th and 11th March 1939 in front of the Mayor and Mayoress of Bolton [Fig. 63].[379] Thomas commented that the 'behind the scenes tribulations were the most interesting things', but the reviews in the *Bolton Evening News*, both of *Easter* and of the three-scene, one-act play, Cedric Mount's

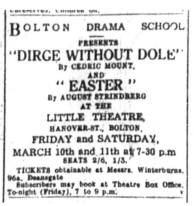

Fig. 63: Advertisement, *Bolton Evening News*, 3 March 1939.

*Dirge Without Dole*, which immediately preceded it and in which Gerald played the part of the adjudicator, were extremely positive. Cedric Mount was the *alias* of Sydney Box who was at this time a controversial experimental playwright and author of one of the essays in William Kozlenko's collection published in 1939 as *The One-Act Play Today*.[380] Thomas's diary account may have been written up with the help of one the reviews, though perhaps due to his constant pursuit of potential love interest in Bolton, he seems to have known the cast well already:

---

[378] MO, Thomas, *Diary*, 25 January 1939.

[379] I am very grateful to Frances Clemmitt of Bolton Little Theatre for her assistance in locating the articles from the *Bolton Evening News* cited here.

[380] Kozlenko's book was largely devoted to the Anglo-American phenomenon known as the Little Theatre Movement. Sydney Box was the brother of film producer Betty Box and husband of Muriel, with whom he founded Verity Films, which produced short propaganda films such as *The English Inn*, during the early 1940s, suggesting possible connections with Mass Observation (*ODNB*).

Since the previous Sunday I had been at the Little Theatre practically every day, so in that time, seeing three rehearsals and helping to paint the flats and put up the scenery, I knew the play and the actors fairly well. The girl who played Eleanor was really nice, small, plump, fair, with a most strange red mouth, and a peculiar voice. Marjorie Wilson. She played her part well. Jack Crompton was a worried Elis, since he couldn't get the part. Jack Inskter [*sic*] was a very good Lin[d]kvist, and the rest fair. The behind the scenes tribulations were the most interesting things. Rows between Jack C and Alice Morris the Irishwoman who played Mrs Heyst. Rows between Gerald and the same Jack.

Still, on the night the play went well, and again on Saturday, when most of the evening I stood in the foyer talking to a girl I didn't know, though I had seen her once before... That night I went back to Jack Crompton's house and had potato pie with beer and a discussion afterwards that lasted till after three. It was surprisingly a working class house in Derby Street with his mother a white haired woman, with a will of her own, and thoroughly nice in a homely way. Gerald was being a perfect beast to everyone, which added to the evening, plus a nasty rabbit faced little young woman, who was IIIII [*sic*] about the stage, and a stupid young man who had driven us up and was her boy-friend...[381]

The regular reviewer for the *Bolton Evening News*, John Wardle, an accomplished actor, translator and one of the founders of Little Theatre [Fig. 64], had already trailed Gerald's production the previous Saturday.[382] This appeared in a feature entitled 'Bolton Drama School', which according to Thomas's account Gerald had created in the previous November:

---

[381] SX MOA 32/102/2 entry dated Sunday 19 March 1939.

[382] I would like to thank John Wardle's son, the theatre critic, Irving Wardle, for help with information about his father and for supplying me with his photograph. Michael Shipley kindly adds that: 'John Wardle of the *Bolton Evening News* was the leading drama man in town, and consistently promoted the best in drama for the town. He was one of our founding members, acted there frequently himself, and eventually became President of the Bolton Dramatic Society... I remember [him] with great affection.'

The public perform-
ance of Strindberg's
'Easter' preceded by the
modern one-act play
'Dirge Without Dole' to
which reference has
already been made in
this column, will take
place at the Little
Theatre on Friday and
Saturday March 10th
and 11th. The perform-
ance on March 10th will
be attended by the
Mayor and Mayoress.[383]

Fig. 64: *John Wardle*
(photo: Irving Wardle, c.1951)

The cast list is then
transcribed more or less as
Thomas's diary has it. The feature immediately below this is
entitled 'Student Producer', confirming one's impression that
the indefatigable Gerald was training select students to produce
as well as perform in plays:

> Mr Jack Crompton included in the above cast [of *Easter*]
> produces the shorter of the two plays. His cast consists of
> Elsie Flood, Sheila Duckworth, Wilfred Brooks, Frederick
> W. Allen, Gilbert H. Jones, James Foster, Joseph Howard,
> Celia Wood and Gerald B. Edwards.

In the *Evening News* for Friday 10 March, a photograph of a scene
from 'Dirge Without Dole' was featured, with a caption reading:
'"Unemployed family" – symbolic group … by Bolton Drama
School at the Little Theatre to-night' and listing the players in
the play within a play (thus not including Gerald, who acted the
part of the adjudicator). In the next night's edition, 'The
Showman' (John Wardle) published an enthusiastic puff
entitled 'Both Sides of the Curtain' and illustrated by a
glamorous photograph of Gerald's leading lady, Marjorie
Wilson [Fig. 65]:

---

[383] *Bolton Evening News*, Saturday 25 February 1939, p. 7

## BOLTON EVENING NEWS, SATURDAY,

# BOTH SIDES
# *of the* CURTAIN

### By " The Showman "

### I—PLAYS

THE event of the week is the emergence into public view of Bolton Drama School in the production of Strindberg's "Easter," preceded by the short play, " Dirge Without Dole," by Cedric Mount. As the "Evening News" has given, in another column of this issue, an account of the first performances, which took place last evening, I propose to withhold my own impressions until next Saturday, except for the payment of tribute which, without any adverse reflection on other members of the two casts, I feel bound to offer at once to Marjorie Wilson for her sensitive performance of the very difficult part of Eleonora in " Easter."

**MARJORIE WILSON**

ach revealed a deftness which threw the two characters into sharp contrast and gave the whole production a sound basis. Another valuable contribution was made by John Heelis, playing the flamboyant Archie Leadenhall. Henry Wolstencroft ably suggested the more sedate John, but should strive for greater ease of movement and a clearer enunciation.

### HOMELY COMEDY

Though its characters are all stock types, Armitage Owen's three-act comedy, " Queen for a Year," which the Georgian Players presented in St. George's-rd. Congregational School on Wednesday, will always " go down well " with a local society's audience, writes B.S. I am not saying this disparagingly, because Wednesday's production, for which Norma Wilson was responsible, was a rollicking success from half-way through the first act when things had got going properly. As the title suggests, the play tells of a local shopgirl who is elected Beauty Queen of England, through the arrangement of a newspaper. She is lifted out of her environment, leaves behind for

Fig. 65: *Bolton Evening News*, 11 March 1939.

The event of the week is the emergence into public view of the Bolton Drama School in the production of Strindberg's 'Easter', preceded by the short play, 'Dirge Without Dole' by Cedric Mount. As the 'Evening News' has given, in another column of this issue, an account of the first performances, which took place last evening, I propose to withhold my own impressions until next Saturday, except for the payment of tribute which, without any adverse reflection on other members of the two casts, I feel bound to offer at once to Marjorie Wilson, for her sensitive performance of the very difficult part of Eleonara in

'Easter'.[384]

The review referred to here appeared under the title: 'Good Acting' and characterised Mount's *Dirge* as:

> a satirical play full of modern cynicism which I found much to my liking. It ... deals with the presentation of an unemployment propaganda play at a drama festival. Jack Crompton was responsible for producing this and he also designed a most effective setting and costumes. The play is unusual, in that it relies on the ancient method of repetition, as in the Greek chorus, to give emphasis to the unemployed man's statement of fact. The repetition is made by his wife and children in turn... The satire comes from the Bishop (Thomas Foster), the Fascist (Gilbert Jones), the Communist (Joseph Howard), the scientist (Celia Wood), and the business man (Frederick Allen).[385]

Given that he established the theatre school it seems likely that Gerald provided overall direction to both plays and was training Jack Crompton in theatrical production. Wardle briefly described Gerald's performance in the role he presumably chose for himself as appropriate, of critiquing the play within this experimental play:

> Caustic in its application was the wit of the adjudicator, Gerald Edwards, when commenting on the play, and also the reflection of the cast after the adjudication.

Where *Easter* was concerned, given the dearth of material on Gerald's artistic life from before the war until the time I met him more than thirty years later, and given also the absence hitherto of this production from the existing histories of Bolton's distinguished Little Theatre,[386] this intelligently enthusiastic review is perhaps worth quoting in full:

> Judging by their ambitious first effort in giving

---

[384] The part of the Christ-like Eleonora was inspired by Strindberg's institutionalised sister. Interestingly Collis discusses this in his *Marriage and Genius*, pp, 125-26, perhaps an echo of conversations with Gerald on the subject decades earlier.

[385] *Bolton Evening News*, 11 March 1939.

[386] Shipley, *The Little Theatre*.

Strindberg's 'Easter,' the members of the Bolton Drama School look like contributing much to the amateur stage in Bolton. It was a most competent presentation of a play far from easy to make convincing to any audience.

The drama is built up of the clash of such abstract qualities as crime and punishment: justice and mercy, pride and humility, and jealousy and love against the symbolic background of the sorrow and despair of Good Friday and the hope and joy of the resurrection. With such material it can well be understood that any false note will of certainty throw the whole out of tune.

Jack Crompton as Elis, the son, left to face the victims of his father's crime, and Alice Morris, as Mrs Heyst, who feels herself to some extent responsible for the family's catastrophe, cleverly built up the sense of despair, with Dorothy Bramwell as Christina, the fiancé of Elis, wielding a sane influence. Underacting rather than too much, tended to keep all the characters in perspective.

The most difficult character to keep in check was that of Eleonara, but Ma[r]jorie Wilson saw to it that the girl was sufficiently fey, to use a Scottish expression, without any strong tendency to the weird. Hers was a balanced interpretation and did much to make Jack Adam's Benjamin convincing.[387]

The final scene was most effective, largely owing to the forthrightness of Jack Inkster as Lindkvist, in setting all to rights, and the whole reflects credit on the producer, Gerald Edwards, for a due sense of proportion all through.[388]

---

[387] In an email dated 27 May 2015, Michael Shipley kindly responded to my request for more information about this review: 'In the reviews of 'Easter' I do see names of actors who at the time and for many years later were acting members of BLT - Marjorie Wilson (a very charismatic comedy actress) and Dorothy Bramwell (Hilton) (in my time, a strong director of gritty plays) in particular, so obviously … Gerald Edwards at Bolton Drama School had a rich fund of talent to draw on for his ambitious production. Incidentally ... Dorothy Bramwell was the mother of Andrew Hilton' (now Artistic Director of Bristol-based Shakespeare at the Tobacco Factory).

[388] *Bolton Evening News*, 11 March 1939. The review concludes: 'Incidentally, the drama school linked up with the junior instruction centre for boys in

## 15: WILDERNESS YEARS

Though Gerald may well have produced, and indeed acted in, more plays through most of the rest of 1939, I have found no record of them; neither have those who have kindly assisted me in my search at the Bolton Little Theatre, which hosted these two productions but would not necessarily have hosted others by his Drama School. For the little that is known of Gerald's wartime activities we have to return to the Mass Observation archive. During his interview with Geoffrey Thomas, Nick Stanley asks him to confirm that Gerald had indeed lived in Davenport Street. Having done so he then provides an account of Gerald's later movements, which though somewhat garbled, is all we really have. Thomas does not even specify where they met up again but given that he found work with the Wartime Social Survey, before eventually being promoted to direct its successor, the Government Social Survey, one can assume it was in London, where Gerald was certainly living by 1945:

> He lived in Davenport Street, yes. And then when we all broke up he disappeared somewhere. The last time I saw him was in 1941 or 2 possibly, when he'd joined the Ministry of Labour of all things. He had a landlady who he called Mrs Mussolini or something like that and he'd have... We had a cup of coffee together in a restaurant before he had to go back to work. I remember that, very odd. Sitting down working at a desk. He also had to deal with the, what were they called? With the conscientious objector[s?] – he had a battle with one of those Boards which he described in great detail. He also had a battle with the Department of Employment because he said 'I have no money' and they expected me to sit for a month with no money and work – so I went to them and I said 'I have to have money' – and broke the financial system of the DOE, Ministry of Labour as it was then of course, gave his money and he was therefore...
>
> The last time I saw him was in 41 or 42 was exactly the same Gerald. What happened to him after that I didn't

---

constructing the play's setting.'

know. I don't think Katie knew either.[389]

According to his 1972 letter to me, Gerald had visited his father in Guernsey in late 1938 for he described going over there 'in the year of the Munich Crisis.' Tom Edwards was by then 77 years old and living with his third wife in the relatively modest house he acquired with the proceeds of the sale of Hawkesbury.[390] By now it must have been clear to Gerald that if, as was likely, his father failed to outlive his wife, he would not inherit. Once war was declared it would also have been clear that he would not earn enough to survive in any other than a mundane occupation. In around 1940, therefore, he seems to have obtained a job at a Labour Exchange. In his reliable but lightly referenced entry on Gerald in *Guernsey People*, James Marr writes that:

> He put in a spell with the Bolton Repertory Company, for which he wrote a number of plays – all of which he subsequently destroyed!... With the coming of the Second World War Edwards took up an appointment in an employment exchange and thereafter remained in the civil service until his retirement in 1960.[391]

Gerald's expertise on the German occupation of Guernsey as evidenced in *The Book of Ebenezer Le Page* was based both upon reading and on interviews he conducted with his few remaining friends on the island, including the cobbler Clarrie Bellot [Fig. 25], and relatives such as his cousin Hilda Dumond. He presumably returned to the island for his father's funeral in 1946, assuming he could face meeting his step-mother Rose Cooke, who now inherited his father's entire estate.[392] In the final

---

[389] Audiotape recording of interview between Nick Stanley and Geoffrey Thomas (Mass Observation Archive, SxMOA 32/102/7). Transcribed by Edward Chaney and Stephen Foote, 2 October 2014. The reference to Kathleen's ignorance of his whereabouts lends some credence to Michael Young's understanding the Gerald left her; see p. 164.

[390] See below, p. 245 and p. 44 above.

[391] L. James Marr, *Guernsey People* (Chichester, 1984), p. 49. This section of Marr's biographical entry is dependent on that part of John Fowles's introduction to *Ebenezer Le Page* which is based on his correspondence with Gerald's daughter, Dorcas.

[392] Tom Edwards died aged 89 on 23 January 1946 in 'Les Rosiers'. He and Rosina

year of the war he was living, with a large number of other lodgers, in the then still very run-down Notting Hill.[393]

A measure of Gerald's stubborn, indeed courageous, loyalty to his beliefs, however wrongheaded, is their survival intact through to when I knew him. For it must have been galling indeed to live, at least latterly, as unadventurously as he seems to have done, when in his first major publication, as a 26-year-old 'genius', he had condemned the author of *Man and Superman* and promoter of 'creative evolution' for failing to promote as preferable a credo of the privileged moment as eternal life.[394] In *The Will to Power* Nietzsche wrote that:

> If we affirm one single moment, we thus affirm not only ourselves but all existence. For nothing is self-sufficient, neither in us ourselves nor in things; and if our soul has trembled with happiness and sounded like a harp string just once, all eternity was needed to produce this one event — and in this single moment of affirmation all eternity was called good, redeemed, justified, and affirmed.[395]

That Nietzsche had been Gerald's principal inspiration in 1926, he made clear in his critique of Shaw: 'He has denied creation

---

bought 'La Rosière', now Les Rosiers, in 1927, but he did not sell Hawkesbury until 1929 and was buried in Foulon cemetery, not with Gerald's mother, Harriet, but with Rosina Cooke's previous husband. According to Clary Dumond, Tom was buried 'in an old Rangers Red and Black shirt ... there was a fuss about him not being buried with Aunty Harriet, Gerald's mother. Mrs Cook like Mrs Crew said, when its Gods goodwill I will go to my rest I will lie in the same grave with my two husbands, so Mrs Cook lies on top of them both.' Upon investigation, however, it appears that in this last detail at least, Clary Dumond was conflating fact with fiction for Rosina Cooke was not buried there, her nieces being responsible for her private funeral. Tom's death certificate describes him by this stage as a 'Fruit Grower' (Civil Deaths Register, Greffe, 23 Jan 1946).

[393] At 23 Chepstow Road, Paddington (ancestry.com, London Electoral Register, 1945). I thank Stephen Foote for this reference.

[394] Keum-Hee Jang, *George Bernard Shaw's Religion of Creative Evolution: A Study of Shavian Dramatic Works*, PhD dissertation (University of Leicester, 2006) which distinguishes Shaw's more intellectualizing definition from Henri Bergson's more intuitive account of 'Creation Evolution'. He clearly did not, as Collis has Gerald say: 'invent' creative evolution (see note 396, below).

[395] Eds W. Kaufmann and R.J. Hollingdale translators (London, 1967), pp. 532–533

for contemplation … it is living, not thought, which is … the one indestructible deed.'[396]

How thoroughly - or creatively - Gerald lived his life during the years of post-war austerity we do not know but from the absence of documentation it would seem he became increasingly reclusive and as disillusioned with men as with women. Even after the publicity associated with the posthumous publication of *Ebenezer Le Page*, which included a BBC Radio 4 series, it is remarkable how few people claimed to have known him. He retired in 1960 and went 'to live rough' in Wales (1960-61), then moved to Penzance (1961-64) and Plymouth (1964-67), before finally settling in Weymouth (handy for visits to Guernsey) from 1967 onwards. It was from Weymouth in 1967 that he crossed over to Guernsey and visited his cousin, Hilda Dumond, asking her for a copy of his mother's photograph whilst staying at Mrs Mead at Torteval.[397]

He had remained in touch with Hilda, writing to her on Christmas Eve 1961 when he was wintering in London and thinking of moving to Southampton in the New Year.[398] In this letter Gerald refers to a visit that seems to have been relatively recent and included one to Le Petit Désert at the Landes du Marché [Fig. 66]. Such a visit, his request for family news and reference to appreciation of his early years, suggest he may already have been thinking of writing about the island and his

---

[396] 'Shaw', p. 32 (*cf.* above, p. 58). As an admirer of Shaw, Collis asked Gerald whether he thought Shaw parasitic upon his own ideas, as he had just described Bertrand Russell and G.D.H. Cole to be. Gerald answered: ' "No." Edwards always admired Shaw's power, as he put it. "No. He invented creative evolution to account for his inner sense of purpose."' ('Memories of a Genius Friend', p. 22); *cf.* note 394 above.

[397] Letter in my possession from her son, Clary Dumond. He and Wilfrid Burgess were the only two people who got in touch with me after the publication of *Ebenezer Le Page*, J.S. Collis being the only other who revealed that they had known him. The Reverend David 'Livingstone' Le Page kindly informs me that Gerald visited him in Anglesey (presumably 1960-1) and then subsequently in Guernsey. He is named as Ebenezer's cousin in the novel on pp. 142 and 171.

[398] Further evidence of Gerald's eternally optimistic streak: 'Odd you should mention that Violet is living in Southampton; for lately I've been thinking of moving down to Southampton this coming year, probably in September. If I do, I shall certainly call on her.'

Fig. 66: *Le Petit Désert, Landes du Marché, Guernsey*
(photo : Stephen Foote).

relationship with it, for this was the house of his mother's family. It is likely that his grandfather, Daniel Mauger, acquired it at around the time of his marriage in 1855 which would mean the family had lived there for almost a century:[399]

> It's sad that there are strangers at Le Petit Désert after all these years. I'm glad I managed to see inside while Edwin Le Page was there.[400] You are certainly right about Guernsey not being the same as it used to be. I probably notice that more than you. There are too many people living on the island, especially strangers: and more visitors than it can cope with, while having its own life. Of course money is made; but that's not everything. The Guernsey we knew when we were young was more of a place.
>
> All the same, there is nowhere else I really want to live now. I hate London. If I get down to Southampton, I'll certainly hop over, if only for a holiday. I'll let you know of

---

[399] They were certainly there by the time of the 1861 census.

[400] Edwin Le Page (1890-1969) was Gerald's first cousin, the son of Nicholas Le Page and the eldest Mauger daughter, Charlotte, sister of Rachel and Harriet, who married the Edwards brothers, George and Tom, Gerald's father; see family tree Appendix 6.

course; and come and see you. I know writing letters is a nuisance, I always put if off myself; but do let me know from time to time how you are. You're the only person I know and like who is a link with my mother and her family; and I think the older one gets, the more one appreciates one's early years. At least, I know I do.

I'm glad to hear Clary and Dorothy have been doing well. Please remember me to them with every good wish. I remember Dorothy's little dark boy, who looked very much like one of the family. He must be quite grown up by now.

It's surprising how quickly children do grow up. When I was in Guernsey this last time, I kept on seeing people I thought I knew, who turned out to be sons and sometimes grandsons of boys I was at school with. I completely forgot for the time being that I too had grown older...

Gerald moved to Bert and Joan Snells' large, but now sadly demolished, house on the Dorchester Road between Weymouth and Upwey village in late 1971 [Fig. 67]. Even here he didn't settle immediately for in May 1972, with help from the Snells, he tried instead to settle in East Coker with a woman called 'Olive', perhaps a former lover.[401] Unfortunately, the combined effect of her poor health and his uncompromising personality seems to have brought this experiment to an end after a few months and he returned to Upwey where, soon after, he and I first met. Though he would strike out from time to time for Wales, the Shetland or Scilly Isles, each time he would return to his lodgings a somewhat chastened man, having been reminded that there was no escape from the modern world (or himself) and that the attempt had in any case proved beyond his meagre means and, increasingly, his physical powers.

---

[401] The name 'Olive' occurs from time to time in May-June 1972 correspondence between Gerald and Mrs Snell, which the latter kindly gave me. It is just possible she is Olive Cassar, who was living at 23 Chepstow Road in 1945, where Gerald was a fellow lodger at this Notting Hill address; see above, p. 221. This Olive married a Gerald Binderman in the first quarter of 1972. Gerald's experiment of co-habitation with 'Olive' in East Coker failed in late June 1972.

Fig. 67: *654 Dorchester Road, Upwey, Dorset* (photo: the author).

By the summer of 1972, when I met him, Gerald was already working on a substantial novel he called *Sarnia Chérie*, set in Guernsey. Having become aware of this fairly quickly I encouraged him to complete it and he did so, handing over the immaculate typescript in his bed-sitting room with a proud flourish two years later. In the novel itself, when Ebenezer hands over his journal to his young artist friend, Neville Falla, he observes: 'He didn't thank me for my book; but I swear he knew I had given him all my secrets for him to read some day'. Though, like Neville, also a motorcycling artist-rebel, I thanked Gerald warmly for his gift, having already gained some idea of its contents. A fortnight after my return to University from Dorset, I received an unsolicited letter which confirmed the symmetry between the fictional and actual donation. Whereas Ebenezer wrote the words: 'THE PROPERTY OF NEVILLE FALLA' upon the first page of his book and bequeathed Neville his house and life savings, Gerald, who owned nothing but a typewriter and the paperbacks he was reading at the time, had dedicated *his* book to me and my wife. Prior to any further correspondence on the subject, however, he completed the gift of his novel by sending me the following, typed declaration:

<u>To Edward Chaney</u>

This is formally to confirm over my signature that on 3rd August 1974, I gave you unconditionally the definitive Typescript of SARNIA CHÉRIE: THE BOOK OF EBENEZER LE PAGE, written by myself: you are therefore free to get it published if and as you think fit, to own the copyright, and to receive whatever emoluments may accrue, without any obligation to me.

<u>G.B. Edwards</u>

Gerald clearly anticipated that his book should eventually appear in print but our struggle to find a publisher for it during his lifetime failed. He received the repeated rejections with extraordinary stoicism, however, even writing civilised replies to the often obtuse publishers' letters. Only after his death, when I migrated to postgraduate work in Italy and met a former Hamish Hamilton editor there, did I manage to locate a sympathetic reader and have it accepted. Though Hamish Hamilton required few alterations to the text I was obliged to agree to their abandoning Gerald's original title and promoting his subtitle in its place, for they insisted that 'Sarnia Chérie' sounded too much like a Barbara Cartland romance. Ironically they then chose as an epigraph the lyrics of George Deighton's 1911 song of the same name, effectively Guernsey's national anthem.[402]

Meanwhile, although I had begun writing the introduction the publishers requested, unbeknownst to me they had sent a complete photocopy of Gerald's typescript to John Fowles who responded enthusiastically and agreed to write one of his own. After almost scuppering the deal, I eventually handed over both my draft introduction and correspondence with Gerald and he did a superior job which attracted far greater attention to the novel than mine could have done.[403]

---

[402] See below, p. 335.

[403] *Cf.* below, pp. 336-38, for fuller account.

# 16: OF RELIGIOUS EXPERIENCE

Though far from flaunting his literary sophistication, Gerald's title, *The Book of Ebenezer Le Page*, which he originally intended as his sub-title, already suggests the 'metafiction' that post-modernist authors so self-consciously parade. Fowles himself had provided alternatively happy and unhappy endings for his *French Lieutenant's Woman*[404] - further complicated by Harold Pinter's screenplay for Karel Reisz's 1981 film, which alternated between the present and the Victorian past. But where Ian McEwan's *Atonement* all too knowingly retracts the happy ending it had seemed to offer in Bryony's fiction-within-*his*-fiction - made the more annoying by Vanessa Redgrave's performance in the Oscar-winning film version - Gerald and Ebenezer's narratives conclude in positive harmony.[405] Describing *The Book of Ebenezer Le Page* as 'a masterpiece', in his *New York Times* review, Guy Davenport wrote: 'I know of no description of happiness in modern literature equal to the one that ends this novel.'[406] Perhaps the contrast between the bourgeois life-style of the successful Oxford novelist, and the bohemian poverty, professional failure and (no doubt anticipated) lonely death suffered by the Islander in exile, help explain the latter's compulsion to create 'something upon which to rejoice', more profoundly positive than Matisse's metaphorical armchair, yet more authentically artful than most modern/ist literature. It is in this respect interesting that in Bolton, Gerald chose to produce Strindberg's *Easter*, which is relatively rare in being a *fin de siècle* Scandinavian play that ends optimistically, one whose very plot indeed, parallels the Resurrection. It is hilarious that when he lost patience with his students and tried to get them to abandon *Easter*, he 'raved at

---

[404] (Jonathan Cape, 1969). No doubt both Fowles and Gerald would have had Dickens's 'improved' conclusion of *Great Expectations* in mind.

[405] In a 1979 BBC2 interview with Christopher Ricks, McEwan says that what he really worries about is 'gratuitous optimism' (www.bbc.co.uk/archive/writers/12229.shtml; accessed 5 May 2014). For a summary of the already vast literature on the ending/s of *Atonement* see: www.diva-portal.org/smash/get/diva2:291657/FULLTEXT01.pdf.

[406] 'A Novel of Life in a Small World', *New York Times*, 19 April 1981.

them [and] read the Psalms he was using for voice practice like a bull.'[407] Gerald remained fiercely loyal to the individualist idea of religion he had begun articulating in the 1920s, indebted but by no means identical to Lawrence's. His 1926 essay on Bernard Shaw had sought to expose Shaw's failure to be a true Nietzschean. Five years on, though still essentially a Nietzschean, in two more essays published in the *Adelphi*, Gerald articulated a more personal credo.

The first of these was entitled 'A Prospective Religion'. In this Gerald managed to criticise the book he was reviewing, Lawrence Hyde's *The Prospects of Humanism*, for (among many other things) criticising Middleton Murry, whilst himself criticising Murry, his older friend, patron and editor, in similarly patronising tones:

> This book is an indirect plea for a modern religion and a new order of priests. Mr. Hyde recognises that modern intellectuals have come, or are coming, to the end of themselves, and will have to look beyond themselves if they are to continue to live. He does not say so, but he means that they will have to look to the Divine Man in them, to the Lord of Life, to God. And then their work as intellectuals will not centre around Art as such or Literature as such, but around Religion. They will be priests.[408]

Parts of this review read as if Gerald were annoyed that someone had gone to print with ideas he would have preferred to publish himself. As with his review of Potter's book on Lawrence, however, his frustration may, in both instances, and more commendably have been motivated by his feeling that neither author had quite got the (or at least *his*) point regarding

---

[407] See above, p. 191.

[408] G.B. Edwards, 'A Prospective Religion', *Adelphi*, III, 2, new series (June, 1931), pp. 257-59. Gerald's review seems to have put Hyde off writing another book for the next fifteen years, when he published the misleadingly-titled *Isis and Osiris* (1946) and *I who am: a Study of the Self* (1954), a work which might have been more acceptable to Gerald, inasmuch as it was 'an enquiry into the limitations of the purely psychological approach to the study of human beings', albeit based on 'an analysis of Carl Jung's conception of the Unconscious'. For Hyde's immediate response to Gerald's review, which he published in the July issue, see below, p. 210.

the ultimate role of religion as the intensification of the authentically physical and intuitive life experience based on a conception of God. This is, however, neither Christian nor even Deist but rather existentialist in nature:

> He says that his primary concern is to 'show that in the end the purely humanistic attitude to the world breaks down, and that in so breaking down points beyond itself to the superior validity of the religious experience.'… But all the time he is perverse and indefinite about the very experience which is the crux of religion and the essential credential of every priest… He is willing to feel the Lord in his spirit, and wants to know Him in his mind, but will not acknowledge Him in his flesh.

He then launches into a somewhat back-handed - and at times facetiously high-handed - but ultimately defensive account of Murry which as well as explaining Gerald's attitude to the latter, reveals much about his 'peculiar personality' and his notion of the nature of religious belief:

> Take as an example his attack on Mr. Murry. During the last years Mr. Murry has laid himself open to every manner of calumny and misunderstanding by writing of the feelings nearest his heart. At the same time he has misled many (and sometimes lost himself) in a maze of self-hypnotic intellectualism by which he would explain his experience. Now Mr. Hyde comes along and completely ignores everything sincere and personal to Mr. Murry, and attacks his philosophy (which surely no one else but Mr. Hyde has ever discovered) as representative of a school of thought. It is a futile procedure, for while all his criticism of Mr. Murry is quite justified … he is really wasting his effort in conflict with his own image, and fails to perceive the growing point in Mr. Murry that is beyond him.
>
> Possibly it is half Mr. Murry's fault for having talked so much about *the* religious experience. All experience is religious: it merely varies in intensity and value. But Mr. Hyde abstracts experience from the person and his context of circumstance, and is then free to take flight into philosophical complexities. Yet the fact remains that Mr. Murry's work has made it clear that his religious experience

was the pinnacle of a sequence of human (and very human) experiences which were inseparable from his peculiar personality and his personal relationships. It is always so. The so-called religious experience is but the highest human experience, and needs every other human experience for its existence. Once this is acknowledged, then it can be given its supreme place as the clue to human life, and becomes essentially simple. It is the experience of a man when he forgives and is forgiven, when he loves and is loved.

If there were ever any doubt that Raymond, whose first sermon earns him the sack, is at least as much based on Gerald as Ebenezer is, then this and his subsequent essay on 'Religion' surely dispels it. In discussing Raymond, Ebenezer boasts a moral relativity that is contrasted with – even as it complements - his younger cousin's quest for an authentic truth. Where Raymond, no doubt like the young Gerald, reads the liberal Methodist, W.H. Fitchett's *The Unrealized Logic of Religion*,[409] Ebenezer advocates *ad hominem* judgements, even devilishly anarchic ones, so long as they are sincerely felt:

> I don't like people who preach. They put themselves on a pedestal and make out what they say is according to the Will of God and that what anybody else think different is of the Devil. I like a chap who say straight out what he think at the moment, and don't care a bugger if he is right or

---

[409] 'For himself, Raymond was reading a book I looked into, but couldn't make head or tail of. It was called *The Unrealised Logic of Religion*, I don't know by who.' (p. 131). The now unjustly forgotten Fitchett (1841-1928) was taken to Australia as a child and became a popular author and headmaster in Melbourne. Inasmuch as his book was sceptical of the uses (and inhumanity) of logic (and an advocate of 'the logic of the unlearned') Gerald would have been sympathetic if not indeed influenced by it if, as I suspect, he read it as a teenager. Gerald is also likely to have read Donald Hankey's *The Beloved Captain* before migrating permanently to England as Ebenezer talks of it as another book Raymond was reading at this time: 'but that book he had bought for his own, because he liked it so much. I liked the bits I read of it, myself. That Captain must have been a nice chap.' (*Ebenezer Le Page*, p. 131). A critical Christian, Hankey was killed in action at the Somme in October 1916. Though his publications don't seem to feature in studies of Wilfred Owen one suspects he would also have read Hankey's articles in the *Spectator* which were published posthumously to great acclaim as *A Student in Arms* in 1917; see Ross Davies's fascinating: '*A Student in Arms': Donald Hankey and Edwardian Society at War* (London, 2013).

wrong.[410]

Ebenezer's speculation regarding Raymond's motive for alienating the Church authorities might even provide a clue as to Gerald's only part-conscious motive/s for alienating a circle of English (and Irish) friends who had been so supportive of this outspoken outsider. Though he enjoyed his status as a 'genius' among this coterie, Gerald was unusually ambivalent about public recognition. Referring to Raymond's sermon, Ebenezer says:

> When he told me he was going to do it, he laughed and said, 'The Lord hath delivered them into my hands.' I have wondered since whether he didn't engineer the whole thing to get out of what he had let himself in for on the other side. Raymond was deep…[411]

Gerald's follow-up essay on 'Religion' appeared in the October 1931 issue of the *Adelphi* and was prompted by Hyde's dignified response to his 'spirited assault' on his *Prospects of Humanism*, which had appeared in the July issue.[412] It begins with a sort of apology but one still couched in his characteristically lofty tone. Referring to Hyde having 'bravely shot his last arrow at the Murry-Rees-Edwards-etc.-etc.-Neo-Romantic monster', he says he does not want to reply directly:

> … at least, not in public. In private I would have an apology to make to him, and some explanations… But my review of his book was too combative to permit him to read it: it blinded his eyes to the sympathy it concealed.
>
> I am sorry. And I will frankly admit that my review was far less merciful than just, and disproportionately

---

[410] *Ebenezer Le Page*, p. 174.

[411] *Ibid*. For what remained of Raymond's religion, see below, II, note 186.

[412] Hyde, 'Religion and "The Adelphi",' *The Adelphi*, II, 2 (July 1931), pp. 275-82. Hyde critiqued Gerald as an extreme manifestation of Murry's Neo-Romantic grouping, associating the latter with 'that accomplished wizard, Mr Santayana'. He accused Gerald of interpreting 'all purely intellectual activity' as 'nothing more than a sort of incidental accompaniment of spiritual activity' and of 'kicking the intellect downstairs' rather than seeking a new synthesis of mind and heart. The reference to Santayana was no doubt encouraged by the *Adelphi*'s publication his *The Genteel Tradition at Bay* in this year.

antagonistic in temper. But, to be just to myself also, it was at the same time a condemnation which presupposed a positive vision and a definite belief.

He then launches into his own, post-Nietzschean, post-William Jamesian account of religion. Though still couched in the language of Christianity, or at least the Bible, Gerald's Christ, like that of Raymond, who is defrocked for elaborating on this belief, is an entirely human one. He begins by re-emphasising his refutation of Hyde's categorisation of Murry and his followers (at least this one) as 'New Romantics':

> I don't believe in Romanticism, Neo or otherwise: I don't believe in any cultural religion of to-day. I believe in religion which is neither old nor new. I can't define religion. It is not any of the little religions: yet everything all the little religions have said is true. Religion is all human wisdom and every divine revelation that ever has been or will be: it is the sum of all hope, purpose, faith, endurance, love and courage, both discovered and undiscovered in the world; and it is every device of the human soul, spiritual, mental, and physical, whereby we human beings live and grow striving continually to rise into the fullness of our divine humanity.

> I believe that religion is necessary and always will be. And I believe that it is the one crying need of people, of all people, to-day. I believe it is that for which, unknown to themselves, they are hungering and thirsting, and which is more vitally necessary to them than food or drink ... religion is necessary even though it may mean another or many more little religions. There is but one place where man shall have no religion, and that is in the Kingdom of Heaven.

> So I would see a revival of religion in any and every form. Every religious practise (and excess) that the modern cultured intellectual abuses (and fears) I would welcome again among us… I would see new churches being built… I would have Pagan rites of the body mingling with Christian rites of the soul, and giving birth to new symbols of the hope of man re-born…

> For the purpose of religion is beyond culture, beyond

civilisation, in fact beyond history (as we know it) altogether. It goes on through history shedding civilisations from itself like leaves from a tree, but at every moment in its progress the direction of the true religious soul is towards that assured but unimaginable state where man shall emerge in the full glory, at last, of the power that is nascent in him.[413]

It is a pity that Richard Rees, who participated in this debate on religion that Gerald had prompted, seems to have accepted Gerald's disappearance by the time he published *A Theory of my Time*. I nevertheless suspect that like Murry and Plowman, who, unlike Potter and Collis, also failed to acknowledge Gerald in their published writings, Rees would have been thinking of his former travelling companion as he recalled the great religious debate between Eliot and Murry:

> This debate between an orthodox Anglican and a Christian heretic was probably the most serious intellectual controversy in England during the period, but it attracted little interest in spite of the eminence of both parties to it.

It is surely significant in this respect that Rees concludes this paragraph on a note which suggests that, although he appreciated the significance of the less specifically Christian advocates of religion, he was himself too sensible to join them:

> Nor has much attention ever been paid to the religious preoccupation of D.H. Lawrence, in spite of his ever-increasing fame.[414]

If this were true in 1963, better-known now is Lawrence's post-Jamesian credo:

> My great religion is a belief in the blood, the flesh, as being wiser than the intellect.[415]

---

[413] G.B. Edwards, 'Religion', *Adelphi*, III, 1, new series (October, 1931), pp. 50-53. For all their shared origins, Gerald's ideas on religion clearly influenced his friend Collis's; Richard Ingrams's Christian critique of the latter applying to both; see his *Collis*, pp. 143-47. In a more mature form, they are epitomised in the poem he sent to Murry in 1947: 'Song of a Man who saw God' (see Appendix 1).

[414] *Theory of my Time*, p. 44; *cf.* above, p.68, for his comparison with Simone Weil.

[415] *Letters of D.H. Lawrence* (17 January 1913), I, p. 503.

# 17: GUERNSEY GATTOPARDO

It is perhaps unfair to compare the more popularly-esteemed, yet class-conscious mainlander McEwan - who informs us that he has 'no patience whatsoever' with religion[416] - with the still underestimated and classless islander Edwards. Where fellow-islanders, indeed fellow fishermen, are concerned, more appropriate might be a comparison with Giovanni Verga's *I Malavoglia*.[417] Verga left his native Sicily and wrote about it from the mainland with an obsessive combination of realism and nostalgia that inspired D.H. Lawrence to call him 'Homeric'. In 1923, Lawrence translated Verga's *Mastro-don-Gesualdo* - featuring a Sicilian peasant whose integrity is not recognised by the family he marries into - and two years later published Verga's *Novelle Rusticane* as *Little Novels of Sicily*. If only because of Lawrence's involvement, Gerald would have been familiar with both these works and no doubt noted the parallels between his island identity and Verga's. Unlike Gerald, however, Verga returned to his childhood home in his fifties and died there a celebrated Senator of the Republic.[418]

More qualitatively challenging, however, would be the comparison between *The Book of Ebenezer Le Page* and Lampedusa's *Il Gattopardo*, not quite accurately translated as *The Leopard* (the 'gattopardo' or serval is an even rarer beast).[419]

---

[416] *Daily Telegraph Review*, 30 August 2014, p. 5.

[417] I owe this suggestion to Vittorio Gabrieli's article on 'Il libro di Ebenezer Le Page' in *La Cultura*, no. 2 (2001), pp. 295-301. We have seen that Gerald produced a play about a fisherman in November 1930; see above, p. 135.

[418] In the introduction to his translation of *Mastro-Don Gesualdo* (1923), Lawrence wrote that 'the deepest nostalgia I have ever felt has been for Sicily, reading Verga. Not for England or anywhere else – for Sicily, the beautiful, that which goes deepest into the blood. It is so clear, so beautiful, so like the physical beauty of the Greek!' Elsewhere he described Verga as 'the only Italian who does interest me' and 'extraordinarily good' and that 'Poor old Verga went and died when I was about to meet him in Catania'; *Letters of D.H. Lawrence*, IV, pp. 109-110 and 186; *cf*. E. Chaney, 'British and American Travellers in Sicily…', *The Evolution of the Grand Tour*, 2nd ed. (London, 2000), pp. 1-40.

[419] Both Verga's *I Malavoglia* and Lampedusa's *Gattopardo* were transformed into films by Luchino Visconti, who also created a film out of D'Annunzio's *L'Innocente*, unfashionably admired by Lampedusa. Although I don't remember Gerald referring to Lampedusa, he would certainly have been all too conscious

Fig. 68: Giuseppe Tomasi di Lampedusa and Gioacchino Lanza
Tomasi in the ruined castle of Montechiaro, Sicily.
(photo: Giuseppe Biancheri, 1955)

Lampedusa and his creation, Don Fabrizio, are both nostalgic vestiges of a pre-modern world, casting critical eyes on the new, mercantile and mechanical vulgarity that encroaches upon their island.

Gerald and his creation, Ebenezer, respond in similar ways to equivalent encroachments. The fact that Don Fabrizio is an aristocrat and Ebenezer a peasant, only sharpens the symmetry and highlights the common enemy, for both are anachronisms whose ancient wisdom encourages them to resist changes which are essentially bourgeois-driven.[420] Don Fabrizio's relationship

---

of the 1958 posthumous publication of the *Gattopardo* and its 1963 translation, which coincided with the release (in both Italian and English) of Visconti's film.

[420] *Cf.* Lampedusa's aphorism: 'Se vogliamo che tutto rimanga come è, bisogna che tutto cambi.' ('If we want everything to stay the same as it is, everything will have to change.') with Ebenezer's 'things got to change … but they ought to

with his impetuous nephew, Tancredi, parallels the real Lampedusa's friendship with Gioacchino, the son of a second cousin he eventually adopts, just as Ebenezer's relationship with artist-rebel Neville Falla, the young man who marries his illegitimate grand-daughter and becomes his heir, resembles Gerald's 'adoption' of me [Fig. 68].[421] Though the childless and far from sexually liberated Lampedusa seems not have submitted to psychoanalysis *per se*, he read Freud and was married to an analyst to whom he occasionally related his dreams.[422]

Recently retranslated as *The Professor and the Siren*, the relationship between the old Sicilian Senator in exile, La Ciula, and his young protégé, Paolo Corbera, in Lampedusa's *La Sirena*, includes still more striking parallels.[423] Three years younger than Lampedusa but outliving him by almost twenty, Gerald set his great novel in the late 19th and 20th centuries, a generation ahead of his own. Lampedusa set the *Gattopardo* further back in the period of his great-grandfather, Prince Giulio's encounter with the Risorgimento, which threatened what was sacred and customary about his beloved island. For Lampedusa and Gerald, both in fact and fiction, the Second World War was perceived as deeply destructive of their islands' cultural memory. In *The Professor and the Siren* Paolo's precious souvenirs of his mentor are destroyed in the war. In *The Leopard*, Bourbon Sicily is invaded by Garibaldi and his Redshirts as the advanced guard of an invasion by middle-class bureaucrats from mainland Italy. In Lampedusa's lifetime, Sicily was dominated first by Mussolini and his agents and then by the

---

change so as you don't notice.'; *Ebenezer Le Page*, p. 167.

[421] Though Gioacchino's father was Lampedusa's second cousin, they only became acquainted in 1952, five years before the latter died; see G.L. Tomasi, *A Biography through Images*, p. 79; *cf.* alainelkanninterviews.com/lanza-tomasi/; *cf.* the wonderful interview with him at NYU: www.youtube.com/ watch?v=J50cWxwK2n4. For both Lampedusa and Gerald predicting problems for the marriages of their fictionalised protégés, see below, p. 322.

[422] See for this, and his admiration for Freud, Tomasi, *Biography*, pp. 75 and 122.

[423] *La Sirena*, introduction by Gioacchino Lanza Tomasi (Milan, 2014), newly translated by Stephen Twilley for Gerald's American publisher, NYRB, as *The Professor and the Siren*, introduction by Marina Warner (New York, 2014).

Germans whose eviction by the Allies involved the destruction of his family Palazzo in Palermo, an event that so distressed Lampedusa it prompted him to write his great novel. During his post-war visits to Guernsey, Gerald questioned his fellow-islanders about the German occupation and subsequent liberation, meanwhile observing what he describes as the next invasion, by tourists and tax-escapees from mainland Britain.[424]

Gerald lost the home he was supposed to inherit, not like Lampedusa, due to Allied bombing but to his father's remarriage. As in *The Leopard*, it is difficult to distinguish the author's more or less political protest from the poignancy of personal loss and periodic angst. Gerald must have had such dreams and aspirations when, like James Joyce he decided 'to fly by those nets' of nationality, language and religion flung at him by his native island, as also by his formidable mother. Like Joyce, however, his imaginative soul broke free even as it also fed upon these cultural memories. It could be argued that although both men exiled themselves from their respective islands, Joyce and Gerald constructed more positive (albeit homesick?) images of their native lands than either Thomas Hardy or Lampedusa, who travelled rather than migrated, even if all four authors ultimately envisage their birth-rights in quasi-tragic or at least melancholic terms.[425]

Gerald has Liza Quéripel express her feelings for Guernsey after at first alienating Ebenezer with her enthusiasm for London:

> … she stopped dead in her tracks and gripped me by both arms and turned me to face her in the wild way she had. She had a grip of steel. She said, 'I swear every day and

---

[424] One of the reasons for the lack of official enthusiasm for, or promotion of, the greatest work of art by a native Guernseyman, not least on the part of the Guernsey Tourist Board (see the *Ebenezer*-less, two-page spreads in the Sunday supplements), may be statements such as that which Gerald included in his preface-turned-appendix to the novel, 'Guernsey English': 'Tourism is an incubus that saps the natural and spiritual vitality of the island'. For the argument that Sicily might even benefit from tourism were it more judiciously distributed, from Cefalu and Taormina (whose 'parterre of English weeds' was already critiqued by D.H. Lawrence), to Palermo, Messina and Catania, see Chaney, 'British and American Travellers in Sicily…', pp. 39-40.

[425] For Gerald on *Ebenezer's* 'tone of tragi-comic irony', see below, p. 320.

every hour I am away from Guernsey, my heart is bleeding secretly to be back. When I stand on the deck of the ship coming down the Russel and see Herm and Jethou and Sark behind, and the Brehon Tower, I know I am home!' I liked her then.[426]

Having never been further than Jersey, Ebenezer expresses his own poignant nostalgia for the *genius loci* in these terms:

I have lived all my days to the sound of bells of the Vale Church, coming to me on the wind over the water. When I was a boy I used to hear them playing a hymn of a Sunday evening, and then the quick ding-dong, ding-dong, before the service began; and I would hear them practising of a Wednesday night... [Fig. 69].[427]

Fig. 69: *Vale Church, Guernsey* (photo: States of Guernsey).

Elsewhere, however, Gerald merges Ebenezer's voice with his own, as he migrates from the specificity of the island to its microcosmic significance, only returning in order to depict his *alter ego* as an internal exile, lamenting the loss of the ancient authenticities and so many 'improvements for the worse':

---

[426] *Ebenezer Le Page*, p. 140.

[427] *Ebenezer Le Page*, p. 57. Poignantly, the mere title of a poem, entitled: 'Sailing Down The Russell', survives among Gerald's manuscripts.

Mind you, I am not one of those who say living on Guernsey in the good old days was a bed of roses. I think living in this world is hell on earth for most of us most of the time, it don't matter when or where we are born; but the way we used to live over here, I mean in the country parts, was more or less as it had been for many hundreds of years; and it was real... When I think what have happened to our island, I could sit down on the ground and cry...[428]

In *The Professor and the Siren*, Lampedusa, to a significant extent also an internal exile, imagines *his* curmudgeonly *alter ego*, Senator La Ciura, as having, just like Gerald:

scarcely visited [his] island for fifty years, and yet his memory of certain minute details was remarkably precise. 'Sicily's sea is the most vividly colored, the most romantic of any I have ever seen; it's the only thing you won't manage to ruin, at least away from the cities. Do the trattorias by the sea still serve spiny urchins, split in half?'... 'What flavor! How divine in appearance! My most beautiful memory of the last fifty years!'[429]

Albeit then elaborated in graphically sexualised terms, this celebration of an island speciality cannot fail to remind one of Ebenezer's paean in honour of the ormer:

The food I like best of all foods is ormers; but you can't always get them. My father used to take me with him ormering ... I can't say what ormers taste like. They are not like fish, flesh, or fowl. They are like no other food on earth. I have heard of the nectar of the gods. Or is it ambrosia they feed on? That must be ormers.[430]

Though closer to Lampedusa and Gerald than to Lawrence and

---

[428] *Ebenezer Le Page*, pp. 171-72.

[429] *The Professor and the Siren, ed. cit.*, p. 11; *cf.* the original *La Sirena*, republished this year by Feltrinelli with a CD of Gioacchino Tomasi's precious recording of Lampedusa reading the story in February 1957, a few months before he died. I greatly regret not recording Gerald reading at least a part of *Ebenezer Le Page*, though in 2012 I managed to persuade AudioGo (now Audible) to record Roy Dotrice reading the entire book after the BBC failed to locate his original, abridged 'Woman's Hour' reading.

[430] *Ebenezer Le Page*, p. 17.

Joyce in publishing relatively little and then leaving it to the next generation to have the bulk of his writings printed, perhaps only the similarly depressive Shakespeare got the balance between life and art right, retaining a foothold in his native Stratford and significantly enlarging this to return home and retire in prosperity. Gerald resembled Shelley in his determination to live the dream to the more or less bitter end. For all his denials he was an incurable, indeed uncompromising Romantic but one who refused to die young because he hadn't yet fulfilled his destiny.[431] Like Shelley, his refusal to compromise with the requirements of society, friends or family, brought a more minor version of the trauma suffered by Shelley's friends and family down upon all concerned, but above all upon himself.

A more pragmatic literary exile of whom Gerald (like fellow-exile Joseph Conrad) was particularly conscious was Victor Hugo, whose *Les Travailleurs de la Mer (Toilers of the Sea)* of 1866 was set in the Guernsey that became his adopted home after he left France in 1851. Published in Brussels in 1866, four years after *Les Misérables*, the exiled Hugo dedicated it: 'au rocher d'hospitalité et de liberté, à ce coin de vieille terre normande où vit le noble petit peuple de la mer, à l'île de Guernesey, sévère et douce, mon asile actuel, mon tombeau probable.' Gerald has Raymond read the whole of *Les Misérables* in French when recuperating from influenza, but more relevant to his own novel was *Toilers of the Sea*, to which he referred in conversation and correspondence with me.[432] Hugo's principal protagonist, Gilliatt, however, is an epic hero who has to fight the sea and indeed an octopus in order to win the hand of his beloved. When, despite his success in these testing enterprises he loses her to another – as it happens a young clergyman called Ebenezer - he drowns himself in the very sea over which he had previously prevailed.

By comparison with the Romantic grandeur of Byron, Shelley and Hugo's protagonists, though he manages to kill a German soldier who was trying to sodomise an East European

---

[431] See his letter of 8 July 1975 when he silently references Shelley and states 'I am not a Romantic'; below, p. 295.

[432] *Ebenezer Le Page*, p. 123.

slaveworker, Gerald's bandy-legged tomato grower is not most people's idea of an *Übermensch*. His equivalent struggle to Gilliat's with the octopus was his successful landing of a conger eel.[433] Yet Gerald leads the reader through Ebenezer's long life and loves with such artful authenticity, he encourages a sort of evolutionary identification with his *alter ego*. His unpretentious insistence on maintaining Ebenezer's unintellectualizing identity provides us with a kind of consolation that the more conventional (but less down to earth) tragic hero does not. In seeking precedents for this rare combination of archetypes, some of Chaucer's creations come to mind, even if underpinning these, Gerald's youthful Nietzscheanism persists and indeed re-emerges in the quiet climax of the novel.

Shelley drowned like Hugo's hero and Lampedusa's La Ciula, though he took an innocent party with him. Hugo himself, however, returned to prosperity in France, as Sinuhe returned to Egypt, Shakespeare to Stratford, Ibsen to Norway, Strindberg to Sweden, Verga and Lampedusa to Sicily (inasmuch as the latter ever left it), and Solzhenitsyn to Mother Russia.[434] Like La Ciula, Gerald remained an exile to the end, even if Ebenezer never left his native land. If Lampedusa's Professor could not have the sublime erotic experience he had had with his beloved siren off the coast of his native Sicily, he would not settle for second best anywhere else. In the end both Gerald and Lampedusa took the advice that Ebenezer extracts from the Book of Isaiah (51:1): 'look unto the rock whence ye are hewn, and to the hole of the pit whence ye are digged.'[435] Only in Hugo's fiction does the hero sit on a Guernsey rock awaiting death by drowning, or in that of Lampedusa does the Professor finally cast himself overboard to join his beloved Siren.

---

[433] *Ebenezer Le Page*, p. 286. This might even be a parody of the Hugo episode though at the time Ebenezer is close to starving due to the German occupation; *cf.* Peter Goodall, '*The Book of Ebenezer Le Page*: Guernsey and the Channel Islands in the 20th Century', *The 2nd International Small Island Cultures Conference, Norfolk Island Museum* ed. H. Johnson, 9-13 February 2006, pp. 54-60.

[434] For Gerald on Solzhenitsyn see below, p. 257.

[435] For this and other comparisons with Hugo, see the articles by Peter Goodall, culminating in '"The Rock whence ye are hewn".' Ebenezer's own name is derived from the Hebrew for stone.

# 18: EBENEZER CONCEIVED

When Lampedusa's great novel was finally published, Gerald had been living as a solitary lodger, first in the slums of Notting Hill and then the suburbs of south London, since the Second World War. On 24 December 1961 he wrote to his cousin, Hilda, in Guernsey that he was 'feeling depressed and worn out and not at all like Christmas'.[436]   From the same Balham address fourteen years earlier, he had sent a magnificent poem to Middleton Murry, who had returned to editing the *Adelphi*. Whether or not Murry replied, he seems not have published the poem, which to this day remains attached to Gerald's letter by a rusty paper clip [Fig. 70 and Appendix 1].[437]

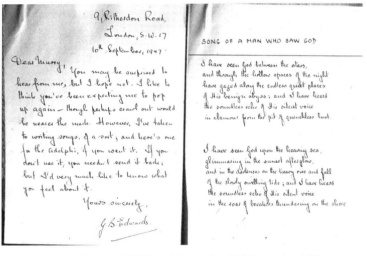

Fig.. 70: Letter to Middleton Murry, dated 10 September 1947 with first page of poem attached.

---

[436] He lodged at 23 Chepstow Road in 1945 and then, from at least as early as September 1947, at 9 Ritherdon Road, his landlady being Miss Violet Mary Beresford, who lived there from 1895 until her death in 1988; information from Martin MacDonald, who was her lodger in the 1980s. This was not far south of 36 Old Park Avenue, the house in which  Stephen Potter was born and which Gerald used to visit, to preach Nietzsche and take a bath.

[437] See below, Appendix 1, p. 347. The letter and poem form part of the collection I acquired from Robin Waterfield's Oxford Bookshop in 1985; see *Waterfield's Catalogue 50*, item 1378.

This poem, entitled 'Song of a Man who saw God', shows that Gerald needed no lessons from the likes of McEwan on the darker side of life but, rather than follow the even darker Samuel Beckett into aesthetic 'impoverishment', into 'taking away, in subtracting rather than in adding,' he persevered in evolving his own far richer, religio-humanist aesthetic.[438] Thus do these lines rather remind one of the similarly conflicted Wilfred Owen's 'I, too, saw God through mud…' in his *Apologia pro Poemate Meo*, or Whitman's 'Song of Myself':

> … and I have heard
> the soundless echo of His silent voice
> in the last fierce death-gasp from the entrails torn.[439]

In preparing this chapter, based on the 'post-fazione' I wrote for the Italian edition of *Ebenezer*, I noticed that Gerald re-uses these concluding lines of this 1947 poem in a poem he sent me in 1975. Somewhat disingenuously he told me he was enclosing a couple of 'spontaneous' lyrics, 'as L'Envoi to Sarnia Chérie'.

The first of these lyrics, which I transcribe here, is entitled 'Benediction', and is clearly indebted to Gerald's 1947 poem:

> Between the syllables of babble,
> mine and thine,
> in blast of thunder
> and fall of dew,
> in vow of lover
> and troth of friend,
> in first bleak cry
> of babe new born,
> in last fierce death-gasp

---

[438] James Olney, *Memory and Narrative: The Weave of Life-Writing* (Chicago, 1998), p. 348; *cf.* God in *Exodus*, 33:20: 'there shall be no man see me, and live'.

[439] See Appendix 1 for the complete poem. In his fine 1929 *Adelphi* review of Krishnamurti's *Life in Freedom*, Gerald writes that: 'it does not satisfy me as some human utterances which say the same thing *do* satisfy me – Whitman's "Song of Myself," for instance, or the Sermon on the Mount.' Middleton Murry was an early appreciator of Wilfred Owen, writing to Katherine Mansfield of the poems published in the Sitwells' 1919 *Wheels* that: 'It's what Sassoon might have done, if he were any real good'; see Max Egremont, *Some Desperate Glory: The First World War the Poets Knew* (London, 2014), p. 247.

from entrails torn,
he silent is: nor condemn,
nor pardon, He is benign.[440]


The second lyric was entitled: 'Canticle' [Fig. 71].

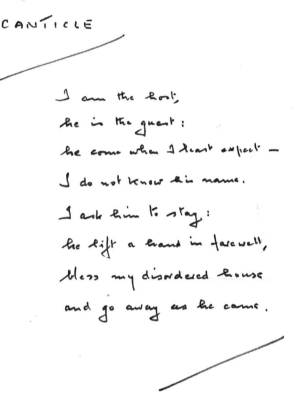

CANTICLE

I am the host;
he is the guest:
he comes when I least expect —
I do not know his name.
I ask him to stay:
he lift a brand in farewell,
bless my disordered house
and go away as he came.

Fig. 71: *Canticle*; as sent to the author in 1975.

Gerald's 'atonement' for a life of worldly failure (or relative indifference to worldly success) is a reminder of the redemptive role that art can still play in our lives. He remained resolutely faithful to a notion of authentic life and love as religion, and art

---

[440] See below, p. 296, for further discussion.

as inseparable from this sacred combination.

In the *Spectator* article on Gerald already quoted, his one-time intimate, J.S. Collis, concluded on an exaggeratedly despairing note [Fig. 72]. This was no doubt due to a variety of personal

Fig. 72: *J.S. 'Jack' Collis* (1900-1984). (c. 1982)

regrets, but prominent among them must have been that he had ever abandoned his belief in Gerald's 'genius'. Implicit also was Collis's acknowledgement that towards the end of Gerald's life, albeit with a single book to Collis's dozen, the creator of *Ebenezer Le Page* had confirmed his superior status in their artistic relationship. Recalling their profound but occasionally fraught friendship, one which may have contributed to the less cultured but undying fictional friendship between the young Ebenezer and Jim Mahy, he concluded by quoting one of the surprising number of female authors who have recognised Gerald's climactic genius.

My relations with him became strained on the literary front. 'I have just burnt some of my MSS' he would say, 'including *The Idea of Ideas*, perhaps my best work'. I thought this silly and pompous. 'Here are five poems' he wrote, 'which I enclose for the good of your soul'. I … replied that they interested me but did not move me much. And I said something about lacking 'magic of phrase'. This brought me a 20-page letter on my own shortcomings. 'It is not my inadequate little poems that are at fault, John. Forgive me for saying so, but for you to appreciate those poems you must first *know* the same Lord. On reading them you feel that you do not or cannot or will not acknowledge the same Lord as I do – so you are hurt and hit back'. And much more in the same vein. Then – 'Oh, John when you start talking magic of phrase at me I fear for you! We don't read books for their tone or their rhythm or their magic of phrase – but as Human Documents.....' I now think that he was right to be annoyed, for he was eventually to be the author of *Ebenezer Le Page*. In *Ebenezer* there is no magic of phrase: the whole thing is so intensely magical an evocation that 'the reader is rendered speechless'.[441]

[441] Collis, 'Memories of a Genius Friend', p. 22. Collis's final quotation is taken from Isobel Murray's 1981 review of *Ebenezer Le Page* in the *Financial Times*; see below, p. 229. Professor Murray is now Emeritus Professor of English Literature at King's College, University of Aberdeen.

Fig. 73: *Gerald Edwards, Upwey*
(photo: Anthony Willey, c.1972).

# PART TWO:
# THE BOOK OF G.B. EDWARDS

## 1:  RECEPTION OF *EBENEZER*

In March 1981, Hamish Hamilton, soon followed by Penguin in Britain, Knopf, Avon and Moyer Bell in America, published a fictional autobiography entitled *The Book of Ebenezer Le Page.* Next to nothing was known of its author, G.B. Edwards, a reclusive Guernseyman who had died in Weymouth aged 77 in December 1976. These English language editions were succeeded by a prize-winning French translation published by Maurice Nadeau, followed by Editions Points, and eventually an Italian version by Elliot Edizioni.[1] Meanwhile, in 1982 the first abridged and dramatised version of the original, movingly read by Guernsey-born Roy Dotrice, was broadcast in twenty-eight, 15-minute episodes on BBC Radio 4's *Woman's Hour.* A decade later, the latter's half-French series producer, Pat McLoughlin, confirmed that this was: 'without question, the most popular serial I have ever done in the five hundred or so I have produced in the last twenty-one years...'[2]  In the new millennium, largely thanks to Edwin Frank, New York Review Books reissued the novel in their Classics series and have kept it in print in both Britain and America ever since, latterly in e-book form [Fig. 74].[3]

The film rights have been sold several times but although play-scripts have been produced and very successful theatrical

---

[1] Janine Hérisson's French edition won the 4th (1983) Prix Baudelaire for the 1982 translation of what they published as: *Sarnia,* which title was closer to Gerald's intended one: *Sarnia Chérie* but lacks his subtitle which would have been *Le Livre d'Ebenezer Le Page*. A new paperback Italian edition of *Il Libro di Ebenezer Le Page* was published in 2014.

[2] In a 1992 letter to Martin Ellis (who had acquired the film option for the *Book*), forwarded to the author. McLoughlin's obituary in the *Daily Telegraph* (28 February 2000)  singled out the production of *Ebenezer Le Page* as one of her greatest successes 'after early doubts from colleagues and listeners alike'.

[3] For this edition, R.B. Kitaj kindly allowed me to use his 2006 oil sketch of *Blake's God* for the cover.

productions have been staged in England and Guernsey, the novel has yet to make the transition to cinema or TV, in the case of the latter partly because I have resisted proposals to turn it into a 'series'. Finally, in 2012, AudioGo issued the first audiobook version, in both CD and downloadable format, a 21-and-a-half-hour recording of the now 92-year-old Roy Dotrice reading the entire novel.[4]

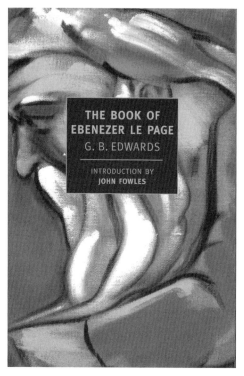

Fig. 74: *The Book of Ebenezer Le Page*, NYRB Classics edition (2007) with cover featuring R.B. Kitaj's oil on canvas of *Blake's God* (2006).

Most of what was known about the author, was included in a eulogistic introduction to the book written by John Fowles. Fowles had not known Edwards personally but responded enthusiastically to the publisher's suggestion that he promote this unknown work as a major new discovery. Set entirely in

---

[4] AudioGo's list has since been taken over by Audible, a branch of Amazon.

Guernsey, as Ebenezer tells his story he shifts back and forth between near present ('I am the oldest on the island, I think') to distant past (as far back as the end of the nineteenth century) and still nearer present (up to the 1960s) in an apparently unstructured way. As one reads on, the gap between even the recent past and present closes, disappearing entirely as the narrator puts down his pen upon completing the last of his 'three big books' and falls asleep for the last time. Ebenezer bequeaths his manuscript, along with a pot of gold sovereigns, to a young artist he has befriended. He never marries but loves (and is often infuriated by) a remarkable woman, Liza Quéripel, whose illegitimate grandson turns out to be the artist he has chosen as his heir. Ebenezer discovers that he too has a grandchild he never knew was his and that this is the girl the artist has chosen to marry, thereby effecting at least a vicarious conjunction between himself and Liza. He also, in an equivalently ambivalent way, loves Guernsey, or *Sarnia Chérie* as the novel was supposed to be called, but he is ever more scornful of the tourist-and-tax-avoiding occupation which succeeds the German one.

The book is rich in plots and subplots via which the author explores a fascinating range of human relationships at the deepest level. Once one has entered the world he creates with almost obsessive thoroughness in the first few chapters, one can scarcely fail to be moved, often to tears, by much of what happens to the various characters during the rest of them. As William Golding said in his *Guardian* review of 'this extraordinary book', full of 'wonderful writing':

> The texture of Edwards' writing is so dense, the detail of such inbuilt authenticity you hardly seem to be reading at all, but living, in the peculiar circumstances of peasant life.[5]

Of Ebenezer himself Golding wrote 'Nor are simple adjectives

---

[5] *Guardian*, 19 March 1981. In view of the life-art balance discussed elsewhere, it perhaps says more of his own relatively unsatisfactory concluding experiences that Golding also wrote: 'I do not believe that in the twilight of his [Ebenezer's] life he would come across two young people so perfectly suited to his requirements as Adèle and the rioting artist, nor that they would have bothered with him…'; *cf.* John Carey, *William Golding: The Man who wrote Lord of the Flies* (London, 2009), *passim.*

adequate ... there is epic stature in his individualism...'. In *The Daily Telegraph,* Nina Bawden wrote of his 'strong, compelling, seductive voice, both wily and innocent ... it holds the reader in an Ancient Mariner grip throughout this brilliant, unusual, and - very sadly - posthumous novel'.[6]

In *The Financial Times* of 17 July 1981 Isobel Murray wrote that:

> the achievement is so intense and universal that the reader is rendered speechless. Ebenezer would interject that that was a fine thing for a reviewer... His heir is a painter. He says 'All I want to paint is the real feel of the actual thing in front of me. I will never get to it, I know; but I can try'. This seems to me the attitude of the novelist, G.B. Edwards, and in an extraordinary way I think he has succeeded in writing a great novel.[7]

In *The Sunday Times,* the following December, Golding chose *Ebenezer Le Page* as 'my first choice' for 'Book of the Year'.[8] In America, *The New Yorker* devoted two full pages to 'this lovely book', *Newsweek* called it 'a breathtaking novel' while Guy Davenport, writing on the front page of *The New York Times Book Review* called it 'one of the best novels of our time...', concluding: 'I know of no description of happiness in modern literature equal to the one that ends this novel'.

In his review in *Le Monde* of the French edition, *Sarnia,* Hubert Juin likewise dwelt upon the book's ultimately positive vision and its extraordinarily authentic expression:

> Cette sorte de miracle tient à l'étrange fraicheur de l'écriture, sinon à la merveilleuse naïveté de l'écrivain. G. B. Edwards ne songe pas à *écrire*, il a pour seul impératif de *parler.'*[9]

I hope from Part I and what follows that it will be clear that no

---

[6] 19 March 1981.

[7] *Financial Times*, 17 April 1981; *cf.* above, p. 225.

[8] 6 December 1981.

[9] 'This type of miracle carries a strange freshness of writing, if not the marvellous naivety of the writer. G. B. Edwards does not seek to *write*, his sole imperative is to *speak.'* In *L'Express* of 22-28 July 1983, Michel Braudeau praises 'la réussite de G.B. Edwards' to that of Michel de Montaigne.

such straightforward identification between the author and his apparently provincial creation is possible. American author-reviewers, most recently Anne Tyler, have been perhaps the most appreciative of the *Book*, apparently less worried about its failure to conform to modernist (and/or post-modernist) criteria, perhaps less snooty also about encountering emotionalism in a provincial setting.[10] Despite being a prominent American member of a fashionably French literary society by the name of Oulipo, Harry Mathews registered a powerfully personal response to the climax of *Ebenezer Le Page* in the entry dated '6/16/84' in his Stendhalian *20 Lines a Day*. Addressing himself, stream-of-consciousness style, not knowing more than was in Fowles's introduction to the novel, Mathews grasped what it was that Gerald was communicating through Ebenezer:

> Are you going to wait until you are on the point of death to give up this model: your old, old self, tiny, terrified, aware of his power only through the intensity of the anxieties that shrivelled him? A lifetime of refusal ending in a revelation that melts the past in one moment or movement of surrender to the truth makes a fit drama for literature, as you just rediscovered in finishing *The Book of Ebenezer Le Page*. The copiousness of your tears (as you the 'modernist' abounded in the 'romanticism' of Ebenezer's last pages) suggests the intensity with which you deny yourself the process of opening-up that so touched you in that imaginary old man. Why else were you crying? What burial were you mourning over, if not that of your own unrealized life?[11]

In 2000, partly due to the prompting of her husband, Michael Holroyd (who with A.N. Wilson and Richard Ingrams had re-

---

[10] Apparently undeterred by Gerald's pejorative portrayal of the female, Anne Tyler cites *Ebenezer Le Page* as one of a handful of 'books she returns to again and again' (*New York Times,* 5 February 2015). I thank her warmly for confirming her enthusiasm for Gerald's writing (and for my daughter's singing) in an email (11 February 2015): 'Years ago, the New York Times asked a bunch of writers what literary character they would most like to be, and I named Ebenezer Le Page.'

[11] Harry Mathews, *20 Lines a Day* (Chicago, 1988), p. 128. I thank Jaspreet Singh Boparai for drawing my attention to this remarkable passage.

discovered Gerald's friend and admirer J.S. Collis), Margaret Drabble added an entry on G.B. Edwards and *The Book of Ebenezer Le Page* to her revised (6th) edition of the *Oxford Companion to English Literature*.[12] More recently, on a 2004 website recommending summer reading to his Stanford University students, the Shakespearean scholar (and fellow Inigo Jonesian), Stephen Orgel, wrote: 'G.B. Edwards, *The Book of Ebenezer Le Page*. I'd never heard of it. A friend gave it to me. It was written by an 80 year old recluse on the island of Guernsey, which is where it's set, and it seems to me one of the greatest novels of the 20th century. Really'.[13] Since then, stimulated by the 2007 NYRB Classics edition, the Anglo-German-American, author and translator, Michael Hofmann, eulogised 'G.B. Edwards's miraculous novel *The Book of Ebenezer Le Page*':

> There is a rare wholeness about *The Book of Ebenezer Le Page*. You get the entire man, in a way that isn't usually within the gift of literature to procure... Edwards's great accomplishment is to have constructed a stately, almost imposing ... narrative out of such crooked, personality-steeped sentences ... one wouldn't have thought it was load-bearing, or could go in a straight line, but it is and does... I have read few books of such wide and delightful appeal ... [it] is vast fun and vast life, a *Kulturgeschichte* and a *roman à thèse*.[14]

Finally, launching what will inevitably become a more academic but hopefully still human response, the Australian literary scholar, Peter Goodall, writes:

> As the story moves to its conclusion, the simplicity of its events and the lives of its characters take on a transcendent cast, as if the small island were a microcosm on which matters of mythical scope and significance were being played out. At first sight the materials of the narrative seem unprepossessing [but] one of Edwards's great

---

[12] Margaret Drabble's entry seems to have been abandoned by her more restrictively academic successor, Dinah Birch, in the 7th edition of the *Companion*.

[13] Stanford University Department of English: Summer Reading: Top Picks 2004.

[14] 'Reading with No Clothes on', *London Review of Books* (24 January 2008), p. 23.

achievements is to make Ebenezer's story and the story of his island so moving in spite of this.[15]

## 2: 'GENIUS FRIEND'

But I should perhaps have begun by attempting to explain why an English art historian (of sorts) should be discussing Guernsey's greatest novelist at all. And I suppose the best way of doing this is to explain how I came to meet Gerald Edwards in the first place and then quote from some of the many letters he wrote during the last four and a half years of his life. In the process of doing so I hope I can shed new light on the way in which *The Book of Ebenezer Le Page* was completed, perfected, repeatedly rejected, and only after its author's death, at last published. The letters reveal much about a remarkable man whose uncompromising efforts to produce a literary masterpiece of which he could at last be proud, took a lifetime.

Fig. 75: Beloved great-aunt
Josephine Chaney.
(oil on canvas, H. Ricketts, c.1966)

As a rather-more-rebellious-than-average teenager, lead guitarist in an unsuccessful folk-rock band and aspiring art student, by the summer of 1969 it was felt that I would benefit from a lengthy spell as far as feasible from the drug-culture of London. My parents were relieved when, with my one 'A' level in Art, I expressed a willingness to go and stay in Dorset with great-aunt Josephine for a dose of bourgeois civilisation [Fig. 75].

Since I was, of course, an aspiring intellectual as well

[15] Goodall, '"The Rock whence ye are Hewn".'

as artist, my aunt's library as well as her piano, painting studio and the romantic setting of Bankside Cottage in the village of Upwey near Weymouth, helped persuade me to go - though the relative proximity of another cottage belonging to the parents of the drummer in my band and often used for dissolute parties, made the prospect of Dorset that bit more alluring.

Things worked out better than could have been expected. My octogenarian aunt and I became the closest of friends and, despite my disreputable appearance, I was soon deemed sufficiently respectable to be introduced to her cronies in and around the village. Among these was Nye Norman, a wealthy connoisseur of music who had retired to a nearby manor house and patronised a local student pianist. The latter, Elizabeth Snell, would come to my aunt's house to perform to small, invited audiences while I passed round the cucumber sandwiches.

During this period of about four months I painted enough to get a place on an art school foundation course which in turn led to a place at Reading University. Though I returned to my parents in the suburbs of London and subsequently moved to Reading, I now visited my aunt and other friends in Dorset fairly regularly, motorcycling down when I had a long weekend to spare. The next two summers I also worked on a nearby farm. During one of these visits, Elizabeth Snell, whose parents took in lodgers, mentioned that their new incumbent had known D.H. Lawrence and was vaguely literary himself. Her mother, Joan Snell:

> Opened her door one morning and was confronted with a tall, handsome, elderly gentleman who asked if she did lodgings. He had got her name from a post office.[16]

Gerald stayed at the Snells for several months but in May 1972 moved in with a woman in East Coker for a month or so before returning to 'Snelldonia', as he would call it. According to the date on his first substantial letter to me it must have been soon after his return from Somerset in the summer of 1972 that we

---

[16] David Wilson, 'The Quiet Man of Upwey, now about to be discovered by the literary establishment', *[Dorset] Evening Echo Weekly Review: Mid Week Magazine*, 18 March 1981.

arranged to meet. Our first encounter took place on neutral territory in the Mason's Arms, half way between my aunt's village and the Snells. We arrived on foot at almost the same moment and were introduced by a friend of Elizabeth's, Margaret Nelson, who had walked down with him.

Gerald Basil Edwards was by then 73 years old. He wore blue canvas shoes, casual baggy trousers, an artist's smock and a Guernsey beret which, though tilted somewhat rakishly to one side, disguised the extent to which his grey hair had disappeared on top.[17] He was neither short nor bandy-legged like his great creation but more than six foot tall and rather wiry, though distinguished, indeed almost military in his bearing. When he walked, although he looked his age due to a degree of stiffness, he seemed jaunty at the same time. When he sat down and began talking, the physical aspect of his age became irrelevant, his intense, authoritative personality overriding such considerations. After a minimum of small-talk he would roll a cigarette, pass his tobacco and papers to me and then launch a literary, religious or socio-political theme upon which he would then pronounce judgement with extreme clarity and confidence.

All of this was delivered in a fine, deep, English voice which resembled Ebenezer's Guernsey English only in its aphoristic tendency to articulate in short periods. Proposing that you might have complementary thoughts on the matter, he then sat back to fix you with what J.S. Collis would call: 'his very brilliant eyes shining with intelligence and warmth'. Gerald's less forthright but no less admiring friend and protégé of the late 1920s, Stephen Potter, said of his first encounter that 'the frankness and candour' of his eyes made him feel 'fidgetty'.[18] These almost black eyes were set beneath a high, veined forehead and to either side of a slightly aquiline nose.[19] His cheeks would hollow as he sucked on his thin cigarette and then

---

[17] At the beginning of the final chapter of *Ebenezer Le Page*, when Neville drives him to visit Lisa Quéripel, Ebenezer says: 'I had to take off my beret and was ashamed for her to see my bald head' (p. 389).

[18] See above, p. 51.

[19] Which Potter, revealing perhaps as much about himself as of Gerald's proboscis, describes as 'a pleasant plebeian nose' (see above, p. 51).

relax around a slightly sardonic smile. The smile looked as if it were about to break into a short laugh and occasionally did. I was perhaps less put off by this almost theatrical style than others during the previous half-century or more. Gerald could be very charming as well as fiercely assertive and this, combined with an extraordinary faith in his own ideas, ensured that he seemed to have no difficulty in accepting interruptions and even criticisms from a student some fifty years his junior. In any case, despite or thanks to his several idiosyncrasies, I was delighted to have discovered such a fascinatingly literate conversationalist buried away in the suburbs of Weymouth. I got back to my aunt's late that night for we had talked for hours.

Since that first meeting I have increasingly appreciated how blithely I took for granted its success and the fact that it began so fruitful a friendship. Interviewed by David Wilson in March 1981 when *Ebenezer Le Page* was first published, Joan Snell said:

> He was a remarkable man with such an intellect... But he was very moody. Sometimes he would go for days without speaking, then when I could see he wanted to chat, I would make a cup of tea and he would talk. He used to come out with some profound things. He abhorred modern science and television. He used to say that information was not education...

Wilson then explains that Gerald was:

> writing his book while at Upwey. It was while there he met young Edward Chaney ... to whom he later gave the book rights. 'He took to Edward right away', said Mrs Snell. 'They just clicked. If you could take to him, and he to you, he was a wonderful person. He didn't take to everyone. There were many hundreds he would not look twice at, nor they at him. But that's their loss I think. He really was a remarkable man. He had piercing eyes, and a sort of magnetism. In his day I should have said he was a very handsome man.[20]

The Irish-born Collis, who was perhaps Gerald's closest friend in the 1920s, but who like others lost touch when he apparently

---

[20] Wilson, 'The Quiet Man of Upwey.'

failed to fulfil their high expectations of him, wrote a long and almost exaggeratedly poignant eulogy in the *Spectator* after the publication of *Ebenezer Le Page*. In it he enlarged upon what could happen when Gerald met someone new:

> To Stephen Potter and myself he seemed always a genius. He was the most dynamic person we had ever met. To be dynamic may mean no more than fully alive; but he had something to *say*, he spoke from an inner centre, as one having authority and not as the scribes and the pharisees... He reacted to life almost with an animal's lack of calculation. He was really *affected* by people he met, and made little attempt to conceal his version of their character. Introducing him to someone was like conducting a chemical experiment. If he found this person alien to his taste, say an intellectual sophisticate, he would be unable or unwilling to conceal his reaction. He would grow pale. He would not only lower his eyes but his whole head, slanting his face away from the person. He might not say anything at all, only bow his head still lower. He had a flair, like D.H. Lawrence, for spotting what was *wrong* with other people. Some people shirked meeting him for fear of his insight into their defective interiors. But he was really all warmth and concern, and friendship was a life-need for him. Stephen Potter and myself were close friends of his for several years, though he was difficult, for one never knew when he might take offence. But in spite of rows we always thought of him as 'our genius friend'.[21]

Gerald informed me that he never actually met Lawrence, only his widow, the German-born Frieda. Years later I discovered that, put in touch by their mutual friend, Middleton Murry, Gerald had in fact corresponded with Lawrence prior to the latter's final illness and death in the south of France in 1930. No doubt thanks to Murry, in whose *Adelphi* magazine Gerald had already featured, in 1928 (two years after getting married) he was commissioned by Jonathan Cape to write a book on Lawrence. In that year he moved to Switzerland with his wife and young son largely in order to meet the ailing author,

---

[21] Collis, 'Memories of a Genius Friend,' p. 21.

remaining there until April 1930 when his second child was born in London. Though he abandoned the book on Lawrence for one on that even more influential messiah, Jesus (which Cape then rejected), Lawrence's life and works remained a fundamental influence on Gerald both as a writer and man. As well as his particular version of what Lawrence called 'blood consciousness', something of Gerald's determination never to be dominated by a woman, a determination he be-queathed to Ebenezer (and

Fig. 76: *Frieda Lawrence* (1879-1956)
(photo: Howard Coster, 1937)
(National Portrait Gallery)

encouraged in me), came from his knowledge of Lawrence, as reinforced by his familiarity with the formidable Frieda, both in person as well as via conversation with Murry, who renewed his intimate acquaintance with her after Lawrence's death [Fig. 76].[22]

Had Gerald been less uncompromising (or merely more worldly) and managed to complete even an imperfect book on Lawrence before or immediately after the latter's death, he would have been en route to at least that degree of literary success enjoyed by Collis and Stephen Potter. Collis had already published a book on Bernard Shaw and Potter effectively inherited Gerald's Cape commission in the last months of Lawrence's life. When this was published, probably the worst review Potter received was from the man who had introduced him to Lawrence's work in the first place, G.B. Edwards, writing

---

[22] See Part I, p. 11. The part played by his parents was no doubt fundamental, his father apparently dominated both by his second and third wives (the last with negative practical consequences for Gerald); see p. 40.

in *The Adelphi*.[23] When in April 1930, with a second child to support, Gerald proposed to write 'a new and shorter' book on Lawrence, Cape rejected the idea, 'expecting crops of them just now'.

So discreet is the wealth of literary expertise that underpins *The Book of Ebenezer Le Page* that readers of the novel alone, even when guided by John Fowles's preface, might not appreciate quite how extraordinarily well-read Gerald was. When I first met him I had met a handful of learned people and have since met many more, but I have rarely met anyone with so profound and passionate an acquaintance with such a wide range of the world's greatest works of literature. As well as Shakespeare and the King James Bible (the latter, he wrote, 'is a complete cure from being a Christian'), he was intimately familiar with the works of Dostoyevsky, Joseph Conrad, Lawrence and most more nearly contemporary novelists of any quality.[24] He would either quote them from memory or, if we were in his room, turn and pull from his bookcase a paperback in which he immediately found the relevant passage. In a thinly disguised account of Gerald who featured prominently as the genius figure in a novel Collis wrote in the late 1920s but never published, he records 'Edward Newman' behaving in just this way:

> During conversation of this kind Newman had a habit of going to the bookshelf, taking down a volume of Nietzsche or Walt Whitman or Edward Carpenter or the Bible or Blake, and quoting with felicity the right sentence for the

---

[23] For more detail, see Part I, p. 118.

[24] In his 1981 letter, Gerald's boyhood friend, Wilfrid Burgess, informed me that he and Gerald 'were members of Mr. Carrington's Bible Class' at which Gerald would give readings, on one occasion with a pointed *double entendre* at the expense of a mutual friend, Aubrey Heaume, who was 'enamoured of a young lady by the name of Marion Fowler'. Mr Carrington appears in the novel on p. 72. In the same letter, Burgess informed me that Gerald presented him with a copy of Kipling's *Barrack-Room Ballads*, signed 'With sincerest good wishes from an old pal, Gerald 6/7/18'. Middleton Murry published an enthusiastic *Critical Study* of Dostoyevsky in 1923 though D.H. Lawrence more than once expressed deep dislike of his work. On the other hand, in correspondence with me Gerald references André Gide (1869-1951) and his younger, more radical contemporary, Jean Genet (1910-1996).

occasion.

He reached up now, then taking down 'Towards Democracy,'[25] quoted 'Have faith. If that which rules the universe were alien to your soul, then nothing could mend your state – there were nothing left but to fold your hands and be damned everlastingly. But since it is not so – why, what can you wish for more? – all things are given into your hands… These things I say not in order to excite thought in you – rather to destroy it'.[26]

Gerald remained loyal to the Whitmanesque libertarianism of Edward Carpenter [Fig. 77]. On the previous page to that from *Towards Democracy* which Collis remembered him quoting, Carpenter wrote something that seems even more appropriate to Gerald's life as he ended up living it:

Have Faith. Do not hurry: have faith. Remember that if

Fig. 77: *Edward Carpenter* (1844-1929), wearing what Fry described as his 'anarchist overcoat' (oil on canvas: Roger Fry, 1894) (National Portrait Gallery).

---

[25] Carpenter, *Towards Democracy* (London, 1883), p. 164 (198).

[26] 'Chapter X' from Collis's unpublished typescript, kindly loaned to me by Richard Ingrams, copyright Michael Holroyd, and now in Trinity College Library, Dublin, pp. 134-35. This wide-ranging conversation is based on those which took place in Collis's flat in Rotherhithe, before he moved to Guilford Street. Collis recalls the same phenomenon in his 'Memories of a Genius Friend',

you become famous you can never share the lot of those who pass by unnoticed from the cradle to the grave, nor take part in the last heroism of their daily life; If you seek and encompass wealth and ease the divine outlook of poverty cannot be yours nor shall you feel all your days the loving and constraining touch of Nature and Necessity; If you are successful in all you do, you cannot also battle magnificently against odds; If you have fortune and good health and a loving wife and children, you cannot also be of those who are happy without these things.[27]

But Gerald was also at least as up-to-date as I was, persuading me to read Kazantzakis and Solzhenitsyn, when all I had known of the former was *Zorba the Greek,* and of the latter, politically-oriented reviews I had read in the press.[28] Of Gerald's other relatively original enthusiasms, Patrick White (fellow islander of a kind) was not to receive the Nobel Prize until a year after we met and remained under-appreciated.[29] In 1972 White was merely a name to me, yet Gerald had read almost all his novels and persuaded me to do likewise. Thus this Guernsey exile introduced me to the Australian author I came to believe shared with him and few others the status of great 20th-century novelist.[30]

---

p. 21.

[27] *Towards Democracy*, p. 162 (197); Carpenter was also a major influence on D.H. Lawrence, *cf.* Martin Green's view that he was 'the kind of man Lawrence was determined not to be, the kind that Frieda saved him from being. *That* was his basic importance to Lawrence'; *The Von Richthofen Sisters*, p. 382.

[28] Writing this note as I am in April 2014 I cannot resist citing Solzhenitsyn in *Der Spiegel* in 2006 on the dangers of promoting NATO and encouraging Ukrainian opposition to the Russians (now complemented by the EU). Gerald seems to have been familiar with the full range of the Cretan (and fellow Nietzschean) Kazantzakis's writings, including his *Saviours of God*, 'spiritual exercises', which were written between 1922 and 1944, and *The Last Temptation*, first published in 1953 (in English in 1960).

[29] Though the Prize was for *The Vivisector* which was published in 1970 it was not awarded until 1973. By this time my similarly well-read Australian father-in-law, Keith Jacka, had confirmed the recommendation.

[30] For his enthusiastic reading of *Riders in the Chariot* soon after its publication in 1973, see below, p. 256. Gerald has continued to educate me in these respects. Noting Ebenezer's approval of something Raymond had been reading, Donald Hankey's *The Beloved Captain* of 1917, I acquired a copy and encountered the

Gerald was a demanding conversationalist not merely because of his great literary range but because he was also, for someone with such a large and assertive ego, an extremely attentive listener. His 'taste' in literature was also subordinated to a quasi-religious conviction of its crucial role in our lives. Despite his somewhat haughty manner, he was passionately interested in an unusual range of people. The extent to which he might value interaction with, or essential information about, anyone with whom he came into contact occasionally bordered on the absurd. He would talk at great length and in intense detail about, say, an obscure friend of his landlady's daughter, when there was no apparent reason for his fellow-conversationalist to be interested in that person. Yet the quality of *his* interest and the particular angle he adopted often lent surprising significance to what he had to say, persuading one into complicity with his unusually egalitarian spirit. This spirit complemented his particular brand of Romanticism. '"Romantic" is not a dirty word' he told me almost angrily, when criticising my tough-minded hero, Wyndham Lewis.

Inasmuch as Lewis had ever been a Romantic he had also been a Nietzschean one but retained an elitist belief in the privileging of the artist-intellectual.[31] More than Lewis and perhaps even Lawrence, to the end of his life Gerald dismissed what elites had to offer if this did not 'speak from the heart'. In this respect he never abandoned Nietzsche's advocacy of 'amor fati,' or love of one's fate. In his novel, as in life, Gerald set himself that most

---

quietly emotive prose that does not merely exemplify Gerald's formative reading but is, surely, an essential context for an understanding of Wilfred Owen and Robert Graves (see above, p. 209).

[31] What Gerald and Lewis shared, however, was a disregard for worldly goods, which went hand in hand with an assumption that others should support them (and yet sometimes be scorned for doing so). Gerald was as extreme as Lewis in this, his lofty disregard for worldly achievement being a primary reason for his friends' abandonment of him. One could not say the same of Lawrence, still less of Frieda, who fought his family to secure his royalties (John Worthen has informed me that family papers he has seen suggest that Lawrence's sister, Ada, in fact supported Frieda's campaign in accordance with her belief that Lawrence would have wanted her to control the estate); *cf.* Norman Douglas's 29 March 1930 letter to her regarding her proposed sale of Lawrence's manuscripts for £25,000 ('you won't get £2,000') in Holloway, *Douglas*, p. 376.

challenging of tasks of investing an apparently mundane existence – so far from Übermenschean that Ebenezer might almost be parodying  the popular notion of the Nietzschean project – with the flawed nobility of *Ecce Homo,* Nietzsche's last and posthumous publication.[32] William Golding recognised that 'there is epic stature in [Ebenezer's] individualism'.[33] Given the crucial roles Shakespeare gave to the humblest of his characters, this greatest of all authors might also have appreciated Gerald's elevation of Everyman.

It seems unlikely that the personalities Gerald created for *The Book of Ebenezer Le Page* would have appealed to the author of *Also sprach Zarasthustra,* or for that matter, *The Apes of God*; perhaps even *Women in Love.* The character who might most have appealed to Nietzsche, Lewis or, indeed Lawrence, is he who bears an embarrassing resemblance to myself, the dynamic dedicatee of the book within the *Book,* that 'rioting artist', Neville Falla.[34] But revisiting Gerald's novel in the light of his correspondence and the articles he published in the 1920s and '30s, it became even clearer to me how courageously committed he remained to truths as deep as those articulated by the ambivalent Nietzsche. Conscious of the rationalist limitations of Darwin and Freud - to some extent even of Nietzsche himself in his anti-Christianism - he stubbornly held to his 'religious' brand of existentialism. Neither he nor Nietzsche lived very Nietzschean lives but if his philosophy of sacralised life and love – his own version of 'amor fati' - failed to bring him the worldly rewards that others achieve by compromising in middle age and following more mundane idols, in the end he fulfilled his artistic ambition, even to the extent of enhancing the lives of some he left behind.[35]

---

[32] Despite advocating Nietzsche to Potter (above, p. 55), Gerald was in this more like Murry, who intended the *Adelphi* to be 'deliberately middle-brow'; mikalsonengl4620.wordpress.com/contextual-material/the-adelphi/.

[33] For Golding's review, see above, p. 229, note 5.

[34] *Ibid*. Interestingly, in a subsequent letter, dated 26 March 1976, he anticipated that in the second part of his proposed trilogy, Neville would suffer an 'early death'. For the 'rioting artist', see Golding's review, p. 229.

[35] By mundane idols one should include those worldly gods elevated in the wake of true religion: 'such collectives as race, state and nation'; viz his attack on

But returning to 1972, we parted company knowing we would remain firm friends. I visited him briefly in his austere bed-sitting room at the Snells before leaving Dorset. Leading a particularly disorganised life at this time, however, although I may have received a message in Reading, it seems I didn't reply until November when I was about to move out of a squalid flat there. Apparently I didn't even get his surname right (or merely addressed him as Gerald), but he responded immediately with a long and important (indeed strangely prophetic) auto-biographical letter, written in his clear script on cheap ruled paper. From what he says towards the end of this letter it is clear that I had already begun encouraging him to complete and publish something:

> I was ever so pleased to hear from you and hasten to reply, so you may get something from me before you leave your present address. The name is Edwards, by the way. A fairly common name in Guernsey. My particular branch, no doubt, stems from Wales, as do the others, but the earliest ancestor I know of on my father's side was Zackariah Edwards of Dalwood, Devon, who married a gipsy and begat a breed of stalwart sons, who migrated to every quarter of the globe. He was my great-grandfather. My grandfather, Tom, married one Mary Organ of Honiton and migrated to Guernsey at the age of 19 for the 'stone-rush', when the quarries of the north were opened. It was a hard life. My father, the eldest son, also Tom, was born on Guernsey, but at twelve ran away from his strap-wielding father and his mother, who had a bosom of iron, to the softer usages of sailing ships. He sailed and 'saw the world' until he came home and married at the age of 26.[36] He wouldn't have come home then, except that he never overcame his tendency to sea-sickness. He worked for his father, who was by now a quarry-owner, and in due course

---

Murry's Communism; see Michael Burleigh's discussion of Voegelin in *Earthly Powers: Religion and Politics in Europe from the Enlightenment to the Great War* (London, 2006), pp. 6-8. It would have been interesting to read what Gerald might have said to Murry when the latter was considering ordination in the later 1930s but by then the two men had parted company.

[36] As we have seen, he in fact married at 20; see above, p. 20.

inherited the quarry and the house, Sous les Hougues, where I was born [Fig. 6].

I was the only child of his second marriage, from the first of which two half-sisters of mine survived.[37] My mother died in 1924. A couple of years later he married the house-keeper and sold up to disinherit me, buying another property which he could legally leave her.[38] Hence my exile. (It won't make sense to you; but it's Guernsey law.) He was a very tough man, my father: with a very tender core. He was passionately attached to Guernsey and refused to leave before the Occupation. He lived for more than a year after the liberation and must have been well over ninety when he died.[39] I have to be vague on this, for it was not considered decent for a Guernsey child to know the precise age of its parents. I was only truly in touch with him on one occasion; and that was in 1938, the year of the Munich Crisis, when I visited him at Les Rosiers, where he ran a small growing concern, the quarry having been worked out.[40] He was rather humiliated, though over 80, by being reduced to so effete an occupation. He regarded quarrying granite as the only work fit for a man.[41]

My mother was a Mauger. I cannot claim she was pure Guernsey, for the purest Guernsey are Neolithic; nor can I brag that my family came over with the Conqueror. As a matter of fact, the first Mauger on the island, of whom there is any record, was dumped there by the Conqueror for being a nuisance. He had the effrontery to reproach William for wanting to conquer England.[42] Thereafter, he lived as an

---

[37] See above, pp. 22-25.

[38] For a detailed discussion of Gerald's inheritance, see Chapter 3, above.

[39] He was in fact 89 when he died; see above, p. 199.

[40] After Guernsey's quarrying boom of the mid-19th-century, when Gerald's grandfather and his brothers arrived on the island, the industry peaked c.1910 but declined between the wars; see James Marr, *A History of the Bailiwick of Guernsey* (Chichester, 1982), pp. 213-15 and Peter Girard, 'The Stone Industry', *Transactions of La Société Guernesiaise*, XXI, ii (1982), pp. 202-08.

[41] Since he was born on 28 May 1861 Tom Edwards would only have been 77 at the time of the Munich Crisis.

[42] The Archbishop's offence actually seems to have been that of critiquing the

exile, oscillating between sorcery and sanctity, in which state he prolifically begat the beginning of the Mauger clan on a girl called Guille. There is an old lady at the Pilgrim House Old Age Pensioners' Club in Weymouth, who is one of them. Naturally posterity and the Tourist Industry are inclined to stress the sanctity; and the bay where he had his hide-out is called Saint's Bay.[43]

My boyhood, adolescence and young manhood was an increasingly intense fight to the death against my mother; and indeed all my relationships with women have been a fight to the death. I survive, but in grief; for I have sympathy with what I fight against, and sorrow at the necessity. That should make clear to you my disorientation from Lawrence, with whom in other ways I have much in common. I can coo like a dove, but deceptively; for underneath [I] am steel against the female will. I do not mean the feminine nature. D.H. submitted. To my mind, his is the saddest story. The White Peacock becomes the flaming uterus of Lady C. They are the same. The Phoenix is swamped.

When I began this letter I had in mind a dozen themes I wanted to write to you about; but have let myself be side-tracked into the purely personal. I am glad. I want you to know the odd sort of mixed creature who is at the other end of this pen. The rest can wait. As for reading me in print, that also can wait and may never happen. I live from day to day, at the edge of living: can give no promises, make no plans. I go on while I can. I have, though, arranged for any Guernsey manuscripts I leave, in whatever state of completion, to be deposited with a Guernsey friend in Weymouth, from whom you could borrow them on enquiry. I am hoping, however, to hear from you many times before then; and perhaps see you again a few times. It means much to me to be in touch with you at all across

consanguinity between William and his wife, Matilda (which was also criticised by the Pope) rather than the King's intention of invading England; see above, p. 20.

[43] A corruption of 'La Baie des Seines' (The Bay of the Fishing Nets); I thank Stephen Foote for this observation; *cf.* MacCulloch's *Guernsey Folk Lore*, p. 444.

more than half a century, and I trust it will remain so while I am around. Meanwhile, all blessings!

Affectionately,

Gerald.

## 3: SHAKESPEARE & COMPANY

In January 1973 I went skiing with my brother and evidently sent a card to Gerald. Since receiving his long autobiographical letter of the previous November, we must have corresponded or talked on the phone, or I may have revisited Dorset. What is clear is that he had recommended I read Patrick White's *Voss*, and I, pleased to have known a fine poet (like-minded libertarian and Old Leightonian) with whom Gerald was unfamiliar, had suggested he read Basil Bunting's *Briggflatts*. Evidently I also wrote that I had injured my hand, presumably skiing. All I can establish from my scrappy diary of this period is that by 28 March 1973, the day Gerald wrote the next letter I possess, I was in Hillingdon Hospital with glandular fever. Since he was not sure where I was, he had addressed his letter care of Reading University's Fine Art Department, so I probably didn't receive it until the following term.

I got your card from Austria months ago, and was delighted to get it. I was distressed though about your right hand; I hope it has completely recovered and that you now have full use of it.

I would have replied to your card had I known of an address to write to. On your first letter, you did put an address at the bottom, but I took that to be only the address you were leaving. I have often thought of writing to you there on the off-chance of its being forwarded; but, not knowing the circumstances, didn't want to land you into complications... It happens I now have something definite I want to let you know, and was discussing with Joan (Mrs Snell) the best thing to do, when she got the bright idea of my writing to you direct at the University, who would be sure to have your address, and would forward it, if by chance you are already on vacation.

This is not intended to be a letter of much interest; but only to settle a practical matter. Since you were here I have been sorting out and destroying MSS, everything except what I am still willing to be responsible for. The one completed book left I have typed; and am at work on typing the part draft I have of the second. As the typing of the first is too slap-dash for my liking, I intend doing it again before submitting it to anybody. My first approach will be through Victor Coysh, the most distinguished of our writers on Guernsey who is only six years younger than I am; and then we'll see.[44] However, that is not the point at the moment. I hope to be able to hang on long enough to get at least the first one in print, but at my age anything may happen: therefore I want you to have the address of the person who will have my MS: Cynthia Mooney, 71, Radipole Lane, Weymouth. She also is of Guernsey.[45]

I tried to order Briggflatts from Smith's, but they wouldn't take an order for a Falcon paper-back.[46] I am wondering if you have made anything of Voss. Are perhaps wondering why I, of all people, think it great? The answer must wait until we can talk. I hope you will be down in Dorset sometime soon...

I do want to see you again; and I do want to have news of you.

<u>Gerald.</u>

1973 was an eventful year. I visited Dorset at Easter. Later in April I moved into another flat in Reading with a new girlfriend.

---

[44] Victor Coysh (1906-1994) was, like Gerald, a Guernseyman descended from West Country immigrants, who attended the States Intermediate School, and had spent a period of exile in Dorset (in Coysh's case 1926-45). Having written a guidebook to the island by the early 1970s he was a Chief Reporter for the Guernsey Evening Press and a prolific contributor to the periodicals of La Société Guernesiaise and the Guernsey Society. See below, pp. 286 and 321 for references to Coysh's 'pedantry', referring to his having pointed up topographical errors in the typescript which were in fact deliberate.

[45] I visited Cynthia Mooney with my daughters in the mid-1990s but failed to discover any new information about Gerald's biography.

[46] Perhaps I had written 'Fulcrum' illegibly, the press set up by the enterprising Stuart Montgomery in order to publish Bunting from 1965.

In June I went on a University trip to Paris where I called in at Shakespeare & Company Bookshop and met and befriended its eccentric owner, George Whitman. I had meanwhile taken over the editorship of the University Arts magazine *Tamesis,* mainly in order to publish a provocative poem promoting the work of Wyndham Lewis. I now promised George copies for his bookshop if the girlfriend and I could stay and work there later that summer. On 25 July I drove to my aunt's and the next morning visited Gerald and introduced him to Lisa, before driving on to Wales to meet her father who had a house there. We returned on 3 August and left for Paris on the 9th.

In the event, Lisa and I not only stayed in 'the writer's guest-room' at Shakespeare & Company for the rest of the long vacation but on 15 September, after an epic dose of French bureaucracy, we got married in the Mairie of the Cinquième Arrondissement, George standing proudly alongside our other

Fig. 78: The author's wedding on the steps of the Mairie of the 5eme Arrondissement, 15 September 1973, Paris. Centre: Lisa, the author, brother Philip; below him, witness Bernard Mendès France; to his left, other witness George Whitman; far right Australian cousin, Richard Chaney.

witness, the son of a socialist Prime Minister of France [Fig. 78].[47]

Whilst in Paris, I acquired a first edition of Lewis's 1927 book on the role of the hero in Shakespeare: *The Lion and the Fox*. As soon as I got back, I sent Gerald my now spare paperback copy with a covering letter. He replied on 27 September:

> Thanks very much for your letter, and the book (which I have read; but of that anon). I am enclosing one of two Conrads I had long planned to give you and Lisa - the other hardback I've had on order from Longman's for weeks. When it does arrive I'll send it on. I recommend especially to your notice the magnificent preface to The Nigger of the Narcissus. It is Conrad's Manifesto. Of the rest, read Amy Foster, if you haven't. The only pity is it isn't called 'The Castaway' as he originally intended.[48] It's sublimely moving; as is its companion piece 'The Secret Sharer' (rightly titled) in the volume I hope to send you soon. Together they are Conrad's vulnerable human testimony. Having said that I think you will realise how I must dislike Wyndham Lewis and The Lion and the Fox.[49]

---

[47] Gerald was amused by my tale of befriending the stylish mathematician, Michel Mendès France (now Professor Emeritus and father of author, Tristan), who offered to be our witness when he heard that our first choice, the American expatriate, Jack Belden, proved ineligible. Due to the amount of time it took to navigate the bureaucracy, which included blood tests and appearing before a high court judge due to Lisa being Australian, under 21 and not having parental consent (I hadn't yet met her mother), by the time we finally obtained permission to marry, Michel had to be back in post at the University of Bordeaux. He therefore very kindly arranged for his brother, Bernard, whom we had never met, to turn up on the day of the wedding to act (also very kindly) as witness in his place. Their father, Pierre Mendès France, was Prime Minister for eight months between 1954-55 when with Communist support, he withdrew French troops from Vietnam which prompted their replacement (and more) by America.

[48] Amy Foster is indeed the young wife of the principal protagonist, Yanko, the East European castaway who meets and marries her only to frighten her off when he falls ill and feverishly calls for water in his native language, as Conrad had done in the early years of his marriage.

[49] *The Lion and the Fox* was critiqued by 'The Journeyman' (perhaps Murry himself; intelligent enough and certainly an admirer of Keats who is praised in the review), in *The Adelphi* in 1927, pp. 510-14: 'His criticism is essentially destructive and disintegrating' though reference is also made to 'Mr. Lewis's

I wish, rather than write, I could talk with you at ease and length about it.[50] Reading it I was mentally annotating in the margin:

Yes!

NO!

But - ?

Well, go on -

The last is his most irritating evasion. He starts hare after hare, and doesn't follow up any. His approach to Shakespeare is invalid, anyway. The 'colossi' are not Shakespeare's last word. I know he says they are: but he uses his scholarship slip-shod and slap-dash, often to downright inaccuracy. For instance, Ibsen was not kept out of the *Swedish* theatre.[51] Worse, is his rasping, harsh, abusive manner. His remarks re Shaw for instance.[52] It all adds up to no more than a chaos of logical positivist deductions, heartless and intellectual. He doesn't speak with a human voice. Conrad does, incidentally. He's a good antidote.[53] All

---

dazzlingly brilliant mind.' (p. 514).

[50] This had been a characteristic refrain in his letters to Murry (Part I passim).

[51] Gerald would in any case have spotted this all-too-typical piece of Lewisian slapdashery (on pp. 296-97 of *The Lion and the Fox*), but as well as having directed a play in Bolton in 1939 by Strindberg, who was genuinely Swedish, he also had a special interest in the Norwegian Ibsen, having published a fine essay on *Rosmersholm* in the *Adelphi*, IV, 1932 (pp. 292-95). He no doubt identified with Ibsen's interests in the sins of the fathers (as also in Strindberg's *Easter*), the individual's struggle against society's failure to recognise superior morality and, at this transitional stage in his marriage, the dangers of domineering, or at least unknowable women: 'The character of Rebecca West is the mystery element in the play, and it is its unfolding that holds our interest to the end'.

[52] See above, p. 63, for both Gerald and Lewis, satirising Shaw, the former no more gently than the latter. In fact, Lewis may well have been influenced by Gerald's 1926 jibes about Shaw being inadequately Nietzschean, jeering as he does just a year later that: 'Shaw, it is true, produced a "Superman", of sorts; but his Superman was dressed in Jaeger underclothing and ate nuts…'; *The Lion and the Fox*, p. 64.

[53] In his skilful summary of the thousand pages that Lampedusa wrote on British writers from Bede to Graham Greene in 1954, having remarked on his great admiration for Conrad in general, David Gilmour quotes him on Conrad: 'as an antidote to the unbearable stagnation of Palermitan life.' (*The Last Leopard*, p.

the more, as like Lewis, he constrains himself to remain within a human and material continuoum [*sic*]; but masterfully with controlled passion and exquisite tenderness. 'Romantic' is not a dirty word, you know.

I went down to see Jo [my great-aunt] this afternoon. Trixie was there and a girl came in whose name I didn't catch - she's going to be a vet.⁵⁴ I am disappointed not to be seeing the two of you before you go back to Reading. I look forward to hearing from Lisa.

I think I've said all I can say in this inadequate note.

Every good wish,

<u>Gerald.</u>

While we were in Paris, my mother had driven down to Upwey with an elderly Irish friend of my aunt's, Maura McDonagh, and on 14 August fetched Gerald from the Snells to join them for dinner.⁵⁵ We visited Jo and Gerald in the autumn and that Christmas my parents and brother again descended on Jo, Lisa

---

131).

⁵⁴ These were Beatrice Blackwood (1889-1975), the distinguished Oxford anthropologist, daughter of the Victorian publisher, James Blackwood, and my aunt's life-long friend (see *ODNB*), and Gillian Kestin, the daughter of the local photographer. Gerald met 'Trix', as Jo called her, more than once and one wonders whether the subject of Malinowksi ever came up, given Gerald's knowledge of him through Mass Observation and Trix's early interest after reading his *Sex and Repression in Savage Society* in 1929 on the eve of her field trip to Melanesia, which culminated in *Both Sides of the Buka Passage* (1935); see Frances Larson, '"Did He Ever Darn His Stockings?" Beatrice Blackwood and the Ethnographic Authority of Bronislaw Malinowski', *History and Anthropology*, 22, I (2011), pp. 75-92. (Tom Harrisson was also something of an expert on Melanesia and no doubt known to her). I inherited Trix's personal copy of this, along with the rest of the library she kept at my aunt's. Unfortunately, their discovery and sale of a first edition of Whitman's *Leaves of Grass* pre-dated this and indeed Gerald's acquaintance with them.

⁵⁵ Maura McDonagh, Beatrice Blackwood and Jo had shared a flat together in Finsbury Park at the beginning of the 20ᵗʰ century. All three spinsters remained devoted friends for the rest of their long lives. Maura lived in a tiny flat near the British Museum where she had a small but distinguished library of Irish literature, including a complete set of the publications of the Dolmen Press. These were sent to her as they appeared by the proprietors, Liam and Josephine Miller, who were close friends, and to whom she bequeathed them back at her death.

and I arriving separately. Gerald was then invited round to meet the family. On Boxing Day I visited him in his room and the following day we returned to Reading. Since we were increasingly concerned about Jo being on her own, and since the Snells were planning to move and in the shorter term Joan was due to stay in Cambridge with their daughter for a while, a somewhat unrealistic plot was hatched whereby Gerald would go and live at my aunt's while Joan was away. He wrote to me about this on 29 December, saying he was looking forward to the move. His depression having no doubt been deepened by the recent Christmas festivities and the anticipation of more of the same over the New Year period, he articulated his incapacity to cope with modern family life:

> It is my lowest ebb at Snelldonia. The great juggernaut god Machine moves triumphantly, lubricated by sentimentality; and I am driven inwardly to near extinction.

With other members of the family arriving at 'Snelldonia', including, significantly, young children, he continues, with only the merest hint of Ebenezer's self-mockery, in melodramatic mode:

> It was their last visit drove me into the suicidal adolescent state when I pitched 'The Boud'lo' into the dustbin.[56] I will have to summon every effort of will of which I am capable not to pitch anything, including myself, into the dustbin this time.

> It's good to know you two are around, anyhow. My love to you both.

Gerald

Plans for the move advanced even to the point that rent was discussed. An excited Aunt Jo refused to hear of receiving any, so, since the Snells would not be charging him in his absence, Gerald formulated a sub-plot whereby with her approval he would forward the £7 per week he had been paying them to subsidise us in Reading.[57] Despite his writing: 'You must let me

---

[56] This was the second 'part draft' typescript he referred to above, p. 248.

[57] By 14 April 1975 Gerald writes that he is paying the Snells £10 per week; see below, p. 277.

do this because it will give <u>me</u> pleasure!', I refused to accept his offer. Gerald's somewhat self-dramatising but scrupulous style, as well as his increasing tendency to prioritise our/my interests, are conveyed in this letter, dated 3 February 1974.

Dear Edward,

I'm posting with this last week's Sunday Times magazine which has the article on Lucian Freud in it and another on the Bloomsbury clan - in case you don't manage to get a copy elsewhere.[58]

I've broken the news to Joan and Bert that I'm definitely going down to Jo's. They took it very well and I will go with their blessing. Bert talks of taking me and props down in car, but when the crisis arrives, he'll probably have quite enough to do to close up here and get himself Joan and dogs to Cambridge in time. I propose to take your advice and get a taxi to move me...

Cheers to Philip and remember me cordially to your father when you see him. I'm glad Lisa may be there some of the time. She was very quiet. May be very wise. She also looked very lovely; but anything she might care to say to me would interest me.

As for you, you can take it for granted, without my having to say it, that I am whole-heartedly for your well-being.

<u>Gerald.</u>

Partly because the Snells' plans were postponed, the plan for the move to Upwey came to nothing and for the time being Gerald stayed put. That it had progressed as far as it did, founded on the almost flirtatious relationship he had struck up with my 84-year-old aunt [Fig. 75], was evidence that he had mellowed since the era of great expectations evoked by J.S. Collis and Stephen Potter. As an egocentric teenager whom she saw through rose-tinted spectacles, it had been easy for me to appreciate her. To a formerly fierce, Neo-Romantic radical,

---

[58] Lucian Freud and his brothers were sent to Dartington School in 1933, so, albeit older, would have been there with Gerald's children; see above, p. 165.

however, an anti-bourgeois bohemian a mere decade younger than her, this retired schoolteacher, spinster and more or less conventional Christian, forever fussing over her spoilt dog, must have reminded Gerald of the generation against whom he and his friends had rebelled throughout 1920s and '30s. Her quintessential Englishness might, moreover, have prompted further prejudice on his part. And yet he became her friend as well as mine. She would in fact outlive him and share my sorrow at his death.

On 5 March 1974, my mother repeated the routine of the previous August; she had driven Maura McDonagh down from London to Jo's and then picked up Gerald to join the three ladies for dinner. By chance Gerald had received a letter from me the same morning. He expressed his delight in this, saying it 'couldn't have been better timed' as it encouraged him to include an amusing account of the evening in a long, typed reply the next day. This letter also contained details of his health problems (including, ominously, a somewhat dismissive comment on his GP's concern about his heart), a no less detailed appreciation of my mother and her concern about my brother, Philip's health, a response to my enquiry as to whether he had voted in the election which had that day returned Harold Wilson to power (following Edward Heath's failure to form a coalition with the Liberals) and a typically fascinating discursion on his recent reading. On the subject of Maura, or 'Moira', as he insisted on calling my aunt's octogenarian Irish Catholic friend, Gerald was at his most Ebenezerish:

> I had a private session with her. I can't say conversation. It would be like trying to converse with a Catherine wheel going full whiz. The sparks fly in all directions. Occasionally they impact. I let out our people were Norman. Ye gods! For some esoteric reason to do with the ancient history of Ireland, the Normans have always been and still are the spawn of the Devil. 'Then, by all the saints, I want nothing to do with yer!' she announced. Fortunately I was at that stage still quick-witted enough to let her know Guernsey was originally Christianised by Celtic saints. 'Ach, praise be to God, then there be some little good in you after all!' she said. I forebore from letting her know that

insofar as I personally was Christianised at all, it was by the
spiritual descendants of John Wesley. So I got off lightly;
but your unfortunate mother didn't.[59] She entered the fray
with her sociological mind in top gear to extract from Moira
a reasonable explanation of the present situation in Ireland.
It was a battle royal. I can only leave it for you to imagine.
It went on for forty minutes; and, in the end, your mother
could only thump her brow with her two clenched fists in
despair and incomprehension. I got up to go. My mind was
a whirligig, I was dizzy, I could hardly stand. This morning
Jo rang up to ask how I was; and I said good-bye again to
the others. To Moira, 'Good-bye, you Celt!' She said to me,
'Good-bye, you old Norman, God bless yer!'...

No, I didn't vote. I don't vote in English elections;
though I'd have voted for Moira's Devil himself to kick
Heath out.[60] My dislike of that man, like my aversion to TV,
is near the pathological. I can't say I'm all that keen on any
of the others but, on the whole, I think the change is for the
better; though being brought up in a different tradition of
government, I have never been able to take seriously the
national schizophrenia of English party politics. At home
we vote for a person, not a party.

I am re-reading Riders in the Chariot in Penguin English
Classics.[61] I have now read all of White, except Happy
Valley, his first. The Riders seems to me the summit of his
achievement; though, when the Literature Factory gets
cracking, it may pronounce his last, The Eye of the Storm,

[59] My mother was the daughter of atheist engineer, Paul de Gruyter, and
granddaughter of Jan de Gruyter, author of books on Dostoevsky, Joseph
Conrad and a life of the anti-colonial novelist, 'Multatuli' (Amsterdam, 1920), for
whose Max Havelaar, D.H. Lawrence wrote an introduction in 1927.

[60] Edward Heath (1916-2005). Elected PM in 1970 (one of only four never to have
been married). Took Britain into the EEC (now the … EU) in 1973. Lost election
to Harold Wilson the following year; failed to resign but in 1975 was ousted as
Conservative party leader by Margaret Thatcher, whose relentless critic he
became. When his Salisbury neighbour, the author Leslie Thomas, was asked by
a BBC producer if Heath was gay he replied 'No … he's bloody miserable!'

[61] Patrick White's novel was first published in the previous year, so he may then
have read a library copy. The title refers to the four figures in Ezekiel's vision of
the chariot.

to be his masterpiece. The only book I know comparable to The Riders is The Brothers Karamazov; or rather, what it could have been if Dostoievsky had lived to write the second half. His nearest approach to White's rounded completeness is The Idiot. I can never understand why White is compared with Tolstoy.[62] By the way, did you read Solzhenitsyn's manifesto to the Commintern [sic] in last week's Sunday Times Review? I've kept it, so you can read it if you haven't.[63] It confirms Tolstoy's Resurrection and Conrad's Under Western Eyes. The last is absolutely shattering, and the book cost Conrad most to write. Words from the Cross.[64]

Well, I think I've written enough, if not too much. Some of it is meant for Lisa. I know painting has to be your chief pre-occupation for the present. Good luck to it! Please remember me to Philip. I hope he gets a good sum for his bike. I gave your message to Jo, who received it with a beatific smile. I can't use the big words, or those of formal

---

[62] White himself greatly admired Tolstoy though after reading Henri Troyat's 1965 biography, he decided that 'although I still admire [him] as a writer, this book has torn to shreds the respect I had for him as a man'; 1968 letter to Geoffrey Dutton in *Patrick White Letters*, ed. David Marr (London, 1994), p. 332.

[63] *A Letter to the Soviet Leaders* (London, 1974), Solzhenitsyn's manifesto was published in the wake of his exile from Russia and the publication of *The Gulag Archipelago*. Gerald's response reminds one of his independence of mind and long-standing insistence upon individual freedom whilst most about him in London, Bolton and elsewhere subscribed to Communism, his patron Middleton Murry opting to be an ardent proselytiser at a time when Stalin's purges were at their most lethal. Though it had its roots in Nietzsche and Lawrence, Gerald's scorn for 'mere thought' or the unfeeling intellectualism of ideology or political theory (and their consequences) is shared by Ebenezer as he observes twentieth-century history through the prism of Guernsey.

[64] Tolstoy's *Resurrection* was his last novel and, in its first English translation (illustrated by Boris Pasternak's father, Leonid), as significant an influence on Gerald and his friends as on the sandal-promoting socialist, Edward Carpenter. In 1932, 'in furtherance of the advocacy of Freedom for All Mankind, the Libertarian Group of Los Angeles,' published Thomas H. Bell's *Edward Carpenter: The British Tolstoi; cf.* now, Sheila Rowbotham, *Edward Carpenter: A Life of Liberty and Love* (London, 2008). Collis published a short 'pictorial biography' on *Tolstoy* in 1969 after his more substantial study of *Marriage and Genius: Strindberg and Tolstoy*, both of which Gerald would certainly have been aware.

good wishes to you and Lisa. Take it for granted. I hope to see you both soon.

Gerald.

This letter was typed on 6 March 1974. On 19 March he reverted to his felt-tipped Parker to write a letter 'in haste, hoping you will get it before you leave for Holland'. In response to the Snells' latest change of plans, he had decided to be independent of both them and my aunt and find a bed-sit in Salisbury. 'If I can't,' he added, 'I'll be on the main line and can move somewhere else. I'm seeing Jo this afternoon and will tell her. I'm sorry if I disappoint you.' He continued:

> I haven't bothered you with the criss-crossing and double-crossing that has been going on. There would be no point. I hope, though, perhaps without foundation, I may even be able to do some more writing. I can do nothing here; and I am sure I wouldn't be able to at Jo's. My one anxiety is the fear this may put me out of touch with you and Lisa. Anyhow, I will let you know where I am.

Gerald.

In the event, this potential crisis re-resolved itself. Gerald remained at the Snells and ironically - though the crisis may itself have acted as a catalyst - he finally completed the typescript of *Sarnia Chérie: The Book of Ebenezer Le Page*.

According to my diary we visited Upwey with my family on 14 April and at seven the next evening I drove over to the Snells to pick up Gerald for dinner, bringing him back at about eleven. In view of the significance of the visionary drive on which Neville Falla takes Ebenezer at the end of the novel, I should perhaps mention that I had previously taken Gerald on a drive into the Dorset countryside.[65] We left Upwey on the road behind my aunt's cottage, via Waddon through Portesham to Abbotsbury - beneath the hill on which I had painted St Catherine's Chapel – and down to Chesil Beach. We then drove back through Abbotsbury and up to the Hardy Monument where we parked

---

[65] Like Neville I had graduated from motorcycle to car in the period I knew him; see *Ebenezer Le Page*, p. 367.

and admired an evening view of the Chesil reaching as far as Portland - a match for the magnificent Guernsey sunset Gerald imagined for Ebenezer and Neville - before I drove him home.

In Richard Ingrams's moving *Memoir* of J.S. Collis, there is a passage which is particularly poignant when read in the light of the emotional review-article Collis wrote for *The Spectator* after the posthumous publication of *Ebenezer*. Collis had not seen Gerald for decades before his 'genius friend' died and, at least implicitly, regretted this profoundly, though he seems to have transferred his feeling of regretful guilt for his own failure into bitter scorn for the failure of potential publishers. How ironic, therefore, in an appropriately Hardyesque way, that:

> once, during a stormy period of weather in 1974 [Collis] decided he had to re-visit Chesil Beach, driving all the way to Dorset from his home in Ewell to stand on the shingle, like King Lear in the storm, relishing the wind and the rain and the huge waves: so enraptured was he that he very nearly lost his car to the incoming sea.[66]

If life were a novel, Gerald and I might have met him there, in front of the Old Coastguard Station, part of which he used to rent from Middleton Murry [Fig. 79].[67] But in life itself, had

[66] Ingrams, *Collis*, p. 31; *cf.* Collis's fine account of walking between Chesil and Maiden Castle in *An Irishman's England*, pp. 70-77. Potter and Collis, who had been at Oxford together, kept in touch with each other somewhat erratically but apart from Potter's meeting with Gerald in the 1950s, both ceased contact with him, partly because of the frequency (and lofty tone) of his begging letters. Interestingly, Ingrams concludes the account of Collis's impetuous journey to Chesil Beach with one about a similarly spontaneous, but even more Gerald-like journey to Mount Etna in 1928. This was undertaken at the height of the two men's friendship, albeit after Gerald's marriage. In his autobiography, *Bound upon a Course*, which Potter encouraged him to write, Collis reveals that although he remained closer to Potter than to Gerald yet 'a shadow fell' over that friendship also: 'Nothing was going right for me and I did not confide in him, I was too proud' (pp. 106-7).

[67] Murry loaned the ground floor to Stephen and Mary Potter for their honeymoon in July 1927; Jenkins, *Potter*, p. 84; Collis was meanwhile upstairs pining for a girl that had left for America; Murry was next door having just discovered that his second wife, Violet, had T.B. and H.M. Tomlinson, living nearby was mourning his son who five weeks earlier had drowned off Chesil Beach. Murry's son ('another John Middleton, ye gods' exclaimed D.H. Lawrence) had been born in the Old Coastguard Station on 9 May 1926. For Collis's account of the situation and Violet's decline, following the precedent of

Fig. 79. *Old Coastguard Station, Chesil Beach, Abbotsbury, Dorset*
(photo: the author).

Collis kept or got in touch, he could have called in at the Snells and read the long-gestated masterpiece in time to praise its living author. He might well have helped us get it published, for his own literary fortunes had recently revived: his highly-praised autobiographical *Bound upon a Course*, clearly - albeit briefly - acknowledging Gerald's crucial influence, appeared in 1971, and the two anthologies of his earlier writings: *Vision of Glory* and *The Worm forgives the Plough* appeared in each of the two years that followed, being further reissued by Penguin in 1975.

Though I do not remember Gerald talking of Collis at this, or indeed any other time, it has since occurred to me that reading enthusiastic reviews of his one-time best friend's books might

his first, Katherine Mansfield, see his *Bound upon a Course*, pp. 119-20. Murry and Violet were first directed to Chesil Beach by Thomas Hardy and purchased the Coastguard Station with his £1,000 royalties from Katherine Mansfield's books; see Lea, *Murry*, pp. 124-25. Hardy and his second wife stood as Godparents to the Murrys' first child, born there just over a year earlier and ominously named Katherine. In a 1916 letter to the Dutch author, Augusta de Wit, Lawrence described Hardy as 'our last great writer' (*Letters*, VIII, p. 18). Now that *Far from the Madding Crowd* has twice been turned into a film, perhaps the time has come for *Ebenezer Le Page*, ideally featuring Carey Mulligan as Liza Quéripel...

have spurred him on to complete his novel. He must surely have thought of Murry and Potter, as well as Collis when we visited Chesil Beach together.

Following our visit at Easter, I find one short letter, dated 23 May 1974, reporting my aunt's poor health, the postponement of his intended visit due to the breaking of his teeth at breakfast ('Joan is taking them down to Weymouth to get them repaired'), and his 'distress' at hearing from Jo of Lisa's flu and my sprained ankle. He concludes:

> This is only to say how soon I hope you both recover. I think of you both every day.
>
> Love,
>
> Gerald.

That I must have answered relatively promptly, teasingly questioning him and/or his catastrophising source for the melodramatic account of our ailments, is implied in his second letter, dated 28 May:

Dear Edward,

> Yes, you were right: I wasn't being ironic, though I did think the phrase I wrote rather heavily charged, even as I was writing it; but I was still under the sway of Jo's afflatus by telephone, from which it sounded as if you two poor things had been rescued as wrecks by your mother and brought home... However I'm relieved you're both better and back at Copse Cottage.[68]

It is also clear I had enquired about progress on *Sarnia Chérie*. His response concludes with a reference whose significance I had not yet guessed at:

> Yes, the book is well up to schedule and the typing should be finished in a fortnight. Then the tedious task of re-reading the thing and, doubtless, re-typing a page here and there. Remains to punch holes and bind it ready for its rightful owners.

Meanwhile I vaguely remember acquiring for him a second-

---

[68] A communal cottage in Earley on the outskirts of Reading.

hand book on Conrad's seamanship, so obscure I thought he might not know it:

> Thanks for getting the book on Conrad for me. I've seen the title in lists of books on Conrad, but never the book. I look forward to reading it. C. himself wrote an essay on submarine warfare. It filled him with horror and compassion: even more so than visible fighting on land. It was the sudden disappearance of a whole ship and its human load appalled him.

> Well, every good wish for good luck to Lisa in her exam and my love to you both.

<u>Gerald</u>

We may have paid another visit that summer but if so the typescript could not have been complete. Then on 2 August, late in the afternoon, Lisa and I drove down to Upwey and stayed the night at Jo's. The next morning I encouraged Lisa to accompany me to visit Gerald for coffee and as soon as we had squeezed into his tiny bedsitting room,

Fig. 80: *Rear view of 'Snelldonia'* (654 Dorchester Road, Upwey). Gerald wrote *Ebenezer Le Page* in the upper-storey bed-sitting room (photo: the author).

with something of a flourish he handed over a heavy, rectangular package.

# 4: THE PROPERTY OF NEVILLE FALLA

Demonstrating something of what Renaissance Italians called 'sprezzatura' (the art of achieving something difficult without apparent effort), Gerald said next to nothing about the substantial typescript he had given me. In the *Book* itself, having presented his autobiographical journal to Neville Falla, Ebenezer comments: 'I swear he knew I had given him all my secrets for him to read some day.'[69] Although, from the moment I met him I had been personally convinced of his exceptional talents, for his own satisfaction and that of a wider audience, I had tried to persuade Gerald to complete and publish the novel he seemed tirelessly to write and rewrite. Like Neville, I could guess that what I had been given to read was of great personal significance to its author. Where the secrets of Gerald's youth were concerned, however, his novel was only very obliquely revelatory and it would be decades before I discovered the half of them, with even now his later middle age remaining a mysteriously dark wood.

We left Dorset a couple of days later and returned to Uxbridge. Lisa and I had left our cottage outside Reading and were staying temporarily with my parents, pending moving into a house nearby, Uxbridge being conveniently situated between Reading, where I was to complete my degree, and London, where Lisa was to begin hers. As soon as I had read the typescript I phoned Gerald to congratulate him on his magnificent achievement and thank him as best I could both for presenting me with the result of so many years labour and, as I discovered on turning over the immaculately typed title-page, for dedicating it to us both. I confirmed what I had always promised, that I would do my best to get it published.

A fortnight later, I received a letter which underlined the symmetry between the fictional and actual donation. Where Ebenezer had inscribed the words: 'THE PROPERTY OF NEVILLE FALLA' on the first page of *his* Book and bequeathed him his house and life savings, Gerald had dedicated his *Book* to me and Lisa. Prior to any further correspondence on the subject,

---

[69] *Ebenezer Le Page*, p. 376.

however, he confirmed the gift of his novel to me by typing and signing a formal declaration, giving me the sole rights 'to get it published if and as you think fit, to own the copyright, and to receive whatever emoluments may accrue, without any obligation to me'.[70]

His covering letter, dated 12 August 1974, explained:

> I am enclosing the statement I promised over the 'phone. It may never prove necessary for you to use it … but, for the time being, it will serve to cover you, if ever you are challenged as to why you are making independent arrangement for the publication of SARNIA CHÉRIE.
>
> I am not going to deal now with the objections I know you will raise; nor with the book itself. I wait for an opportunity when we can talk at ease together. I wish to emphasise, however, that when I say 'without obligation' I mean without obligation - on any level. Consideration of neither money nor book must be allowed to impair what is more important. All the same, I am egotistic enough to have wishes regarding publicity which you need or need not abide by. I want none. It is not from modesty either. The mere thought of having a public image appals me.[71] Consequently I would prefer an approach to a publisher to be in terms of the merits of the book, rather than any particulars of my personality or career. I would not myself willingly supply 'the public' with any autobiographic data whatever - as distinct from to you. Also the possibility of profit on future work cannot be used as a bait. I don't contemplate embarking on another full-length work. At present I am steering against the wind with two parts in view only. LE VIER GUERNÉSI: TALES OF GUERNSEY FOLK.[72] LA ROCQUE QUI CHANTE: SONGS OF A GUERNSEYMAN.[73] It is for the second I am hoping most my sails will fill. Anyway, neither can ever be completed

---

[70] See above, p. 205  for the full text of this typed document.

[71] See above p. 210. [public recognition]

[72] See Appendix 2, p. 350.

[73] See Appendix 3, p. 355.

and, possibly, none be published while I am alive: but at least what gets done will get done, and I won't leave you with chunks of arrogantly conceived colossi.

By the way, in view of the possibility of my presence being needed, I am not going to Guernsey this year.[74] When the Snells leave here, which may be in September, I may move to Salisbury as I previously intended. Anyhow, I'll keep within relatively easy touch. I hope soon to hear Lisa's news of her exam.

As ever,

Gerald.

P.S. Glancing through this it reads to me rather as though I am shifting a burden on to you. It is not my intention. So long as I am around I will give you every help I can.

Gerald remained needlessly concerned about the tone of this letter and returned to the subject in his next, dated 29 August. He linked this to his concern about the promise of further writing:

Dear Edward,

Another note only, but I have been feeling uneasy about my last (perhaps unnecessarily) and, in any case, have an amendment to make. The typed statement I'm quite satisfied with: but in recollection my personal note does seem to have been hard or putting-off, or something: or at least putting difficulties in your way and Lisa's, which God forbid I should do.

The amendment is re future writing. Readingly and writingly I've been going through a most frustrating time. Details of any reading would take too long to tell you now: but I have emerged with the feeling it is hopeless for me to

---

[74] Somewhat poignantly (wishful-thinkingly) he writes as if a visit to Guernsey was a regular occurrence but to my knowledge he didn't go there during the entire period I knew him, *i.e.* the last four and half years of his life. *Cf.* the slightly later letter below, in which he says he is thinking of going over to Guernsey in the New Year but didn't then either (below, p. 270).

try writing anything head on - it has for me, I think, always to be done obliquely. That knocks out the Stories and Songs I suggested, both of which were contemplated as being done head on. Oh, I can be verbally competent enough, but for some reason it feels to me phoney when I'm not allowing an incubus to speak in a circumscribed context. So if anything follows S.C. it will, I think at present, have to be THE BOUD'LO, if I retain strength, years, and mental coherence long enough to complete it.[75] Philip Le Moigne, the B. in question, is like the weight of an unborn creature I carry round with me quite unlike Ebenezer. He's born (as a freak) in a quite different social and cultural strata of Guernsey society - a strata I also know by instinct - to which English fashionable sophistications come. Philip, who may be mad from birth (I don't know) naturally doesn't play - he writes his story in old age in a mental home: it's FOR DR ERIC KENNEDY TO READ. It's not at all in Christian images like S.C; nor is it a sequel, but it does dovetail at the edges. For instance, the later life of Neville and Adèle come into it; and parts of Raymond's that are only glossed in S.C. As I said, the conception possesses me, has for years: whether I'll bring it to birth or not remains to be seen. I get very tired.[76]

However, I don't feel saying the foregoing is unfriendly, which is what I feared my last note was. I would love to hear from Lisa - humanly, the result of her exam and so on. She seems nervous of writing to me - as if I had to be written up to. Good God, I'm not a judge - certainly haven't got the right to be.[77]

My love to you both,     <u>Gerald.</u>

---

[75] *Cf.* above, p. 253, where on the 29 December 1973 he says he has 'pitched 'The Boud'lo' into the dustbin.'

[76] I possess only scraps of Gerald's work in progress on this project, one sent or handed over soon after this and another given to me by Joan Snell some time after his death; *cf.* his development of this theme below, pp. 312-14 and Appendices.

[77] In his penultimate paragraph, Ebenezer writes: 'I have judged people. I do not want to judge people. I want to bless...' (*Ebenezer Le Page*, p. 394, and below, p. 345).

# 5: REJECTED BY CASSELLS

On 13 September 1974, by prearrangement with a reader I had met at an exhibition opening, I delivered the typescript of *Sarnia Chérie* to Cassell and Company in London, my first attempt in what was to become a litany of failures to persuade publishers to accept the novel. More than a month later, having not heard from my contact, I was already prepared for the worst and had suggested to Gerald that if it were to be rejected I should send it to Cape's. Gerald never mentioned what I only discovered long after his death, that almost half a century earlier Jonathan Cape had commissioned him to write a book on D.H. Lawrence and, after his failure to deliver, transferred the commission to his friend Stephen Potter, and then rejected a book on Jesus which Gerald had offered instead. Instead he wrote, on 30 October:

> Of course, Edward, you can let Capes see it, if Cassells reject it: you are free to let anybody see it without asking me. I have given the carbon copy to Joan, but inscribed it 'This copy is for Joan Snell only.'…

> I have read the thing through again. Spotted a few typing slips and there are doubtless countless others. Also a wrong tense that ought to be put right, a right tense that ought to be put wrong, and a local surname mis-spelt. I have retyped these pages. They are, in fact, reversions to the original script. If you get the typescript back from Cassells, will you please make the corrections and substitute the three pages, before you pass it on to Capes. If, by any chance, Cassells take the book, let them have the Amendments and do it themselves before it goes to the printers.

> There is one bait for a publisher I must withdraw. S.C. is a first and last novel. Nor do I think I shall write any shorter stories. I have made a break through into verse; but whether I shall be able to write another line I, naturally, don't know. In any case, the project is hardly likely to be publishable during my life-time. If ever...

> This house is sold (D.V.) to be considerably enlarged and converted into a commercial Home for Old People. The buyers want it vacated at latest by January 1st. The Snells

haven't found another house yet, but Cornwall is indicated. They want me to go with them. I don't. I'd rather be a hermit-crab than live 'en famille'.

Gerald's anxiety about where to live and his proud resistance against accepting the Snells' offer that he should continue lodging with them wherever they went is still the theme of his next letter, dated 2 December:

Dear Edward,

I'm sorry to have to pester you again via the parental mansion, but I shall be leaving here on Monday, the 16th, and don't know what my address will be after. It will be in Weymouth somewhere, but possibly only a Board-Residence for an uncertain period, while I search for a bed-sitter - If I haven't found one before. All I ask of you is that, in the meantime, you let me have your own address, so that I can let you have mine when I get one, in case you want to contact me.

Love to you and Lisa,

<u>Gerald.</u>

It seems that, having finally received a rejection letter from Cassells, I had postponed writing, thereby failing to confirm our new address in Uxbridge. I now replied by return and on 6 December, Gerald wrote the first of what became a series of seemingly stoic responses to the blindness of the great British publishers:

Dear Edward,

I was ever so glad to hear from you this morning (the understatement of the year). Believe me, I didn't feel even the slightest tinge of personal grief at Cassell's turning the book down; but I did feel sorry for the trouble you have been to when you must have plenty to concern you of your own. I hope you will be luckier with Cape - I don't know now the set-up and policy of the firm - but I fancy they go for fiction more than Cassell's. If they turn it down, the only other publisher I can think of as likely - and, I expect this will astonish you, is Faber and Faber. They published in 1964 by far the best empirical book on the Channel Islands:

INTRODUCING THE CHANNEL ISLANDS by Henry Myhill; and S.C. is not so far from the Eliot tradition. Strip T.S.E. of implied dogmatic beliefs and moral absolutes (to neither of which he was wholly committed) and you're afloat on the same stream of intimations as gave S.C. its circular form. After all, the begetter of Ebenezer Le Page can't help loving the man who wrote THE HIPPOPOTAMUS and HOW UNPLEASANT TO MEET MR ELIOT! So I may not be wrong in thinking the firm may still have a reader who can spot meaning by indirection, and not be altogether literal-minded, or literary. However, what matters is that success or failure to get it published must not disturb you. Anyhow, now I have your address, I intend to write to Lisa this week-end an answer to her letter - generous and all the more appreciated for her reservations. Even when she flares up in anger I like her. At least she won't go to heaven 'on ice'.[78]

This next week I shall be sorting my things out and packing and room-hunting...

I much look forward to seeing you both.

Love

<u>Gerald</u>

P.S. I want you to thank Lisa's father for arranging for the duplication of MS.

Gerald's punctilious expression of gratitude here refers to my father-in-law, Keith Jacka, for having kindly photocopied the typescript on its return from Cassells. I had asked him to do this both for safety's sake and to enable an extra reader to judge or simply enjoy the book (as Keith himself did) for I was beginning to suspect this would be a long haul. Were I trying to get an old man's book published without an agent today I would have sent it to several publishers simultaneously.

---

[78] This seems to be a reference to Jo having told Gerald of her mother (my great-grandmother who had lived with her in Upwey till her death at the age of 94), joking about the icepack that was applied to her throat when she was dying of oesophageal cancer and relating it to the sort of TV entertainment Gerald so disliked.

When in early September I had reminded Lisa of Gerald's earlier message that he would appreciate her feed-back, she read rapidly through the typescript before I handed it over to Cassell's. We compared our conclusions; I encouraged her to write to Gerald and he replied as promised. Though he had talked to me on the phone about the book, he now put his thoughts to paper. Despite writing on 7 December 1974, the day after receiving the news from me of Cassell's rejection, he made only one oblique reference to this, characteristically taking our responses to his novel far more seriously than those of the supposed professionals:

> Dear Lisa,
>
> I got an immeasurably welcome letter from Edward yesterday giving your address and news re book. I replied briefly and mainly on only practical matters, promising myself the indulgence this week-end of writing more discursively to you.

After several pages about an unsuccessful visit to Jo, the Snells' latest plans, whether or not we were coming down that Christmas and his own plans for moving, Gerald wrote:

> I am thinking of going over to Guernsey for at least a couple of weeks in the New Year - especially if I can get a pied-à-terre to leave my books in Weymouth (they really are a burden); but I won't think of going until after term has begun and you're both back at the grindstone again.
>
> I've written all this and yet haven't got round to acknowledging and thanking you for your marvellous letter. For it was a marvellous letter; and if the book is ever published, it will certainly never get a review within light years as good. The generous response, the acumen of your intuitions, equally with the questionings and reservations, seemed a miracle to me across the gulf of more the half a century. It provoked me to check up by reading the whole damn book through again. It was an odd experience, for I found I was reading a book [that] might have been written by somebody else. The umbilical cord had withered, and only now and again did I feel a twinge of the original birth pangs. On the whole I was pleasantly surprised - it was

better than I thought, and a few chapters in particular I thought really quite good. Of course I was biased and read it with a sympathetic, rather than critical, approach. Had I got on to my intellectual high horse, I would no doubt have reduced it to a shambles from the start. I can't truly feel violent about Cassell's Reader.

You were quite right, of course, in being aware that I know exactly what Ebenezer was doing: yet he is definitely not me under cover, nor my mouthpiece. He often says things I know to be untrue: at others doesn't say all he knows, and sometimes things which say more than he knows he means. It was his arrival set the book going in my mind; and he is the only character created anywhere near in the round. I see him quite objectively. Of the others, the ones I see as best done are his mother and Jim. The others leave much to the imagination, and are really only presented in so far as they impact on Ebenezer - as in fact are the history and geography of Guernsey itself. I leave at least half the work to be done by the reader.

It's true there are chapters surface more than others - these are the ones I think well done. They include a chapter in the first part (9 or 10?) beginning, 'I am Church, me...' and including the Seamen's Mission scene and Ebenezer climbing the greasy pole; a chapter in the second part (I think it's 9) which includes Raymond's service in the Birdo Mission Hall (the same sermon in other words, really); and the pseudo ghost-scene (I think again chapter 9) in the third part. It's the nearest to an intellectual statement - but I, when possible, avoid intellectual arguments conducted on 'sound' logical principles. My experience is that, even in real life, there are skew lines that don't really contact because they start off, however logically they may proceed, from different premises - i.e. different persons. So that you are quite right in your sense of the illusory and the vague, in spite of the obviously solid and factual basis.

Also, in sensing a whole was being made - though, to be more precise, I would say an imperfect whole was trying to be made. Actually, the complex of pre-occupations I was trying to unify is never explicitly stated, and can't be - or, from my point of view I'd have no impulse in writing the book. I'm not interested in documentary or 'shock of recognition' fiction. As to its relation to my personal life and experiences, I must leave that for conversation. It's enough for me to say here they are none of them me in their personalities, circumstances, or relationships, but there are slithers of me in quite a number, not only Ebenezer and Raymond, but Archie Mauger and Horace among others.[79] Only in the nominally male, though. I am congenitally incapable to projecting a woman from the inside out - hence my total incapacity of writing head-on an impersonal 'classical' novel. Voss and Nostromo are far beyond and above me.

Remains the end: concerning which both you and Edward agree in disapproving. Though (rightly, I think) for different reasons. From what Edward said over the phone when he had just finished the book, I gathered his disapproval was of the blood relation between Neville and Liza; and Adèle and Ebenezer. It had never occurred to me before it could be otherwise; and it still seems to me consistent psychologically with the thing 'as a whole'. Incidentally, Edward also said he wouldn't have me alter it.

I have to join issue with you for your reason, if I've got it right. You talk of plot; of 'tucking in the ends.' I never thought of plot. I often faced a blank sheet of paper without any idea what Ebenezer was going to say next. I wrote down what he said. True, I was 'clever' enough (with the top of my head) to try and arrest a reader's attention and keep it - dramatic, instinct. Your word 'mesmerise' is quite right. As for 'plot', I was myself flattered by how intricately the various strands of the different themes had interwoven - I was more aware of 'correspondence' than of weaving a

---

[79] Of the minor characters, there is at least one 'slither' of Gerald in Archie Mauger when he writes: '[he] was a clever boy and went to the University of Bristol after the War and got a B.Sc. and became a Science Master in England...' (*Ebenezer Le Page*, p. 114). Perhaps Gerald also saw himself in Archie Mauger when the latter is punished for objecting to go on Church parade in the army 'but wasn't dishonest enough to change his religion when it suited him' (*ibid.*, p. 134).

plot. Therefore the ends are NOT tucked in. For instance, Neville and Adèle are not necessarily in for a 'happy ending'. There are possible storms ahead. Edward saw that, and on those grounds didn't object.[80] More seriously, I think it is the near mystical end is the root of the variance; but that I cannot change, for I didn't think it out. The last two pages, or so, I didn't even write. They occurred to me almost word for word as they are now, while I was lying in bed one night in Plymouth, when I think it was only three or four chapters were actually written.[81] Read carefully, even the end is left 'open'. The unrepentant sinner is forgiven, true; but a few lines later Ebenezer is wishing he could live his life again. He wants to bless, genuinely; but in his blessing describes Sarnia Chérie as 'this whore of an island'. Seems true to me. Another significant fact is the time gap between what he is writing about and what he is living shortens, and the last words, purely human, he is actually living and writing simultaneously. His end is conveyed by the dedication.

The difficulty is that it is a Guernsey story; and he, of course, of the generation before mine, has not terms to think in but those of our bibliodrous, puritan, Calvinist tradition; but to that he is a heretic. There is no evidence he *believes* in 'personal immortality:' only he is honest enough to acknowledge an 'intimation' of something more. There I am with him. Nobody will be more surprised than me if, when I die, I wake up and find myself alive. I won't deny the possibility, though I don't like the idea much. The point of view of the absolute mystic or the absolute logician is not mine: I feel it to be self-loving, inflated and pretentious. Many finer minds than mine, however, don't and haven't.

Well, that's all for now, dear Lisa (except a P.S.)

---

[80] Among so many other coincidences (perhaps too many to be mere coincidence), Lampedusa anticipates a difficult life for Don Fabrizio's heir and his wife, Angelica: 'Those were the best days in the life of Tancredi and Angelica, lives later to be so variegated, so erring, against the inevitable background of sorrow. But of that they were still unaware.' (*Leopard*, Colquhoun translation, p. 124). I am unlikely to have objected as already anticipating such problems in our parallel lives; see also below, pp. 312 and 322.

[81] Gerald lived in Plymouth in the mid-1960s; see above, p. 201.

Love,

<u>Gerald</u>

P.S. I much, much prefer - a free and easy talk with friends than writing to them. There is so much I'd like to know about your studies and so on. I imagined you both going to see the Turner Exhibition.[82]

Having announced that he would be leaving the Snells on 16 December, Gerald wrote on the 17th:

As you will see from the date, the zero hour has gone by and I have somewhat shamefacedly to confess I am still here: and will remain put until the Snells quit. I don't know when that will be. The house is 'sold subject to contract' and the contract is in their possession and the buyers clamouring for it to be signed; but ... I wouldn't be surprised if they are still here in a year's time... Anyhow, as far as I am concerned, it means I will be here when you come down, as I certainly hope you will, after Christmas.

I did, as a matter of fact, find one place in Weymouth I could have taken. I'd have had a quiet room to myself, furnished with only those objects I needed; but it entailed communal meals, the idea of which I didn't like at all. I feared I'd be jumping out of the frying pan into the fire.

So here I am for Christmas, which was my basic dread. It will be relatively quiet this year, anyway... Also my lack of 'the Christmas spirit' is by now taken for granted without giving offence. I look forward to seeing you.

Meanwhile, cordial greetings to Melissa, Tim and Philip.

My love to you both,

<u>Gerald.</u>

---

[82] The bicentennial: *Turner 1775-1851*, at the Royal Academy, which ran from November 1974 - March 1975, which we indeed visited.

# 6: REJECTED BY CAPE

Between Christmas and returning to our respective degrees we squeezed in another visit to Jo and Gerald. This being my final year, having decided to graduate in art history rather than fine art (largely due to the orthodoxy of the avant-garde that prevailed in Reading's Fine Art Department since the premature retirement of Claude Rogers), I had to begin some serious work in order to obtain a post-graduate place and funding. In March I must have phoned or written to Gerald informing him that, subject to my getting a good result, I had won places at both the Courtauld and Warburg Institutes in London University. But my other news was disheartening. I had delivered the typescript to Cape's and heard back within the month. Gerald responded on 24 March 1975:

> Dear Edward and Lisa,
>
> I'm ever so happy to hear from you - and delighted, Edward, at your two acceptances. I want to know more.

On first re-reading this, I imagined for a moment that Gerald was referring here to some sort of acceptance of his novel but *pace* Collis's account of him of having 'died of discouragement ... not of a heart attack but of the killing cancer of rejection,'[83] his stoicism and at least short-term, instinctive charm were such that he began his letter by enthusing over my good fortune before even referring to what was the second rejection of his novel:

> Sorry about Cape's, of course - but not to worry. You did your best. I'm not surprised, though. It's not only the economic, it's the contemporary mood.[84] I won't enlarge on that - in fact, don't intend to spread myself now. This is really only to thank you and let you know I'm still here. I suggest you don't send it to anyone else till we've had a talk

---

[83] Collis, 'Memories of a Genius Friend', p. 22.

[84] Gerald was unlucky in that 1973-75 saw a period of serious inflationary recession which indeed manifested itself in a kind of malaise that diminished many forms of enterprise, including publishing. March 1975 is often thought to have signalled the beginning of the recovery.

- just make a list of the publishers, as I frankly don't know half of them now. For instance, I don't know those you mention. However, whatever happens, the book is yours. The mood may change, will, has to, if not before, after I'm around; and then you may get it in somewhere. It's not all that good: but I still think it is in toto humanising - and there are readers, I perhaps fondly imagine, would feel it so, if it could be got to them.

Typically, Gerald waxed more indignant on behalf of fellow-exile Joseph Conrad, the subject of a television programme on which I had commented, than on his own predicament:

> The poem [*sic* for programme?] on Conrad. I didn't see the Omnibus, but read a review of it denigrating him (another symptom of 'the mood').[85] God, there has never been a sad, lonely soul who wrote less from his 'brain'!

> I haven't been to see Jo. The truth is I haven't been up to it - physically. So the other effort I just could not have made. It's been a low long winter... Moaning over!

> Be seeing you,

> Love,

> Gerald.

A fortnight later, on 9 April 1975, Gerald sent something from his very meagre pension as a birthday present. I had meanwhile suggested that this time he might compose a letter with which we could approach Faber and Faber:

Dear Edward,

> A widower's mite for your 24th birthday on the 11th, also for Lisa's, as I don't know the date of hers. I meant to send you a couple of Book Tokens, but am too dithery to go down to Weymouth on my own steam and Bert [Snell] is not well enough to go out, and therefore unable to drive me down. I hope you won't mind it this way.

---

[85] The BBC TV 'Omnibus' programme on Conrad, presumably a repeat of the one first shown on 27 October 1974. The series started in 1967 but was unfortunately scrapped in favour of Alan Yentob's 'Imagine' in 2002.

I've been trying out approaches to Faber's, but the knot of inhibitions won't untie, nor can I at present believe it would be effective if they did. At the same time I can't have you burdened with the trouble and humiliation of touting that book round, when I feel you should for the next two months be completely absorbed in your own vital preoccupations. It may be when the weather gets warmer and I feel better, as I hope, I shall be able to draft something for you to see when you come down; or we can again discuss tactics. In the meantime, many happy returns to you both.

Gerald.

I must have replied promptly for his next letter is dated 14 April. Apparently I had begun by asking him how he knew my birthdate. I then suggested that, given his inhibitions about writing to Fabers (which I now realise may partly have been due to rejections dating back decades), I should send the typescript to Calder and Boyars, who had recently been enterprising enough to republish several titles by Wyndham Lewis.[86] It seems that I still recommended that Gerald should send a preliminary, or covering letter. Meanwhile the Snells' plans to move had again been postponed:

> Thanks for your thanks. It was no deprivation, though. I pay only £10 a week here, including heat, light and laundry; which my Old Age Pension covers and leaves some to spare. My monthly Government Pensions mount up in the Bank adequate for any move over or under ground. I don't think it will be over, as I doubt whether Bert and Joan really intend to sell this house. In my opinion, they will be foolish if they do... It suits me, anyhow. I will stay here, if they do. This room is quiet, has in it all I need, and quite big enough for me to keep tidy. If they move, I shan't move with them. It would mean an unsettled, camping-out state for some time, which I am sorry to have to admit I am not up to now. I got your date of birth from Jo, of course, last year. Almost by violence. I had to chase her up the stairs to get it for me

---

[86] For his negotiations with Faber and Faber in the early days of T.S. Eliot's directorship, see pp. 113-18.

(and pay the price by giving her my own). I daren't ask her for Lisa's as well that day. As you know, when I used to visit Jo, you two were like the couple in the weather house - one in the sun and one in the shade. It was all right: it worked out fair. Lisa got her turn. Unfortunately, the day she was gloriously in the sun, Margot turned up and I had to curb my violent impulses.[87] By the way, I laughed out loud when I read of Jo taking anti-forgetting pills that succeeded in making her forget to take them. It might be a Guernsey joke.

Yes, let Calder and Boyars have *S.C.*, if you like. Odd, yesterday I saw their name for the first time in the Observer Lit. Supp. A book of theirs was reviewed which, from what I could glean, didn't sound very flash, but genuine. Described by the condescending reviewer as 'thoughtful.' I just can't write to them first, though. (a) I don't know their address, and (b) I am still stuck with a chronic inhibition against writing to an anonymous blank wall. What I am going to do is to write you a more formal letter than this (typed) authorising you to let them see the book and suggesting a few things you might let them know about it beforehand. You could then write them asking them if they will read it, make any comments you want to, and enclose my letter, if you think it might help. I also suggest you enclose a stamped and addressed envelope for them to let you know whether they want you to deliver it. Otherwise a direct attack; but I think the way I suggest would make it easier all around.

I have in mind the desirability of altering the Preface somewhat. I haven't tried it yet, so don't know whether it will work. My idea is to scrap the Disclaimer beginning, I think: 'Local names are used throughout...' and entitling the Preface GUERNSEY ENGLISH AND GUERNSEY NAMES. All the pages on linguistics would remain as they are, but instead of the pyrotechnic last paras, I would name which

---

[87] The elegant Margot Hodges was my aunt's Upwey neighbour. I have a vague recollection of her revealing that she was an old flame of the Dorchester-born Llewelyn Powys (1884-1939), who had dedicated poems to her as a girl.

people in Ebenezer's story actually existed, and admit to geographic liberties, and the careful misplacing of houses and deliberate misuse of Guernsey names. It will not be as exciting as the present end, but would not provoke initial antagonism in some; when, after all, the same thing is said obliquely in the book, and I think to better effect. Blitz begets blitz - which is the last thing I want to do. Undercut, rather. However, I'll have a shot at it; and, if I succeed, you can use which you think better. I do feel now the Preface should be only interestingly informative, without the intrusion of my own emotion. I'd scrap the date (when the emotion was true) and just sign it.

I am made slightly uneasy by your remarks on Van Gogh and Rembrandt - not because your facts are untrue, but because they can be used in such a way as to inflate the present 'with-it' trend in criticism. I mean helicopter thinking. That is to de-bunk from a superior height and remain safe. I am all for de-bunking; but it's the bunkers who need de-bunking, not the bunked. I think, however, the query you are up against is too near the raw nerve of your job for me to presume to deal with it clumsily in a few words. It applies also to all writers whose works I like, who all in some way or another are sorry specimens; but they are the ones out on a limb, and do shed seeds of light. Possibly criticism ought to be salvage, really.

I'll send you the typed letter as soon as I can get it done and, if I succeed, the amended pages of the Preface.

My love to you both.

<u>Gerald</u>

Gerald sent the formal letter three days later with a covering note informing me of his latest change of mind:

Here's the letter. I hated writing it and I don't have to say I'm not satisfied with it but it's the best I can do, as I am at present. I hope it will be some use to you.

I have decided NOT to re-write the Preface, or remove the Disclaimer. It's all part of the book as a whole, and I feel it's phoney to tinker with it now. If Calder and Boyars *do* ask to see it, I think it would be all right to let them have the original typescript. You would be delivering it in person at their invitation, and it should be safe enough; but I leave that to you.

I won't write more as I want Joan to post this when she goes out with the dogs. I haven't been well enough to go out since you were here. I hope I revive in the spring - if there is one this year.

The typed, formal letter, from 654 Dorchester Road, Upwey, Weymouth, and dated 17 April 1975, ostensibly addressed to us, but in fact intended to explain and thereby sell the book to the publisher, is of considerable interest in providing an insight (albeit a somewhat anaesthetised one) into what Gerald thought he had achieved:

Yes, by all means let Calder and Boyars read S.C., if you think they might take it... It is an odd book. It fits into the category of 'novel', I suppose; but from many points of view it does not. Certainly not in the classical mode; but then, though I spent 20 years of my life lecturing on Literature, I still don't know what a novel is. I think of it as a book. SARNIA CHÉRIE: THE BOOK OF EBENEZER LE PAGE.

Ostensibly it is the rambling record of an ancient Guernseyman, who lives on Guernsey from before the Boer War until the 1960's. He has never been further from the island, except for one trip to Jersey, than a few miles out to sea in a fishing-boat. His view of the world is circumscribed by the sea and rocks and other islands and the distant coast of France; and his culture only extended by contact with British and foreign seamen and a more educated cousin. He knows little of the history of his own island, and it would never occur to him to rhapsodise over its scenery and charm. A tourist knows more about Guernsey from the outside, by reading one of the dozen or so guide books available, than he does. On the other hand, he experiences living in Guernsey for most of a century, and expresses from the inside out the effect of world events as they impinge on its coasts.[88]

---

[88] A few months previously Gerald had described himself of being incapable of

On that level, the book might appeal to a publisher as unexploited territory in imaginative writing. Victor Hugo and Elizabeth Goudge have both written of Guernsey, but one was a Frenchman and the other is an English lady; and, whatever merits their stories may have, they are completely unconvincing to a born and bred Guernseyman.[89] They might as well be set in Normandy, or Devon. In that respect I can claim to be authentic; being a Guernseyman on my father's side of two generations, and on my mother's side as far back as local records go. English for me is an acquired language, and I am not even yet quite at home in it.[90] I am sure I write more subtly in Ebenezer's 'Guernsey English'. A Guernseyman can mean quite a lot by saying very little, especially through the medium of his quirky, tragi-comic, down-to-earth humour. I have occasionally let Ebenezer lapse into patois, the speech I was born into, but only in contexts where the meaning is apparent. The brief

---

'projecting a woman from the inside out'; see above, p. 272.

[89] Though born in Wells, Somerset, her father the Reverend Henry Goudge, Elizabeth Goudge's mother was, in fact, Ida de Beauchamp Collenette, of an old Guernsey family (see *ODNB*). She elaborated on her Guernsey roots in the 1947 issue of the *Quarterly Review of the Guernsey Society*: 'I paid my first visit to Guernsey when I was eighteen months old… My grandfather was Adolphus Collenette, famous for his weather lore, and my grandmother was Marie-Louise Ozanne, who was brought up in Hauteville House, now the Victor Hugo Museum. My great-grandfather sold the house to Victor Hugo. He came to see it before buying it, and my grandmother took him over it on her eighteenth birthday. So that on one side I am proud to call myself a Guernseywoman.' She goes on to write: 'I had had no success with my writing until I began to write about Guernsey… I have enjoyed writing about Guernsey more than any other place…'. Moving to Devon, she found herself thinking about Guernsey again, 'and in odd times all through the war I wrote *Green Dolphin Country*, and once again Guernsey brought me luck.' (She won a £30,000 prize for the novel and it was turned into a Hollywood film). She also remarks, as would Gerald, that, 'As all that I wrote about Guernsey has been written away from it, I have never made any attempt to be topographically correct.' Though one of her characters in *Island Magic* concedes that 'you can't be an individualist on our Island,' she concludes in positive mode: 'there's so much magic packed into so small a space. With the sea flung round us and holding us so tightly we are all thrown into each other's arms—souls and seasons and birds and flowers and running water. People understand unity who live on an island. And peace. Unity is such peace.'

[90] See above, pp. 33-34.

introduction on GUERNSEY ENGLISH should clear the ground for subsequent linguistic irregularities.

I think a publisher ought in honesty be warned not to expect an exciting story. The exploits of the First Battalion of the Royal Guernsey Light Infantry in the First World War make brave reading; but I was only old enough to serve more or less unadventurously in the Second Battalion, and Ebenezer serves only in the Guernsey Militia. Neither have I played up the desperate heroism of some of our islanders under the German Occupation during the Second World War. In my book that period has some tense and poignant moments, but only in so far as they affect Ebenezer and his relatives and friends.

I expect most English people know by now the Channel Islands were occupied, but not conquered; so the set-up was different from, say, the German Occupation of France, Holland, or Norway. The Germans are not, therefore, presented as altogether black. It is true they had spasms and panics, when victims were sent to camps on the continent, sometimes with tragic consequences, for little or no reason; but, on the whole, the opposite numbers, in so isolated and limited a space, had to settle down to peaceful, if somewhat strained (and often very funny) co-existence. The stolid, literal German mind was no match for the Guernsey wink. The Herrenvolk lost on points.

The religious tradition of Guernsey is more Calvinist than in England; and though the entanglements of love, which have been the analysed subject of so much English, American and French fiction, happen in Guernsey as elsewhere, there is a difference. To this day, Guernsey is only reluctantly admissive, but not permissive. Ebenezer had never heard of Freud and, as far as he knows, French literature from Gide to Genet does not exist.[91] The

---

[91] This rare reference to Freud begs the question as to his influence on Gerald (as also that of libertarians, André Gide and Jean Genet). Despite his 'disorientation from Lawrence' in boasting superior resistance to 'the female will' (see above, p. 246), Gerald seems to have shared Lawrence's scepticism regarding Freud's tendency to see 'the serpent of sex coiled round the root of all our actions', in favour of the sacredness of sex (and the sacralisation of love). Soon

ambivalences do, though. They comprise also the anomaly of the island's geography and history. It is geographically part of the continent; and its pro and contra relationship to the British Crown has been a recurring motif since the Conquest. I, as you know, have no political axe to grind, but have to admit Ebenezer's amusing double-thinking is not antipathetic.

Alas. I am only reminding you of what you know already, and I fear providing you with little help in approaching a publisher; but as neither of you knew anything of Guernsey before reading the book and both found it interesting, I think you might point out it has a human relevance outside its insular subject matter...

Having confessed that it embarrasses him to write about his 'own stuff', Gerald concluded this rather too low-key letter with the hope that his book would be read 'sympathetically as a human document, and only after consider publication policy', adding apologetically (and no doubt unproductively given the letter's *raison 'd'être*):

I know how if I (the cultured English facade of me) picked up such a book and sampled a few pages here and there with a cold critical eye, I would throw it aside.

Well, whatever the result, thank you for trying.

Every good wish, as always,    Gerald

---

'psychoanalysis had become a public danger... The Oedipus complex was a household word, the incest motive a commonplace of tea-table chat.' (Lawrence, *Psychoanalysis and the Unconscious* [Harmondsworth, 1971], p. 201). Thus Lawrence responded negatively to Oedipal interpretations of *Sons and Lovers*, preferring Jung's more mystical approach to life and literature, one based, as Gerald also recommended, on quasi-religious authenticity. (Jung published 'Woman in Europe' in the September 1928 issue of the *Adelphi*). For Frieda's views on Freud, whom, following Otto Gross, she thought erred on the side of 'civilized' repression, see *Frieda Lawrence: The Memoirs and Correspondence,* p. 15; *cf.* David Holbrook's more wholesome critique in *Where D.H. Lawrence was wrong about Women* (Lewisburg, 1997). For an interesting discussion of Auden's use of Freud, Lawrence and Gide in relation to his own sexual liberation, see Richard Davenport-Hines, *Auden*, pp. 108-12. Married to an analyst, Lampedusa 'was a great admirer of Freud's *Beyond the Pleasure Principle* (1920)'; (Tomasi, *Biography,* p. 122). This focused upon the struggle between the opposing drives of *eros* and the death instinct, subsequently entitled *thanatos*.

# 7: APPROACHING FABER

Despite Gerald's best efforts and this rare gesture of practical compromise on his part, our plans again came to nothing. His next letter, responding to mine, is dated 7 May 1975:

Dear Edward,

I was surprised having a verdict from Calder and Boyars so soon. No I, for my part, am not at all put down by the rejection. My heart is really set on Fabers doing it. All the same, I'm sorry you had the trouble for nothing - especially as I doubt very much whether my letter helped. In fact, I think you'd have had a better chance without it. It was a cross-eyed effort. Aiming at two birds with one stone and missing both. Don't on any account use it again.

I will write direct to Fabers: at least, try my best to. It will be more formal; and not ingratiating. Their two books on the Channel Islands provide a context to start from; though I will have to attack both. John Uttley's STORY OF THE CHANNEL ISLANDS must be the deadliest history of any part of the world ever written. (I am going to compel myself to read the thing through again to be sure of my ground).[92] Henry Myhill's INTRODUCING THE CHANNEL ISLANDS is innocuous in so far as it contains much interesting and accurate information: but it proceeds from

---

[92] I inherited a still pristine copy of this 1966 book from my aunt which is inscribed: 'For Jo, on her 85th Birthday. From her old Guernsey Donkey, Gerald.' Jo was 85 on 11 September 1973. Despite his disparagement, it is interesting that as soon as he had settled in Shetland he made sure Joan Snell sent him '(1) Map of Guernsey (2) Patois Dictionary (3) Uttley's two books [the other presumably being *The Bailiwick of Guernsey*] and (4) Press green-covered "Guernsey Ways";' letter dated 12 July 1975. (*Guernsey Ways* was compiled by J.E. Moullin for the Guernsey Society in 1966). Uttley was a tragic figure, with a domineering mother, Alice or 'Alison', who wrote children's books, and a father who drowned himself in 1930. He himself committed suicide by driving over a Guernsey cliff in 1978 two years after his mother's death; see Denis Judd, *Alison Uttley: The Life of a Country Child* (London, 1986; 2nd ed. Manchester, 2011) and *cf.* the bizarrely inadequate *ODNB* entry on 'Alice Uttley', which mentions neither of the said suicides nor Denis Judd's definitive biography; he also edited her disturbing *Private Diaries* (London, 2009). For Gerald taking a map of Guernsey to the Scilly Isles, see below, p. 317, note 143.

the gaffe I read to you, and ends with iniquitous chapter on 'The Channel Islands as Places of Residence,' encouraging English people to go and settle there. His book was published in 1964, and thousands seem to have taken his advice; leading to the deadlock of the 'English Occupation,' which even the dimmest-witted local people are now beginning to deplore.

I don't intend in the letter to say much about my book, and even less about myself. I just must leave the book to speak for itself. If the Reader is deaf, it's just too bad. I may, however, risk a quite genuine tribute to the thread of humane, religious and distinguished cultural values their House has preserved intact throughout my English-reading life to this day.

In the meantime, forget about S.C., until your examination anxiety is over - you can wait until the results are out, if you like. I don't mind. Of course, you can let anyone sample the photostat, if somebody happens along.

I have read CANCER WARD and THE FIRST CIRCLE (each twice) and am tempted to dilate upon those miracles, and how they are rightly being acclaimed in the West though for the wrong reasons; but I will not tempt you to raise your nose from the grindstone, which is the proper place for it just now.[93]

I haven't forgotten Lisa. I wonder what is going on behind those beautiful big bland eyes that see so much and show so little, as she wanders among the academic anatomists of philosophy. I am quite quite sure, anyhow, she has more innate wisdom than any of the foolish philosophers: as well as being determined and astute enough to 'satisfy the examiners' with ease. I am less easy about you; for you're a gentler soul and headstrong with an awkward conscience (leavened, fortunately, with a spice of mild unscrupulousness). It is a combination which makes it harder for you. All I can do is keep my fingers crossed and

---

[93] After initial banning in Russia, Solzhenitsyn's *Cancer Ward* and *First Circle* were first published in English in 1968.

hope you get a first. 'Render unto Caesar...' and it is
certainly Caesar who sets examinations.

I won't send the letter to Fabers, if I manage to get it
done, until I hear from you that you are free in mind and
body to deal with the consequences. If you come down first,
you can read it before it goes: otherwise I'll send you a
carbon copy. I also have in mind to write a few pages on
GUERNSEY NAMES AND GUERNSEY PEOPLE and, if I
succeed, will send them to you to be inserted at the end.
THE GUERNSEY ENGLISH introduction is for English
readers: the end-piece for any Guernsey people who may
chance to read the book.[94] An amplification of the disclaimer
at the beginning really. I think it necessary to stress the
ubiquity of a few names on the island. The result is there
are probably numerous people living there today with
names the same as those of characters in the story. Le Pages
are as common as Smiths over here; but there is no Ebenezer
Le Page living at Les Moulins for the simple reason it isn't
there, nor can La Petite Grève be found on the map. There
are Careys galore in all the upper echelons; but none who
could have been living at Castle Carey during the Liza-
Ebenezer association with it; for the Carey family sold
Castle Carey some years before the First World War. The
same coverage, by mis-naming and misplacing, applies to
many other instances. To spike the guns of the Coysh type
of pedantry, I want to admit to knowing which places are
there, and which aren't, in Ebenezer's story; and which
have magically moved, or changed names.[95] The houses of

---

[94] Gerald's 'Guernsey English' appendix was in many ways the most provocative
part of the package, concluding with a scornful account of the current state of
the island, 'where the great Goddess Smug can reign supreme…'. Meanwhile, a
few interesting notes of local linguistic interest, as for example variations on the
theme of 'Houmet' or 'Hommet', were omitted by the publishers, as apparently
was his short (quasi-)disclaimer: 'Local names are used in this book; but apart
from some topographical features and a few peripheral figures who play no
['very' added by Gerald in pen]] active part in the story, are not to be identified
with places or persons of those names, or any others, existing on the Island of
Guernsey at any time.'

[95] See above, p. 248 for Gerald's intention to send his typescript to Victor Coysh
who seems to have replied by pointing out errors in topography, which were in

the Martel brothers could not have existed where they are placed, for it was an open green meadow until well after the end of the First World War. Nor, to my knowledge, were there ever any houses on Guernsey called by those names. In fact, they have never existed on Guernsey at all. I am under an obligation also to acknowledge who were 'the peripheral figures'. They are all dead now. I may divulge the more I know of them than Ebenezer did: which may not always tally with his sentiments. I feel I should close it with a personal reference to Guernseymen of today - not contradicting the pyrotechnics of the introduction, but counteracting it somewhat by a sympathetic recognition, forced upon me by recent reading, of the survival of some who still stick their heads in and lash out from time to time, and lift up their heads to heaven and bray, as a good Guernsey donkey ought to do.[96]

Well, that's all for now, and perhaps too much.

My love to you both,

Gerald.

We didn't go down to Dorset in May for I was at last working hard for my finals. Meanwhile my Dutch grandfather died, not long after visiting England with my grandmother. With characteristic consideration, Gerald waited until the day I finished my exams before writing on 5 June 1975:

Dear Edward

Sorry about your grandfather. It's good he saw you that last time.

Today for you must have been Liberation Day! I eagerly await the result and hope for the best. Does Lisa have an

---

fact intentional.

[96] Not the only instance in which Gerald identifies himself in Ebenezerish terms as a Guernsey donkey, a corrective to those who doubt his patriotism? (see e.g., p. 216). One should also remember that he called his novel *Sarnia Chérie*, and though it was not his idea to preface it with George Deighton's lyrics he would have been fully aware of that song's (and thus his title's) sentimental connotations; *n.b.*, the lines: 'I left thee in anger, I knew not thy worth…'.

Inter Exam, as we used to?[97] However, I don't expect she's worried.

Have just done the letter to Fabers and will post it the same time as this. One bird one stone this time. I'm quite pleased with it.

I feel it's a pretty good shot - though, of course, I can't see the bird. Anyhow, it's a straight aim not the circuitous self-conscious rigmarole I let you have last time. I've said nothing of the content of the book, or about myself. I have introduced you I hope acceptably, and confirmed you are fully authorised by me to negotiate. I have given them your address and hope you get a decent reply.

If it comes to an interview, I advise you not to expatiate on my 'literary' past.[98] Confine yourself to the book and your own views - I'm best left out. I haven't written an 'end-piece'. Decided it would be bathos and is unnecessary. Guernsiana recently published prove me right. I've made no reference to their two Channel Island books and there's no point in your doing so. I have referred to the 'Guernsey English' preface. I felt it necessary to give an assurance that the lingo in which Ebenezer writes is easily intelligible to an educated English reader.

Anyhow it's the best I can do.

My love to you both.

Gerald.

According to my journal it was on 10 June 1975 that I was informed I had got the 'first' that Gerald had hoped for and would therefore most likely get a full grant to go to the Warburg Institute, as my preferred option. On 22 June Lisa and I drove down to Dorset for three days during which I visited him. Partly perhaps because we were planning to go to Florence, he was already planning one of his periodic expeditions for he deposited with me almost all his worldly goods, some books

---

[97] This may be a rare reference to his time at Bristol University; see above, p. 40.

[98] This suggests that he had told me about his literary past, or indeed anything very much about his past at all, which he had not.

and clothes in a suitcase, his typewriter, the heavy second-hand coat I had acquired for him and a few manuscripts. He said he intended going to Shetland where, wishfully thinking, he thought he might remain forever.

Meanwhile, somewhat more practically, partly in order to improve my Italian in preparation for post-graduate work, Lisa and I had decided to spend as much of the summer as cheaply as possible in Italy. Before we left, however, there was a mini-crisis relating to Gerald's daughter. Gerald can never have been an ideal husband though his own experience of both mother and wife seems likewise to have been far from ideal. Largely as a result I believe, he was a far from ideal father. When his marriage collapsed in the early 1930s the children were sent to the recently founded progressive Dartington School where they were cared for by Leonard Elmhirst and his wealthy American wife, Dorothy.[99] He saw very little of them again. Gerald seems not to have seen his son, Adam, for more than half a century before he died, even though at least one of his poems, the 'Song of a Man who saw God' poignantly recalls what was presumably an experience in Switzerland, when 'a headstrong child, / swaying at the cliff-edge reckless of the height, and shambling to his mother's anxious arms, [is] affronted by her fears'. The last line of this verse even more poignantly recalls the 'sobs at night of the orphan's muffled grief.'[100]

Gerald's daughter, Dorcas, who became a doctor in Devon, was the only member of his immediate family with whom he maintained even minimal contact. He had talked of her on a couple of occasions and once went to stay with her for a day or two, but on 28 June 1975, having phoned to inform her of his plan to migrate to Shetland, he now reported to me that she had 'asked about the book - wants to read it, even if it is not published'.[101] He therefore asked that if my photocopy was not

---

[99] See above, Part I, p. 165.

[100] See Appendix 1, below, p. 347.

[101] When writing the introduction to the *Book*, John Fowles contacted Dorcas and on the basis of their correspondence wrote: 'His marriage finally broke down about 1933. One of its four children tells me that her father disappeared entirely from her life between that date and 1967, and the gap had become too great by the time relationship was renewed to be very successfully bridged'. Perhaps

being read by anyone else, could I send it to his daughter, whose address he supplied. A P.S. indicated that he had already told her I would send the photocopy and that she could keep it till the autumn: 'I've told her not to return it till the end of September.' After a brief account of a 'farewell' visit to Jo's, during which he presented her with a copy of Powys's *Weymouth Sands*, he concluded this letter with his most generous expression of gratitude to date:

> I think she was pleased with the present/dear old Jo!
>
> It's too deep in me and damn silly to try and say how sad I felt after you had gone. From the moment we met, you, and then Lisa, have been unremittingly good to me.
>
> Hope your visit to Florence is rewarding.
>
> <u>Gerald.</u>

Perhaps partly because of the warmth of his tone here and because in my partisan youth I was more critical of Gerald's children for ignoring *him* than *vice versa*, but partly also because I had planned to lend the photocopy to someone else to read whilst we were travelling in Italy, a journey for which I was earning money in a London bookshop, I rashly requested the £5 postage from Dorcas when I dispatched the heavy parcel to her in Devon. Whether I or his daughter informed Gerald of my supposed *faux pas* I cannot remember but within a few days I received the nearest I ever got to a ticking off from him.

> 1st July, 1975
>
> Dear Edward,
>
> Thanks for sending the Photostat to Dorcas but why the hell not ask me for the Postage? I know, Edward, you did it to spare <u>me</u>... I could easily have let you have a fiver - in cash, too; as Barclays have <u>not</u> got a bank in Shetland. I've already got my ticket, sleeper booked, and a wallet of notes. Besides, I do get £20 a week coming in...

A second, undated note must have been written later the same day. Gerald explained that he had now written to his daughter

---

significantly, 1967 was the year in which Gerald asked his cousin Hilda Dumond for a copy of his mother's photograph.

to apologise, complete with 'exonerating explanation' for what had happened. He seems to have enclosed the £5 in question, wishing us the best for our journey. He explained that I could continue to write care of the Snells who would forward letters to Shetland 'until the end of September, at least.' It seems I was forgiven, for the note concluded: 'Oh, you two! Love, though - Gerald'. Indignant that he should have sent me the cash himself, somewhat Gerald-like I now sent him back a cheque for the same amount. This in turn provoked a long letter, dated '3 July Snelldonia':

> Idiot, of course I don't take offense at your sending the cheque. I'm not tearing it up (nor endorsing it): just putting it in my wallet.

> I thoroughly enjoyed your letter - both instalments. I think you may have been partly right, being irked by my request - though, had I known you were leaving it with somebody of your choice, I wouldn't have asked you to send it to Dorcas. I did it to reciprocate in substance her last astonishingly cordial move – but my ambivalent relations to my biological daughter (as far as she is concerned being a parent in no other way), I can't make clear in a few words – or, for that matter in many…

There followed three pages about his daughter which beyond being un-fatherly, betray that tendency to Weiningerian misogyny which, mediated via Ebenezer ('Man is doomed to Woman'; 'She [Christine Mahy] wasn't a friend: she was a woman'), also manifests itself in his novel:

> her enthusiasms … are my detestations – hunting for instance; and her delight in equestrian acrobatics. I was brought up with horses; but our rough brutes really were 'the friend of man'. They served us well – I mean men: they were not degraded by being bred to be subservient to the dominance of vain females, or for social status blood rituals.

As if to confirm the likely influence of Nietzsche where both horses and women are concerned, he then pauses as if to apologise, only to do so in facetiously religious terms:

> I'm not being quite fair; but then I never am, and pray God I never will be. I have no ambition to take on His job.'

Yet he cannot help reverting back to his bitter and ultimately irrational tone; doubting that Dorcas will read his book or take it on her scheduled visit to New Zealand but concluding with the more or less egocentric aspiration that she might still:

> be mildly interested to discover what sort of person her father 'really' is, was, or will be. The book won't help her far with that. So let her read it, if she wants to. Thank you for sending it.

This train of thought (or articulated emotion) then leads him to respond to comments I had made on *Ebenezer* when I had first read it a year before:

> There's one question of yours I've never had the presence of mind to answer properly. You ask me to change the end. I say 'No'! That is not because I think it perfect, or even good or right. The true answer is 'can't' because it is implied in the whole book. The end is the beginning - the dedication Ebenezer inserts - because he can't think of 'a text in the Bible to suit.' In actual fact the beginning and the end were conceived simultaneously; and the book grew out of the pivotal image of the gold under the apple-tree. To alter the <u>substance</u> of the end is impossible without scrapping the whole thing.

To the extent to which this account is entirely convincing and not somehow hind-sighted, it is hardly surprising that Gerald resisted suggestions that he modify his happy ending.[102] In fact my comments had been concerned with tone rather than with content, and somewhat self-consciously, implausible aspects of the greenhouse-smashing (green but mean?) character of Neville Falla. I was also slightly worried that the style and pace of the concluding chapters of the novel were not consistent with the more detailed, authentic quality that prevails throughout the rest. Gerald was correct about the inevitable symmetry of the

---

[102] It is remarkable that, acquiring Gerald's letters to Middleton Murry years later, I discovered a letter, dated 29 April 1929, in which he conducts an almost identical (both defensive and defiant) discussion over the 'they-lived-happily-ever-after' ending which he insisted on retaining in his unpublished play *Margaret*; see above, p. 92. *Cf.* the similarly positive conclusion of Strindberg's *Easter*, which Gerald chose to direct a decade later in Bolton.

ending, however, and in my less cynically self-conscious old age I now find it harder to separate quasi-sentimental passages from those that can reduce even the most anti-Romantic or Modernist reader to tears, moving one as profoundly as only (?) great music can.[103] As in an opera by Handel, a powerful passage of emotional, even metaphysical beauty surprises one all the more effectively for its sudden emergence out of an insistent period of plotting, couched in relatively mundane *recitativo secco*. But in both music and literature, such irresistible effects arise from exceptionally artful manipulation of timely empathetic triggers, the product of instinct and experience, inseparable from deep-rooted religious feeling which is both the result and origin of art itself.[104]

Gerald now turned precisely - albeit disingenuously - to the issue of self-consciousness, seeking to disarm my residual doubts by distancing us both (indeed all) from his principal protagonists:

> I have wondered whether you ever imagined Neville and Adèle had anything to do with you. Nothing whatever. The book was complete in MSS before I met either of you two. My dedication of it to you two – as distinct from Ebenezer's - done without your knowledge, serves to show the difference in orientation between me and Ebenezer - or any of the others:[105] as do the pyrotechnics at the end of the preface.[106] Also its last line. I think I've answered your query as honestly as I can.

Though the reference to his orientation may hint at revelation,

---

[103] *Cf.* Harry Mathews' response, above, p. 231.

[104] An unusually large number of readers of Gerald's novel have remarked on its capacity to provoke tears; *cf.* Michael Trimble, *The Soul in the Brain* and *Why Humans like to Cry* (London, 2012 and 2014) and the left-right brain dynamic as it functions in the arts and, longer-term, the crucial role of the right brain in relation to our social well-being, in McGilchrist, *The Master and his Emissary*, who quotes Nietzsche on the superior capacity of music to move, p. 74.

[105] He no doubt had Raymond in mind here, in which case he perhaps protesting too much, at the same time revealing perhaps too much in his use of the word 'orientation.'

[106] By which he presumably means what became his appendix on Guernsey English.

Gerald's concluding sentence here may be his most significant. Where his greatest achievement was concerned, it seems he found it hard to be entirely honest - or at least straightforward - as is evident from the indirectness of his letter to Calder and Boyars. Neither is his comparison between Ebenezer's dedication of his book to Neville and his own to myself and Lisa the most relevant or revealing one. The closer comparison here is surely the symmetry between Ebenezer's formal gift of his book to Neville and Gerald's real-life one to me alone. This, and our respective roles in the lives of our elderly friends, our shared identity as long-haired, painting, motorcycling, blue-eyed bad-boys with hearts of gold, each of whom gets the girl he undoubtedly deserves, surely brings Neville too close for coincidence (and, perhaps, comfort).[107]

The rest of Gerald's letter of 3 July concerned other people's literature, starting with his gift of Powys's *Weymouth Sands* to my aunt. (This, incidentally, I eventually inherited, complete with its inscription: 'For Jo, with love from Gerald - who, though he is going away, hopes to see you again. 27th June 1975'):

> I don't suggest you bother to read Weymouth Sands. It's good in its way, mind you. Written in impeccable classical English - long undulating sentences - and I hope interesting to Jo, as it is very much in her setting. It's true some of the people are rather odd, but 'nicely' presented. (Apparently Riders in the Chariot knocked her out. I don't know what she'd say about the Nancy Lightfoot episode in the Vivisector, which I think one of his best-done bits!)[108]

---

[107] See above, p. 214, for the similar parallels between Lampedusa's fictional and actual protégés, Tancredi and Gioacchino Lanza Tomasi.

[108] There are several 'episodes' between the artist Hurtle Duffield and his model/prostitute/girlfriend, Nance Lightfoot, in his Nobel Prize-winning novel *The Vivisector* (London, 1970), which would have shocked my great-aunt. Gerald's mention of this novel reminds one of the difficulties most writers have with depicting painters and sculptors, including, it has to be said, his own depiction of 'the handsome, sarcastic' Neville Falla and his 'wildscapes' (see the discussion on p. 357 of *Ebenezer Le Page*). Gerald would meanwhile have been aware that White dedicated *The Vivisector* to Sidney Nolan, who was still designing his dust-jackets in 1973 (prior to falling out with him). David Marr argues that White failed to get the Nobel Prize in 1970 because *The Vivisector* suggests the impossibility of being an artist and 'human' at the same time; see

Anyhow, he's not in my line, and I doubt if he'd prove to be in yours - and it's a tremendous number of words to have to read.

This letter is getting that way and I'd better end it. I'm only thinking now of when I'm going to see you both again. It will have to be up there - I think it very unlikely I'll come South again. So keep it in mind; and this time, if there's any difficulty over fares, for Christ's sake, ask me and I'll contribute, if I can...[109]

# 8: SHETLAND ISLES

Gerald left on his ambitious expedition, via Bristol Temple Meads, to the Shetland Isles on 7 July 1975. He had sent a final farewell note on the 5th, enclosing two poems:

Dearest Edward and Lisa,

A few words to say 'Tcheerie!'

God and love are words I dislike to use - in my own person. I always feel I'm being slightly piffling - and sacrilegious.

Two words are too often profaned

For me to profane them.[110]

I am not a Romantic.

I enclose a couple of spontaneous lyrics - as L'ENVOI to SARNIA CHÉRIE. Though don't imagine I am not admitting evil. To my mind, it is the non-existent. The -ism, the -ist, the abstract, the dead-end reached by extra-

---

*Patrick White: A Life* (London, 1992), p. 534.

[109] Re-reading this I am reminded of the extent to which 'genius' requires a larger than average measure of fantasy. Awaiting the boat on 8 July, Gerald wrote to Joan Snell that the train journey from Edinburgh to the 'shambles' of Aberdeen docks: 'made me certain I'll never come south again.'

[110] These two lines I did not recognise at the time as being adapted from Shelley's 'One Word is Too Often Profaned'. They are thought to have been addressed to Jane Williams, whose common-law husband Edward, Shelley eventually took sailing to his death.

polation. At present, nearly all-prevailing. May you two reduce its dominance!

Gerald.

Though these two poems were intended to conclude his novel, he later changed his mind (back and forth) about whether to include them at all. 'Benediction' has already been transcribed; see above, pp. 222-3, where 'Canticle' is illustrated as Gerald sent it [Fig. 71].

### CANTICLE

I am the host,
he is the guest:
he come when I least expect –
I do not know his name.
I ask him to stay:
he lift a hand in farewell,
bless my disordered house
and go away as he came.

The degree of spontaneity Gerald claims for these lyrics becomes questionable when we read a poem he would have assumed had been long since lost. This was the superb 'Song of a Man who saw God' which I purchased in 1985 in Robin Waterfield's Oxford bookshop along with all but one of his surviving letters to Middleton Murry.[111] After more than a decade, during which there had been no contact between them, on 10 September 1947 Gerald sent this magnificent poem as a possible contribution to the *Adelphi*, of which Murry had resumed the editorship in 1941 (see Appendix 1). It remains to this day attached to his letter, was presumably never published and perhaps never responded to, despite Gerald writing: 'if you don't use it, you needn't send it back; but I'd very much like to know what you feel about it.' The concluding line of its penultimate stanza reads:

in the bleak first cry of babe new-risen to the day.

The concluding line of the twelfth and last verse reads:

in the last fierce death-gasp from the entrails torn.

---

[111] See above, p. 146.

Given its similarity to these lines, therefore, far from being a spontaneous lyric, 'Benediction' may be read as a brilliant condensation of the far longer original, its essence no doubt itself distilled during Gerald's 'missing' post-war years.

After a week or so in Rome, towards the end of July we settled in a monastery-cum-student hostel in Florence. Gerald had by this time phoned my parents and asked them to forward his address in Lerwick when we got in touch. Thus in mid-August I wrote to him from the Casa di Ospitalità, Viale dei Mille, and, on the 20th (according to the postmark on his neatly addressed envelope), he replied.[112]

Meanwhile, however, he had been corresponding - to begin with almost daily - with Joan Snell, combining rather un-Nietzschean comments on the temperature of his tea, with commentaries on the Apocalypse. When I began compiling material towards a biography, Joan Snell very kindly gave me the interesting series of letters Gerald sent her during the seven weeks he was in the Shetland Isles. These begin with the one he wrote in a very positive mood on the morning of the 9 July from 'St Clements, North Sea', that is the ferry, the elderly 'St Clement', he had taken en route to Lerwick [Fig. 81]:

Fig. 81: The *St Clement*: 'a small but smart, privately run ship, leaving tonight' (Gerald to Joan Snell, 8 July 1975).

---

[112] His letter arrived on Monday 25 August according to my Italian journal.

Had a marvellous trip, or rather, having. Another 6 hours to go. Saw from deck the last of Aberdeen. Sailed at 22.00.

Cabin to myself, every facility. Slept like a log for ten hours. Awakened with tea and toast. Am now down in the Saloon having a coffee. Having lunch aboard. Dock at 18.00. May not have the chance to write on arrival…

It's marvellous being at sea with no land anywhere in sight. Not going to Orkneys, of course: but direct. I don't regret it. This direct trip on a small boat is best…

On 15 July, Gerald reports that he has found satisfactory accommodation at 88 St Olaf Street, Lerwick, and still sounds optimistic, walking more than 5 miles a day and meeting a variety of mainly younger and non-native people, reminding one of D.H. Lawrence on his solitary travels:

I can write sitting among the trawlers. Or anywhere. I shan't need the typewriter, for some time anyhow. Shetland has resurrected Guernsey, but it is here I think I'll end…

He concludes somewhat ominously however:

I may sound cheerful; but I am more than ever aware the world is warped (as we are) and all we can do is make the best of it by never knowingly and willingly taking the side of the warping. Here endeth the first lesson…

By 30 July the tone of a longer letter to Joan Snell has become significantly less positive in tone:

The landscape is quite unlike any I have seen (or sea-scape, for you come upon the sea when you imagine you're inland) and on the west particularly mostly unspoiled, but pockmarked already with 'houses' manufactured not built. On the East coast, the Oil Fiend really has his claws in; and Tourism is being encouraged. In ten years these islands will be uninhabitable by any but machine men. Has not Scalloway appeared on T.V.? Sure sign of doom.

It wouldn't matter if the old were being destroyed for the creation of the new; but it isn't. Technocracy knows nothing of creation: only construction. It is a shingle short. The only consolation is the cosmopolitan crews remain human – even on things afloat that might have come out of a Science Fiction nightmare. The sea saves men from abstraction ... according to the Revelation of St John the Divine, in the New Jerusalem 'there is no sea'.[113] That damned City! An exclusively male obsession, in its earthly counterpart kept going by women in trousers – if only metaphorically speaking. Thank you, but I want none of it. The technocrats and the Christian Dogmatists can have it all to themselves.

*The Book of Revelation* is the subject of Lawrence's last, in fact posthumous publication, *Apocalypse* (London, 1931), which Gerald is no doubt remembering here, though he would have known the original at least as well. Lawrence's still quite Nietzschean account in *Apocalypse* - and elsewhere - has been recently well summarised:

> Nor is Lawrence a fan of the New Jerusalem. In his Introduction to Frederick Carter's *The Dragon* he writes: 'Of all the stale buns, the New Jerusalem is one of the stalest ... only invented for the aunties of this world.' It is full of impudent and revengeful saved people, insisting on wiping out the whole universe, but also, in true 'bourgeois' spirit, containing flowers that never fade. And to add insult to injury, Lawrence sees in the atheistical revolutionary Lenin the same resentful, egalitarian, and soul-destroying impulses as he finds in the Christian saints.[114]

Gerald's reply to my Florentine letter tells the tale of his tragi-comic defeat at the hands of modernity's machine man - whether communist or capitalist - more maddingly manifest in its (for him) unexpectedness in this should-be remote corner of the world than in the suburban environment he had left behind:

---

[113] *Revelation* 21:1: 'And I saw a new heaven and a new earth: for the first heaven and the first earth were passed away; and there was no more sea.'

[114] Natasha and Anthony O'Hear, *Picturing the Apocalypse: The Book of Revelation in the Arts over Two Millennia* (Oxford, 2015), p. 268. For more on Lawrence's *Apocalypse* and the circumstances of its publication, see Ornella de Zordo, *Una Proposta Anglofiorentina degli Anni Trenta: The Lungarno Series* (Florence 1981). The modern edition is *Apocalypse and the Writings on Revelation*, ed. Mara Kalnins (Cambridge, 2002).

Dear Edward,

God, it's good to hear from you! That ejaculation is neither heathen nor Christian. While you are basking among the crustacea of Christianity, I am moving among the cool shades of Norse paganism. I am for neither. When Saint Olaf converted the Vikings to Christianity, he did so at the edge of the sword. Like to like. However, at present here, both are irrelevant. The magic word is OIL. Spiritually it means more and more people going faster and faster - nowhere. Materially it means accommodation for any other service is next to unobtainable; and then only at colossal prices. A gimcrack hotel, made of angles, charges £11 for bed and breakfast; and £15 for bed, breakfast and evening meal. I pay £24.50 a week for bed, breakfasts and evening meals. That includes use of room during the day and other perks. John and Beryl Constable are against the stream and more than decent; but it is ruinous. I can live on my pensions at the rate of £60 a month with a few pounds to spare. Fortunately I had some extra cash but that is exhausted. I got the idea of hitch-hiking off the beaten track. John forbad it. I put the idea to the test by scouring Scalloway which is where Beryl Constable was born. Even with their credentials, there was only one dicey and rather ghoulish possibility. I shan't know till Monday, if it is available; but, if it is, it could only be temporary and I think it would be outside reason to accept it.[115] Unless the unforeseen happens, I shall probably leave Shetland Tuesday and be back at Snelldonia on the 28th - having to borrow money from Joan to manage it. I don't feel <u>too</u> bad about that: they didn't want me to leave and do want me back; and the debt will soon be repaid.

I wrote a note to Lisa at Wilmar Close a week or so ago TO AWAIT RETURN and another to you this morning, warning you not to write to me here, unless I let you know

---

[115] Two complementary letters to Joan Snell confirm that in desperation Gerald had explored the possibility of migrating across mainland Shetland to the far smaller and less oil-dominated Scalloway as a possible place to settle but decided against that also.

to the contrary. I haven't in the circumstances written to anybody except Joan and you two. I will post this tomorrow to Firenze, unless the postage is prohibitive: in which case I will re-address it to you at Wilmar Close.

These islands have the beauty of a dream. Ultima Thule [Fig. 82].[116] Unattainable. I feel they should never have been humanly inhabited: only by sheep and birds and small long-tailed ponies.

Fig. 82: Lerwick – *Ultima Thule*.

I am in a very good health for me; but will nevertheless return feeling chastened. I hope you will make it to Upwey fairly soon. I will drop you another note at Wilmar Close as soon as I am back; or let you know any change of plans.

My love to Lisa, and to you.

<u>Gerald</u>.[117]

---

[116] 'Ultima Thule' was coined by Virgil (*Georgics*, I, 30) as an elaboration on Thule, an ancient Northern land, to symbolise a far-off or unattainable goal. The Thule Society or 'Thule-Gesellschaft' was a Munich-based occultist organization which sponsored the *Deutsche Arbeiterpartei*, later reformed by Hitler as the Nazi Party. For an evocative recent account of Shetland, see Malachy Tallack, *Sixty Degrees North: Around the World in Search of Home* (London, 2015).

[117] The information in this letter is complemented by two to Joan Snell with more

In one of his letters to Joan Snell, written the day before this, on 19 July 1975 he writes similarly about feeling chastened and moreover returning 'ready to be really an old, old man,' but continues:

> I may or may not see Guernsey again, and will always be heartsick for Shetland (as an impossible dream); but when I've got square with you and build up my account enough, I may go and see Guernsey for a week or fortnight. That I don't think of as possible until late October or November. We'll see.
>
> I hope you will find me improved. At least, I can't possibly have got any worse.[118]

Arriving home in late September we were greeted by Gerald's 'To await return' letters and the presumably rejected typescript which Fabers had returned without comment. These were followed almost immediately by another letter from Gerald, dated 23 September, which reversed its predecessor's more or less positive account of his welcome home at 'Snelldonia' on 28 August. Though still ostensibly ignorant of Faber's decision (for I had not hastened to inform him of this), he was nevertheless very depressed, not merely discounting his welcome as insincere, but somewhat melodramatically comparing his existence at the Snells with that described in Solzhenitsyn's novels: 'I can now take it as axiomatic that I have no home and never will have', he wrote, but then consoled himself with the thought that 'It is at least something to have a quiet prison cell'.[119]

---

of the practical and financial detail involved in his decision-making and travel arrangements.

[118] Letter to Joan Snell in my possession, from 88 St. Olaf Street, Lerwick, dated 19 August 1975. Having settled at this address a week earlier Gerald had already asked Joan to send him a pullover and some Guernsiana, suggesting his ongoing work on poems and/or trilogy; see above, p. 264, and below p. 284.

[119] There is an odd reference in the letter to Joan Snell from Lerwick dated 30 July 1975 already quoted which, unless he was merely anticipating the rejection, means I must have been told that the typescript had been returned and somehow, perhaps by phone, communicated this to him. He writes: 'By the way, Fabers have turned down S.C. I'm not surprised, not disappointed (in fact, relieved I shan't have any proof-reading to do); but they returned it to Edward without comment – not even a formal letter "We regret etc".'

# 9: RETURN TO SNELLDONIA

I should in fairness to Gerald's long-suffering landlady, Joan Snell [Fig. 83] and her husband Bert, emphasise here what should by now be obvious, that due to his uncompromising nature and borderline manic-depression, Gerald could be a very difficult person to live with. That he was aware of the extent to which his anger was

Fig. 83: *Joan Snell*
(photo: the author, c.1990).

disproportionate is suggested by remarks made by Mass Observation colleagues when he shared a house in Bolton. Geoffrey Thomas remembered him saying that he was so furious with his drama group 'that it was almost funny'. He explained his anger in relation to his feeling there was something in him which was capable of doing things but that 'the comparison between that and what he actually does arouses him to the bitterest damnation of himself'.[120] Interestingly, at one point he attributes something similar to Ebenezer who elaborates on the phenomenon beyond the extent to which it is really called for in the novel, though it may be significant that it is associated with mourning the death of his beloved Jim Mahy in the Great War:

> I have dreamt of him many times over the years; but, thank God, it have never been in mud and blood. It have been the happy Jim coming to meet me across the meadow with his big smile and his hand up; and I feel in my sleep that a great happiness is coming to me, but then I wake up.
>
> I have something bad in me. I think it is a devil. I get very angry. I get so angry sometimes I feel I am going to break in two. The worst of it is that it is not for reasons

---

[120] See above, p. 191.

anybody else would get angry; and nobody else would understand. I don't understand why myself half the time. When the fellows at work, and many others, all with the best intentions in the world, said to me 'Hard luck about Jim,' I felt I could have murdered them.[121]

Given also his highly critical view of women, or at least his determination never to be dominated by one, Mrs Snell could hardly have done better by Gerald, providing a reliable base for him and a sympathetic ear when the patience of other members of her family, with whom he often fell out, was exhausted.[122] She recalled to me an occasion when Gerald got up from the table after arguing loudly with the entire family, strode theatrically

Fig. 84: *Living room at Snelldonia* (1972/3): Gerald and Anneliese Snell (seated), Jonathan Snell (above), Chris Rees, Elizabeth Snell and Dinah Walker (foreground).

---

[121] *Ebenezer Le Page*, p. 120.

[122] The letters Gerald addressed to her in May and June when he moved to East Coker after only a short residence with her, begin 'My dear friend Joan' and are full of gratitude to her and other members of her family for assistance in his moving out and then (in effect) permanently back to Upwey. He certainly never called her 'Mrs Mussolini' as he called his landlady, perhaps in Notting Hill, during the war; see above, p. 198. The scarcity of pictures of Gerald is largely the result of Mrs Snell's warnings to family and visitors on his behalf that he hated being photographed.

from the room (other family members confirm this to have been something of a habit) and slammed the door behind him. Unfortunately, he slammed it so hard that the door handle remained in his grip. Instead of putting it down and completing his retreat, Gerald re-entered the room still holding the handle, glared at the seated family, some of whom were failing to disguise their amusement, and flung it at Bert Snell. Fortunately he missed his target who managed to catch it instead. It seems that Gerald never apologised.

Not a presence that could easily be ignored, seeing Gerald on a daily basis, the earth-motherly Joan often experienced him at his most depressed. Though she told John Fowles that 'it was a great privilege to have known him', and that he could be: 'full of feeling and sympathy. Proud but humble … charming and endearing', she conceded that at his worst he was 'despairing and moody. A man of heights, and of deepest, blackest depths.'[123]

I was already aware that I tended to see Gerald at his most impressive best. Even in his perfectly composed letters he might exaggerate or become obsessive about a subject and then abruptly switch mode. In his letter of 28 August 1975, he concluded his account of what it was like to live in the supposedly Stalinist Snelldonia, with the exclamation: 'Enough', and proceeded in satirical mode to describe a visit to my great-aunt and his sceptical response to *her* over-dramatised account of a robbery we had experienced in Florence:

> From the summit of horror on which she began (and for which I was apparently to blame) I literally had visions of you two either killed in a motor crash, or at least crippled for life. Eventually it came down to the theft of your camera and the loss of your money. She can easily say I gave no sign of being sorry to hear it. Actually I had no more chance

---

[123] Quoted by Fowles in his 1981 introduction to *Ebenezer Le Page*; *cf.* his *Wormholes*, p. 174. This passage is prefaced by his account of Gerald's letters which, he says, 'show an impressive blend of honesty and self-humour, besides a frequent Orwellian excellence of plain English prose. They would do very well as a contemporary appendix to the Grub Street side of Dr Johnson's *Lives of the English Poets*, and I hope that one day Mr Chaney will consider publishing parts of them.'

than a pigmy under Niagara. I was too angry at the source
of her rage, anyway. MONEY. She is certainly a mono-
theist.[124] Privately I was upset at the loss of an instrument to
which you must have naturally felt attachment, it already
having served you well in the past; and even more, that it
might contain pictures you had taken for use this next year.
The loss of the money was an inconvenience, I understand
too well; but on that score I had no doubt you would
somehow cope...[125]

Gerald's account is amusing in ways that are largely intentional
but having justifiably satirised my Victorian aunt for her focus
upon financial security, less deliberate is what he reveals
regarding his attitude to worldly goods; an attitude that had left
him with fewer means than any highly educated (non-alcoholic
or drug-addicted) person I have known, and certainly less than
Ebenezer or indeed his hero, Walt Whitman, who built an
expensive tomb for himself.[126] He then returned briefly to the
subject of his daughter and the postage saga (she had not yet
returned the photocopy) before turning to *Sarnia Chérie* itself
and the related matter of how he was to retrieve those
belongings he had insisted on leaving with me prior to his

---

[124] Beyond having a low regard for money, Gerald was no doubt a follower of
Nietzsche in believing the invention of monotheism 'the most monstrous of all
human errors'; see my review-article of R.H. Armstrong, *A Compulsion for
Antiquity: Freud and the Ancient World* (Ithaca, NY, 2005), in *Psychoanalysis and
History*, IX, no. 1 (2007), pp. 123-30.

[125] In view of his own tendency to dramatise in just the way he accused my aunt
of doing, it is perhaps revealing that on this occasion she was nearer the mark in
her estimate of our/my loss, for it was not so much that the black and white
photographs I had taken during the previous weeks in Florence were to be of
use in my research but they would have been of sentimental value, a commodity
about which Gerald was almost wilfully ambivalent. I wrote a poem about the
loss of my photographs, no doubt discarded by the Eastern European mother
and son who stole them from our room while we answered a phone call along
the corridor of the Casa di Ospitilità.

[126] He, like Raymond, most closely resembles Wittgenstein in this respect, in the
gesture of destroying his mother's will and living the rest of his life so close to
poverty. Wittgenstein returned home from the Great War: 'one of the wealthiest
men in Europe, owing to his father's financial astuteness in transferring the
family's wealth, before the war, into American bonds. But within a month of
returning, he had disposed of his entire estate'; Monk, *Wittgenstein*, p. 171.

proposed migration to Shetland:

> Myself, I have borrowed Joan's Carbon Copy and flogged myself into reading it right through to decide finally whether it was worth preserving. Rightly or wrongly, I have decided it is but also not to write of Guernsey any more. (Shetland was a very toughening experience). If I write any more it will be in my English, such as it is, and much less appealing. Also, head on.

> If you come down to see Joe before term starts will you please bring down my things. If not, I'll have to have a think. There are none of the books I really need; but a few I'd like for a thing I've actually started. At present I'm thinking the best plan would be for you to pack the typewriter in the rug in the case and shove in the type-writer accessories, the Croxley Box and a few books; and send it by British Road Services, or something like that, which delivers from door to door. I ought to be solvent again with a bit over by the middle of October and could let you have the where-withal. However, that's only a possibility occurs to me at the moment.

> I still hope you will be coming to see Jo before term starts. I want to see you and have your presence, of course; and hear your impressions more fully than you hinted at in your letter.

> Looking forward to hearing from you, anyway.

> Love,

> <u>Gerald.</u>

> I have been romantically imagining Philip astride a dromedary. Is he?

This last was a reference to my brother's working in Saudi Arabia. I apparently found time to drive down to Dorset and deliver Gerald's things before I started work at the Warburg Institute and Lisa resumed her philosophy degree at University College. In so doing I confirmed the implicit rejection by his preferred publishers, Faber and Faber. He not only bore this with customary outward calm and good humour, it actually seemed to raise his spirits, his deeply ambivalent attitude to any form of celebrity no doubt partly accounting for this. (Meanwhile he never revealed to me what I discovered when I acquired his letters to Murry that Fabers had rejected something of his - which he presumably then destroyed - as long ago as 1930).[127] His first response was to insist on extracting an explanation as to why they had rejected his novel. Thus on 1 October he wrote an indignant-sounding letter to Fabers and sent a copy to me with a covering letter:

Dear Edward,

Enclosed is a copy of the letter I am sending to Fabers. (I don't want it back.) It is the whittled down quintessence of about a dozen drafts and is now, I imagine, irreproachably deadly enough possibly to extract a response. If it doesn't you will have to forgive me. I've done my best to do my damnedest.

I have also written to Dorcas. Hers without difficulty and quite affably. I've asked her to return S.C. to you as soon as possible as you have some-one waiting to read it 'Samizdat'.[128] I mentioned the other copy had been turned down by Fabers who 'have not, as yet, disclosed the reasons.' I've given her your address 'in case she didn't have it handy.'

If those two lines of supply produce results and converge on you, let me know and I'll send you typed copies of L'ENVOI and the list of ERRATA. For the present, I'm sure you have plenty else to occupy your mind, anyway.

I have, thanks to your bringing my things. Reading, if not writing. By the way, I said I wouldn't do any more Guernsey stuff. I have to revoke that. Typing MADAME BOISSEL and glancing at the other beginnings, I decided I

---

[127] See above, p. 115.

[128] Dorcas sent the photocopy back to me from her GP's practice in Torquay on 24 September with a friendly message, adding: 'I enjoyed reading it but should like to have had more time so that the gaps between readings weren't so long.' She also asked for Gerald's address and any news, presumably believing him to still be in Shetland.

must let both series of verse go on, if they are willing to go - even if they have no visible practical outlet (and my friends don't like them!) [see Appendix 3].

All good to Lisa. Thank Melissa from me for letting you have my address. My request was hurried and very brusque. My respects to Tim – and I trust in due course I will get a snap of Philip on that beast. I hope also the 'party' didn't turn out too bad; or, if it did, you two were able to watch it from afar like two buddhas, non-committally but serenely amused. I find it the only way to live in the Kremlin - but I can't say I'm all that good at it.

Ever,

Gerald.

The typed letter to 'Messrs Faber and Faber Ltd', dated the same day, was indeed skilfully - if somewhat self-defeatingly - worded:

Dear Sirs,

Early in June, I think it was, I wrote to you concerning a book of mine, SARNIA CHÉRIE: THE BOOK OF EBENEZER LE PAGE. It is an odd sort of book purporting to be written by an ancient Guernseyman who lives on Guernsey from before the Boer War until the early 1960's; and he writes it in a variant of Guernsey English which I, in a brief preface, relate to 'good English' and 'good French' as an aid to the educated reader. The original Typescript was with my friends, Edward Chaney and his wife, Lisa, who live in Uxbridge and are students in London. They both like the book (with reservations) and suggested they show it to a London publisher. It was then I wrote to you asking if you would care to see it; and, if so, would you please write direct to Edward Chaney for him to bring it in. That you very kindly did and I heard from him he had delivered it. He was not acting, of course, as an agent in any sense. It was a purely disinterested gesture on his part.

In the meantime, I went to Shetland for the summer and the Chaneys to Italy. When he got home, he found the Typescript had been returned without comment, or enclosure of any sort. As it seemed so unprecedented a discourtesy coming from you of all people, he assumed you had sent the rejection notice to me; but when he came down, only to learn I had received nothing, it did seem something had gone wrong somewhere.

I was naturally disappointed it had been rejected, but not surprised. It was the manner of it I was at a loss to account for. I thought it must be either an Office slip-up; or a deliberate brush-off. The last I find difficult to believe. It is too crude to be the Faber and Faber way of doing things.

I am therefore presuming to ask if you will disclose the reasons for refusing the book: I mean in so far as they are other than economic pressure. Actually, it would be a kindness and helpful to be told the worst. As it is, one is left in the air with no idea what it may mean.

If you are good enough to do this, will you please address it, as before, to:

Edward Chaney,
24, Wilmar Close
UXBRIDGE
Middlesex.

I remain

yours respectfully,

G.B. Edwards

Gerald's letter had the desired effect of producing a polite explanation from senior editor, Rosemary Goad, which Gerald could now get his teeth into. It was accompanied by a covering note addressed to me.[129] Evidently I forwarded both with a somewhat scornful comment. I vaguely remember reminding Gerald, in the form of a facetious enquiry, that it was a director of Fabers by the name of T.S. Eliot who had rejected *Animal Farm*.[130] Coping with rejection was clearly the habit of a lifetime

---

[129] Rosemary Goad, formerly fellow-secretary at Faber and Faber with Valerie Fletcher (the future Mrs Eliot), and latterly a director. She started working at the publishers in 1954 and retired in 1989.

[130] Eliot had already rejected *A Scullion's Diary*, the original version of *Down and Out in Paris and London*, submitted soon after Orwell had had his preliminary

but the positive tone of this letter suggests that there was an element of relief involved, complementing a rebellious anger which, albeit sublimated, spurred him on to new efforts, until these too bore fruit he could not quite bring himself to enjoy:

Thanks. Your query made me roar. Trust you two to put your finger on the spot.

I am keeping the letter for the present, but will let you have it back eventually. I am writing to Rosemary Goad, marked Personal c/o Faber and Faber. I feel she deserves a human response. The letter to me was unbreakable glass, but hers to you is quite human. It's quite an achievement to have extracted that much from the Kremlin of High Culture. Though whether she will think my letter is 'charming' when she has read it, is doubtful. I intend to point out Publishing Houses are putting the cart before the horse; and by extension undermining their intention. This economic pressure obsession is an abstraction. I have a feeling she may really agree.

Her letter to me actually did me good. Its net effect was to make the old donkey spirit stick his heels in; and start on the next book of the series. I think I told you the first time you came to tea here I had three books in mind: each separate and not sequels, but interlocked and covering roughly the same period. The second, the one I'm on, THE BOUD'LO: THE BOOK OF PHILIP LE MOIGNE is set in a different Parish and social status, more educated, 'cultured', and outside the Calvinist Puritan tradition.[131] Philip is one odd throw-back. He enacts quite unconsciously the role of the Boud'lo in this century, by which 'religion', 'education', 'science' are sent up. He ends up in the Country Hospital (our Herrison) which is where he writes his book. It dovetails with Raymond's story, among others: his school life, his honeymoon in Sark, his

---

essay, 'The Spike', accepted for the *New Adelphi* (though this was not published until April 1931). A review of a book on Carlyle by Orwell, under his real name, Eric Blair, had appeared in the previous issue, directly after one by Plowman of William Rothenstein's *Men and Memories*.

[131] See above, p. 266, and Appendix 2, p. 350.

years in Victoria Road, and what is really happening when Liza hears him talking to himself. Also Neville and Adèle's story: glamour and tragedy. I think you will get more reconciled to them as they develop. By the way, I trust you realise they bear no relation whatever to you and Lisa - they existed independently before I met either of you. Odd.[132] For Philip marries Sheba Hardwickson from Baltasound long before I went to Shetland: yet when I went to and was in Shetland I had no thought I would ever get down to writing it.[133] Now I can with conviction.

The last of the triplet, whose heart is beating is LA GRAN'-MÈRE DU CHIMQUIÈRE: THE BOOK OF JEAN LE FÉNIANT. He is a young drop-out, who has dropped in: but he has not dropped in what he had dropped out of - which is what most drop-outs who drop in do. It begins with the Centenarian Celebration of his great-grand-mother: the Bailiff is paying her homage, she holds the Queen's telegram in her hand, and her innumerable clan is gathered around her in apparent admiration. Except for one ruthless, pure young face she cannot see: the only one she wants to see. He is not there. He is lying on a rock in the sun. It is he writes her Memorial, unveiling the generation of his relatives backwards. He doesn't know it; but he is the only one she hasn't perverted or destroyed.[134]

I mean to call the whole LE VIER GUERNÉSI - and transfer the dedication of the whole to you. Reasonably speaking, it sounds an impossible undertaking; but I may make it. I have always wanted to write only one book. Wish me luck.

When you have time (there's no hurry) let me know whether, in view of what I have said, you want to go on trying to place S.C. by itself. You can, if you wish; or you can wait till the second is done (at least a year, at a generous guess); or wait till all three are done. In any case, I suggest

---

[132] Odd indeed; *cf.* above, pp. 293-94.

[133] Baltasound is the largest settlement on Unst, Britain's northern-most inhabited island and once the largest herring port in Shetland.

[134] See the poem 'Lying in the Sun' in Appendix 2.

Dents. I could write to them quite differently from to Fabers: that is, not diplomatically. If it is S.C. by itself, I'll let you have L'ENVOI (and the ERRATA). The other verse I've written, except for two, only fragments, I've kept: but not for publication, if the books are. The themes are really stolen from the books - though used in a differing context - escape exits from inhibition on THE BOUD'LO.[135] The photostat copy, of course, anybody can read. However, <u>don't put yourselves out</u>; you have a full-time job both to assimilate and recover from your present preoccupations.

Not all that 'charming', you know!

### Gerald.

My next letter from Gerald was dated 8 November and announced his re-abandonment of the three volume idea. I had meanwhile written to say I would persevere with trying to get *Sarnia Chérie* published on its own:

Thanks for writing to me. Odd. I had in my drawer a letter I had written you the day before, but decided not to butt in term time.

It was only to let you know (a) I had written to Rosemary Goad and (b) there will be no trilogy. Fits in with your wish to try and get S.C. out on its own.

I'm returning Rosemary Goad's letter. Keep it: she deserves it.[136]

I wrote her a brief, unofficial note marked PERSONAL, c/o Faber and Faber: thanking her for the trouble she had taken, acknowledging the Readers had been very kind to me and by no means discouraging, and complimenting her on remaining human within 'the inevitable Kremlin of a huge and distinguished Publishing House such as yours'. Ending 'Gratefully'.

The complex of reasons for shelving the trilogy

---

[135] For *Le Vier Guernési*, see Appendix 2, p. 350. The 'stolen' poems include the carefully-typed but incomplete 40-stanza 'Old Boud'lo' (see p. 355, note 5).

[136] I interpret this as further evidence of Gerald's confidence that I would eventually succeed in having his novel published.

would be tedious to relate; and only half true, anyway. Age and infirmity, if you like; though not to be interpreted as a Jo-moan. It is true I tire easily, get pain and headaches, and have deteriorated generally since my return. The ethos of this ménage has something to do with it. Though I am solvent again and can move, if I want to; but don't feel up to making another desperate bid for escape, especially in winter.

I don't think it wise to approach Dent's until the New Year. I've done typed copies of L'ENVOI you can have [at] Christmas, as well as the few ERRATA I want made. In any case, I'd rather we talk it over first. I suggest a rather different approach, and they just <u>might</u> do it.


# 10: THE SCILLY ISLES

Christmas was always a bad time for Gerald, as it had also been for his friend Collis.[137] Clary Dumond gave me the copy of a letter dated 24 December 1961 addressed to his cousin, Clary's mother Hilda Dumond, in Guernsey, from the house at 9 Ritherdon Road, Balham [Fig. 85],[138] in which he had lodged from at least as early as September 1947 when he sent the poem to Murry. Responding politely to a card from his cousin containing family news, he revealed that he hated London and was thinking of moving to Southampton and if he gets there: 'I'll certainly hop over, if only for a holiday.'[139] Having been

---

[137] Bernard Shaw consoled his young friend, Collis, with a £50 cheque in the late 1920s, writing: 'Courage, friend! We all hate Christmas but it is soon over.' Jenkins, *Potter*, p. 86.

[138] This is the house on which, supported by Roy Dotrice, I suggested English Heritage erect a Blue Plaque in Gerald's honour, a suggestion, which was turned down in 1996. The official letter from EH, dated 12 August 1996, states that 'the Working Group decided that it is unable to adopt the suggestion as they felt his work was not of sufficient significance to warrant a plaque, particularly as his novel relates so strongly to Guernsey rather than London.' Under current rule this means that one can re-apply in 2016; one hopes that at least the size of this book may weigh in favour of the re-application.

[139] See above, p. 202, for more of this letter and details about his movements during the 1960s.

effectively disinherited by his father in much the same way as Raymond in the novel, Gerald could never afford to return permanently to his native island. This makes his concluding words all the more poignant: 'It's Christmas Eve, bitterly cold outside, but clear with no snow. I'm spending Christmas on my own: at least I shall be quiet.' (He was to use almost the same words in a letter to me thirteen years later).

We saw Gerald during the Christmas vacation of 1975-6 but as expected the season had proved difficult for him, as he hints in a letter of 10

Fig. 85: *9 Ritherdon Road, Balham, London SW17*, where Gerald lodged from 1947-1961 (photo: the author).

February 1976 in which he reveals his plans for another would-be permanent escapade, part-prompted (it seems from a later letter), by differences between him and Bert Snell.

> I've been very unwell all ways but, thank God, have perked up again. Let that pass. This is only a note to let you know I am leaving here on Monday, 16th February, from Weymouth via Bristol, via Cardiff, via Swansea, via Carmarthen to Haverfordwest. I leave at 10.05am and am due to arrive at Haverfordwest at 6.04 p.m. There is no change of station en route, though a rather tight schedule at Temple Meads, Bristol.
>
> I am only taking a rucksack and my typewriter. Apart from change of clothing and toilet necessaries, the rucksack contains as much of La Rocque qui Chante as I have done and, of books, the essential Guernsiana. Dead bones. I have

to be, if anything, a mini-Ezekiel.[140]

Meanwhile hold your horses on S.C. (my typed copy). The photostat copy is yours, of course, exclusively, and you can let anybody see it without my disapproval. Otherwise, I have a scheme in mind which may enable to get it out eventually. We'll see.

I'm intending to make Haverfordwest a centre for finding a place on my own. I shall have three weeks to explore the district before it will be necessary for me to have a fixed address for collection of Pensions. It means, however, I can't give you a 'permanent' address; nor will the Snells have one. They are keeping my living books, as well as clothes I couldn't take - including, alas, your coat, which is too heavy. I experimented with both it and my mack, but it was impossible. Joan has the Carbon Copy of S.C., but no rights of publication. She also has a typescript of MADAME BOISSEL from La Rocque qui Chante[141]; but unsigned. I have a typescript and carbon with me (signed).

I am now confining my remarks to the practical. That does not mean I am not always aware of your existence, and wonder daily how things are going with you - what is, and what is not happening. I will let you have an address relatively permanent, as soon as I have one.

Love,

Gerald.

The next day, written on blue airmail paper he had no doubt bought for the journey, Gerald wrote what is headed the '3rd last Epistle (for a time)'.

It's all right. I'm not going + 1 - 1 = 0. I mean to Haverfordwest. I find I can't. Feel bereaved. Impossible to

---

[140] Gerald would not have needed to look up the significance of Patrick White's title: *Riders in the Chariot*, referencing as it does Ezekiel's vision; see above, p. 256. Here he no doubt identifies with his status as an exile, Ezekiel being one of 3,000 Jews expelled from Judea by the Babylonians. Appealing also to Gerald might have been Ezekiel's status as the unheeded prophet of the latters' destruction of Jerusalem.

[141] See Appendix 3, p. 355.

say that 'Good-bye'. Balaam's ass speaks and I have no choice. So I'm only going to the Scillies. That is not as silly as it sounds; for I lived in Penzance for 3 years.[142] I can manage to take typewriter as appurtenances, paper and script of La Rocque qui Chante, and the minimum of books I need. The rest is stored and sorted here, and can be sent for and when I want any. They do not know here yet; but will have to - I have a map of South Wales to return to Bert. Am taking mine of Guernsey instead.[143] I'm letting you know first to clear up the confusion - and dispel any unease you may have.

It's the same train, anyhow; except that I change at Yeovil Junction: then Exeter, then Penzance, and the Scillonian at the first sailing.

I'll write to you soon.

Meanwhile

Tcheerie!

<u>Gerald.</u>

A week later I received a letter on the same paper dated 'St Mary's, Isles of Scilly, Wednesday, 18th February, 1976.' He had stayed two nights in Penzance and even whilst awaiting the next boat wrote ominously to Joan Snell that:

Cornwall since ten years ago, has changed (for the worse) almost beyond recognition. Overbuilt with pretentious, or ugly, or just ramshackle erections; and 'light' industries springing up everywhere. Tonight there is a cold foggy drizzle.

To us, two days later he wrote:

This is just to let you know I've got here. Also have a bed for 2 nights. Meanwhile I can get my bearings. I'm desperately keen to stay on these islands.

---

[142] See above, p. 201.

[143] He had had Joan Snell send him his map of Guernsey when he was in Lerwick, then as now, presumably, so as to facilitate ongoing work on the trilogy and/or poems; see above, pp. 284 and 302.

Your letter arrived just before I left Snelldonia on Monday morning. Actually, the note I sent with that typescript answers it as much as I can for the time being. I'll write to you again as soon as I can let you have an address.

I'm glad to be here - and sorry you are so far away.

<u>Gerald.</u>

The next day he sent us a postcard of Hugh Town from Peninnis, St Mary's [Fig. 86], looking significantly like the Guernsey coast, but apparently suffering from a similar problem:

HUGH TOWN FROM PENINNIS   ST MARY'S   ISLES OF SCILLY

Fig. 86: Gerald's postcard from Peninnis (sent 19 February 1976).

These islands are out of this world for loveliness; but in total grip of Tourism. Impossible to settle here. Am returning to the mainland by helicopter this afternoon. Am I disappointed? Yes, but not bitterly. The dim spark hasn't quite gone out yet. Which is all that matters.

His next letter was dated 25 February and addressed from the Snell's. It confirms that the typescript he had in the meantime sent me was his poem, 'Madame Boissel', from the proposed sequence, *La Rocque qui Chante*.[144]

---

[144] See Appendix 3.

This is just a note to let you know I'm back. I could have stayed on in Penzance and to my advantage financially, but my hazardous choice was to return and now, rightly, I am sure. I cannot foresee my leaving the Snells again - unless it is to go to Guernsey – not even Bert, with whom it is all right now. I could only in intimate conversation tell you what all this is about; which, in any case, I think would be irrelevant, and of no particular value to you. I am much more interested in gleaning a hint of what has been happening to you, which is surely more important.

Naturally, I am egotistic enough, to be eager to know your reaction to MADAME BOISSEL. However adverse. Though again, naturally, I cannot help hoping you got something from it, for what it is. That, however, makes no difference to my going on with La Rocque. I have in my mind the germ of a possibility of using it to winkle a way for your S.C. I will let you know more later, either by writing to you at greater length, or as and when we can meet. In the meantime, hoping to hear from you.

Am feeling very well. Trust you are,

Gerald.

Gerald now returned to the further perfecting of *Sarnia Chérie*. He reported on progress on 21 March 1976 in one of his most significant letters, the second and third sections of which provide us with our best account of his intention in the existing work and his aspiration to perfect and complete it:

If you come down at the end of the month, as I hope you will, and the copy of SARNIA CHÉRIE I typed is not being read by anybody, will you please bring it with you and let me have it; otherwise, will you please send it to me by post, as soon as it is available.

The photostat is yours for keeps, of course, but I would not myself sign anything for its publication as it stands. I am re-typing (with carbon) the whole thing, and making sundry changes. Apart from a few feeble passages I remember need re-writing, the changes come under three heads.

First, I am scrapping GUERNSEY ENGLISH and

319

L'ENVOI (also the Disclaimer, which is now quite unnecessary). It will mean more of the Guernsey names will be spelt 'correctly' and not as Ebenezer says them. How he does pronounce them will be let out, however, more explicitly in his conversation with the French master, and, possibly in other contexts.

Second, the scene of Ebenezer in the Vale Church, I have always felt missed fire. I am reluctant to explain empi[ri]cally how; but, privately to you, will risk it. It is not, as it stands, made clear in that scene, that the Cross is a necessary symbol, not because of a man being born, growing, decaying and dying, but because for every person that process is vitiated. It is the inescapable crux of what the Christian myth calls 'The Fall' and the T.L.S. 'the human condition.' Incidentally, it is what the whole of Greek Drama is about, as well as the 'Holy Bible'. Its symptoms in present-day terms are, on the political level, the ambiguity of commitment and, on the personal level, the tangled flame of love. In philosophical terms, the transcendental is <u>not</u> imman[en]t. That knocks out creative evolution, historical utopianism and personal romanticism. Also pantheism, of course; and its sterile twin, logical positivism.

Third, it follows the end has to be changed. Though not all that much: only enough to maintain the tone of tragi-comic irony. Ebenezer himself doesn't change; except that he expresses himself finally more in Christological terms, rather than by a mystical syllogism. He does say elsewhere: 'Perhaps I am more like my mother than I think.' The chief change is the way in which Neville and Adèle are to be presented. Ebenezer sees them in a romantic glow. I don't; and the reader should not. The blood relation remains, though; and they are rather fine, even if conky like the rest of us. Anyhow, if I complete THE BOUD'LO, both their and Raymond's story will be more complete. If I don't get it done, faut de mieux, S.C. could stand by itself (I hope).

Try and come down. It is what you are doing and thinking, I am eager to know.

<u>Gerald.</u>

I forgot to mention I have scrapped all VERSE in progress. Also I can get along temporarily with Joan's Carbon of S.C: but I can't tear it asunder, as I want to mine. It is a replica of your photostat copy.

I wrote back to say we were hoping to come down to Dorset with the typescript on 7 April and return on the 11th; Gerald replied on 26 March:

Thanks very much for your card - for letting me know. I'll now hope to see you in April. As I said, there's no hurry for your copy of S.C. I can work from Joan's Carbon; but I'd rather the original as I can tear it apart, and make some of the amendments on it before I type the final. Apart from what I told you, I'm not changing anything else much. If, however, anybody does get interested, they must be told. I am not allowing it to be published as it stands; GUERNSEY ENGLISH must go; and L'ENVOI. The titlepage is to be SARNIA CHÉRIE: THE BOOK OF EBENEZER LE PAGE by - my name in full. (There are numerous Edwards on Guernsey; and, to my knowledge several G's, and possibly, a G.B.) It will also squash Coysh's accusation that it is 'biographic, possibly autobiographic,' though only a born fool could imagine any one of the people in it having formed the whole, even as it was when he read it. I want it even more objective - that doesn't mean less sympathetic. Also I must fix the date more clearly. It ends in the 1960's. The Foreword to the one you have is dated 1974; but since then a lot has changed (mostly for the worse) in Guernsey. Anyhow, all the living people mentioned in it, with the possible exception of Clarrie Bellot (a passage which has to be re-written) are dead now.[145] The Official History of the

---

[145] This casual-seeming mention of Clarrie Bellot, one of Gerald's closest Guernsey friends, comes across as oddly unsentimental. He once posed with Bellot for a studio photograph which resembled his hero Walt Whitman's with Harry Stafford and according to Clary Dumond, he visited Bellot in 1967 [Figs 25 and 58]. Ebenezer's closest friend, Jim Mahy, includes ingredients derived from Bellot and Wilfrid de Lisle Burgess, both of whom lived well into their nineties, yet Gerald kept up with neither. At a deeper level, Ebenezer's account of Jim, may express, later, no doubt more intimate relationships, which along with worldly failure may partly explain his failure to return to old friends. That Gerald met Bellot after the war tends to be confirmed by Wilfrid Burgess's

Occupation (a deadly book) has been produced and is in my drawer of dead bones.[146] Though I don't have to worry. I got my impression from living sources, and find no reason to alter any of that. In any case it is not the pivot of the book - about 7 chapters in the sweep of an arc of 60. There <u>are</u> serious hiatuses: Raymond's school life: his honeymoon on Sark: what is happening when he is heard talking to himself; for instance. Also, the subsequent lives of Neville and Adèle, the birth of their children, his development as a painter - and his early death; but all those come incidentally into THE BOUD'LO, though not the main theme.[147] However, even if THE BOUD'LO is never done - nor the third dove-tailed 'sequel'; you do not have to fear I'd not let you have S.C. by itself, for publication on its own, when I feel, in spite of defects and hiatuses, it can stand on its own. The Dedication remains, of course. As also, in different wording, to THE BOUD'LO (subject to your consent).[148] It will be more difficult to take - balances more, I think, to the tragic than the comic - in tragi-comic terms: if I get it done, I will certainly thereby graduate out of the charm school.

Enough. I've written too much as it is. Today is Friday, when I read the T.L.S. and the Weekly Press;[149] and find it

---

quotation of a letter from him recalling Gerald 'living at Pleinmont awhile, and becoming "friendly with a Steve Picquet who was living in a Jerry (German) dugout with some goats".' Picquet is the subject of 3 pages in the *Book* and was clearly one of Gerald's sources for his account of the occupation; he died in 1963; Bellot in 1990. Picquet called his adapted bunker 'Onmeown'.

[146] This second, more specific reference to one of the 'dead bones' of his Guernsiana must refer to Charles Cruickshank's *The German Occupation of the Channel Islands*, commissioned in 1970 to mark the 25th anniversary of the liberation of Guernsey. It was published in 1975 by the Imperial War Museum and indeed seems a lifeless work that Gerald was justified in believing did not require him to alter his chapters on the occupation.

[147] Interestingly, Lampedusa's Tancredi also dies an early death, whilst his widow Angelica, is in her late sixties: 'already suffering from the illness which was to transform her into a wretched spectre three years later.' (*Leopard*, p. 203).

[148] Confirmation of an earlier remark that he intended to hand over the other parts of the trilogy as continuous with *Ebenezer Le Page*, see above, p. 312.

[149] *The Guernsey Weekly Press* is the weekly digest of the island's local daily newspaper, the *Guernsey Evening Press*. Although the number of subscribers is dwindling, it is still posted weekly to all corners of the globe. Before the internet,

hard to keep my head above water.

Be seeing you,

Love,

<u>Gerald.</u>

A somewhat mysterious letter follows, dated 9 April 1976 (as per the previous year), suggests that we did not after all make it to Dorset on the 7th. Gerald writes:

> I hope I am not committing a gaffe, but I have the idea that your birthday is on the 11th. I only know from memory, as I destroyed all correspondence and personal records, including my address book, before I went to the Scillies, in case I didn't come back. I kept in my wallet only my birth certificate or pension docs, as being necessary practicalls [*sic*]. Your date of birth was in my address book; so I may not have remembered it right.

> I won't say happy returns – as it is an insultingly meaningless phrase to me, and I am not out to inflict it on you / rather to convey solicitude.[150] I can't even send a widower's mite as token because, though not in the red, I am nearly so until the 15th. Not, as I know, that the lack matters.

> I ponder often, nowadays, how you (and Lisa) are getting along with your 'education.' I am not doubting for a moment that you can perform the requisite tricks to get your 'qualifications'; but otherwise in terms of value. The more the echoes of the Education Industries redound on me, the more deeply I become depressed. That perhaps you should discount, as it is for the most time my present state – if not worse. I live here as a non-entity in limbo.

> It follows I am not writing anything, and am loath to. I

---

it was the only way of expatriate islanders keeping abreast of island news.

[150] He had in fact already used the expression (above, p. 277) but the reluctance he expresses here may in part be the result of Nietzsche's initially negative notion of 'Eternal Return' (or the certainty of repeating one's life in infinite time), which can and should, however, be countered by the positive philosophy of 'Amor fati.'

do read – an odd range from Norse Sagas via the Authorised Version and Shakespeare to grail legends. My response is always the same. Questions; and for answer Yes/No. With one exception. The present. The ambiguous, sentimental commercial technocracy of the Kingdom of Snelldonia – and equally, of course, though in terms I will not define, the cultural and economic heritage of the Virgin Queen of Chaneydom.[151] To both of whom my answer is NO. NO. NO.

Consequently, if you do come down this month, I hope we can meet on neutral territory. The Masons Arms, say. Or any other idea you may have. It's your news I want to hear. I have none.

An odd birthday greeting, this; but we are not altogether strangers to each other.

<u>Gerald.</u>

## 11: POSITIVE RESPONSES

What is presumably Gerald's next letter is undated but its opening paragraph clearly refers to Lisa's first pregnancy, confirmation of which we received in May 1976. I had meanwhile suggested I send the photocopy of *Sarnia Chérie* to John Mellors - the father of friend and fellow student, Catherine, at the Warburg Institute. He reviewed regularly for the *Listener* and, given that he was publishing his *Memoirs of an Advertising Man*, with the London Magazine that year, I had asked him if he might be willing to help. Still tinkering with the typescript I must have returned in late April, Gerald had misunderstood me to mean that I was sending Mellors his Guernsey-English poem rather than the novel:

Dear Edward,

First and foremost, your news has gladdened my heart as nothing has for a very long time. To say more would be

---

[151] My spinster great-aunt Josephine Chaney (born 1888).

324

gush, or understatement.

I hadn't heard of it from Jo; or I'd have written. I rang her this morning and am going to see her tomorrow afternoon.

Yes, it's O.K. to let John Mellors see MADAME BOISSEL. I have several others in progress: one a long ballad three-quarters done. In so far as I am able to write at all in future, I think it will be verse. At present I have two folders going: each to one epigraph from SARNIA CHÉRIE. (I may have told you this before: if so, you must forgive me for repeating myself.) They are:

LA ROCQUE QUI CHÁNTE

> This island down the years have been a singing rock.   EBENEZER LE PAGE

GOD'S STEP-SON

> MISS LOUISE COHU: It has never occurred to me before; but HE was a Jew.

> MISS ANNETTE COHU: That is quite all right, my dear: it was only on His mother's side.[152]

MADAME BOISSEL comes from LA ROCQUE, of course. They are each by a different person singing about others, but revealing himself as much as those he is singing about. He doesn't, however, know what the song as a whole is about; but, for the nonce, I do. They are in variants of Guernsey English from the very Guernsey of MADAME to the nearly 'good' English of others. The form, rhythm, rhyme etc, some more regular than others, differ for each and are 'given' when the particular singer presents himself. Then I have no choice.

GOD'S STEP-SON is head-on dramatic and in 'good' English.[153] Well, more or less; and it plays havoc with traditional English prosody without being 'modern.' I may be confusing you. THE NOYADE by C. H. Sisson in last

---

[152] Misses Louise and Annette Cohu ran the Misses Cohu's School at Albion Terrace, Vale Road which Gerald attended; see p. 33 for this and missing page.

[153] See Appendix 4, p. 366.

week's T.L.S. is 'modern.' It left me cold, Wilfred Owen's APOLOGIA PRO POEMATE MEO, which overwhelms me by its magnificence, is 'traditional prosody'.[154] Anyhow, I will type a copy of the first of mine as a specimen and send it to you in a day or two. It's only three pages.

The problem of SARNIA CHÉRIE remains unsolved; or, rather, in suspense. I've read it through and will confess I was, on the whole, pleasantly surprised. I would not, could not write it now and, as it is, there are many minor alterations - the wrong right word in places and the right wrong word in others - would be better; but I can't see any way of altering the end substantially (or, perhaps, I should say insubstantially) without doing violence to what I feel are the better parts of what is there. The fact is the ending was written nearly simultaneously with the beginning; and clues pointing to it crop up all the way through. L'Envoi should definitely be removed. The place for that is at the end of La Rocque. I'd like to get rid of the Foreword. The part on linguistics could pass; but I object to the personal pyrotechnics of the last para. Ebenezer himself does it better. Anyhow, I'm not bothered about it now. I'd appreciate your advice and look forward to the opportunity of our having some leisurely talks.

I'll close now, I've just had a personal interruption which has rather put my nerves on edge. Lisa always says 'Look after yourself' to me, when she says 'Good-bye.' It's my turn to say that to her now.

Salaams to the Shah! [reference to my brother, now in Persia (now Iran)]

Gerald.

The next day, 26 May [1976], Gerald sent a typed poem as promised with a brief note about an unexpectedly successful visit to Jo. Evidently he had mentioned Wilfred Owen to her and she had informed him of my long-standing enthusiasm for his poetry:

---

[154] For 'The Noyade', see Sisson, *Collected Poems* (London, 1998), p. 215

Here it is. I don't want it back – I've kept a carbon.[155]

Just back from Jo's. Glad I went. Enjoyed it and hope she did too. Didn't discuss persons much, but her ideas mostly; and some of the things she said were very good. Clear. She has humour too. I've not liked her so much. It was I was more scatty by straying out of her context. Incidentally, I mentioned Wilfred Owen: it being on my mind to wonder whether my reference to him yesterday would contact. Apparently, it might. Good. His marvellous dictum in a letter 'Christ in No Man's Land' might have been the motto on his buckler. His end was absolutely right.

It's painful to see, though, the trouble Jo has now to get on her feet. I'll certainly go down and see her again soon.

G.

I had intended to visit Jo and Gerald the first weekend in July but a return of glandular fever prevented me. Whether because of renewed problems with the Snells, or he had already decided to leave after our previous visit, Gerald now wrote to announce yet another migration, in fact a revival of his plan to move to South West Wales.[156] This 6-page letter confirms that he was intending another major, potentially permanent move:

I've given Joan some of my books - including all of White and Camus: except two philosophic ones Lisa might care to glance at (they're in the book-case.) When you do come down to see Jo, you can have any, or all of the books in the bookcase; and from the bottom drawer of the chest-of-drawers. Those are only novels. Anyhow, Joan will show you: take anything you fancy. Myself, I'd rather like you to have the Collected Wilfred Owen. Also the Oxford Book of English Verse and the Cambridge A.V. of the Bible are quite expensive editions. The A.V. has marvellous things in it: and is a complete cure from being a Christian.

---

[155] 'The Immaculate Conception of Jesus They Call Christ' from 'God's Step-Son' – see Appendix 4.

[156] The interest in Wales may in part be explained by his belief that his father's family ultimately hailed from there. For Gerald on Wales via Jim Mahy's enthusiastic letters to Ebenezer, see *Ebenezer Le Page*, pp. 104-05.

I've leaving [*sic*] here quite amicably [*sic*]. There's a possibility they may be migrating to North Wales in the near future. I will remain South. I know what I'm letting myself in for. I did a day and a night journey from Newport to Milford Haven and back. Cardiff is the Inferno: but there's a no-change train from Weymouth, which is why I'm starting from there.

Well, I think that's all the practical details. I'll let you have an address, perhaps; when I have one.

Meanwhile, luck to the Thesis, blessing on the Unborn!

As ever,

Odd,

<u>Gerald.</u>

Before I had a chance to answer this he wrote again, on the day I was seeing a specialist at Hillingdon Hospital and the morning of his departure, 5 July 1976:

Dear Edward,

I was hoping to see you this week-end; but Jo tells me your gland trouble has recurred - trust you will soon recover. She says Lisa is keeping well. Good.

I am leaving for Wales today and don't expect to return. I am taking only a light rucksack and leaving behind a case of heavy clothing to be sent on when I have a more or less settled address.

Bert and Joan are amiably reconciled to my leaving and will be pleased to see you. I am not taking my books and would be glad for you to have any you fancy. I want you to have the type-writer, as well as accessories in the top drawer under the bookcase. There are in folders typescripts of two things you already possess - you can do what you like with them. The second drawer contains Guernsiana, mostly deadly; and I doubt if they're worth your while burdening yourself with - that's up to you. The bottom drawer is off [*sic?*] odds and sods - to me of little merit. The bottom drawer of the chest-of-drawers is all novels - take what you want…

Meanwhile, a wholesome and handsome infant and successful careers.

By the way, I've got rid of all fragments, correspondence and records (except for those essential for my official survival.)

### Gerald.

Mrs Snell remembers an abortive journey during which Gerald went to Haverfordwest, slept in the station, was overwhelmed by the heat, stayed three nights in a bed and breakfast place and returned to Weymouth. By 19 July, I was sufficiently recovered to drive down with Lisa and spend six days in Upwey during which time we visited the resettled Gerald as if nothing had happened.

Then, soon after our return to Uxbridge, I received a welcome report on the photocopy I had sent John Mellors which I immediately forwarded to Gerald. Though it was not an exclusively enthusiastic review, Gerald was delighted that a professional reader had at last responded humanly and positively to his magnum opus. Though Mellors did not know Guernsey, he was first of all impressed by Gerald's treatment of the island:

> The description of Guernsey before, during and after the German occupation, and its final abandonment to the depredations of tourists, has an authenticity which makes the book quite fascinating.

I consider that to be the most successful theme in the book. Next I enjoyed the vignettes of eccentric characters - the 'great-aunt-in-sin' who preached in the Seamen's Bethel chapel, finishing with drinks all round, Aunts Hetty and Prissy, Cousin Horace who sold 'Bang's Enerjim' to Americans, the widow with the wooden leg, and a host of others.

Of the relationships between major characters, I was not really convinced by Ebenezer's happiness with Neville, crucial as it is meant to be to the final stages of the work. Ebenezer's love for Liza, on the other hand, is always delicately, and at times movingly, treated – especially at the end, when Ebenezer sees her as 'a little old woman feeding the fowls ... wearing a scoop and sabots'. Best of all, I think, is the treatment of Raymond vis-à-vis Christ, Christine, parents and Ebenezer.

Having begun with praise, Mellors now ventured a few criticisms and comments on the problems we might face with potential publishers. I had informed him of the rejections to date:

> I know the whole narrative is meant to be by an old, garrulous and, for all his insights, slightly potty recluse, but I don't think the author has entirely solved the problem of maintaining that persona without losing impetus…

> However, I hope you can gather from what I have said that if the book were an already published work sent to me for review I would give it a good one. It has great character. It is vivid, truthful, entertaining, about 'important' things, and altogether original. My guess - and it's only that - is that a publisher might boggle at its length, at the leisurely, discursive style, and at its general 'unfashionableness'; I mean by 'unfashionable' that it contains little explicit sex or violence, is about a world the publisher himself is unlikely to know, is not an escapist fantasy, is lacking in the received notion of plot, and does demand some effort from the reader.

Mellors kindly concluded with advice but, rather disappointingly, with only one potentially useful contact:

> It would be a pity, in my view, if Sarnia Chérie did not get into print, and I hope my guesses about publishers' reactions are off the mark. But in case they aren't, it might be worth the author's while to edit out some of the digressions and 'family gossip' in the early chapters in order to get a reader involved that much more quickly. It might, too, be advisable to relegate that part of the introduction which deals with the local language (though personally I found it most interesting) to a post scriptum or footnote at the back; that might allay any publisher's fear of something too 'academic' in the author's approach. Finally, it occurs to me that if the writer does have difficulty in getting acceptance for the book as a whole, Alan Ross might

be interested in publishing extracts in his London Magazine.[157] If it comes to that, I would be only too happy to talk to him about it and suggest which extracts might be of particular interest to him (e.g. passages dealing with Guernsey during the occupation).

Gerald replied to my letter, accompanying Mellors' report by return on 19 August:

Dear Edward,

What a surprise! I thought it was MADAME BOISSEL you were sending to Mellors; but I'm glad it was S.C. You've certainly scored a bull this time. It's an excellent critique. I don't agree with him, but rather with you, about the beginning; and, as regards the end, I won't write anything now. I absolutely agree with him about the foreword. As a matter of fact; I have started revising it, I mean the whole book, so it can do without an introduction (or a glossary); and correcting a few gaffes on the way. It is completely wrong to intrude personally. I've only done 10 chapters, and those are the ones he thinks should be edited; but I still think they are good and true - and necessary. They set the background of Guernsey at the beginning of this century - atmospherically. If the book is ever published as a whole, they must remain as they are. What can be done at the end I will wait to see when I get there. I do know I am not easy about it myself: though I think some implications are being missed. It is very congested - the last dozen or so pages.

All the same, I am immensely grateful to him (and to you for sending it.) He has so obviously read it well, and his reaction is honest, straightforward and justified. I will write to him and thank him during the next week or so, and send you the letter to post on to him with a carbon for you, and your copy of his. I am not averse to extracts being published in the London Magazine.

---

[157] Alan Ross (1922-2001), sports writer and poet, took over editorship of *The London Magazine* from John Lehmann in 1961 and remained there until his death 40 years later.

Jo rang me the week you left and I went down to see her. It really wasn't very good - possibly my fault. She was comatose and muddled, and I didn't appreciate Sheba sufficiently.[158] However, we parted 'friends' and I asked her to let me know when she'd like me to go and see her again. She hasn't rung, so I haven't been. I would go if she asked me; but I know from experience on two previous occasions, it works out even worse if I go on my own initiative. It behoves me to await a summons to the Presence.

I hope Lisa is keeping well and your work going as you wish. I'm keeping well in parts at times, and now and again fit.

Gerald.

Three days later, Gerald returned Mellors's review with a note that reflected a decline in his mood:

Dear Edward,

Here's Mellors' Report back. I've been trying for days to concoct a letter to him; but it's no go. I get tied in knots of insincerity. As usual in the pickles into which you land me – doubtless with the best of intentions! I don't know the man, nor what you're up to. It's your business, not mine.

Myself, on a final count, I'm against the publication of extracts, particularly on the Occupation out of context. If I had to choose passages as appetisers, I'd say Chap. 10 of Part I, Chap. 8 of Part II and Chap. 9 of Part III; but could only really approve of publication in full without trimmings. However, do as you like.

Gerald.

That autumn my parents visited Jo on at least two occasions in Upwey, but I could only manage a single trip, visiting Gerald and picking up the revised typescript of *Sarnia Chérie*. I was very busy writing my dissertation and on 30 November our daughter Jessica was born [Fig. 87].

Following up Mellors's suggestion, I sent the typescript to Alan

---

[158] Sheba was Jo's highly-strung mongrel dog.

Ross but he was not interested in publishing even extracts. Gerald's aversion to Christmas and preference for being 'quiet' on such occasions meant that when Jo joined the family and new baby at my parents in Uxbridge he did not accompany her. Lisa and I were in any case obliged to spend Christmas Eve and the day itself with her Australian mother, with whom Gerald would certainly not have got on. I drove to Dorset on the morning of 22 December, briefly visiting a university friend near Bridport before returning to my aunt's for the night.

Fig. 87: The author and daughter Jessica in front of Aunt Jo's Upwey home (photo: Lisa Chaney, 1977).

The next morning, before returning to Uxbridge with my aunt and dog, I called in on Gerald for coffee. I recorded in my journal that:

> he was complaining of shortness of breath and was fairly depressed but I seemed to have cheered him up considerably; we planned new projects for him; sending a poem to the London Magazine (as they didn't want *Sarnia Chérie* or its extracts). He talked extremely well as usual about Tolstoy, Conrad, P. White, and less well about T.S. Eliot whom he knows I prefer above most.[159]

Christmas chez my mother-in-law was as bad as Gerald might have anticipated, though daughter Jessica more than compensated where I was concerned. Then after an exhausting night back at home, on the morning of New Year's Eve I went downstairs later than usual and found a letter postmarked

---

[159] Entry for 9 January 1977.

Weymouth. Joan Snell had written, apparently in preference to 'phoning, on 29 December:

Dear Edward and Liese,

I am sorry to have to tell you that Gerald had a heart attack early this morning and died. Dr Sloan was in attendance at the time. [160]

He will be cremated on Friday morning at 10 o'clock, and his ashes scattered at sea. No fuss.

She added that she had told Gerald's daughter - whether by letter or phone she didn't say. Since it was Friday 31 December and about 10.30 when I read this, adding to my dismay was the realisation that the cremation was already taking place 120 miles away. This event, on the last day of 1976, was apparently attended only by Bert Snell and the undertaker.

## 12: POSTHUMOUS PUBLICATION

Soon after this, Alan Ross rejected the poems as well as the novel. With Gerald dead I lost my sense of urgency in attempting to get his now orphan book published, preferring to lend the photocopy to friends who might be interested, though I see from a rejection letter from Frederick Muller Ltd dated 26 January 1978 that on at least one occasion I pestered a publisher.

Later in 1978 I won a Leverhulme scholarship and became a 'ricercatore' at the European University Institute enabling us to live in Florence. There I met fellow-student, John Henderson, who had recently ceased working as an editor for Hamish

---

[160] Joan Snell's son, Jonathan, kindly informs me that only he and his mother were present in the house when Gerald actually died. 'I can remember one morning the sound of Gerald moving around as he normally did before breakfast attending to his ablutions. My mum made breakfast and wondered why he hadn't come down stairs as usual. She asked me to knock on Gerald's door to remind him of the time. There was no reply and being the type of person that wasn't inclined to invade people's privacy. I returned downstairs to relay the news. I then went upstairs with my mum and we found him dead in his bed; I remember that he looked at peace with the world. It seems he had returned to bed and died of a heart attack.'

Hamilton.[161] Given that this firm was the only suitable publisher which had not seen *Sarnia* we agreed that he would forward the typescript to someone relatively senior at the publisher. I hoped that in this way it might be considered more carefully than when farmed out to an underpaid reader. And so things turned out. Hamish (Jamie) Hamilton himself was still alive - in fact resident in Florence where I subsequently got to know him - but his firm was now being run by Christopher Sinclair-Stevenson, a discriminating author in his own right. The editor, Caroline Tonson-Rye, into whose hands the typescript had fallen, immediately recognised its quality and recommended it to Sinclair-Stevenson. He read it and enthusiastically endorsed her positive appraisal.

According to Edwin McDowell of the *New York Times*, Sinclair-Stevenson told him:

> When one of our editors passed it to me with a strong recommendation, I thought it was one of the most remarkable scripts I'd ever read. Publishers say that every day of the year but in this case it was true. I couldn't think of another book like it.[162]

In September 1979 I was offered a contract. I successfully fought to retain certain passages the editors wanted abridged, whilst having to agree a few cuts of specifically local interest, in order to get the whole into print at last. More serious was our struggle over the title. The marketing 'experts' were determined not to use *Sarnia Chérie* because, they argued, it would sound too much like a Mills and Boon romance and no-one would know what Sarnia was anyway.[163] I was obliged to agree that they should use Gerald's subtitle as the sole one. Somewhat inconsistently I thought, they seemed delighted to discover George Deighton's lyrics to the song 'Sarnia Chérie', which they added at the front

---

[161] John is now Professor of Italian Renaissance History at Birkbeck.

[162] McDowell, Edwin, 'Guernsey Novel, Publishing Success,' *New York Times* (8 July 1981).

[163] I have since realised that another reason for choosing Gerald's subtitle instead of *Sarnia Chérie* might have been that Hamish Hamilton had published a romantic novel set in mid-Victorian Guernsey by Hilary Ford, *vere* Sam Youd (1922-2012), called simply *Sarnia,* published as recently as 1974.

of the book, looking rather as if Gerald had chosen it as an epigraph.[164]

More momentously meanwhile, albeit without mentioning it to me in far-away Florence, Sinclair-Stevenson sent John Fowles a copy of the typescript in the hope he might write an introduction. I had been asked to write this myself but whilst I was completing it, quoting as now from our correspondence, Fowles responded enthusiastically to the suggestion.[165] Initially his introduction was envisaged as complementing mine. Although, due to the undoubtedly greater impact Fowles's name would make, the publishers were thrilled at his acceptance, I was less keen. In all our literary discussions Gerald had never mentioned Fowles and I thought him rather over-rated. If what was to be called *The Book of Ebenezer Le Page* had to be introduced by any living novelist I somewhat unrealistically thought the publishers should try Patrick White, whom Gerald had esteemed so highly. Fowles had meanwhile asked for a copy of my 'biographical preface' and when he discovered that it was 'appreciative as well as biographical' he proposed to incorporate it into his own stand-alone introduction, adding 'But you may not like that idea at all, and feel good wine needs no bush from names like mine'.[166]

To the horror of those who had set up the deal, I expressed a

---

[164] Although I don't remember Gerald mentioning this song (music by Domenico Santangelo), he would have been very familiar with it. It emerged as the national anthem of Guernsey after being first performed at St Julian's Hall in 1911, which features frequently in *Ebenezer Le Page* (as St Julien's) as a venue for films, music and spectaculars such as the sinking of the *Titanic*. Ebenezer recommends the composer's band by name: 'the Santangelo's quartet was good' (p. 97) and one of his more unusual sexual partners sold chocolates there (p. 118: 'I had never imagined before that Saturday afternoon that there was so many ways of doing the same thing.') The irony was probably not lost on Gerald that Guernsey's national anthem was the work of an Englishman and an Italian (at least the latter remained a resident). Nor could he have refrained from comment had he survived to see the Gaumont cinema - as St Julian's became in 1929, albeit German-dominated throughout the occupation - turned into a bank in 1985.

[165] In his letter to Sinclair-Stevenson, dated 22 March 1980 Fowles congratulated him on accepting the novel, writing: 'I think you are very right to have taken it on,' but added 'I feel I must see the legatee's preface before I can write mine.'

[166] Letter addressed to me in Florence from 'Belmont', Lyme Regis, dated 10 April 1980.

version of my views to Fowles and proposed, if anything, a joint introduction with some control over what he would say. He now responded with a dignified (only mildly indignant) letter in which he offered to withdraw, acknowledging 'my special right to do the appraising.'[167] The courtesy of his response, combined with further pressure from Sinclair-Stevenson, persuaded me to withdraw instead. I sent him copies of the rest of Gerald's letters to me and on the 9 July he thanked me fulsomely, saying he 'felt he knew the writer much better now.' In the end he kindly sent me his draft introduction for comments and on 30 September, the day after incorporating, 'in the nick of time … the great bulk of your justified criticisms', he thanked me again for my suggestions and additions. He had meanwhile managed to extract from Gerald's daughter, Dorcas, most of what little information we have about his movements after he retired and, through Harry Tomlinson, discovered the details of Gerald's birth at the Greffe and two other references relating to his school days.[168] He also, again with Tomlinson's assistance, compiled the glossary which was appended to the novel, adding a note on Guernsey's first poet, Georges Métivier (1790-1881), 'who can stand comparison with William Barnes of Dorset and should surely be more widely known.'[169]

Fowles's by this time quite passionate commitment to the *Book* and its author is communicated by his conclusion to his very gracious letter of 30 September:

> I'm afraid going to proof means we cannot now effectively add or change very much, but I hope further information will appear when the book comes out. I suspect other people will want to research him one day much more diligently than I have been able to and obviously you will have to decide what your policy will be.

---

[167] Letter from Lyme Regis to Florence dated 27 May 1980, enclosing undated letter from Harry Tomlinson.

[168] See above, p. 35. Fowles also told me he corresponded with Collis, 'but alas he died before a meeting could take place.' (letter dated 28 February 1986).

[169] Fowles was sufficiently proud of his introduction to republish it in his *Wormholes: Essays and occasional Writings* (London, 1998), pp. 166-174. This no doubt encouraged his friend, William Golding, to write his enthusiastic review of *Ebenezer* in the *Guardian* in March 1981, *cf.* pp. 229-30.

At any rate, I've greatly enjoyed doing the introduction and I pray the book will at least meet some critics who have got beyond 'helicopter thinking'.[170] Tomlinson was obviously a little shocked by the criticism of some aspects of Guernsey in the extracts I sent him, and I am a tiny bit afraid that that may be a not uncommon first island reaction. But I shall be surprised if it is more than that – just a first reaction.

Let me end by thanking you for your help - and I have inserted a little passage in the final draft making it clear how vital becoming friends with you was for Edwards in those last years. It should have been there from the start.

After such a faltering start I thought the final product so good I managed, this time unwittingly, to add insult to earlier injury by praising it as one of the best things he had written. Despite or even due to this we remained firm friends and continued to communicate on the subject of the novel we were united in admiring for the rest of his life [Fig. 88].[171]

Fig. 88: John Fowles (1926-2005) with the author at the re-opening of the Town Mill, Lyme Regis: 26 May 2001.

---

[170] See above, p. 279.

[171] On 27 August 1997 for example he wrote to me enthusiastically about the possibility that the author Zachariah Edwards of Combpyne might be related to Gerald's grandfather, see p. 18.

# 13: GENIUS LOCI

Whilst concluding this memoir, I was tempted to repeat the final paragraph of Fowles's introduction to *The Book of Ebenezer Le Page* by way of conclusion:

> Gerald Edwards died after a heart attack, in his small room near Weymouth, on 29 December, 1976. His ashes were scattered at sea. I should like to think that some at least were washed up among the *vraic* and granite of his long-lost native shore.

This might suggest that Gerald's ashes were scattered on the sea near Weymouth. Talking to Mrs Snell a few months after his death, however, I discovered that some weeks after the cremation, more or less spontaneously and unbeknownst to myself, Bert Snell, together with their daughter Anneliese and her boyfriend and brother, took the ferry to St Peter Port and scattered Gerald's ashes on his own sea, as they entered the harbour. More recently, Anneliese's boyfriend, now husband, Tony, informs me that as they were arriving into the port, Bert Snell attempted to scatter the ashes, most of which blew back in their faces, his own in particular, an Ebenezerish incident that, given their sometime rivalry for Mrs Snell's attention – and even affection - Gerald would surely have enjoyed.

In the end therefore, after all his attempts to escape to a far-flung haven that might remind him of the Guernsey he increasingly dwelt upon in his imagination, Gerald returned in death to the imperfect reality of his place of birth. 'I may or may not see Guernsey again', he wrote in the summer of 1975 from Lerwick, 'and will always be heartsick for Shetland (as an impossible dream,' but intended to visit Guernsey after his return to Dorset. Such unusually ambivalent phrasing is surely expressive of his profound feelings of, yet resistance to, nostalgia for the *genius loci* of his native island. Gerald identified himself more closely with Conrad and Lawrence than with Lampedusa or Joyce but it is the latter's explanation for his self-exile, complementing an abiding obsession for the island of *his* birth, that best expresses the conflicting complexity of this quest:

> When the soul of a man is born in this country there are nets flung at it to hold it back from flight. You talk to me of

nationality, language, religion. I shall try to fly by those
nets.[172]

Though Gerald and Joyce both flew by these and the many other
nets flung at their souls, they nevertheless drew rich inspiration
from the nationality, language and religion of their respective
islands. Meanwhile, fellow-exile D.H. Lawrence, who likewise
harked back to his native land, encouraged in Gerald a
passionate belief in the value of emotional authenticity.[173]
Though Joyce and Lawrence may be regarded as greater
novelists in the world of academe, Gerald came to admire
Joseph Conrad and Patrick White as much, sounding, on more
than one occasion, uncharacteristically modest in the face of
their achievement. In December 1974, a few months after
completing *Sarnia Chérie*, he wrote that where 'writing head-on
an impersonal "classical" novel' was concerned… Voss and
Nostromo are far beyond and above me.' It may be significant
that he cited a single novel by each author when pronouncing
on this aspect of their superiority.

Thanks partly to his passionate absorption of at least three of
these four great moderns in the course of a lifetime's reading
ranging from the Old Testament to Solzhenitsyn, Gerald's own
novel eventually matched any of theirs. According to J.S. Collis
he outshone both Joyce and Lawrence, even to the extent of
matching the American poet who had proved such a bond
between their band of *Adelphoi* half a century before. In that
emotive posthumous tribute to his former intimate and literary
mentor, Collis imagined a conversation he might have had with
Gerald in their old age, reminiscent of those 'Socratic dialogues'
they had once enjoyed in his Rotherhithe flat as the sun set over
the Thames.[174] To the 'Genius Friend' with whom he had so
regretfully lost touch but who had finally completed a *magnum*

---

[172] *Portrait of the Artist as a Young Man*, Chapter 5. William Blake refers to 'the
Net of Religion' spreading over the cities in *The Book of Urizen* (London, 1794).

[173] Though sensing a longer life ahead of him Gerald crafted his writing less
spontaneously.

[174] In his unpublished novel, Collis talks of the 'genius' 'Edward Newman'
coming to see him for tea there after his mother had died (Gerald's mother died
in 1924); see above, p. 239.

*opus* which surpassed any of his own, Collis would have said:

> Give me *Ebenezer* rather than *Ulysses*; give me *Ebenezer* before any novel by Lawrence, *and* I would have said, though only he would have understood my meaning – it is a sort of *Leaves of Grass*.[175]

Stephen Potter concluded the book on Lawrence that Gerald failed to finish with a quotation from the same collection.[176] 'These lines', he wrote, 'make, I think, a good epitaph'. Yet, as Collis reminds us, it was Gerald who inspired both his and Potter's devotion to the life-enhancing literature of both Whitman and Lawrence in the first place.

In a survey of six new books by or about Walt Whitman, J.M. Coetzee concluded that:

> Whitman's democracy is a civic religion energized by a broadly erotic feeling that men have for women, and women for men, and women for women, but above all that men have for other men.[177]

Lawrence wrote ecstatically about Whitman: 'the great poet [who] has meant so much to me. Whitman, the one man breaking a way ahead. Whitman the one pioneer…'.[178]  In 1923, he  also wrote that:

> All my life I have wanted friendship with a man – real friendship, in my sense of what I mean by that word.

But Lawrence goes on to specify that it is 'not something homosexual' he seeks:

> besides this term is so imbedded in its own period. I do not belong to a world where that word has meaning. Comradeship perhaps? No, not that – too much love about it – no, not even in the Calamus sense, not comradeship –

---

[175] 'Memories of a Genius Friend', *Spectator* (31 July 1982), p. 22.

[176] *D.H. Lawrence,* p. 153, quoting the first lines of Whitman's final stanza of *Song of Myself*.

[177] J.M. Coetzee, 'Love and Walt Whitman', *New York Review of Books*, LII, no. 14 (22 September 2005).

[178] Bloom, *Western Canon*, p. 289; *cf.* now Bloom, *The Daemon Knows: Literary Greatness and the American Sublime* (New York, 2015).

not manly love.[179] Then what Nietzsche describes – the
friend in whom the world standeth complete, a capsule of
the good – the creating friend, who hath always a complete
world to bestow? Well, in a way. That means in my words,
choose as your friend the man who has centre.[180]

Centring suggests duality. In his *Marriage of Heaven and Hell*,
long before Nietzsche argued the necessity of conjoining the
Apollonian with the Dionysian, William Blake preached that
'without contraries is no progression'. Since Freud's *id, ego, eros*
and *thanatos*, we have (more scientifically) discovered the
importance of right and left brain co-ordination. Though Gerald
created two very different characters to represent his thoughts
and, more importantly, his emotions and intuitions, the
relatively centred character through whom he chose to sustain
his dialogue with the world (or at least posterity) would not
have known of Blake, Whitman, Nietzsche or even Lawrence,
unless news of the cultural revolution proclaimed by the (re-)
publication of *Lady Chatterley's Lover* reached Les Moulins in
1960. In resembling the young Gerald more intimately than
Ebenezer, however, Raymond would have known of all four.[181]
Though he was able to read the New Testament in Greek, 'he
ought never to have been born' and was destined for death in
middle age. Gerald has him and his beloved cousin Horace, with
whom he shared his wife, Christine, blow themselves up,
Karpos- and Kalamos-like, on a German mine. This left
Ebenezer to live on alone after the war and continue writing in
his three big books, just as Gerald wrote his, after all the angst-
filled intensity and disappointment of his middle age.

Though he may have been tempted to end his life like Raymond,

---

[179] In Nonnus's late 4th century epic poem, the *Dionysiaca*, Calamus, or Kalamos,
allows himself to drown after his friend had drowned ahead of him a race.
Whitman named a group of poems in his *Leaves of Grass* after him.

[180] Meyers, *Lawrence*, p. 210, quoting Lawrence on *Thus Spake Zarasthustra*.

[181] The only novel Ebenezer read was that other island 'autobiography', Defoe's
*Robinson Crusoe*, which he chose as a memento of his friend Jim Mahy after the
latter's death; *Ebenezer Le Page*, p. 120. Telling (as if self-mockingly?), Gerald
has Ebenezer say of it: 'It is a good book. It show how if you go gallivanting all
over the world instead of stopping at home where you belong, you only land
yourself with a load of trouble.' (*ibid.*, p. 147).

Gerald chose to struggle on as he has Ebenezer do. In this he maintained his young man's belief in Nietzsche's aspiration to 'love one's fate,' evolving a personalised means of coping with the ancient Egyptian idea of 'eternal return', as he had advocated in his article on Bernard Shaw as long ago as 1926.[182] Gerald's profound love of literature and concomitant scorn for machine-man's 'progress' complemented his concern with posterity. In this he could hardly have been more different from Shaw, about whom he knew Collis had written:

> I am convinced that Shaw is not in the smallest bit concerned with what posterity will say of him. He would much prefer fame in his own generation than in the years to come.[183]

Gerald avoided fame in almost any form but focussed instead on constructing 'something upon which to rejoice' in the longer term; something of which he could be proud enough to bequeath to a Neville-like friend. It was through this project that he finally found fulfillment; in a friendship across more than a generation but based on a shared appreciation of art as inseparable from life.

However closely Gerald might have identified with Raymond, it was to his older and more resilient cousin, Ebenezer Le Page, that he donated the credo to which he had so courageously clung throughout his life. Though he had profoundly identified with Nietzsche, Gerald not only survived in better personal shape; in the end he bequeathed a more positive message to posterity. He did so above all in the dying words he gave the seemingly un-Nietzschean hero he created out of a Guernsey peasant. Yet, whether consciously or not, there is surely still more than an echo of Geralds's favorite philospher in these last words.

On New Years Day 1882, Nietzsche had written:

> I still live, I still think; I must still live, for I must still think … and what thought first crossed my mind this year, a thought which ought to be the basis, the pledge and the

---

[182] *Adelphi*, IV, i (July 1926), pp. 31-32; see above, p. 58.

[183] Collis, *Shaw*, p. 172.

343

sweetening of all my future life! I want more and more to perceive the necessary characters in things as the beautiful… Amor fati: let that henceforth be my love! I do not want to wage war with the ugly. I do not want to accuse, I do not want even to accuse the accusers. Looking aside, let that be my sole negation! And all in all, to sum up: I wish to be at any time hereafter only a yea-sayer![184]

Gerald's New World did not depend on destroying the Old, however; rather did it attempt to bless and preserve it, *i.e.* God's island in the sun as a microcosm of the world at large. In this respect, it recalled Nietzsche's account of the cosmos as: 'The primordial poem of mankind.'[185] Gerald maintains the voice with which the reader has become intimate yet has this relatively primitive persona express with unprecedented poetry, his thoughts on a post-Nietzschean God and the Cosmos. Apart from conceding that he has been judgmental, Ebenezer is by now beyond good and evil and in that state of animal innocence Nietzsche envisaged for his *Übermensch*. Except in the most sophisticated sense there will, however, be no infinity of eternal returns, 'only now'. He addresses the future only through Neville, who in turn has Adele and his art. Then, returning to himself, the past merges with the present and he feels sure that he will sleep soundly.

Retaining Ebenezer's emphatic style, he begins his end by confirming his intuition that: 'There is SOMEBODY THERE'. But that somebody is not a metaphysical entity:

He is like my father was, behind me, on the ladder. He is like my mother was, when she was cooking me ormers… Neville is in Him; but don't know it yet. I wonder how he will shape out, that boy. He say he is a pagan; and I say he is a puritan. I hope he will not stick his heels in over getting married in a Catholic Church. He is honest in the mind. He must not expect to find what's what in any religion, or any person in this world. I hope he will not let his wild ideas

[184] Nietzsche's 1882 New Year's Resolution in: *The Joyfull Wisdom (La Gaya Scienza)*, translation by Thomas Common, *The Complete Works of Friedrich Nietzsche*, X (1924), (Book 4th, §276: 'For the New Year').

[185] Bloom, *Western Canon*, p. 334.

run away with him. As bad as Guernsey is, I hope he will not butt in and try and change it. It will change quick enough without his help; and for the worse and worse. He must endure it. He have Adèle to love and a living to make and his pictures to paint. They are his way of prayer and praise…

It was a fine clear night and the sky was full of stars. The Casquets light was doing its round: three flashes and down, three flashes and down; and far out to sea ships was passing without a sound. I don't know how many, but I must have seen a dozen, or more. Some was cargo boats with port and masthead lights, and the glow of a cabin or two, but others was great liners lit up like floating palaces on the way to America. I don't want to die, me! I want to stop alive for ever, if only to see the ships pass.

I came indoors. I made up my mind I would write this very night what have happened to me today. I have never written so much at one go. It is near on midnight, and I am writing yet; but now it is death and what come after I am thinking of. There is no after: it will only be now. I don't believe, I don't believe in the harps and the big fire, and the wheat and the tares, and the sheep and the goats; for the Day of Judgment is the Day of Forgiveness, and the repentant and the unrepentant sinner are with Christ in Paradise. I hear Christine singing:

> O Love, that will not let me go,
> I rest my weary soul in Thee![186]

Sing, Christine: sing! Be not bitter, as Lot's wife was. Forgive them, forgive them; for they have loved much!… I wish I could live my life again. I wish I could write my story again. I have judged people. I do not want to judge people.

---

[186] The blind George Matheson's 1882 hymn. No doubt Gerald knew the heart-breaking story that lay behind its composition; *cf.* the status he accords these words elsewhere in *Ebenezer Le Page*, p. 178: 'I know they are the words of Raymond's religion and the whole of his religion. He came to turn against it and deny it and try and tear it out of himself; but I know he didn't ever quite tear the roots from his heart.' For the 'modernist' Harry Mathews' response to 'the "romanticism" of Ebenezer's last pages', see p. 231.

I want to bless. I want to bless every soul who have ever lived and laughed and suffered on this whore of an island, this island in the sun, this island in God's sea!

I am on the last page of the last of my three big books. Who will ever believe I have written these three big books? I want to write another. Next time I go to Town, I will buy another from the Press. I want to write down in it all the good thoughts I have left out in this. Now it is high time I thought of going to bed. I mustn't forget to wind the clock; and I will turn the lamp down, but not right out. I don't like it in the dark. I like to be able to see my two china dogs while I am falling asleep. Damme, I am tired, me! I will sleep well tonight, I know. Ah well, that is all for now. A la prochaine!

# APPENDICES

## APPENDIX 1

### SONG OF A MAN WHO SAW GOD [1]

I have seen God between the stars,
and through the hollow spaces of the night
have gazed along the endless quiet places
of His benign abyss: and I have heard
the soundless echo of His silent voice
in clamour from the pit of quenchless lust.

I have seen God upon the heaving sea,
glimmering in the sunset afterglow,
and in the darkness on the heavy rise and fall
of the slowly swelling tide; and I have heard
the soundless echo of His silent voice
in the roar of breakers thundering on the shore.

I have seen God before the dawn,
a lambent pallor on the scalloped waves,
a mist departing from the fissured cliffs
of the unexpected island: and I have heard
the soundless echo of His silent voice
in the wrenching of the timber as the frail ship sank.

I have seen God beyond the garish noon,
a stalking dragon of devouring arrogance,
so a great and equal anger in my breast arose
to confront Him laughing; and I have heard
the soundless echo of His silent voice
in the  belching wrath of storm and hurtling rain.

---

[1] Sent by Gerald to Middleton Murry from 9 Ritherdon Road, London, on 10 September 1947, for possible inclusion in the *Adelphi*. Presumably unpublished; original now in the author's collection; see above, p. 221-23.

I have seen God at evening creep
from gorse and fern, down hollow, over hillock,
while the sheep crouched close for sleep and the
        wide-eyed goat
stared expectant on a rock: and I have heard
the soundless echo of His silent voice
in the spiteful evening gossip of the birds.

I have seen God beside the fire
that cheers the hearth-stone and the homely room,
where the crone sits dreaming of her brave lost sons,
and the old man sleeps; and I have heard
the soundless echo of His silent voice
in the cracking fury of the burning dunes.

I have seen God home from the wars
in the township's bustling market-place,
his jaunty thighs and twinkling eyes apprizing
a pert delicious maid: and I have heard
the soundless echo of His silent voice
in the call of pipe and the blood-song of the drums.

I have seen God a headstrong child,
swaying at the cliff-edge reckless of the height,
and shambling sulky to his mother's anxious arms,
affronted by her fears; and I have heard
the soundless echo of His silent voice
in sobs at night of the orphan's muffled grief.

I have seen God a flaming youth,
standing tip-toe on the earth and unbewildered
reaching for the fair unconquered world,
eager as the dawn; and I have heard
the soundless echo of His silent voice
in the brazen shouts of boys at ruffian play.

I have seen God behind the lover's eyes,
a nether creature pleading for release,
till I have been humbled, shamed and blinded
by so much beauty shown; and I have heard
the soundless echo of His silent voice
in curse and groan and the forbidden words of dark.

I have seen God on the beloved's face,
pallid reflecting the blazing glory of the Lord,
and would fain of stayed  that moment from the dead
to have my godhead reassured; and I have heard
the soundless echo of His silent voice
in the bleak first cry of babe new-risen to the day.

I have seen God in the countenance of death,
all passions quelled as in a marble tomb,
and marvelled that such strong agony could leave
a monument so calm; and I have heard
the soundless echo of His silent voice
in the last fierce death-gasp from the entrails torn.

# APPENDIX 2

## LE VIER GUERNÉSI :

## TALES OF GUERNSEY FOLK

In his 1981 introduction to *The Book of Ebenezer Le Page*, John Fowles observed that :

> The present book was to form the first part of a trilogy. The second and third were to be called *Le Boud'lo: the Book of Philip Le Moigne* and *La Gran'-mere du Chimquière: the Book of Jean Le Féniant*. Edwards left enough hints in his letters to make it plain that he saw the first part as something of a humorous contrast to the other two. Readers may be interested to know that Neville Falla, the cause of much of the final sentimentality here, was in fact earmarked for an early death in the second part, and that its tone was to be much more tragic than comic. Edwards himself remarked wrily of it: 'I will certainly thereby graduate out of the charm school'.[2]

Fowles added a footnote, translating Gerald's proposed titles as:

> Literally, 'The Puppet: the Book of Philip the Amputated' and 'The Grandmother of the Cemetery: the Book of John the Sluggard'. Edwards' full title for the present book was *Sarnia Chérie: the Book of Ebenezer Le Page*, in symmetry with the other two.

Fowles reports Gerald's daughter, Dorcas, as saying that as early as 1967 the first draft of the novel was completed, 'and the second part, Le Boud'lo, half done.' Towards the end of his introduction Fowles, however, records my opinion that 'there were never more than brief drafts for the rest of the intended trilogy; and most of those Edwards seems to have destroyed before he died.' Although Gerald indeed had a tendency to destroy his possessions before moving on, and indeed says at one point that in a 'suicidal adolescent state [he] pitched 'The Boud'lo' into the dustbin' (above, p. 253), we have also seen that

---

[2] Fowles, 'Introduction,' *Ebenezer Le Page*, p. x ; *cf.* pp. 312-13.

he tended to exaggerate the completeness of a project in progress. *Ebenezer Le Page* was not completed until almost a decade later and given that he talks of resuming work on *Le Boud'lo* and kept the fragments published here, it seems unlikely he destroyed anything very substantial.

Apart from the typed and hand-written poems he sent me from time to time he left a few fragments in his room which Joan Snell kindly hand over after he died. I have transcribed most of those that may be of interest or are more-or-less self-contained as well as a few fragments which provide a glimpse of what might have been had he survived to see the success of *Ebenezer Le Page* and been asked to produce more of the same:

## THE BOUD'LO [3]

The Boud'lo, that's me. In Guernsey a boud'lo is anybody who is ugly, or funny-looking, or who behave in a funny way. Well, I'm all three! He is also the Johnnie they burn on Guy Fawkes night; though how it can have come about for any Guernseyman to care if the Houses of Parliament got blown up, I don't know. I know I wouldn't have. The word 'boud'lo'; is short for Le Vieux Bout-de-l'An (Old End-of-the-Year) and thousands of years before Guy Fawkes was thought of, it was a tree? dressed as a man, or perhaps a living man, was burnt on the night of the shortest day for some reason or another; but I've no idea what for and it got nothing to do with me. All I know is I am a bundle of old rubbish have been put in here out of the way because I have been making a nuisance of myself…

It's alright in here really. The food is not bad and plenty of it; and I got a little room to myself upstairs where I can sit of an evening. I could go down in the big room with the others, if I wanted, but they always got the T.V. on. I can't bear the T.V. It is like having a lot of crackling devils coming at you. I am not mad, but there are some in here who are,

---

[3] This is alas merely a hand-written fragment; something Gerald may not even have realised had survived. It is included largely to provide an idea of what the successor to *Ebenezer Le Page* might have been.

and they are taken away when they become dangerous and given electric shocks, but I am given pills sometimes. I don't think that fair. I make out to take them, but I don't, and hide them away after. The nurse don't notice, but the new young doctor who come round with her yesterday, he saw. He come up to my room after tea and knock on the door.

'May I come in please?' he say. 'Yes, come in, come in!' I call out. He come in. He is a nice young chap and I was glad of his company. 'Stay as long as you like' I say. I get up for him to have my armchair by the stove, but he make me the sign to sit. 'I can't stay long, I'm on duty' he said. 'I really only came to ask you a question. What have you done with those pills you refuse to take?' Golly, I had to do a quick think! I put on my stupid look. 'Pills?' I said, 'I don't know what pills you are talking about.' 'I think you know perfectly well what pills I am talking about,' he said: 'I spotted your slight of hand, my friend, ~~Come on, where are they~~?' I thought then I'd better remember. 'Oh those!' I said: 'I expect I threw them down the loo, when I wasn't thinking. I am mad, aren't I?' 'I'm quite sure you're not as mad as that' he said: ~~He looked at me hard.~~ 'Come on, where are they?' I got up and shambled across to my bed, where I got some hidden in a screw of newspaper under the mattress. 'Are those the ones you mean?' I said. He hold out his hand. 'A chap could do himself in who got hold of that little lot,' he said. 'I was not thinking of doing that' I said. 'I am not saying you were,' he said: 'but I am not taking any chances, if you don't mind.' I had to let him have them, watch him put the screw of newspaper carefully in his wallet and in his inside pocket. 'It's not fair!' I said and flounced back onto my chair in a sulk: 'I didn't ought to be given pills!' I said: 'There's nothing wrong with me! If it comes to that, I didn't ought to be in here at all! I ought to be let out!' He was standing looking down at me, considering me. 'I would not say but that you may not be right' he said: 'I am not at all clear in my own mind as to how, or why you were admitted.'

I tell him. It was my daughter got me put in here, and she is paying. She live […]

## IN THE COUNTRY HOSPITAL [4]

I.

It is not fair
me being in here
and shut away
because I say
things some think are bad for the visitors.
I am not mad
but only sad
bcause I am alone
and got no one
who is a friend and can understand.
In here they pretend
and do attend
to my every need
and see I feed
and profess to take an interest in me
but don't, unless
it is, as I guess
to learn more, if they can
of the mind of any man.
I am not any man! I am Philip Le Moigne

I will never forgive
as long as I live
my mother nor my father
for bringing me into the world.
He do it for profit
to have son to inherit
she to keep a hold
on a man not so old
from the start I am made for cross purposes.
My heart is sound
and I weigh ten pound
and got a head as big
as the bladder of a pig.
I am no beauty, you know. I was born a boud'lo!

---

[4] A merging of two surviving manuscripts versions, this was apparently intended as Part I of a series.

## FOR DOCTOR ERIC KENNEDY TO READ

Well, Doctor Kennedy,
here is your remedy –
you get me to write
to keep me quiet,
decide the appropriate treatment is occupational
       therapy.
In you I confide
nothing do hide,
which when you have seen
you feed to a machine
diagnose I am harmlessly but incurably insane.
This patient is indisposed to adjust
as a sane man must,
suffers from a religious neurosis
worse than thrombosis
and is therefore unfit to live in a modern community.
All right, if that's it –
I don't care one bit –
I have had my say –
I am of yesterday.
Who is to know, though? I may be of tomorrow!

----------------

## LYING IN THE SUN

Ah, Gran'-mère du Chimquière,
your day is done,
I, Jean Le Féniant swear,
lying in the sun !
Mais verre, Gran'-mère,
You have had your way,
You have had your say,
Too long!

# APPENDIX 3

## LA ROCQUE QUI CHÁNTE :

## SONGS OF A GUERNSEYMAN [5]

This island down the years have been a singing rock.

EBENEZER LE PAGE

### MADAME BOISSEL

Mondays Madame Boissel
come to do the washing.
Fridays she come to do the rough.
She is as strong as a horse
and as big as the side of a house.
She is a good woman, mind you -
she is Salvation Army
and of a Sunday afternoon
stand in the crowd around the band
on the grass on L'Ancresse Common
and lift up her voice
above the cornets and the drum,
when they play her favourite hymn:
   O happy day! O happy day!
   When Jesus washed my sins away…

Jean Boissel she is married to
go fishing for a living
and drink like a fish
and live to drink.
He don't fear the Devil
or the deep blue sea,
and got big hairy arms

---

[5] Gerald was working on these during 1975 and early 1976. He wrote: 'They are each by a different person singing about others, but revealing himself as much as those he is singing about.'. They start with the longest complete poem, 'Madame Boissel', which Gerald was especially proud of, as he had typed it out neatly and made carbon copies for me and Joan Snell. The second longest poem to survive, 'Old Boud'lo', is incomplete and therefore not included here.

and hands like hams,
and he breed and breed,
and Madame Boissel on her back
she sing and sing,
while the bed-springs creak
and the brass knobs rattle:
  O happy day! O happy day!
  When Jesus washed my sins away…

Yes, she got a tribe of children -
I don't think she know how many:
some are dead and gone to heaven,
some gone to sea and gone to hell;
but she got one good daughter,
Isobel,
who manage to hook
an English swell
who come to the island
to sell Monkey Brand,[6]
and have gone to live in England
where nobody know
Madame Boissel,
nor do anybody guess
in Nelson Crescent
that nice Mrs Travers-Smith
who drink her tea
with a little finger crooked,
got for a mother in Guernsey
a rough old washer-woman who sing:
  O happy day! O happy day!
  When Jesus washed my sins away…

Isobel don't write to her mother -
it would be too much bother,
and Madame Boissel can't read anyway;
but every morning on her way to work
she stop the postman and she ask him
if today he got a letter,

---

[6] Brooke's Soap Monkey Brand was a household china and metal scouring and polishing product, acquired by Lever Brothers in 1899.

and when he shake his head and say
n'e'che pouis au jour d'orgniet,[7]
she go plodding up the road
as if she was a heavy-shod mare
pulling a full cart–load,
and not till she got on to the flat
got the heart in her to sing;
  O happy day! O happy day!
  When Jesus washed my sins away…

She got another daughter,
who have gone to the bad -
she don't live at home, of course,
but in a room up Cornet Street
all done up in tinsel and plush.
She work by night
and sleep by day;
but sometimes take a night off,
if she is feeling flush,
and the next day go
to Le Cuoqn-au-Vraic[8]
at Le Clos-du-Valle[9]
and leave five quid
on the kitchen table,
which when Madame Boissel come in
she put in her purse quick
and sing in thanksgiving to God
like a lark in the spring:
  O happy day! O happy day!
  When Jesus washed my sins away…

It make an honest woman of her -
she can face the baker and the grocer,
and pay the coal-man and the milk,

---

[7] An odd form of Guernésiais, presumably for: 'There is none today'.

[8] Guernésiais: literally 'Seaweed Corner'. *Couogn* = quoin/wedge/cornerstone; *Vraic* = seaweed. Like Thomas Hardy in his novels and poems, Gerald also invented likely-sounding local names.

[9] Clos du Valle, however, is the old name for the northern part of the Vale parish when it was separated from the rest of the island.

and the butcher what she owe.
She is pretty hard up -
it isn't much she get from Jean,
except for stacks of fish
and chancres by the dozen;
but she don't like fish
and crab make her sick.
It is beef she want;
but when he drop asleep dead drunk
and she fish in his pockets,
she is lucky if she find
a five-franc piece,
and then can only twitter
like a sparrow in the winter:
  O happy day! O happy day!
  When Jesus washed my sins away…

He is not a bad husband, though -
as husbands go:
he don't knock her about
and is a jolly fellow.
He is the most popular chap
among the Corbets and the Noyons
and all the pilots of Birdo,[10]
and it don't matter how rough it is
will put out in La Suzette,[11]
so there isn't a boatman isn't sorry
when one day in a squall
she is sunk in the Russel[12]
and he is drowned and never found,
and poor Madame Boissel
left a widow for years;
but she don't have to buy mourning
because she always wear black,

---

[10] *Cf. Ebenezer Le Page*, p. 6: 'He didn't have any schooling to speak of, but knocked around with the Noyon and Corbet boys of Birdo in the pilot boats…'.

[11] Presumably the name of a pilot boat?

[12] Little Russel – stretch of water between Guernsey and Herm; Great Russel – stretch of water between Herm and Sark; *cf.* above p. 217.

and the way it happens
save funeral expense,
so when she is going to shed a tear
in her sorrow,
she remember God's mercy
and sing instead:
  O happy day! O happy day!
  When Jesus washed my sins away…

Ah well, every dog have its day
and Madame Boissel pass away,
Though nobody in the Parish of the Vale believe she is
        gone.
I know I don't, for one -
she was always there;
I am but a boy of four,
I call her big fat 'oomie[13] -
my mother say that is rude,
but Madame Boissel don't care.
She say she got to have me
in the black shed at the back
to help her do the washing -
the work is too heavy for one person.
I watch her light the fire under the copper
and fill it with buckets of rain-water from the butt,
and the three zinc tubs on the bench when it boil:
the first is for the dirty,
the next the second wash,
and the third for the rinse in Reckitt's blue.[14]
The shed is a fog of steam -
I can smell the stench of wet clothes yet;
and while she rub and she scrub
in the tub of grey scum,
she sing as if she was in heaven on earth:
  O happy day! O happy day!
  When Jesus washed my sins away…

---

[13] Abel Martel calls his mother, Christine Mahy, 'Oomie', *Ebenezer Le* Page, p. 216.

[14] Used to whiten laundry, before the introduction of optical brighteners.

I am happy too,
stirring the chemises in the blue
with a bamboo;
but am not thinking the same thoughts as she is.
I am looking at the shelf
where the blacking and the brushes
for the boots and shoes are put,
and wishing I could black myself all over
and be a little nigger boy -
and then I would be happy always!
It is all right, I have grown up white
and sit on the Douzaine,[15]
and every Sunday go to Church and say my prayers.
Church don't make so much fuss
about being saved or being lost -
they sort of think the best is there for after,
at least hope it won't turn out to be the worst,
and in the meantime keep well in
with the powers-that-be on earth;
but sometimes when I, Peter Tostevin,
think how black I am within,
I wonder if it isn't a hot place I am bound for,
and then would give anything to be as sure
as was Madame Boissel when she sing:
  O happy day! O happy day!
  When Jesus washed my sins away…

She was clean in and out, was Madame Boissel,
and the cottage she live in as clean as a new pin -
as our house is Fridays when she have gone.
She start on l'âtre[16] and shovel
the ashes from underneath the terpid,[17]
and wipe with soap and flannel
the stone floor of the kitchen,
until you could eat your dinner off it.
Herself she won't sit down to table,

---

[15] Guernsey equivalent of a parish council.

[16] *l'âtre*: Guernésiais for hearth.

[17] *terpid*: Guernésiais for trivet, a three-legged stand, used for cooking over a fire.

only munch a Guernsey biscuit,[18]
or gobble a chunk of gâche[19]
and gulp down a mug of tea,
while she keep on going on the war-path against dirt.
She come to do the rough,
but do the smooth as well -
sweep the carpet on the stairs
and of the up-stair bed-rooms and the parlour -
flutter with a feather duster
like a big bird round the furniture,
and shine the looking-glasses
so you can't see the glass
and walk into yourself and say I am sorry!
She got a dust-pan and a brush,
but in her fluster she forget -
she put on a dazzling bright white apron in the
     morning,
but carry most of our dirt away on her at night;
and take the two francs she have earnt twice over,
but won't take a penny more and go home along the
     Braye,[20]
singing black as soot from head to foot:
  O happy day! O happy day!
  When Jesus washed my sins away...

All of a bustle and a hustle
is how I remember Madame Boissel
when I am a boy and a young man:
now father of a family,
I can't believe she is quiet,
yet stand at her death bed -
though not, I am ashamed to say,
to pay homage where it is due,
but because it is my duty as Le Procureur des
     Pauvres,[21]

---

[18] Bread roll or bap.

[19] *gâche* is traditional Guernsey fruit loaf.

[20] Main road in the Vale, where Gerald grew up in 'Hawkesbury'.

[21] Parish officer responsible for the administration of relief for the poor.

She have been out working since the age of ten,
but got to be buried on the Parish:
she got no relations living -
or any who will claim her carcase, if they are.
The last was Marie Antoinette -
that is not the name which she was christened with,
but the trade-name she was known by
in Cornet Street;[22]
and when the English soldiers come to Guernsey
to learn to kill the Kaiser,
she get the bad sickness
and go out of business
and end up in the mad-house,
gone in the head.
Madame Boissel say it only go to show -
she won't go in the head, she know,
so long as she can sing:
  O happy day! O happy day!
  When Jesus washed my sins away...

She is found by the neighbours
lying in a coma,
and when the ambulance is fetched
it take four strong men
to lift her on the stretcher.
The doctors are at a loss,
for she can't tell them where the pain is,
and if they cut her open
it will be a major operation -
and even then they won't know where to look!
They keep her living as best they can,
but the end is near are willing to bet;
and I am there and I will swear
her breath stop breathing
and her heart stop beating
and the doctors all agree
time of death eleven-thirty,

---

[22] Street in St Peter Port that was formerly the town's red light district; *cf. Ebenezer Le Page,* p. 43.

cause of death heart failure;
and Sister Mansell, who is Chapel,
say a happy release,
and Nurse Piprell, who is a Catholic,
say I will pray for her salvation,
when Madame Boissel open wide her mouth and croak
as loud as the fog-horn on the Casquets:[23]
  O happy day! O happy day!
  When Jesus washed my sins away...

It throw the whole of the hospital
into a flusteration -
the doctors and the nurses
go nearly off their heads,
and the dying patients
sit bolt upright in their beds.
Old Humbold, the head surgeon,
say it is a pure hallucination,
Sister Mansell say
it is a divine revelation.
Nurse Piprell say
a manifestation of the Devil;
but young Doctor John Sebire, M.B.,
who in nothing do believe,
but know all there is to know
about the central nervous system,
say there is no need to be a sceptic -
it is quite scientific:
a hen will run about
after its head is chopped off;
when to everybody's horror,
before she die good and proper,
they hear a wheezy whisper
come from God knows where:
  O happy day! O happy day!
  When Jesus washed my sins away...

---

[23] Les Casquets is an outcrop of rocks off the coast of Alderney. The lighthouse includes a powerful fog horn that can be heard within a range of 3 nautical miles. The Guernsey aficionado, A.C. Swinburne, published 'Les Casquets' in 1883/4.

## UNTITLED

I was born in the Haut Pas
of St Pierre-du-Bois
in a house built of stone
in sixteen-o-one –
the year is carved in the round arch over the door.
Three centuries it have been
before I appear on the scene,
the same and unchanged,
for living in arranged
as natural as a nest among the leaves of a tree.
The harvest of the fields,
the fish the sea yields
our bread, cider and pork
and long days of hard work
and no worry make our old stock last out.
My mother was a de Garis
before she marry,
my father of the Le Pages
live on the island for ages.
I am as Guernsey as Guernsey! If I'm not, then who is?

## PASTOR McCREE

Pastor McCree come to the Stone-workers' Hall
to preach the Gospel is Good Tiding for all.
I am no worse than many and better than most
but he make me to see I am predestined to roast.
I will never forget the night Pastor McCree
preach the Gospel is bad tidings for me.

## LEN CARRÉ, THE RAKE

Matthew, Mark, Luke and John
went to bed with their trousers on,
the bad boys used to sing at school;
but I was a good boy then and a fool
and until I became Len Carré, the Rake, I never knew
what wicked boys sing is often true.

## MESS ANDRÉ PRIAULX FROM LE MONT

Mess André Priaulx from Le Mont is my neighbour
and the Good Book say I ought to love my neighbour as
      myself;
but I don't love myself and therefore I cannot love him,
and he love himself and therefore he do not love me.
It is not for me to say the Good Book have led me up the
      garden
but I wish I could ask whoever wrote it what on earth am I
      to do –
I can never, never love Mess André Priaulx from Le Mont!

Mess André Priaulx from Le Mont is my neighbour
and I have to admit he is a man of very upright character,
and not a person in the Parish of the Câtel think different,
or but would look sideways on anybody who say otherwise;
and I am only Mister Fred de la Mare from La Maison à Bas –
which put in a nutshell all there is to be said on the subject –
I can never, never love Mess André Priaulx from Le Mont!

Mess André Priaulx from Le Mont is my neighbour
and his family tree is as straight up as a pine
without a notch in it from before the days of the Crusades,
or any by-blows on the wind anybody know of;
but mine is more like a knotted oak with branches right
      and left
sprouted on the right side and the wrong side of the blanket -
I can never, never love Mess André Priaulx from Le Mont!

Mess André Priaulx from Le Mont is my neighbour
and Elizabeth his good lady was de Compte of the Des
      Comptes
who was very important people in the reign of King John
and she have a pale thin face and a back without a bulge.
but my Amelia got a face like an apple and a bottom like a pear
and is of the Le Cheminants who was vraic-pickers at Albecq
      since the year dot -
I can never, never love Mess André Priaulx from Le Mont!

# APPENDIX 4

## GOD'S STEP-SON

### THE IMMACULATE CONCEPTION OF JESUS THEY CALL CHRIST [1]

#### 1

Bastard born, immaculate begot
in love incarnate by lust undefiled
among those far green Galilean hills,
mortal, immortal Son of God.

#### 2

Wingless angel, fire engendered,
Grecian youth of stalwart limb,
golden as the dawn is golden,
ruthless as the sun at noon.

#### 3

Hebrew maiden wandering lonesome,
humble, of unrecorded birth,
in the fading red of evening,
from the mean city of Nazareth.

#### 4

Was it by chance that fateful meeting,
when from the mist the new moon arose,
of those two alien, aimless wanderers,
or was it from the beginning decreed?

#### 5

They have no words to speak,
for divers tongues are silent:
hand touch hand and lip touch lip,
ears are deaf and eyes are blind.

---

[1] Gerald's Calvinist upbringing may account for his apparent belief that the Immaculate Conception refers to the conception of Jesus rather than that of the Virgin Mary, who was born free of Original Sin in anticipation of the birth of Christ. Likewise in his 1926 article on Bernard Shaw (see above p. 58), he refers to St Joan's inquisitor, John Lemaitre, as a 'Dominican monk', instead of a friar; *Adelphi*, p. 26. Raymond loses his job after a single sermon because 'he didn't believe in the Virgin Birth or the Resurrection'; *Ebenezer Le Page*, p. 190.

<u>6</u>

He in the darkness see
the pallid image of his wish,
she in willing weakness sense
the strong hunger of her need.

<u>7</u>

Equal in strength entwined,
writhing reach the abysmal height,
nor of before or after think,
nor of cause or consequence.

<u>8</u>

Light and dark a single star,
heaven and hell one place,
God and Satan reconciled
in a man-child conceived.

<u>9</u>

Striding away lithely over the hills,
singing blithely from desire satisfied,
unknowing, nor ever will he know
who is bequeathed to the world.

<u>10</u>

She in quiet rapture returning
to mother and home and household cares,
unaware of the Holy Infant
the secret womb enfolds.

…………

Where have you been, my girl, out all hours?
Only for a walk on my own, mother dear.
It is not right for a virgin
betrothed to a righteous man
to be gadding about half the night
with the riff-raff of the town!
I have done nothing bad, mother,
nothing bad:
I have never been so good,
so good.

## THE NATIVITY

The stars of night are silent
the silly sheep asleep
huddle soft and warm
against the bristling frost.
The good shepherds' crooks erect
lest one stray and get lost,
watching their flocks forget
they are for wool and meat.

## THE TEMPTATION [2]

Jesus beware! O mortal, beware!
Angels console when devils cease
to torment. They do not heal,
are not whole: will attend, will contend
to the end. Only then, Peace.

## THE SQUIB

Technicolor majesty
seriocomic travesty
of the divine right of Kings.
Constitutional monarchy,
mask of schizophrenic anarchy
whichever party reigns.

## THE BITTER WIND

The bitter wind from Eden
fans the angry flames
when the fire from heaven falls
on the Cities of the Plain.
God's sunset breaks in splendour
while those vile people burn
and through gates of broken glory
they pass into the dark.

---

[2] See Gerald's remarks to Murry on Christ's Temptation; *cf.* note on Kazantzakis, *Temptation of Christ*, p. 111.

# APPENDIX 5: CHRONOLOGY

1899     Gerald Basil Edwards born 8 July at Sous les Hougues in the Vale, son of 44-year-old Thomas Edwards, quarryman, and his 30-year-old, second wife, Harriet Mauger (whose sister is married to Tom's brother).

1901     By the date of the census, Tom and Harriet Edwards had moved with the 16-year-old Kathleen, one of two daughters by his previous wife, and their one-year-old son Gerald, to the more substantial 'Hawkesbury' in Braye Road.

1904     Kathleen Maud Smith born 16 May at 97 High Street, Peckham, daughter of Robert Frank Smith, Master Ironmonger, and his wife Harriet (*née* Roberts).

1905     Postcard addressed from Alderney to Gerald at Hawkesbury. Tom's mother lived on Alderney and when Archie Edwards got a girl pregnant she was sent there to have the baby.

1909     From the Hautes Capelles School, Gerald wins scholarship to the Boys' Intermediate School.

1913-14     October 1913-March 1914; sketches in surviving school sketchbook (signed 'Gerald Bazil Edwards') [Fig. 89].

1915     Pupil teacher at Hautes Capelles but left after his mother thought he was getting too fond of fellow-teacher Miss Waymouth and transferred to Vauvert School in St Peter Port.

1917     Called up to the Royal Guernsey Light Infantry. Serves as sergeant-instructor in gunnery but doesn't see action and ends up in Portsmouth. Half-sister, Rose, dies in London in February.

1919-23?     Attends Bristol University but leaves without graduating. In 1920 he passed his Intermediate Exam for the degree of B.Sc.

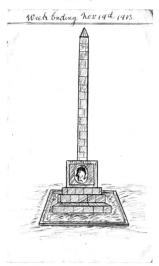

Fig. 89: *Saumarez Memorial*, from Gerald's 1913 sketchbook

1923      Works as an elementary school teacher. Obtains copy of birth certificate 5 July.

1924      Gerald's mother dies of a heart attack age 53 on 3 February. Funeral on the 7th with burial at St Sampson's cemetery. Tears up his mother's will leaving her possessions to him pending his father's death. His father 'sold the lot for old Mrs Cooke, the house-keeper.' Collis publishes *Shaw*.

1925      Teaches at Toynbee Hall. Moves to Ide Hill, Sevenoaks, Kent. Finishes a play entitled: '*Millstones*'. Begins writing for Middleton Murry's *Adelphi*. Visits Guernsey with his fiancée, Kathleen, around this time.

1926      July issue of the *Adelphi* features Gerald's critique of Bernard Shaw. Collis had published book on Shaw the previous year. On 14 September marries 22-year-old Kathleen Maude Smith, elementary school teacher and daughter of engineer Robert Frank Smith.

1927      17 December 1927; birth of first child, Adam, at 60 South Hill Park, Hampstead.

1928      At the Sanctuary, Vera Pragnell's Sussex commune. Commissioned by Cape to write book on D.H. Lawrence. In late spring they leave for Switzerland planning to meet Lawrence. June 1928 c/o Gerhard Spinner, Erstfeld, Kanton Uri. Sends Murry his play *Margaret*.

1929      23 February 1929, about to leave Erstfeld; moves to Alfredo Weilenmann, Carpanteria, Ascona. Writes to Murry from Weilenmann's on 7 March and Collis on 11th. 28 March sends Collis telegram 'wire twenty francs'. Writing *Jesus*. Back in Erstfeld 15 July. Murry takes review of Geoffrey West's *The Life of Annie Besant*, which appears as 'Humanism versus Theosophy' in September-November issue of *The New Adelphi*. By 9 November 'bei Frau Rami, "Konsum,"' Flüelen, Switzerland. Review-article of Krishnamurti's *Life in Freedom* in *The New Adelphi* (December 1929).

1930      1 January reports to Murry he has written to Lady Lutyens. Kathleen and Adam return to London in January to have second baby. Sends Murry manuscript of another play: *Waysmeet*. Death of D.H. Lawrence 2 March 1930. Seven more weeks in Flüelen, then returns to London where daughter, Dorcas, was born on 16 April. To early summer address remains 59 Victoria Road, Finsbury Park, London N4. By mid-May at Moor House, Westerham, Kent. Critical review of Potter's book on Lawrence in the June-August issue of the *Adelphi*. In August 1930 asks Murry to recommend him to Dorothy Elmhirst. Richard Rees takes over editorship of *Adelphi* in October 1930 (-1938). Publishes review of Velona Pilcher's *The Searcher* in *Adelphi*, November 1930. Play featuring Gerald, Kathleen and Solomon Ben Simon scheduled to be performed at Dartington. *News of the Day* for Tuesday 25 November is the announcement of: 'a play called "*Sonny*" by G.B. Edwards'.

1931    Writes to Murry from 'Ayreville, Totnes Road, Paignton, Devon', on 9 January, asking him to visit. Discusses 'The Education of John Jones' in February at Dartington. Visits Murry's at Yateley on 3 March; stays the night and drives up to London with him next morning. Murry's wife, Violet, dies 30 March. 18 April writes to Murry from Vue Charmante, Liverton, Newton Abbot, Devon. 31 May lecturing for the WEA (East Devon Extension Scheme); living at 'The Brackens', Raymonds Hill, near Axminster, Devon. Review of Lawrence Hyde's *Prospects of Humanism* in June *Adelphi*. To Holland with Richard Rees early July. Reviews Ede's *Savage Messiah* in September *Adelphi*. October issue of *Adelphi* features article on 'Religion'. Solomon Simon's son, David, born to Kathleen: 31 December.

1932-5  Kathleen has a fourth child, John Enoch, by Gordon Cruickshank, 4 May 1935; registered citing Gerald as the father, 'Lecturer in English Literature'; place of birth and her current residence: 8 Little Bath Street (Clerkenwell/ Holborn). Marriage ends. All four children given the surname Edwards but cared for by the Elmhirsts, who pay Adam's school fees and arrange for him to be fostered by a family in Totnes. When this family moves away, because Kathleen didn't want him adopted, Adam is fostered by John and Peggy Wales at Dartington.

1937    In April, Archie Edwards visits Guernsey from America to see ailing mother Rachel who dies 20 December.

1938    Gerald returns to Guernsey to visit his father at Les Rosiers, Les Effards, St Sampson's.

1938-39 Living in attic of Mass Observation headquarters, 85 Davenport Street, in Bolton, working part-time for M.O., and for Bolton Corporation, establishing the Bolton Drama School and producing plays at the Bolton Little Theatre.

1939-   Plays the part of the adjudicator in Cedric Mount's *Dirge Without Dole* and directs Strindberg's *Easter* at Bolton Little

Theatre: 10 and 11 March. Moves to Chorley Old Road, Bolton. Dorcas goes to America with the Elmhirsts during the war. Gerald finds work with the Ministry of Labour.

1943    The husband of Gerald's half-sister, Kathleen Edwards, Augustus Thoumine, commits suicide in Guernsey, she having long-since left the island with her daughter, with whose husband she had an affair.

1945    Living in lodgings at 23 Chepstow Road, Notting Hill.

1946    Gerald's father dies aged 89. Buried at the Foulon Cemetery 'in an old Rangers Red and Black shirt' with Rosina Cooke's first husband, Sergeant Charles Cooke, rather than with his second wife, Gerald's mother.

1947    Living at 9 Ritherdon Road, Balham (landlady Miss Violet Mary Beresford, who had lived there since 1929). He writes to Middleton Murry enclosing poem for the *Adelphi*: 'Song of a Man who saw God.' (See Appendix 1).

1956-58  Electoral rolls record him living at 9 Ritherdon Road. In the late 1950s Gerald has successful reunion with Potter but not followed up.

1961    Still living at 9 Ritherdon Road, Balham (listed in 1962 electoral roll), having meanwhile retired and spent a year, 'living rough' in Wales. Writes from Ritherdon Road on Christmas Eve to cousin Hilda in Guernsey: 'feeling depressed and worn out and not at all like Christmas.' Thinking of moving to Southampton, where would call on Hilda's daughter and visit Guernsey.

1961-67  Moves to Penzance (1961-64; though *cf.* letter from Balham dated 24 December 1961) and Plymouth (1964-67); *cf.* his references to inspiration in Penzance and living there for three years cited above p. 201. Probably visits Scilly Isles in this period.

1967    Moves to Weymouth and gets in touch with daughter, Dorcas. Visits Hilda Dumond in Guernsey and asks for copy of his mother's photograph. Tells her how he had torn up his mother's will. Stays at Mrs Mead at Les Galliennes, Torteval.

1969    Death of Gerald's wife, Kathleen, aged 65, in Tolmers Park Hospital, Hatfied, 16 February.

1972    1971-72 lodges with Bert and Joan Snell, 654 Dorchester Road, Upwey, Weymouth, in Dorset. In May, moves to 'Rose View', 4 Coker Marsh, East Coker in Somerset with a frail friend 'Olive'. He returns to the Snells and that summer he meets art student Edward Chaney who is staying with his great-aunt in Upwey. They become friends and he informs Chaney that he is writing a novel set in Guernsey.

1973    11 September: gives Josephine Chaney Uttley's *Story of the Channel Islands*, inscribing it: 'For Jo, on her 85th Birthday. From her old Guernsey Donkey, Gerald.'

1974    Works throughout first half of year on completing final draft of *Sarnia Chérie: The Book of Ebenezer Le Page* and on 3 August presents the typescript to Edward and Lisa Chaney. On 12 August he sends Chaney formal document giving 'unconditionally the definitive Typescript' to him, echoing Ebenezer's gift of his *Book* to Neville Falla. Over the next two years Chaney delivers a copy of the typescript to a series of London publishers, including Capes, Cassells, Faber and Calder and Boyars, all of whom reject it.

1975    5 July: Gerald sends Chaney 'a couple of spontaneous lyrics – as L'ENVOI to SARNIA CHÉRIE' on the eve of his departure for Lerwick on Shetland. 28 August: Returns to the Snells. 24 September: Dorcas returns photocopy of *Book*. Fabers reject *Sarnia Chérie*.

1976    16 February: Gerald leaves for the Scilly Isles. Returns to Upwey on the 19th. Asks Chaney for the typescript back as he is 'retyping (with Carbon) the whole thing, and making sundry changes'. He goes to south Wales in July, having 'got rid of all fragments, correspondence and records'. 19 August: cheered by a report by John Mellors. Dies of a heart attack at the Snells on 29 December. Some months later his ashes are brought over to St Peter Port and scattered in the harbour.

1977    Gerald's cousin, Hilda Dumond, dies aged 85.

1978    Rejection of typescript by Frederick Muller Ltd. 26 January.

1979    Through a friend in Florence, Chaney persuades Hamish Hamilton to read the typescript and in October 1979 a contract is signed.

1981    Having abridged the title and arranged for John Fowles to write an introduction, Hamish Hamilton publish *The Book of Ebenezer Le Page* to great critical acclaim. Republished by Penguin as a paperback the following year and Knopf in America, where it is subsequently published in paperback by Moyer Bell.

1982    A French translation by Jeanine Hérisson is published by

Maurice Nadeau with a C.N.L. grant as *Sarnia*. Wins the 4th Baudelaire Prize for translation. The *Book* is broadcast on Radio 4's *Woman's Hour* in 28 five-minute episodes, read by Roy Dotrice. Martin Ellis of Crescent Films buys option.

1991    Illustrated features by Nick Le Messurier in *Guernsey Evening Press* for 3 September and 7 September 1991 ('Weekender') entitled 'Ebenezer may 'Go on the Box' and 'The Land of Ebenezer Le Page', reporting visit by Chaney to Guernsey, hosted by Ian and Deirdre Harris.

1994    8 February: Chaney lectures on 'G.B. Edwards and *The Book of Ebenezer Le Page*' to the Guernsey Society, London. Lecture published in a series of articles in *The Review of the Guernsey Society*. The Penguin edition of *The Book of Ebenezer Le Page* re-issued on 27 October.

1995    26 February: Chaney meets Gerald's children, Adam and Dorcas, at Dartington. 21 March: Chaney gives revised version of G.B. Edwards lecture at St James's, St Peter Port and interviewed on BBC Guernsey. Attempts to re-broadcast Roy Dotrice's abridged reading of the Book fail due to BBC's failure to locate the recording.

1996    Jonathan Weeks, 'Old Guernsey Donkey', article in 'Resurrection' section in *Literary Review*, June issue, pp. 56-7 (commissioned by Auberon Waugh).

2001    Vittorio Gabrieli publishes article on 'Il libro di Ebenezer Le Page' in *La Cultura*, no. 2., pp. 295-301. (He had translated the entire book into Italian during his wife's final illness).

2002    6-14 September: Roy Dotrice and Emma Cleasby appear at The Theatre Royal, Lincoln, in an adaptation of the book entitled 'The Islander' by Anthony Wilkinson.

2006    Second French edition of *Sarnia* published by *Editions Points*.

2007    *The Book of Ebenezer Le Page* is republished by New York Review of Books in their 'Classics' series (R.B. Kitaj lends rights of 'Blake's God' for cover). The Italian translation *Il Libro di Ebenezer Le Page* is published by Elliot Edizioni in the same year.

2008    Keith Jacka's essay on *The Book of Ebenezer Le Page* in *The Salisbury Review* (Spring 2008). Guernsey's first Blue Plaque is erected at 'Hawkesbury', the house on Braye Road where Gerald lived with his parents from 1900 to 1916. Unveiled 24 September by Jane Mosse and Chaney [Fig. 90].

2009    Joyce Cook's theatrical production of *The Book of Ebenezer Le*

*Page* by Guernsey Amateur Dramatic and Operatic Company (GADOC), St Peter Port, Guernsey, Easter 2009.

2011    Exhibition organised by Amanda Bennett, Jane Mosse and Edward Chaney, with lecture by latter, at the Priaulx Library for the first Guernsey Literary Festival.

2012    Roy Dotrice makes complete, 21-hour recording of *The Book of Ebenezer Le Page* for AudioGo, now Audible. AQA uses passage from the novel on ormers for A level English language exam (11 June 2012).

2014    Paperback edition of the Italian edition of *Il Libro di Ebenezer Le Page* (Elliot Edizioni).

2015    Launch of *Genius Friend: G.B. Edwards and The Book of Ebenezer Le Page*, at the 4th Guernsey Literary Festival, 17 September.

Fig. 90: The author and Jane Mosse unveiling the Blue Plaque on Gerald's home, Hawkesbury, 24 September 2008 (Guernsey Press)

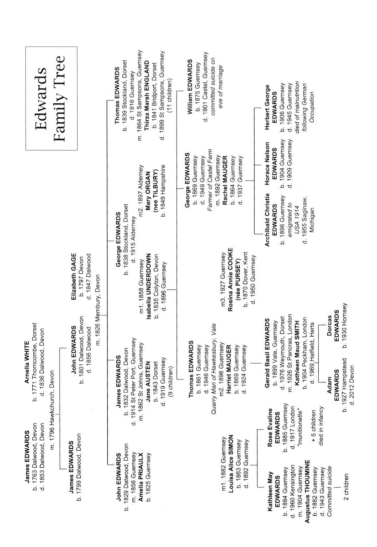

## Edwards Family Tree

**James EDWARDS**
b. 1763 Dalwood, Devon
d. 1853 Dalwood, Devon

m. 1796 Hawkchurch, Devon

**Amelia WHITE**
b. 1771 Thorncombe, Dorset
d. 1836 Dalwood, Devon

**James EDWARDS**
b. 1799 Dalwood, Devon

**John EDWARDS**
b. 1801 Dalwood, Devon
d. 1856 Dalwood

m. 1826 Membury, Devon

**Elizabeth GAGE**
b. 1797 Devon
d. 1847 Dalwood

**George EDWARDS**
b. 1838 Stockland, Dorset
d. 1915 Alderney

m1. 1858 Guernsey
**Isabella UNDERDOWN**
b. 1835 Colyton, Devon
d. 1896 Guernsey

m2. 1897 Alderney
**Mary ORGAN**
(née TILBURY)
b. 1849 Hampshire

**Thomas EDWARDS**
b. 1839 Stockland, Dorset
d. 1916 Guernsey

m. 1864 St Sampsons, Guernsey
**Thirza Marsh ENGLAND**
b. 1841 Bridport, Dorset
d. 1899 St Sampsons, Guernsey
(11 children)

**John EDWARDS**
b. 1829 Dalwood, Devon
m. 1856 Guernsey
**Amelia PRIAULX**
b. 1825 Guernsey

**James EDWARDS**
b. 1832 Dalwood, Devon
d. 1914 St Peter Port, Guernsey
m. 1862 St Johns, Guernsey
**Jane AUSTEN**
b. 1843 Dorset
d. 1919 Guernsey
(9 children)

**Thomas EDWARDS**
b. 1861 Guernsey
d. 1946 Guernsey
*Quarry Man of Hawkesbury, Vale*

m1. 1882 Guernsey
**Harriet MAUGER**
b. 1869 Guernsey
d. 1924 Guernsey

m2. 1896 Guernsey

m3. 1927 Guernsey
**Rosina Annie COOKE**
(née PURSEY)
b. 1870 Dover, Kent
d. 1950 Guernsey

**George EDWARDS**
b. 1869 Guernsey
d. 1949 Guernsey
*Farmer of Castel Farm*
m. 1892 Guernsey
**Rachel MAUGER**
b. 1864 Guernsey
d. 1937 Guernsey

**William EDWARDS**
b. 1875 Guernsey
d. 1901 Castel, Guernsey
*committed suicide on
eve of marriage*

**Archibald Christie EDWARDS**
b. 1896 Guernsey
*emigrated to
USA 1914*
d. 1955 Saginaw,
Michigan

**Horace Nelson EDWARDS**
b. 1904 Guernsey
d. 1909 Guernsey

**Herbert George EDWARDS**
b. 1906 Guernsey
d. 1945 Guernsey
*died of malnutrition
following German
Occupation*

**Kathleen May EDWARDS**
b. 1884 Guernsey
d. 1960 Kensington
m. 1904 Guernsey
**Augustus THOUMINE**
b. 1882 Guernsey
d. 1943 Guernsey
*Committed suicide*

2 children

**Rose Evaline EDWARDS**
b. 1885 Guernsey
d. 1917 London
*"munitionette"*

+ 5 children
died in infancy

**Gerald Basil EDWARDS**
b. 1899 Vale, Guernsey
d. 1976 Weymouth, Dorset
m. 1926 St Pancras, London
**Kathleen Maud SMITH**
b. 1904 Peckham, London
d. 1969 Hatfield, Herts

**Adam EDWARDS**
b. 1927 Hampstead
d. 2012 Devon

**Dorcas EDWARDS**
b. 1930 Hornsey

Louisa Alice SIMON
b. 1863 Guernsey
d. 1892 Guernsey

Fig. 91: Edwards Family Tree (Stephen Foote)

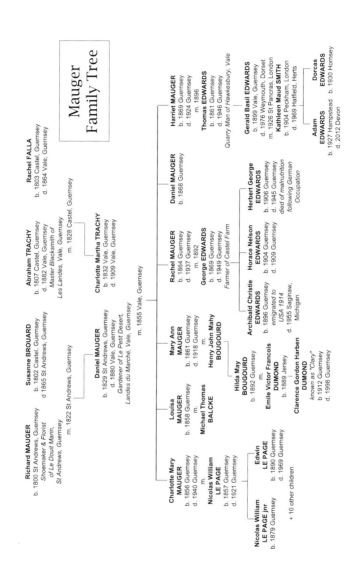

Fig. 92: Mauger Family Tree (Stephen Foote)

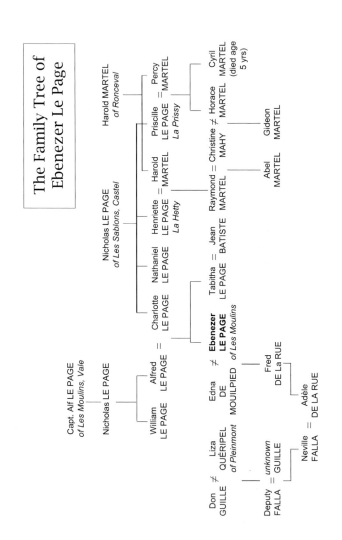

Fig. 93: Family Tree of Ebenezer Le Page (Stephen Foote)

# BIBLIOGRAPHY

**Works of G.B. Edwards:**

Edwards, G.B., Complete typescript, with amendments, of *Sarna Chérie: The Book of Ebenezer Le Page* (1974; revised over subsequent two years); author's collection.

\_\_\_\_\_, *The Book of Ebenezer Le Page*, Hamish Hamilton, London, 1981 (with an introduction by John Fowles). Subsequent editions also in French and Italian. Edition cited here New York Review Books Classics edition (2007) which is a facsimile of the first.

\_\_\_\_\_, unpublished letters to the author (author's collection).

\_\_\_\_\_, unpublished letters to John Middleton Murry (all but one in author's collection with exception in Alexander Turnbull Library, Wellington, New Zealand).

\_\_\_\_\_, unpublished letters to J.S. Collis (from copies courtesy of Richard Ingrams and Michael Holroyd).

\_\_\_\_\_, unpublished letter to Hilda Dumond dated 24 December 1961 (copy supplied by Clary Dumond).

\_\_\_\_\_, 'Shaw ', *The Adelphi*, IV, i (July 1926), pp. 17-32.

\_\_\_\_\_, 'Humanism versus Theosophy', *The New Adelphi*, II, 6 (September-November 1929), pp. 36-48.

\_\_\_\_\_, 'Krishnamurti', *The New Adelphi* magazine, III, 2 (December 1929), pp. 146-70.

\_\_\_\_\_, 'Lawrence and the Young Man', *The Adelphi* (incorporating 'The New Adelphi'), new series, III, 4 (June-August 1930) pp. 310-16.

\_\_\_\_\_, 'The Drama, the War, and Woman', *The Adelphi*, new series, I, ii (November 1930), pp. 161-64.

\_\_\_\_\_, 'A Prospective Religion', *The Adelphi*, new series, III, 2 (June 1931), pp. 257-59.

\_\_\_\_\_, 'The Lost Boy', *The Adelphi,* new series, III (September 1931), pp. 541-44.

\_\_\_\_\_, 'Religion', *The Adelphi*, new series, III, i (October, 1931), pp. 50-53.

\_\_\_\_\_, 'Rosmersholm: A Modern Play', *The Adelphi*, new series, IV (1932), pp. 292-95.

\_\_\_\_\_, *Poems* (first published above from typescripts and manuscripts in the author's possession).

**Unpublished and/or no longer extant writings by G.B. Edwards:**

*Margaret*, *Millstones* and *Waysmeet* (plays). *Jesus* (monograph).

'Essay on Sex' (20,000 word essay, 1930).

*Sonny* (play) (performed Dartington Hall, 18 Nov 1930).

*The Idea of Ideas* (mentioned in correspondence with J.S. Collis).

'The Education of John Jones' (lecture Dartington Hall, 6 Feb 1931).

## A Note on the *Adelphi*:

*The Adelphi* was launched by Middleton Murry in 1923 and ran for more than 270 issues. Between September 1927 and August 1930 it was known as *The New Adelphi* before reverting back to *The Adelphi* (at first 'incorporating the New Adelphi') until its demise in September 1955. Murry edited it from 1923 up to an including the Lawrence issue of June-August 1930. It was monthly until August 1927 and quarterly until this issue and then monthly again until December 1941. Murry's editorial in the June-August 1930 issue announced that he would be unable to continue editing the magazine in its renewed monthly form so that it 'will be henceforward edited by Mr. Max Plowman, assisted by Sir Richard Rees' (though subsequent issues in 1930 had them both listed on the front cover as joint editors, perhaps partly in acknowledgement of the fact that Rees was funding it). In fact Rees seems to have taken at least half-responsibility and this situation prevailed until September 1938 when Plowman continued as sole editor until Murry resumed the reins again in 1941, remaining as editor until 1948. Henry Williamson edited it in 1949, George Goodwin in 1950 and B. Ifor Evans from 1951 until the concluding issue in 1955.

## Unpublished letters and memoirs.

Burgess, Wilfrid de Lisle, Correspondence with the author (1981-83)

_____, 'Letter', 19 September 1981.

_____, 'Comments on "The Book of Ebenezer Le Page" by W. de L. B.', typescript c. 1981.

Collis, J.S., *The Realist,* part of typescript of unpublished autobiographical novel, and correspondence with G.B. Edwards; loaned by Richard Ingrams and Michael Holroyd: now Trinity College Library, Dublin.

_____, *Progress of an Artist*, typescript of unpublished novel; chapter X, copy provided by Richard Ingrams and Michael Holroyd.

Dumond, Clary, Correspondence with the author and copies of correspondence with Hamish Hamilton (1981-97).

Fowles, John, Correspondence with the author and annotated draft introduction to *The Book of Ebenezer Le Page* (1980-1997).

Murry, John Middleton, Diary (unpublished), MS-Group-0411, Alexander Turnbull Library, New Zealand.

Potter, Julian, Correspondence with the author (1986-95).

Potter, Stephen, unpublished autobiography, vol. II (incomplete) and miscellaneous documents, loaned to the author by his son, Julian Potter; now in the University of Texas Library at Austin.

Walter, Franz Wilfred, account of 'The Sanctuary', Storrington (in possession of Josie Walter).

## Archives & Library Sources

Greffe, Guernsey

   Contrats de Partage

Contrats pour la Date.
Contrats pour Lire.
Wills of personalty, Ecclesiastical Court.

Priaulx Library, Guernsey

Parish baptism, marriage and burial records.
Burial Records of the Foulon Cemetery.
Historic Newspaper Collection

'Fatality at the Castel', *Guernsey Evening Press*, Saturday 25 May 1901.
'Death of a Guernsey War Worker: The Late Miss Rose Edwards', *Guernsey Evening Press*, 24 February 1917.
'Son Finds Father Dead', *Guernsey Evening Press*, 4 October 1943.

Alderney

Births, deaths and marriages records for Alderney.

Devon Record Office, Exeter

Baptisms, marriages and burials registers for Dalwood, Membury, Musbury, Hawkchurch, Colyton.

Dorset Record Office, Dorchester

Baptisms, marriages and burials registers for Thorncombe.

Storrington & District Museum, West Sussex

The Sanctuary, Newspaper cuttings file

'Simple Life Colony in Sussex', *The Daily Chronicle*, 24 January 1925.
'The Simple Life', *Daily Express*, 10 August 1928.

Bolton Little Theatre

'Advertisement', *Bolton Evening News*, 3 March 1939.
The Showman [John Wardle], 'Both Sides of the Curtain', *Bolton Evening News*, 4 March 1939.
'Good Acting: "Easter" and "Dirge Without Dole": Competent Presentation by Bolton Drama School', *Bolton Evening News*, 11 March 1939.
The Showman [John Wardle], 'Both Sides of the Curtain', *Bolton Evening News*, 11 March 1939.

National Archives

Census records 1841-1911 for Guernsey, Devon & Dorset.

General Records Office

Births, marriages and deaths 1837-present.

## Published Sources

Aldington, Richard, *Pinorman: Personal Recollections of Norman Douglas, Pino Orioli and Charles Prentice* (London, 1954).

_____, *Frieda Lawrence and her Circle*, eds H.T. Moore, and D.B. Montague (London, 1981).

Allen, Ann Taylor, *Feminism and Motherhood in Western Europe, 1890-1970: The Maternal Dilemma* (New York and London, 2005).

Angelides, Steven, *A History of Bisexuality* (Chicago, 2001).

Armstrong, Richard H., *A Compulsion for Antiquity: Freud and the Ancient World* (Ithaca, N.Y., 2005).

Bachofen, J.J., *An English Translation of Bachofen's Mutterrecht (Mother Right) (1861): A Study of the Religious and Juridicial Aspects of Gynecocracy in the Ancient World*, ed. David Partenheimer, 2 vols (Lampeter, 2003 and 2007).

_____, *Myth, religion, and mother right: selected writings of J. J. Bachofen*, trans. Ralph Manheim from *Mutterrecht und Urreligion*, ed. Rudolf Marx, with a preface by George Boas, introduction by Joseph Campbell (London, 1967).

Barrie, J.M., *Sentimental Tommy, The Story of his Boyhood* (London, 1896).

_____, *Tommy and Grizel* (London, 1900).

Barth, Karl, *Church Dogmatics, III, part 3, The Doctrine of Creation* (London, 2010).

Becket, Fiona, 'Lawrence and Psychoanalysis', *The Cambridge Companion to D.H. Lawrence*, ed. Anne Fernihough (Cambridge, 2001).

Bell, Thomas H., *Edward Carpenter: The British Tolstoi* (Los Angeles, 1932).

Bennett, Alan, 'The Wrong Blond', *London Review of Books*, VII, no. 9 (23 May 1985) (review of Dorothy Farnan, Auden in Love (London, 1984).

Bentley, Gerald ed., *William Blake: The Critical Heritage* (London, 1975).

Berman, Bruce, 'Ethnography as Politics, Politics as Ethnography: Kenyatta, Malinowski, and the Making of Facing Mount Kenya', *Canadian Journal of African Studies / Revue Canadienne des Études Africaines*, XXX, 3 (Ottawa, 1996), pp. 313-44.

Bertschinger-Joos, Esther and R. Butz, *Ernst Frick 1881-1956: Anarchist in Zürich, Künstler und Forscher in Ascona, Monte Verità* (Zurich, 2014).

_____, *Frieda Gross. Ihr Leben und ihre Briefe an Else Jaffé* (Zürich, 2014).

Blackwood, Beatrice, *Both Sides of Buka Passage: An Ethnographic Study of Social,v Sexual and Economic Questions in the North-Western Solomon Islands* (Oxford, 1935).

Blair, E.A., '*Alexander Pope* by Edith Sitwell and *The Course of English Classicism* by Sherard Vines', *The New Adelphi*, III, 4, June-August 1930.

Blake, William, *The Book of Urizen* (London, 1794).

_____, *The Marriage of Heaven and Hell* (London, 1790).

Bloom, Harold, *The Western Canon* (London, 1994).

_____, *The Daemon Knows: Literary Greatness and the American Sublime* (New York, 2015).

Boulton, James T., 'Editing D.H. Lawrence's Letters: The Editor's Creative Role', *Prose Studies*, XIX, no. 2 (August 1996), pp. 211-20.

Browning, Robert, 'Waring', *The Collected Poems of Robert Browning* (London, 2011).

Bunting, Basil, *Briggflatts* (London, 1966).

Burdett, Carolyn, '"The Subjective inside us can turn into Objective outside": Vernon Lee's Psychological Aesthetics', *19: Interdisciplinary Studies in the Long Nineteenth Century*, no. 12 (2011), DOI: dx.doi.org/10.16995/ntn.610.

Burleigh, Michael, *Earthly Powers: Religion and Politics in Europe from the Enlightenment to the Great War* (London, 2005).

_____, *Sacred Causes: Religion and Politics from the European Dictators to Al Qaeda* (London, 2006).

Butler, Samuel, *Way of All Flesh* (London, 1903)

Callow, Philip, *Son and Lover. The Young D.H. Lawrence* (London, 1975).

Carey, John, *William Golding: The Man who wrote Lord of the Flies* (London, 2009).

Carpenter, Edward, *Towards Democracry: A Prose Poem* (London, 1883).

_____, *Art of Creation* (London, 1904).

_____, *Pagan and Christian Creeds: Their Origin and Meaning* (London, 1920).

Carswell, Catherine, *The Savage Pilgrimage* (London, 1932).

Carswell, John, *Lives and Letters* (London, 1978).

Cassavant, Sharron Greer, *John Middleton Murry: The Critic as Moralist* (Alabama, 1982).

Chambers, Jessie, *D.H. Lawrence: A Personal Record by E.T.* (London, 1935).

Chaney, Edward, 'GB Edwards and the Book of Ebenezer Le Page', *Review of the Guernsey Society*, 3 parts: L, iii (Winter 1994), LI, i (Spring 1995), LI, iii (Autumn 1995).

_____, *The Evolution of the Grand Tour: Anglo-Italian Cultural Relations since the Renaissance*, 2nd ed. (London, 2000).

_____, review-article of *A Compulsion for Antiquity: Freud and the Ancient World*, by Richard H. Armstrong  (Ithaca, 2005), in *Psychoanalysis and History*, vol. 9, no,. 1 (2007), pp. 123-30.

_____, 'Warburgian Artist: R.B. Kitaj, Edgar Wind, Ernst Gombrich and the Warburg Institute', in  *Obsessions: R.B. Kitaj (1932-2007)* (Berlin, 2012), pp. 97-103.

Chaney, Lisa, *Hide and Seek with Angels: A Life of J.M. Barrie* (London, 2005).

Chapman, G.M., *Dalwood: A Short History of an East Devon Village* (Bridport, 2002).

Clute, John, 'Richard Cowper', *Science Fiction Writers*, ed. R. Bleiler, 2nd ed (New York, 1999).

_____, 'Murry, John Middleton Murry (1926-2002)', *Oxford Dictionary of National Biography* (Oxford, 2006), online edition May 2014).

Collis, J.S., *Shaw* (London, 1925).

\_\_\_\_, *An Irishman's England* (London, 1937).

\_\_\_\_, *Marriage and Genius: Strindberg and Tolstoy: Studies in Tragi-Comedy* (London, 1963).

\_\_\_\_, *Leo Tolstoy: A Polestar Pictorial Biography* (London, 1969).

\_\_\_\_, *Bound upon a Course* (London, 1971).

\_\_\_\_, *The Vision of Glory* (London, 1972).

\_\_\_\_, *The Worm forgives the Plough* (London, 1975).

\_\_\_\_, 'Memories of a Genius Friend', *The Spectator* (31 July 1982), pp. 21-23.

Collis, Robert, *The Silver Fleece* (London, 1936).

Conrad, Joseph, *The Nigger of the 'Narcissus'* (London, 1897).

\_\_\_\_, 'Amy Foster', *Illustrated London News* (London, 1901).

\_\_\_\_, *Nostromo* (London, 1904).

\_\_\_\_, 'The Secret Sharer', *Harper's Magazine* (New York, 1910).

\_\_\_\_, *Under Western Eyes* (London, 1911).

Corke, Hilary, review of F.A. Lea, *The Life of John Middleton Murry*, in *Encounter* (January 1960), pp. 75-77.

Cowper, Richard, *Recollections of a Ghost* (London, 1960).

Crick, Bernard, *George Orwell: A Life* (London, 1980).

Crockel, Carl, *D.H. Lawrence and Germany: The Politics of Influence* (London, 2007).

Cruickshank, Charles, *The German Occupation of the Channel Islands* (London, 1975).

Cruickshank, Gordon and Philip O'Connor, 'Readers, you are our Writers', *Seven 2* (March 1941).

Culme-Seymour, Angela, *Bolter's Grand-daughter* (Oxford, 2001).

Davenport-Hines, Richard, *Auden* (London, 1995).

\_\_\_\_, *Ettie: The Intimate Life And Dauntless Spirit Of Lady Desborough* (London, 2008).

\_\_\_\_, *Universal Man: The Seven Lives of John Maynard Keynes* (London, 2015)

Davies, Cecil, *The Adelphi Players: The Theatre of Persons,* ed. Peter Billingham (London, 2002).

Davies, Ross, *'A Student in Arms': Donald Hankey and Edwardian Society at War* (London, 2013).

Davies, Rhys, *Print of a Hare's Foot* (London, 1969).

Dennison, Matthew, *Behind the Mask: The Life of Vita Sackville-West* (London, 2014).

De Gruyter, Jan, *Het Leven en de Werken van Eduard Douwes Dekker (Multatuli)* (Amsterdam, 1920).

De Zordo, Ornella, *Una Proposta Anglofiorentina degli Anni Trenta: The Lungarno Series* (Florence, 1981).

Dijkstra, Bram, *Idols of Perversity: Fantasies of Feminine Evil in Fin-de-Siecle Culture* (Oxford, 1986).

_____, *Evil Sisters: The Threat of Female Sexuality and the Cult of Manhood* (New York, 1996).

Dostoyevsky, Fyodor, *The Brothers Karamazov*, trans. Constance Garnett (London, 1912).

Drabble, Margaret (ed.), *Oxford Companion to English Literature*, 6th edition (Oxford, 1998).

Ede, H.S., *The Savage Messiah* (London, 1931).

Edwards, Paul, *Wyndham Lewis, Painter and Writer* (London, 2000).

Egremont, Max, *Some Desperate Glory: The First World War the Poets Knew* (London, 2014).

Eliot, T.S., 'Tradition and the Individual Talent' (1917), *Selected Essays* (London, 1932), pp.13-22.

_____, *Ash Wednesday* (London, 1930).

_____, *After Strange Gods: A Primer of Modern Heresy* (London, 1934).

_____, *Collected Poems 1909-1962* (London, 1963).

_____, *The Letters of T. S. Eliot,* eds Valerie Eliot, Hugh Haughton and John Haffenden, 5 vols (London, 1988-2014).

Farr, Diana, *Gilbert Cannan: A Georgian Prodigy (*London, 1978).

Findlay, Jean, *Chasing Lost Time: The Life of C.K. Scott Moncrieff – Soldier, Spy and Translator* (London, 2014).

Fitchett, William Henry, *The Unrealised Logic of Religion* (London, 1905).

Ford, Hilary, *Sarnia* (London [Hamish Hamilton], 1974).

Fowles, John, *The French Lieutenant's Woman* (London, 1969).

_____, *Wormholes: Essays and Occasional Writings* (London, 1998).

Frazer, James George, *The Golden Bough: A Study in Comparative Religion,* 3rd edition, 12 vols (1906-15).

Freeman, M, 'Fellowship, service and the "spirit of adventure": the Religious Society of Friends and the outdoors movement in Britain c.1900-1950.' *Quaker Studies*, 14 (2009), pp. 72-92.

Freud, Sigmund, *Totem and Taboo* (1913). (New York, 1918).

_____, *Beyond the Pleasure Principle* (1920). (London, 1922).

Fussell, Paul, *The Great War and Modern Memory* (Oxford, 1975).

Gabrieli, Vittorio, 'Il libro di Ebenezer Le Page', *La Cultura*, no. 2 (2001), pp. 295-301.

Gale, Steven H. (ed.), *Encyclopedia of British Humorists: Geoffrey Chaucer to John Cleese*, II (1996).

Gilmour, David, *The Last Leopard: Life of Giuseppe di Lampedusa* (London, 1988; 5th edition, 2007).

Girard, Peter, 'The Stone Industry', *Transactions of La Société Guernesiaise*, XXI, ii (1982), pp. 202-08.

Goldie, David, *A Critical Difference: T.S. Eliot and John Middleton Murry in English Literary Criticism, 1919-1928* (London, 1998).

Goodall, Peter, '*The Book of Ebenezer Le Page*: Guernsey and the Channel Islands in the 20th Century', *The 2nd International Small Island Cultures*

Conference, Museum Theatre, Norfolk Island Museum ed. H. Johnson, 9-13 February 2006, pp. 54-60.

_____, 'The Spell of Sarnia: Fictional Representations of the Island of Guernsey', Shima: The International Journal of Research into Island Cultures, I, no. 2 (2007), pp. 59-70.

_____, "The Rock whence ye are hewn": The Book of Ebenezer Le Page and Guernsey Literature and History', The Modern Language Review, 103, i (January 2008), pp. 22-34.

_____, 'Writing the Literary History of the Channel Islands', Sixth International Small Island Cultures Conference, Guernsey, (23-25 June 2010) www.sicri-network.org.

Goudge, Elizabeth, Island Magic (London, 1934).

_____, Green Dolphin Country (London, 1944).

_____, 'Elizabeth Goudge and Her Books', Quarterly Review of the Guernsey Society, III, i (January 1947), pp. 11-12.

Graves, Richard Perceval, Robert Graves: The Years with Laura Riding: 1926-1940, vol. 2 (London, 1990).

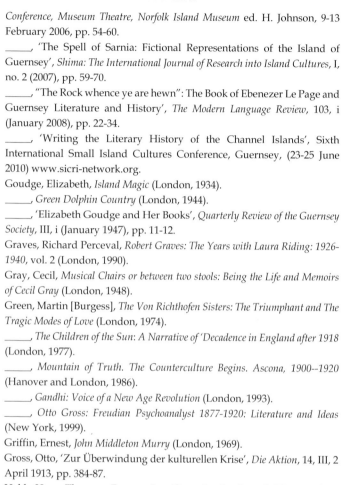

Gray, Cecil, Musical Chairs or between two stools: Being the Life and Memoirs of Cecil Gray (London, 1948).

Green, Martin [Burgess], The Von Richthofen Sisters: The Triumphant and The Tragic Modes of Love (London, 1974).

_____, The Children of the Sun: A Narrative of 'Decadence in England after 1918 (London, 1977).

_____, Mountain of Truth. The Counterculture Begins. Ascona, 1900--1920 (Hanover and London, 1986).

_____, Gandhi: Voice of a New Age Revolution (London, 1993).

_____, Otto Gross: Freudian Psychoanalyst 1877-1920: Literature and Ideas (New York, 1999).

Griffin, Ernest, John Middleton Murry (London, 1969).

Gross, Otto, 'Zur Überwindung der kulturellen Krise', Die Aktion, 14, III, 2 April 1913, pp. 384-87.

Hakl, Hans Thomas, Eranos: An Alternative Intellectual History of the Twentieth Century, trans. Christopher McIntosh (London, 2014).

Hall, David, Worktown: The Astonishing Story of the Project that Launched Mass Obervation (London, 2015).

Hankey, Donald, The Beloved Captain: Selected Chapters from A Student in Arms (London, 1917).

Hare, Chris, The Washington Story: The Forgotten Story of a Downland Village (West Chiltington, 2000).

Harrison, Jane Ellen, Themis: A Study of the Social Origins of Greek Religion (London, 1912; 2nd edition 1927).

Heppenstall, Rayner, Middleton Murry: A Study in Excellent Normality (London, 1934).

Heppenstall, Rayner, Four Absentees (London, 1960).

Heuer, Gottfried (ed.), *Sexual Revolutions: Psychoanalysis, History and the Father* (Hove, 2011).

Hilliard, Christopher, 'To Exercise our Talents', *The Democratization of Writing in Britain* (Boston, 2006).

Hinton, James, *The Mass Observers: A History, 1937-1949* (London, 2013).

Holbrook, David, *Where D.H. Lawrence was wrong about Women* (Lewisburg, 1997).

Holloway, Mark, *Norman Douglas: A Biography* (London, 1976).

Holroyd, Michael, *Lytton Strachey: A Critical Biography*, 2 vols (London, 1967-68).

_____, 'John Middleton Murry in Yateley', *The Yateley Society Newsletter*, no. 27 (July 1986), pp. 2-3.

_____, *Bernard Shaw*, 4 vols (London, 1988-1992).

_____, *Lytton Strachey: The New Biography* (London, 1994).

_____, *Augustus John: The New Biography*, (London, 1996).

Hubble, Nick, *Mass Observation and Everyday Life: Culture, History, Theory*, (London, 2006).

Hugo, Victor, *Travailleurs de la Mer* [Toilers of the Sea] (Brussels, 1866).

Hutton, Ronald, *The Triumph of the Moon: A History of Modern Pagan Witchcraft* (Oxford, 1999).

Huxley, Aldous, *Point Counter Point* (London, 1928).

Hyde, Lawrence, 'Glands and Chakras', *Adelphi*, December 1930.

_____, *Prospects of Humanism* (London, 1931).

_____, 'Religion and 'The Adelphi', *The Adelphi*, II, 2 (July 1931), pp. 275-82.

_____, *Isis and Osiris* (London, 1946).

_____, *I who am: a Study of the Self* (Reigate, 1954).

Ingrams, Richard, *John Stewart Collis: A Memoir* (London, 1986).

Jacka, Keith, '*The Book of Ebenezer Le Page*' ('Conservative Classic'), *Salisbury Review*, XXVI, no. 3 (Spring 2008), pp. 33-34.

Jackson, Kevin, *Humphrey Jennings* (London, 2004).

James, William, *The Varieties of Religious Experience: A Study in Human Nature* (New York, 1902).

Jang, Keum-Hee, *George Bernard Shaw's Religion of Creative Evolution: A Study of Shavian Dramatic Works*, PhD dissertation (University of Leicester, 2006).

Jefferies, Richard, *The Story of my Heart: An Autobiography* (London, 1883).

Jenkins, Alan, *Stephen Potter: Inventor of Gamesmanship* (London, 1980).

Jennings, Humphrey and Charles Madge (eds), *May the Twelfth: Mass Observation Day-Surveys 1937 by over two hundred observers*, 2nd edition with an afterword by David Pocock (London, 1987).

Johnson, Peter, *A Short History of Guernsey*, revised ed. (London, 2014).

Johnson, Samuel, *Letters of Samuel Johnson*, ed. Bruce Redford, I, 1731-1772 (Oxford, 1992).

Joyce, James, *Portrait of the Artist as a Young Man* (New York, 1916).

_____, *Ulysses* (Paris, 1922).

Judd, Denis, *Alison Uttley: The Life of a Country Child* (London, 1986; 2nd ed. Manchester, 2011).

Kaplan, Sydney Janet, *Circulating Genius: John Middleton Murry, Katherine Mansfield and D.H. Lawrence* (London, 2010).

_____, *Katherine Mansfield and the Origins of Modernist Fiction* (Ithaca, 1991).

Kazantzakis, Nikos, *The Saviors of God: Spiritual Exercises* (London, 1960).

_____, *Zorba the Greek* (London, 1952).

_____, *The Last Temptation* (London, 1960).

Kaufmann, Walter, *Nietzsche: Philosopher, Psychologist, Antichrist*, 4th ed. (London, 1975).

_____, *Freud, Adler, and Jung: Discovering the Mind*, III (New Brunswick, 1992).

Kenyatta, Jomo, *Facing Mount Kenya: The tribal life of the Gikuyu*, with an introduction by Bronisław Malinowski (London, 1938).

Keyserling, Count Hermann, *Creative Understanding* (London, 1929).

_____, *America Set Free* (London, 1930).

Kinkead-Weekes, Mark, *D.H. Lawrence: Triumph into Exile 1912-1922* (Cambridge, 1996).

Kinross, Patrick Balfour, *The Ruthless Innocent* (London, 1949).

Knights, Sarah, *Bloomsbury's Outsider: a Life of David Garnett* (London, 2015).

Knowlson, James, *Damned to Fame: the Life of Samuel Beckett* (London, 1996).

Kozlenko, William (ed.), *The One-Act Play Today: A Discussion of the Technique, Scope and History of the Contemporary Short Drama* (London, 1939/1970).

Krishnamurti, Jiddu, *Life in Freedom* (New York, 1928).

Kuh, Anton, *Juden und Deutsche* (Berlin, 1921).

Lampedusa, Giuseppe Tomasi di, *Il Gattopardo* (*The Leopard*), trans. Archibald Colquhoun (London, 1960).

_____, *La Sirena*, introduction by Gioacchino Lanza Tomasi (Milan, 2014).

_____, *The Professor and the Siren*, introduction by Marina Warner, translated by Stephen Twilley (New York, 2014).

Landmann, Robert, *Ascona – Monte Verità. Auf der Suche nach dem Paradies* (Munich, 2009).

Larson, Frances, "Did He Ever Darn His Stockings?" Beatrice Blackwood and the Ethnographic Authority of Bronislaw Malinowski', *History and Anthropology*, 22, I (2011), pp. 75-92

Launer, John, *Sex versus Survival: The Life and Idea of Sabina Spielrein* (London, 2014).

Lawrence, Frieda, *Octavio* (chapter on Otto Gross in unfinished memoir).

Lawrence, Frieda Von Richthofen, *Frieda Lawrence: The Memoirs and Correspondence* ed. E.W. Tedlock (London, 1961).

Lawrence, D.H., *Sons and Lovers* (London, 1913).

\_\_\_\_\_, *The Rainbow* (London, 1915).

\_\_\_\_\_, *Twilight in Italy* (London, 1916).

\_\_\_\_\_, *Twilight in Italy and other essays*, ed. Paul Eggert (Cambridge, 2002).

\_\_\_\_\_, *Women in Love* (New York, 1920).

\_\_\_\_\_, *Sea and Sardinia* (London, 1921).

\_\_\_\_\_, *David: a Play* (London, 1926).

\_\_\_\_\_, *Lady Chatterley's Lover* (Florence, 1928).

\_\_\_\_\_, 'The Man who loved Islands', *The Woman Who Rode Away and other stories* (New York, 1928).

\_\_\_\_\_, *The Escaped Cock* (Paris, 1929).

\_\_\_\_\_, *The Man Who Died* (London, 1931).

\_\_\_\_\_, *Psychoanalysis and the Unconscious* (Harmondsworth, 1971).

\_\_\_\_\_, 'The Lost Girl', ed. John Worthen (Cambridge, 1981).

\_\_\_\_\_, *Mr Noon* (unfinished novel) Parts I and II, edited by Lindeth Vasey (Cambridge, 1984).

\_\_\_\_\_, *The Cambridge Edition of the Letters of D.H. Lawrence,* Vols I-VIII, various editors (Cambridge, 1979-2003).

Lawrence, T.E., *The Selected Letters of T.E. Lawrence,* ed. David Garnett (London, 1938).

Le Messurier, Nick, 'Cousin sheds light on the Life of Ebenezer Le Page author', *Guernsey Evening Press*, 18 June 1981.

Lea, F.A., *The Life of John Middleton Murry* (London, 1959).

Lee, Hermione, *Virginia Woolf* (London, 1996).

Lessing, Theodor, *Der jüdische Selbsthaß* (Berlin, 1930).

Lewis, P. Wyndham, *Blast*, 2 vols. (London, 1914-15).

\_\_\_\_\_, *Time and Western Man* (London, 1927).

\_\_\_\_\_, *The Lion and the Fox: The Role of the Hero in Shakespeare* (London, 1927).

\_\_\_\_\_, *Paleface: The Philosophy of the Melting Pot* (London, 1929).

\_\_\_\_\_, *The Apes of God* (London, 1930).

\_\_\_\_\_, *Time and Tide* (XII, 16, 18 April 1931).

\_\_\_\_\_, *Blasting and Bombardiering* (London, 1937).

Lindfield, Malcolm, 'Jomo Kenyatta', *Longshot: Journal of the Lindfield One Name Group*, XIII, 2 (2010).

Longerich, Peter, *Goebbels: a Biography* (London, 2015).

Lutyens, Mary, *To be Young: Some Chapters of Autobiography* (London, 1959).

\_\_\_\_\_, *Krishnamurti: The Years of Awakening* (London, 1975).

\_\_\_\_\_, *Krishnamurti: The Years of Fulfilment* (London, 1983).

\_\_\_\_\_, *The life and death of Krishnamurti* (London, 1990).

\_\_\_\_\_, *The boy Krishna: the first fourteen years in the life of J. Krishnamurti* (London, 1995).

MacCarthy, Fiona, *Eric Gill* (London, 1989).

\_\_\_\_\_, *William Morris: A Life for Our Time* (London, 1994).

MacCulloch, Edgar, *Guernsey Folk Lore* ed. Edith Carey (London & Guernsey, 1903).

McEwan, Ian, *Atonement* (London, 2001).

_____, *On Chesil Beach* (London, 2007).

McGuire, William (ed.), *The Freud/Jung Letters* (London, 1979).

Maddox, Brenda , *D.H. Lawrence: The Story of a Marriage* (New York, 1994).

_____, *Freud's Wizard: The Enigma of Ernest Jones* (London, 2006).

Madge, Charles and Tom Harrisson, *Britain by Mass Observation* (London 1939).

Malinowski, Bronislaw, *Sex and Repression in Savage Society* (London, 1927).

Marr, David, *Patrick White: a Life* (London, 1992), p. 534.

Marr, James, *A History of the Bailiwick of Guernsey* (Chichester, 1982),

_____, *Guernsey People* (Chichester, 1984).

Mass Observation, *The Pub and the People: a Worktown study* (London, 1943).

Mathews, Harry, *20 Lines a Day* (Chicago, 1988).

McGilchrist, Iain, *The Master and his Emissary: The Divided Brain and the Making of the Western World*, 2nd ed. (New Haven and London, 2012).

Mead, Rebecca, 'Middlemarch and Me: What George Eliot teaches us', *New Yorker*, 14 February 2011.

Meyers, Jeffrey, *The Enemy: A Biography of Wyndham Lewis* (London, 1980).

_____, *D.H. Lawrence: a Biography* (London, 1990).

_____, *Katherine Mansfield: A Darker View* (New York, 2002).

Monk, Ray, *Ludwig Wittgenstein: The Duty of Genius* (London, 1990).

_____, *Bertrand Russell: The Spirit of Solitude* (London, 1996).

_____, *Bertrand Russell 1921-70: The Ghost of Madness* (London, 2000).

Moore, Harry T., *The Priest of Love: A Life of D.H. Lawrence* (London, 1974).

Moullin, J.E. (ed.), *Guernsey Ways* (London, 1966).

Mount, Cedric [vere Sydney Box], *Dirge Without Dole* (London, 1937).

Multulati, *Max Havelaar*, with an introduction by D.H. Lawrence (London, 1927).

Murry, Colin Middleton, *One Hand Clapping: a Memoir of Childhood* (London, 1975).

_____, *Shadows on the Grass* (London, 1977).

Murry, John Middleton, *Fyodor Dostoevsky: a Critical Study* (London, 1923).

_____, *Keats and Shakespeare* (Oxford, 1925).

_____, *Life of Jesus* (London, 1926).

_____, *God: Being an Introduction to the Science of Metabiology* (London, 1929).

_____, *Son of Woman: The Story of D.H. Lawrence* (London, 1931).

_____, *Reminiscences of D.H. Lawrence* (London, 1933).

_____, *William Blake* (London, 1933).

_____, *The Conquest of Death* (London, 1951).

_____, *Unprofessional Essays* (London, 1955).

_____, *The Letters of John Middleton Murry to Katherine Mansfield,* ed. C.A. Hankin (London, 1983).

Murry, Katherine Middleton, *Beloved Quixote: The Unknown Life of John Middleton Murry* (London, 1986).

Myhill, Henry, *Introducing the Channel Islands* (London, 1964).

Neumann, Erich, *The Great Mother: An Analysis of the Archetype* (London, 1955).

Nicolson, Nigel, *Portrait of a Marriage* (London, 1973; illustrated ed. 1990).

Nietzsche, Friederich, *The complete works of Friedrich Nietzsche. The first complete and authorized English translation*, ed. Oscar Levy, 18 vols. (Edinburgh and London, 1909-1913).

_____, *Thus Spake Zarathustra*, trans. Alexander Tille (London, 1896).

_____, *Beyond Good and Evil: Prelude to a Philosophy of the Future*, trans. Helen Zimmern (London, 1909).

_____, *The Joyous Wisdom*, transl. Thomas Common (London, 1910).

O'Casey, Sean, *The Plough and the Stars* (Dublin, 1926).

O'Hear, Natasha and Anthony, *Picturing the Apocalypse: The Book of Revelation in the Arts over Two Millennia* (Oxford, 2015).

O'Keeffe, Paul, *Some Sort of Genius: A Life of Wyndham Lewis* (London, 2000).

_____, *Gaudier-Brzeska: A Absolute Case of Genius* (London, 2004).

Osborne, Frances, *The Bolter* (London, 2008).

Owen, Richard, *Lady Chatterley's Villa. D.H. Lawrence on the Italian Riviera* (London, 2014).

Paglia, Camille, *Sexual Personae: Art and Decadence from Nefertiti to Emily Dickinson* (New Haven, 1990).

Partenheimer, David (ed), *An English Translation of Bachofen's Mutterrecht (Mother Right) (1861): A Study of the Religious and Juridicial Aspects of Gynecocracy in the Ancient World*, 2 vols (Lampeter, 2003 and 2007).

Paskauskas, R. Andrew (ed.), *The Complete Correspondence of Sigmund Freud and Ernest Jones 1908-1939* (Cambridge, Mass. and London, 1993).

Patai, Daphne, *The Orwell Mystique: A Study in Male Ideology* (Amherst, 1984).

Payne, Basil, 'Review of Lea, Studies:', *An Irish Quarterly Review*, XLIX, 195 (January 1960), pp. 338-40.

Pilcher, Velona, *The Searcher: A War Play* (London, 1929).

Pletsch, Carl, *Young Nietzsche: Becoming a Genius* (New York, 1991).

Plowman, Max, *The Right to Live: Selected Essays* with an introduction by J. Middleton Murry (London 1942).

_____, *Bridge to the Future: Letters of Max Plowman*, ed. D.L.P [Dorothy Plowman] (London, 1944).

Potter, Stephen, *The Young Man* (London, 1929).

_____, *D.H. Lawrence: A First Study* (London, 1930).

_____, *One-Upmanship* (London, 1952).

_____, *Steps to Immaturity* (London, 1959).

Potter, Julian, *Stephen Potter at the BBC: 'Features in War and Peace'* (Orford, 2004).

Powell, Anthony, *What's Become of Waring?* (London, 1939).

Pragnell, Vera G., *The Story of the Sanctuary* (Steyning, 1928).

Prideaux, Sue, *Strindberg: A Life* (London and New Haven, 2012).

Proust, Marcel, *A La Recherche du Temps Perdu, Tome 4: Sodome and Gomorre* (Paris, 1921-2).

_____, *Remembrance of Things Past, Volume 4: Cities of the Plain*, translated by C.K. Scott Montcreif (London, 1928).

Purkis, Charlotte, 'Velona Pilcher and Dame Ellen Terry 1926', *Ellen Terry: Spheres of Influence*, ed. K. Cockin (London, 2011).

Rees, Richard, *Brave Men: A study of D H Lawrence and Simone Weil* (London 1958).

_____, *George Orwell: Fugitive from the Camp of Victory* (London, 1961).

_____, *A Theory of my Time: An Essay in Didactic Reminisence* (London, 1963).

_____, *Simone Weil: A Sketch for a Portrait* (Oxford, 1966).

Ricks, Christopher, *Keats and Embarrassment* (Oxford, 1976).

Riding, Laura, *Anarchism is not Enough* (London, 1928).

Roberts, Warren and Poplawski, P., *A Bibliography of D.H. Lawrence*, 3rd edition (Cambridge, 2001).

Robertson, Michael, *Worshipping Walt: The Whitman Disciples* (Princeton, N.J., 2009).

Robin Waterfield Ltd, *Catalogue 50: Twentieth Century English Literature* (Oxford, 1985).

Robinson, Ken, 'A Portrait of the Psychoanalyst as a Bohemian: Ernest Jones and the "Lady from Styria",' *Psychoanalysis and History*, XV (July 2013).

Rowbotham, Sheila, *Edward Carpenter: A Life of Liberty and Love* (London, 2008).

Santayana, George, *The Genteel Tradition at Bay* (London, 1931).

_____, *The Last Puritan* (London, 1936).

_____, *Persons and Places* (London, 1944).

_____, *The German Mind: A Philosophical Diagnosis* (Iowa, 1968).

Schutte, Ofelia, *Beyond Nihilism: Nietzsche Without Masks* (Chicago, 1986).

Sengoopta, Chandak, *Otto Weininger: Sex, Science, and Self in Imperial Vienna* (Chicago, 2000).

Shaw, George Bernard, *Man and Superman* (London, 1903).

_____, *Getting Married* (London, 1908).

_____, *Pygmalion* (London, 1914).

_____, *Saint Joan* (London, 1924).

_____, *Bernard Shaw: The Collected Letters 1926-1950*, Vol 4, ed. Dan H. Laurence (London, 1988).

Shayer, David, 'Compton Mackenzie, D.H. Lawrence and Herm', *Transactions of La Société Guernesiaise*, XXII, ii (1987), pp. 327-32.

Shaw, George Bernard, *Getting Married* (London, 1908).

Shipley, Michael, Andrew Close et al. (eds), *Bolton Little Theatre: 75 years of*

*Drama* (Bolton, 2006).

Sisson, C.H., *Collected Poems* (London, 1998).

Solzhenitsyn, Aleksandr, *Cancer Ward*, trans. Nicholas Bethell and David Burg (London, 1968).

\_\_\_\_\_, *The First Circle*, trans. Michael Guybon (London, 1970).

\_\_\_\_\_, *A Letter to the Soviet Leaders* (London, 1974).

Spender, Stephen, 'New Judgements', BBC TV programme, first broadcast October 1941.

\_\_\_\_\_, *Journals 1939-1983*, ed. John Goldsmith (London, 1985).

Spiegelhalter, David, *Sex by Numbers: What Statistics Can Tell Us About Sexual Behaviour* (London, 2015).

Spinner, Gerhard, 'Die Engel und Wir', *Kirchenblatt für die reformierte Schweiz*, No 18-19 (1937).

Stanley, Nick, *The Extra Dimension: A Study and Assessment of the Methods employed by Mass-Observation in its first Period 1937-40*, unpublished PhD dissertation (Birmingham Polytechnic, 1981).

Stephens, Meic, *Rhys Davies: A Writer's Life* (Swansea, 2010).

Strindberg, August, *Easter and other plays*, trans. E. Classen (London [Cape], 1929).

\_\_\_\_\_, *Easter*, trans. Gregory Motton (London, 2005).

Swinburne, Algernon Charles, *The Complete Works*, ed. E. Gosse and T.J. Wise, 20 vols (London and New York, 1925-27).

Tagore, Rabindranath, *Selected Letters of Rabindranath Tagore*, eds K. Dutta and A. Robinson (Cambridge, 1997).

Tallack, Malachy, *Sixty Degrees North: Around the World in Search of Home* (London, 2015).

Temple, Robert, 'Eranos: Past and Present', in John van Praag and Riccardo Bernardini eds, *Eranos Reborn: The Modernities of East and West ; Perspectives on Violence* (Einsiedeln, 2010).

Tolstoy, Leo, *Resurrection*, trans. Louise Maude (London, 1903).

Tomalin, Claire, *Katherine Mansfield: A Secret Life* (London, 1987).

Toms, Carel, *Guernsey Pictures from the Past* (Chichester, 1991)

Tomasi, Gioacchino Lanza , *Giuseppe Tomasi di Lampedusa: A Biography through Images* (London, 2013).

Trevelyan, Julian, *Indigo Days*, 2nd ed. (London, 1996).

Trimble, Michael, *The Soul in the Brain* (London, 2012).

\_\_\_\_\_, *Why Humans like to Cry* (London, 2014).

Turner, Eric, 'Scandal', *Apollo* (October 2009), pp. 50-56.

Uttley, John, *Story of the Channel Islands* (London, 1966).

Verga, Giovanni, *I Malavoglia* (Milan, 1881).

\_\_\_\_\_, *Mastro-Don Gesualdo*, translated by D.H. Lawrence (New York, 1923).

\_\_\_\_\_, *Little Novels of Sicily*, translated by D.H. Lawrence (London, 1925).

Voegelin, Eric, *The Collected Works of Eric Voegelin*, 34 vols (Columbia, 1989-

2008).

Weeks, Jonathan, 'Old Guernsey Donkey', article in 'Resurrection' section, *Literary Review* (June 1996), pp. 56-7.

Weil, Simone, *Seventy Letters: translated and arranged by Richard Rees* (Oxford, 1965).

Weininger, Otto, *Geschlecht und Charakter (Sex and Character)* (London, 1910).

West, Geoffrey, *The Life of Annie Besant* (London, 1929).

Whimster, Sam and Gottfried Heuer, 'Otto Gross and Else Jaffé and Max Weber', *Theory, Culture & Society*, XV (August 1998), pp. 129-160.

White, Patrick, *Happy Valley* (London, 1939).

_____, *The Tree of Man* (London, 1955).

_____, *Voss* (London, 1957).

_____, *Riders in the Chariot* (London, 1961).

_____, *The Vivisector* (London, 1970).

_____, *The Eye of the Storm* (London, 1973).

_____, *Letters*, ed. David Marr (London, 1994).

Whitman, Walt, *Leaves of Grass* (New Jersey, 1855)

Whitworth, Geoffrey, *The Art of Nijinsky* (London, 1913).

_____, *The Theatre of my Heart*, rev. edn (London, 1938).

Whyte, Eva, 'Biographical Note on L. L. Whyte', *Contemporary Psychoanalysis*, X (1974), pp. 386-88.

Whyte, Lancelot Law, *The Unconscious before Freud* (London, 1960).

_____ (ed.), *Roger Joseph Boscovich: Studies of his Life and Work on the 250th Anniversary of his Birth* (London, 1961).

_____, *Focus and Diversions* (London, 1963).

Williamson, Anne, *Henry Williamson: Tarka and the Last Romantic* (Stroud, 1995).

Wilson, A.N., 'John Stewart Collis', *The Spectator* (10 Mar 1984), pp. 13-14.

Wilson, David, 'The Quiet Man of Upwey: now about to be discovered by the literary establishment', [Dorset] *Evening Echo Weekly Review: Mid Week Magazine* (18 March 1981).

Wilson, Jean Moorcraft, 'Norman Douglas and Richard Aldington: A Literary Feud', *Norman Douglas: 8. Symposium: Bregenz und Thuringen, Vlbg, 10/11/ 10. 2104*, ed. Wilhelm Meusburger (Graz, 2015), pp. 54-59.

Worthen, John, *D.H. Lawrence: The Early Years 1885-1912* (Cambridge, 1992).

Young, Michael, *The Elmhirsts of Dartington: the Creation of a Utopian Community* (London, 1982).

Zimmern, Helen, *Arthur Schopenhauer: His Life and Philosophy* (London, 1876).

_____, *Italian Leaders of Today* (London, 1915).

## Reviews of *The Book of Ebenezer Le Page*

Braudeau, Michel, 'Le monde selon Ebenezer', *L'Express*, 22-28 juillet 1983.

Bull, George, 'The Book of Ebenezer Le Page', *New Fiction Society* (February Choice), March 1981.

Golding, William, 'For Love or Money', *The Guardian*, 19 March 1981.

Grigson, Geoffrey, 'In the Crab Pots,' *New York Review*, 5 November 1981.

Kemp, Peter, 'Rough Island Story', *The Listener*, 19 March 1981.

Tinniswood, Peter, 'Fiction', *The Times*, 19 March 1981.

Sutherland, John, 'Making Strange', *London Review of Books*, 19 March - 1 April 1981.

Kemp, Peter, 'Rough Island Story', The Listener, 19 March 1981.

Bawden, Nina, 'Recent Fiction', *Daily Telegraph*, 19 March 1981.

Morrison, Blake, 'Channel Island Chronicler', *Observer*, 22 March 1981.

Korn, Eric, 'Getting down Guernsey', *Times Literary Supplement*, 27 March 1981.

Murray, Isobel, 'Island Treasure', *Financial Times*, 18 April 1981.

Davenport, Guy, 'A Novel of Life in a Small World', *The New York Times Book Review*, 19 April 1981.

O'Connell, Shaun, 'An Embattled Islander fighting off the Foreign,' *Boston Globe*, 21 June 1981.

Di Paolo, Laurence, 'Ignored Novel is a Treasure', *The Sunday Denver Post*, 10 May 1981.

Balliett, Whitney, 'Guernsey Gossip', *The New Yorker*, 1 June 1981.

Trease, Geoffrey, *British Book News*, June 1981.

Lang, Doug, 'Hidden Treasure in the English Channel,' *Daily News*, 23 June 1981.

McDowell, Edwin, 'Guernsey Novel, Publishing Success', *New York Times*, 8 July 1981.

Golding, William, 'Book of the Year', *The Sunday Times*, 6 December 1981.

Greene, Randall Elisha, 'A Novel of bittersweet Wisdom set on the Isle of Guernsey', *Louiseville Courier,* 26 April 1981.

Holloway, David, 'Books of the Year', *The Times*, 31 December 1981.

Juin, Hubert, 'Rêver Guernesey', *Le Monde*, 1 April 1983.

Orgel, Stephen, Stanford University Department of English: Summer Reading: Top Picks 2004.

Hofmann, Michael, 'Reading with No Clothes on', *London Review of Books*, 24 January 2008.

## Online Sources

Adam Matthew Digital, www.amdigital.co.uk (Mass Observation).

*Oxford Dictionary of National Biography* – www.oxforddnb.com

'*The Adelphi magazine*', mikalsonengl4620.wordpress.com/contextual-material/the-adelphi/

Chaney, Edward, 'R.B. Kitaj: Warburgian Artist'
http://emajartjournal.com/2013/11/30/edward-chaney-r-b-kitaj-1932-2007-warburgian-artist/
*Dartington Hall Archive,* www.dartington.org/archive
'D.H. Lawrence Manuscript Discovered Revealing a Blistering Attack on 1920s Misogyny', *Research Exchange Online*, exchange.nottingham.ac.uk/research/
'The Diaries of Lancelot Law Whyte', *Inquisition 21st Century,* www.inquisition21.com, retrieved 14 November 2014
'From Mass Observation to Big Observation: Anthropologies of Ourselves', *The Photographers' Gallery Blog*, thephotographersgalleryblog.org.uk, retrieved 14 November 2014
Heuer, Gottfried, 'Otto Gross, 1877-1920: Biographical Survey', www.ottogross.org.
Hubble, Nick, 'Review of James Hinton's The Mass Observers' (review no. 1603) *Reviews in History*, Institute of Historical Research, www.history.ac.uk/reviews, retrieved 14 November 2014
Walton, Liz, 'Guernsey Women and the Great War', *Channel Islands Great War Study Group*, greatwarci.net, 2011, retrieved March 2015
*Dictionary of Irish Biography,* dib.cambridge.org (Cambridge, 2009).
Weininger, Otto, *'Letters to Arthur Gerber', Collected Aphorisms, Notebook and Letters to a Friend,* trans. Martin Sudanic and Kevin Solway, www.huzheng.org/geniusreligion/aphlett.pdf (2000-02), retrieved May 2015.

# INDEX

Mitford, Nancy, 142
Moncrieff, Scott, 97
Mond, Henry, 162
Montaigne, Michel de, 230
Monte Verità, Ascona, Switzerland, 75, 88-89, 114
Montgomery, Stuart, 248
Mooney, Cynthia, 248
Moor House, Westerham, Kent, 118, 132, 370-71
Morrell, Lady Ottoline, vi, 15, 54, 76-77, 162
Morrell, Philip, 54
Morris, Jane, 161
Morris, William, 161
Mosse, Jane, iv, 22, 27, 374-375
Mount, Cedric. *See* Box, Sydney
Moyer Bell, 227, 373
Mulligan, Carey, 260
Murray, Isobel, 225, 230
Murry, Colin. *See* Murry, John Middleton Jr
Murry, John Middleton, iii, iv, vi, 9-14, 16, 25, 40, 48-50, 54-55, 57, 60-62, 67-68, 73, 75-78, 82-88, 90-103, 108-20, 127, 129-33, 144-57, 162, 165-70, 177, 207-12, 221-22, 237-39, 243-44, 250-51, 257, 259-61, 267, 292, 296, 308, 314, 347, 368, 370-72
Murry, John Middleton Jr, 10, 149, 167
Murry, Katherine Middleton, 10, 94, 148-49, 167
Murry, Violet (*née* Le Maistre), 48, 94, 97, 147-49, 155, 259, 260, 371
Mussolini, Benito, 71, 215
Mussolini, Mrs, 198, 304
Myhill, Henry, 269, 284
National Theatre, 116
Naughton, Bill, 181, 187
Nelson, Admiral Lord Horatio, 161
Neuburg, Victor, 78
New York Review of Books, ii, v, 215, 227-28, 232, 341, 374
New Zealand, vi, 9, 148, 154, 156, 292
Nicholson, Ben, 164
Nicholson, Nancy, 162
Nicolson, Harold, 142

Nicolson, Nigel, 141
Nietzsche, Friederich, iv, 10, 49, 54-55, 62-63, 70-73, 77, 90, 95, 103-04, 115, 120, 126, 136, 141, 161, 187, 200, 221, 239, 242-43, 257, 291, 342-44
Nietzschean, iii, iv, 10, 14, 53, 67-68, 71, 73, 89, 112, 128, 137, 181, 207, 211, 241, 243, 297, 299, 343
Nijinsky, Vaslav, 116, 126
Norman Conquest, 34, 245-46, 283
Norman, Nye, 234
Oedenkoven, Henri, 75
Oedipus complex, 73, 283
Oeser, Oscar, 184
Ogier, Louis, 160
Olive of East Coker, 187, 203, 372
Organ, Mary, 18-19, 244
Orgel, Stephen, 232
Orioli, Pino, 81, 96
ormer, 218
Orwell, George, 94, 100, 119, 136, 138, 143, 305, 310-11
Otto, Rudolf, 115
Owen, Morfydd, 74
Owen, Wilfred, 209, 222, 242, 325, 326-27
*Oxford Companion to English Literature*, 232
*Oxford Dictionary of National Biography* [ODNB], 10, 49, 57, 61, 71, 94, 113, 117, 142-43, 162, 168, 178-81, 184, 192, 252, 281, 284
Pankhurst, Sylvia, 134
Paris, France, 76, 249-50, 252
Partenheimer, David, 70
Pasternak, Leonid, 257
Penguin Books, 16, 38, 96, 143, 157, 227, 256, 260, 373-74
Peninnis, Scilly Isles, 318
Penzance, Cornwall, 201, 317, 319, 372
Perrottet, Suzanne, 89-90, 161
Picquet, Steve, 322
Pilcher, Velona, 72, 137, 371
Pitt-Rivers, Michael, 143
Plato, 123
Plowman, Dorothy, 94
Plowman, Max, 93-95, 98-100, 117,